# THE USE OF LAND AND WATER RESOURCES
# IN THE PAST AND PRESENT
# VALLEY OF OAXACA, MEXICO

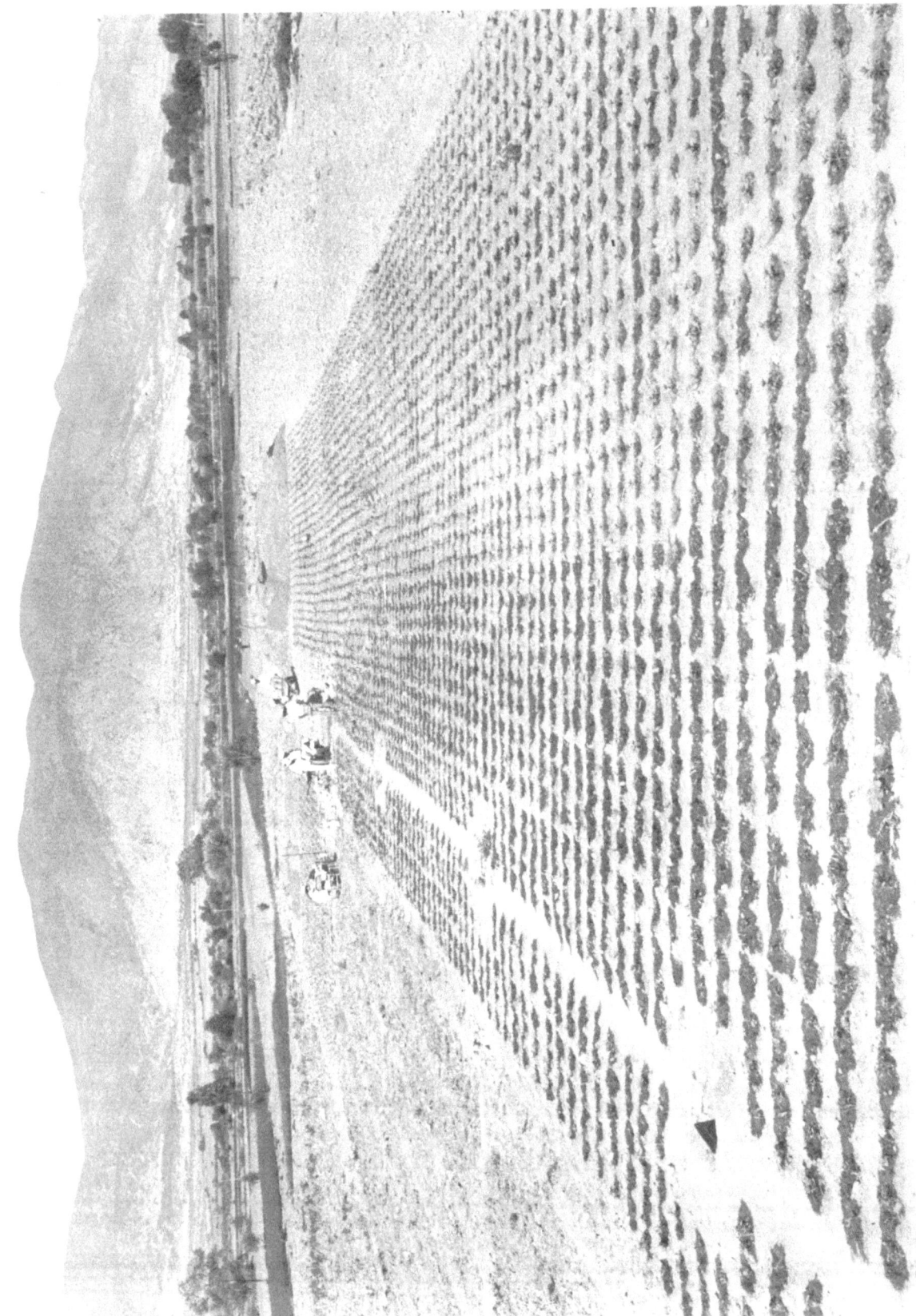

Frontispiece. Pot-irrigated fields at San Sebastián Abasolo, Oaxaca. The dark spots in the foreground are recently-watered cup-shaped depressions (*cajetes*) with individual chile plants. The underlying archaeological levels (being excavated in the background) show this area has probably been pot-irrigated since 1200 B.C.

MEMOIRS OF THE MUSEUM OF ANTHROPOLOGY
UNIVERSITY OF MICHIGAN
NUMBER 5

PREHISTORY AND HUMAN ECOLOGY
OF THE VALLEY OF OAXACA

Kent V. Flannery, General Editor

Volume 1

# THE USE OF LAND AND WATER RESOURCES IN THE PAST AND PRESENT VALLEY OF OAXACA, MEXICO

BY

ANNE V. T. KIRKBY

ANN ARBOR
1973

© 1973 by the Regents of the University of Michigan
The Museum of Anthropology
All rights reserved

ISBN (print): 978-1-949098-46-4
ISBN (ebook): 978-1-949098-67-9

Browse all of our books at sites.lsa.umich.edu/archaeology-books.

Order our books from the University of Michigan Press at www.press.umich.edu.

For permissions, questions, or manuscript queries, contact Museum publications by email at umma-pubs@umich.edu or visit the Museum website at lsa.umich.edu/ummaa.

# AN INTRODUCTION TO THE SERIES AND TO VOLUME 1

by Kent V. Flannery

With this *Memoir,* the University of Michigan Museum of Anthropology begins the publication of "Prehistory and Human Ecology of the Valley of Oaxaca, Mexico." This series of volumes, publication of which will extend over several years, will provide final reports on the University of Michigan's interdisciplinary project in the Valley of Oaxaca. Later in the series, I hope to be joined by my collaborator Richard E. Blanton of Hunter College, who will edit a number of volumes on his settlement pattern and urbanization studies in the same valley. Since the Oaxaca project is still going on at this writing, and much of the archaeological work is yet to be done, the volumes will usually be devoted not to such categories as ceramics, natural environment, and non-ceramic artifacts as in the case of the recent Tehuacán Valley reports edited by Richard S. MacNeish, but rather by individual research topics as was the case with the Maya reports of the Carnegie Institute of Washington.

With the publication of Volume 1, it seems appropriate to sketch the goals and history of the project "The Prehistoric Human Ecology of the Valley of Oaxaca," which began under my direction in January, 1966. Its ultimate goal was the unravelling of cultural process—in this case, the processes by which man made the transition from nomadic hunting and gathering bands to agricultural societies with permanent villages (8000-1300 B.C.) and from simple egalitarian farming societies to urban civilization (1300 B.C.-A.D. 300). A related goal was to determine why these processes took place earlier (and on a larger scale) in the Valley of Oaxaca than in neighboring valleys in the southern Mexican highlands. In the course of this we hope to determine some of the universal processes and mechanisms ancient Oaxaca shares with other areas in which early civilization developed.

Although the overall framework for the Oaxaca project could be described as "ecological" and "evolutionary," we have perhaps defined those terms more broadly than some previous projects in Mesoamerica. We do not believe in linear causality or in prime movers, and we do not view such generalized phenomena as population pressure, trade, or regional symbiosis as sufficient explanations for the course of cultural evolution in Oaxaca. Such terms sometimes *describe* what happened at a given time or place, but they fall short of *explanation* in an epistemological sense. Moreover, the kind of "ecology" in which those concepts are assigned prime-mover status usually fails to take into account a great body of phenomena which motivate human beings, and whose relevance has been convincingly demonstrated by structuralists and cognitive anthropologists over the years. We believe that a disregard for these phenomena—cosmology, world view, religious and ritual systems, pre-Columbian writing, and related topics—has caused many earlier "ecological" approaches to fall short of success.

In our view, human ecology is the study of the subtle and intricate interrelationships of man's exchanges of matter, energy, and information. To concentrate only on matter and energy exchanges and to ignore cognition is to present an unbalanced approach to ecology. This first volume, by Anne V. T. Kirkby, perhaps illustrates a broader ecological approach. Kirkby's expertise in geology, land use, and cultural geography is probably greater than that of any archaeologist who ever claimed to "explain" prehistoric sociopolitical development on the basis of environmental factors and land-use systems. And in the end, rather than resorting to environmental imperatives, she concludes that Oaxacan village farming has probably always been under-productive for reasons which are directly related to the "satisfising" world view of the Valley Zapotec.

We originally selected the Valley of Oaxaca for several reasons. First, it was an important "nuclear" region—the largest expanse of flat agricultural land in the southern Mexican highlands—and the home of Monte Albán, one of pre-Columbian Mexico's largest cities. Second, virtually nothing was known of its history prior to the rise of Monte Albán, Third, the basic ceramic sequence for the area from 400 B.C. to the Spanish Conquest had already been worked out by Alfonso Caso, Ignacio Bernal, and Jorge Acosta. Fourth, Oaxaca lay so close to the recently-investigated Valley of Tehuacán, Puebla as to make it likely that the two areas shared many pottery and flint tool types. This meant that we could start work almost immediately on questions of cultural process after spending only a minimal amount of time establishing a sequence; Oaxaca's later ceramic chronology was already well-known, and its earlier periods would almost surely resemble the already-defined Tehuacán sequence. Fifth, I was promised the support of Ignacio Bernal, John Paddock, and José Luis Lorenzo and encouraged to begin work in Oaxaca "as soon as possible." And sixth, we knew from Richard MacNeish's work that Tehuacán had been dominated by Monte Albán from roughly 300 B.C. to A.D. 700. This meant that by working in Oaxaca, we could not only analyze the cultural evolution of a "nuclear" valley, but also study its impact on a nearby region which was well-studied, but less nuclear.

A pilot project began in January of 1966, financed by Grant 019 from the Smithsonian Research Foundation. It soon became apparent that the Valley of Oaxaca, while it did not have magnificent dry caves comparable to those in Tehuacán, had Formative sites which were second to none. In 1967, the National Science Foundation awarded to Aubrey Williams (University of Maryland) and myself a grant—GS1616—to begin work on a larger scale. In 1968, the N.S.F. granted the University of Michigan a still larger sum—GS2121—which supported our work in Oaxaca until December 31, 1971. In 1972, the N.S.F.'s Office of Science Information Service awarded us a publication grant—GN35572—to cover the printing costs of the first two volumes of final reports. We are very grateful for their financial support.

From the first planning stages of the Oaxaca project, I was interested in finding a geomorphologist—one who could do for us what John T. Hack had done for the old Harvard Awatovi project in the southwestern United States. Hack himself recommended a husband-wife team of British geographers—Michael and Anne Kirkby—who were then resident at Johns Hopkins University. "These are the people you want," he said. "They're fantastic field workers, original thinkers, and charming colleagues." They were everything Hack said and more, as this and their subsequent volumes will indicate.

In this report, Anne Kirkby defines Oaxaca's agricultural potential, and measures the output of all known Valley Zapotec farming techniques. She analyses their decision-making strategies and relates them to their perception of past rainfall. She shows the measureable relationship between corn cob length and yield in kilograms per hectare, and between yield and present-day population density. This unusual combination of geomorphology, cultural geography, game theory and ethnoscience allows her to conclude with a series of models which "predict" the population of the valley and its distribution at various stages since 1300 B.C. These models will serve as the background against which the actual archaeological settlement pattern data can be interpreted as it comes in. Dr. Kirkby's land-use study also served to provide background data for Dr. Susan H. Lees, the author of Volume 2 in this series; Lees will present, from an ethnographic point of view, the sociopolitical aspects of canal irrigation in the Valley of Oaxaca.

Anne Kirkby was a founding member of the Oaxaca project. Her study of *The Use of Land and Water Resources in the Past and Present Valley of Oaxaca* carried her on foot over hundreds of square kilometers and by Jeep over thousands more. When she left for England in August 1966, it was only because Qantas refused to carry her if she waited another week—the birth of her son, David, being roughly a month off. (Two days earlier she had been climbing mountains at 1900 meters with a full pack.) She returned in 1967 with David in her backpack to continue the survey. Three years later, with David on foot and daughter Clare in the backpack, the job was done. In their "spare time" the Kirkbys went east to Iran with Frank Hole and north to Nochixtlán with Ronald Spores, to do the same kind of land-use study. I estimate that they have another 1,000,000 miles left in them, and I will be very disappointed if my archaeologist colleagues let them escape without a chance to do some more "archaeologically-related geo-cultural geography."

In retrospect, those early days of the Oaxaca project, when we knew less and enjoyed it more, were some of the happiest. In addition to my debts to the National Science Foundation, the Smithsonian, and the Kirkbys, I would like to thank a number of people for their help and encouragement. They include Ignacio Bernal, José Luis Lorenzo, and Lorenzo Gamio of the Instituto Nacional de Antropología e Historia; John Paddock and Darío Quero of the Museo Frissell de Art Zapoteca in Mitla, our original Oaxaca headquarters; my colleagues Ronald Spores, Donald Brockington, and Cecil Welte; and of course the Valley Zapotec, surely the aristocrats of ancient and modern Mexico, who made work in Oaxaca such a joy.

Ann Arbor, Michigan<br>
February 1, 1973

## CONTENTS

Figures . . . . . . . . . . . . . . . . . . . . . . . . . . . . . . . . . . . . . . . . . . . . . . . . . . . . . . . . . . . . . . x
Tables . . . . . . . . . . . . . . . . . . . . . . . . . . . . . . . . . . . . . . . . . . . . . . . . . . . . . . . . . . . . . . xi
Plates . . . . . . . . . . . . . . . . . . . . . . . . . . . . . . . . . . . . . . . . . . . . . . . . . . . . . . . . . . . . . . xiii
Acknowledgments . . . . . . . . . . . . . . . . . . . . . . . . . . . . . . . . . . . . . . . . . . . . . . . . . . . xiv

I. Objectives and Research Design

    Introduction . . . . . . . . . . . . . . . . . . . . . . . . . . . . . . . . . . . . . . . . . . . . . . . . . 1
    Definitions . . . . . . . . . . . . . . . . . . . . . . . . . . . . . . . . . . . . . . . . . . . . . . . . . . 3
    Methods . . . . . . . . . . . . . . . . . . . . . . . . . . . . . . . . . . . . . . . . . . . . . . . . . . . 4

II. Agricultural Resources in the Physical Environment

    Introduction . . . . . . . . . . . . . . . . . . . . . . . . . . . . . . . . . . . . . . . . . . . . . . . . . 7
    Land . . . . . . . . . . . . . . . . . . . . . . . . . . . . . . . . . . . . . . . . . . . . . . . . . . . . . . 9
    Water . . . . . . . . . . . . . . . . . . . . . . . . . . . . . . . . . . . . . . . . . . . . . . . . . . . . . 15
    Summary . . . . . . . . . . . . . . . . . . . . . . . . . . . . . . . . . . . . . . . . . . . . . . . . . . 24

III. Social Organisation of Land, Labour and Production

    Introduction . . . . . . . . . . . . . . . . . . . . . . . . . . . . . . . . . . . . . . . . . . . . . . . . . 27
    Land . . . . . . . . . . . . . . . . . . . . . . . . . . . . . . . . . . . . . . . . . . . . . . . . . . . . . . 28
    Labour . . . . . . . . . . . . . . . . . . . . . . . . . . . . . . . . . . . . . . . . . . . . . . . . . . . . 31
    Production . . . . . . . . . . . . . . . . . . . . . . . . . . . . . . . . . . . . . . . . . . . . . . . . . 32

IV. Water Use Techniques and Their Distribution

    Introduction . . . . . . . . . . . . . . . . . . . . . . . . . . . . . . . . . . . . . . . . . . . . . . . . . 35
    Dry Farming . . . . . . . . . . . . . . . . . . . . . . . . . . . . . . . . . . . . . . . . . . . . . . . . 35
    Floodwater Farming . . . . . . . . . . . . . . . . . . . . . . . . . . . . . . . . . . . . . . . . . . 36
    Water-Table Farming . . . . . . . . . . . . . . . . . . . . . . . . . . . . . . . . . . . . . . . . . 41
    Well Irrigation . . . . . . . . . . . . . . . . . . . . . . . . . . . . . . . . . . . . . . . . . . . . . . 41
    Canal Irrigation . . . . . . . . . . . . . . . . . . . . . . . . . . . . . . . . . . . . . . . . . . . . . . 45
    Distribution of Water Use . . . . . . . . . . . . . . . . . . . . . . . . . . . . . . . . . . . . . 47

V. Corn Production and Its Distribution

    Introduction . . . . . . . . . . . . . . . . . . . . . . . . . . . . . . . . . . . . . . . . . . . . . . . . . 53
    Traditional Cultivation Methods . . . . . . . . . . . . . . . . . . . . . . . . . . . . . . . . 53
    Factors Affecting Planting . . . . . . . . . . . . . . . . . . . . . . . . . . . . . . . . . . . . . 54
    Factors Affecting Yields . . . . . . . . . . . . . . . . . . . . . . . . . . . . . . . . . . . . . . . 59
    Areal Variations in Corn Yield and Water Consumption . . . . . . . . . . . . . . . . . . . . . . 65

VI. Subsistence Farming on Unirrigated Land

    Introduction . . . . . . . . . . . . . . . . . . . . . . . . . . . . . . . . . . . . . . . . . . . . . . . . . 71
    Evidence of Fixed Goals in Corn Production . . . . . . . . . . . . . . . . . . . . . . . . 72
    Effect of Local Variability on the Achievement of Fixed Goals . . . . . . . . . . . . . . . . 77
    Socioeconomic Influences on Levels of Satisfaction in Corn . . . . . . . . . . . . . . . . 89
    Summary . . . . . . . . . . . . . . . . . . . . . . . . . . . . . . . . . . . . . . . . . . . . . . . . . . 94

VII. Cash Farming on Irrigated Land

    Introduction . . . . . . . . . . . . . . . . . . . . . . . . . . . . . . . . . . . . . . . . . . . . . . . . . 95
    Sample Land Use Areas . . . . . . . . . . . . . . . . . . . . . . . . . . . . . . . . . . . . . . . 96
    Effect of the Physical Environment on Irrigated Land Use . . . . . . . . . . . . . . . . . . 103
    Effect of the Cultural Environment . . . . . . . . . . . . . . . . . . . . . . . . . . . . . . . 107
    Pre-Conquest Irrigation in the Valley . . . . . . . . . . . . . . . . . . . . . . . . . . . . . 117

ix

VIII. Prehistoric Agriculture and Population
    Introduction . . . . . . . . . . . . . . . . . . . . . . . . . . . . . . . . . . . . . . . . . . . . . . . . . 123
    Land Use Model of Prehistoric Agriculture and Settlement . . . . . . . . . . . . . . . . . . 124
    Stages of Development . . . . . . . . . . . . . . . . . . . . . . . . . . . . . . . . . . . . . . . 129
        Stage I–1300 B.C. . . . . . . . . . . . . . . . . . . . . . . . . . . . . . . . . . . . . . . . . . 129
        Stage II–1000 B.C. . . . . . . . . . . . . . . . . . . . . . . . . . . . . . . . . . . . . . . . . 131
        Stage III–300-1 B.C. . . . . . . . . . . . . . . . . . . . . . . . . . . . . . . . . . . . . . . . 133
        Stage IV–A.D. 900 . . . . . . . . . . . . . . . . . . . . . . . . . . . . . . . . . . . . . . . . 135
        Stage V–A.D. 1970 . . . . . . . . . . . . . . . . . . . . . . . . . . . . . . . . . . . . . . . . 137
    Comparison of Prehistoric Population and Settlement Data from the
        Land Use Model and Archaeological Evidence . . . . . . . . . . . . . . . . . . . . . . 139

IX.   Conclusion: The Effect of Culture on Agricultural Resource Use . . . . . . . . . . . . . . . . . 147

Appendixes
    I. Perception of Annual Rainfall . . . . . . . . . . . . . . . . . . . . . . . . . . . . . . . . . . . 157
    II. Present Distribution of Crops Around the Valley . . . . . . . . . . . . . . . . . . . . . . . 161
    III. Lambityeco Land Use Area . . . . . . . . . . . . . . . . . . . . . . . . . . . . . . . . . . . 165

*Resumen en Español* . . . . . . . . . . . . . . . . . . . . . . . . . . . . . . . . . . . . . . . . . . . . 169

References . . . . . . . . . . . . . . . . . . . . . . . . . . . . . . . . . . . . . . . . . . . . . . . . . . xxx

## FIGURES

1. Map of Valley of Oaxaca to show general features, location of all place names mentioned in text, and position of Valley in southern Mexico ................................................. 6
2. Map of Valley of Oaxaca to show main towns and valleys and locations of sample land use areas .... 8
3. Map of Valley of Oaxaca to show main physiographic zones ........................................ 10
4. *a.* Cross section of Tlacolula Valley ............................................................ 12
   *b.* Cross section of Zaachila Valley ............................................................ 12
5. Map of Valley of Oaxaca to show soils of the valley floor and piedmont .......................... 14
6. Climatic data for Oaxaca de Juárez ............................................................. 16
7. Pattern of annual water deficit for Oaxaca de Juárez ............................................ 18
8. Rainfall map of the Valley of Oaxaca ........................................................... 19
9. Frequency distribution for Oaxaca de Juárez and Tlacolula of years with different R:E-T ratios for June, July and August ............................................................... 20
10. *a.* Monthly rainfall in Oaxaca de Juárez for 1933 and 1948 .................................... 22
    *b.* Frequency distribution of total annual rainfalls for Oaxaca de Juárez ..................... 22
11. Water resources of the Valley of Oaxaca for agriculture ........................................ 23
12. Sizes of irrigated parcels of land in Tlalixtac de Cabrera, San Juan del Estado and San Agustín Etla ................................................................................ 29
13. Map of a series of trincheras along a small valley in Chihuahua, northern Mexico .............. 37
14. Small group floodwater scheme on the Río Salado near Mitla ..................................... 39
15. Cross section of floodwater-farmed area near Tlacolula ......................................... 40
16. Pot-irrigated fields ........................................................................... 43
17. Piedmont canal irrigation systems near San Gabriel Etla ........................................ 47
18. Map of agricultural water use methods .......................................................... 48
19. Simplified flow diagram of corn-planting decisions in dry farming ............................... 56
20. Subroutine A: for matching spatial distribution of milpas to predicted moisture distribution ... 57
21. Subroutine B: for planting and timing decisions within each milpa .............................. 58
22. Relation between cob length and weight of dry grain per cob for modern maize in the Valley of Oaxaca ............................................................................... 60
23. Relationship between slope angle and corn yield for dry farming in the Etla and Tlacolula Valleys .... 63
24. Relationship between measured corn yield and water consumption ................................. 64
25. Distribution of present mean corn yield per hectare for the Valley of Oaxaca .................. 66
26. Distribution of agricultural water consumption in excess of rainfall for the Valley of Oaxaca ..... 67
27. Area of each arm of the Valley giving different mean corn yields per hectare .................. 68
28. Area of each arm of the Valley on which different amounts of agricultural water in excess of rainfall are applied .......................................................................... 69
29. Relationship between area under corn and June rainfall for nine sample areas, 1966 to 1968 ..... 76
30. Land use and physiographic zones of part of the Mitla sample area in 1968 ..................... 78
31. Triangular diagram to show theoretical and actual freedom of planting strategies in the Mitla sample area and measured and extrapolated corn distributions between physiographic zones .. 82
32. Maximin solution for corn distribution among physiographic zones in the Mitla sample area ..... 83
33. Worst possible corn yields for dry farming in the Mitla area for different proportions of corn in the piedmont and high and low alluvium zones .............................................. 85
34. Mean corn yield for dry farming in the Mitla area for different proportions of corn in the piedmont and high and low alluvium zones ...................................................... 86
35. Changing proportions of land under corn, cash crops and fallow for 10 sample areas between 1966 and 1968 ................................................................................. 92
36. Canal system, land use and physiographic zones of part of the San Gabriel Etla sample area in 1970 ... 93
37. Land use, depth to water table and soil texture of part of the Zaachila sample area in 1970 ...... 98
38. Land use and depth to water table of part of the San Antonino Castillo Velasco land use area in 1967 .. 99
39. Land use, depth to water table and soil texture of part of the San Sebastián Abasolo sample area in 1970 ................................................................................... 101
40. Distribution of orchards, alfalfa and corn fields in relation to distance from the main irrigation canal, San Gabriel Etla ......................................................................... 105

xi

41. Mean distribution of pot-irrigation fields in relation to depth to water table for four years in Zaachila, San Antonino and San Sebastián Abasolo sample areas .......... 106
42. Mean distribution of pot-irrigation fields in relation to distance from a transport route for four years in Zaachila, San Antonino and San Sebastián Abasolo sample areas .......... 108
43. Division of water among five communities on the lower Río Mixtepec .......... 110
44. Hypothetical distribution of irrigation water over an area of variable agricultural quality .......... 111
45. Total cash profit in pesos for different proportions of landholding area under pot irrigation of cash crops and under dry farming of corn .......... 116
46. Map of part of archaeological canal system at Hierve el Agua .......... 118
47. Relationship between present mean corn yield per hectare and population in 1960 for different parts of the Valley .......... 125
48. *a.* Increase in mean corn cob length through time, 5000 B.C. to the present .......... 126
    *b.* Mean corn yield per hectare for different lengths of corn cobs measured in the Valley of Oaxaca ... 126
49. Predicted area which could have been cultivated, predicted settlement distribution and location of known archaeological sites for 1300 B.C. .......... 130
50. Predicted area which could have been cultivated, predicted settlement distribution and location of known archaeological sites for 1000 B.C. .......... 132
51. Predicted area which could have been cultivated, predicted settlement distribution and location of known archaeological sites for 300-1 B.C. .......... 134
52. Predicted area which could have been cultivated, predicted settlement distribution and location of known archaeological sites for A.D. 900 .......... 136
53. Predicted cultivated area and predicted settlement distribution for the present .......... 138
54. Present population distribution for the Valley of Oaxaca .......... 140
55. *a.* Increase in cultivated land for each arm of the Valley through time, as predicted from land use data . 143
    *b.* Increase in population density of valley floor for each arm of the Valley through time, as predicted from land use data .......... 143
56. Relationship between predicted number of sites and numbers of archaeological sites for all parts of the Valley from 1300 B.C. to the present .......... 144
57. Relationship between population of Valley estimated from archaeological data and population estimated from corn yield data from 1300 B.C. to the present .......... 145
58. Patterns of rainfall memory and perception among peasant cultivators compared with rainfall records .. 158
59. Annual rainfall for Tlacolula for each year, 1926 to 1968, compared wtih (*a*) the annual rainfall of 3 years before the given year and (*b*) the annual rainfall of the year previous to the given year .... 159
60. Measured proportions of areas under different categories of land use for selected points in the piedmont .......... 162
61. Measured proportions of areas under different categories of land use for selected points on the valley floor .......... 163
62. Physical and archaeological features of part of the Lambityeco sample area .......... 166
63. Land use of part of the Lambityeco sample area in 1970 .......... 167

# TABLES

1. Climatic variation with altitude in the Valley of Oaxaca .......... 9
2. Climatic variation within the valley floor .......... 15
3. Effects of location and physiographic zone on dry farming corn yields as shown by 2-way analysis of variance .......... 61
4. Effects of location and physiographic zone on irrigated corn yields as shown by 2-way analysis of variance .......... 61
5. Effects of soil texture and water use on high and low alluvium corn yields in all areas of the Valley as shown by 2-way analysis of variance .......... 61
6. Effects of location and water use on high alluvium corn yields as shown by 2-way analysis of variance .......... 62
7. Effects of soil texture and physiographic zone on dry and irrigated corn yields in all areas except Zaachila Valley as shown by 2-way analysis of variance .......... 62
8. Costs of corn production per hectare using an ox-plough .......... 72
9. Costs of corn production per hectare using coa, ox-team and tractor cultivation .......... 73
10. Costs and cash profit per peasant agriculturalist for corn production using coa, ox-plough and tractor cultivation .......... 73
11. Cash yield from one hectare of land .......... 73
12. Cash cost and profit per peasant landholding for corn production using coa, ox-plough and tractor cultivation .......... 74
13. Land use of the Mitla sample area, 1966-1968, 1970 .......... 79

14. Land use change matrices for Mitla sample area, 1966 to 1968 .................... 80
15. Comparison of rainfall-predicting methods with actual rainfalls and planting strategies for Mitla sample area, 1966 to 1968 .................................................................. 87
16. Variation of satisfaction level in corn production through time with increasing cash-crop specialisation: San Gabriel Etla ................................................................ 91
17. Land use of sample pot-irrigated and canal-irrigated areas by percentage of total areas sampled ...... 97
18. Land use change matrices for the Zaachila and San Gabriel Etla sample areas, 1966 to 1968 ...... 103
19. Comparative cash production costs and yields for pot irrigating and dry farming ............. 114
20. Comparative labour requirements for pot irrigation of 0.125 hectare and one hectare of dry-farmed corn using an ox-plough ............................................................. 115
21. Number of predicted sites from land use data and known archaeological settlement sites from 1300 B.C. to present .............................................................. 135
22. Predicted size of cultivated area, total possible corn production, and population for each arm of the Valley from 1300 B.C. to present ...................................................... 137
23. Number and percentage of peasant cultivators remembering past rainfalls and believing in rainfall prediction ................................................................. 157
24. Land use in the Lambityeco area by percentage of the physiographic zone area, 1966 to 1968 ..... 168
25. Land use change matrices for physiographic zones in the Lambityeco area, 1966 to 1968 ........ 168

# PLATES

Frontispiece. Pot-irrigated fields at San Sebastián Abasolo, Oaxaca. The dark spots in the foreground are recently-watered cup-shaped depressions (*cajetes*) with individual chile plants. The underlying archaeological levels (being excavated in the background) show this area has probably been pot-irrigated since 1200 B.C.
1. Valley of Oaxaca looking south from above Teotitlán del Valle (village in middle foreground).
2. Eastern end of the Tlacolula Valley looking west towards Mitla, showing piedmont and valley floor. Bed of Río Salado is seen in middle foreground.
3. Central Tlacolula Valley looking south from above the piedmont. The central uncultivated zone crossed by a road is part of the seasonal swamp of the Río Salado.
4. Part of the weekly market at San Pedro y San Pablo Etla.
5. Hoe cultivation in the piedmont zone: San Gabriel Etla. Note the resulting pock-marked surface.
6. Series of dry stone *trincheras* in a piedmont valley which are designed to hold back soil and moisture.
7. Floodwater farming near San Mateo Macuilxochitl
   a. floodwater being distributed along furrows
   b. peak flood discharge half an hour later
   c. destruction of corn and deposition of sediment 12 hours later.
8. Series of soil erosion walls of piled branches one day after flooding of *milpa* in 1966 in the Tlacolula Valley. Position of most concentrated flow was not apparent before the flood.
9. Pot irrigation field near San Antonino Castillo Velasco. The white scale is 15 mm long. A well is indicated in the background.
10. Pot irrigation in the Zaachila Valley. Well is on the left behind the man.
11. Modern well and furrow system for irrigating alfalfa near Tlacolula.
12. Main canal for San Gabriel Etla and San Miguel Etla contouring round the mountain valley side before reaching the top of the piedmont ridge.
13. Ox-plough introduced by the Spanish at the Conquest and in common use today.
14. Ox-cart taking *zacate* from the *milpa*: Tlacolula Valley.
15. Clearing a long-fallowed field by burning vegetation and piling boulders (south of San Andrés Zabache).
16. A partly harvested corn field seen in September 1968.
17. An unirrigated corn field typical of the piedmont zone.
18. Etla Valley and irrigated piedmont landscape looking west from above San Gabriel Etla. The fields in the lower half of the picture are part of the sample land use area.
19. San Sebastián Abasolo and the cultivated valley floor including the sample land use area seen from the north.

## ACKNOWLEDGMENTS

I should like here to record my thanks to all members of the Oaxaca Project from 1966-70 and to others in Oaxaca who helped to form a scientific community in the field and who, through frequent informal discussions in the laboratory at Mitla and in the field, stimulated this research and provided valuable ideas, information and criticism. Those whom I would like particularly to mention are Dr. Kent Flannery of the Museum of Anthropology, University of Michigan, who initiated and led the project and with whom I always enjoyed discussing the most unlikely ideas, many of which now seem acceptable; Dr. Ignacio Bernal, who generously provided us with the unpublished archaeological site data for the Valley used in Chapter VIII; Dr. Susan Lees, formerly of the University of Michigan and now at Hunter College, whose work on the sociopolitical aspects of canal irrigation in the valley is most closely linked to this study; Professor Aubrey Williams of the Department of Sociology and Anthropology at the University of Maryland, who introduced me to ethnography; and Christopher Moser of U.C.L.A., who developed and organised my field photographs and helped both in the field and laboratory.

My thanks are also due to Mr. Cecil Welte of the Oficina de Estudios de Humanidad del Valle de Oaxaca, Oaxaca de Juárez, who surveyed and drew the base map of the Valley on which all the distributions are drawn, provided climatic data from the meteorologic station he set up for us at his own house, and helped in numerous other ways. This research has also profited from the friendship of other anthropologists working in Oaxaca, especially of Professor Ron Spores of Vanderbilt University and Ted Downing of Stanford University.

To the members of the Department of Geography at The Johns Hopkins University I also wish to express my thanks for a happy and profitable two years studying there, particularly to Professor M. Gordon Wolman, who has been my enthusiastic and patient advisor, and to the late Professor John Goodlett who was a good friend and teacher. My thanks are also due to Professor David Harvey, late of Bristol University, England, and now at The Johns Hopkins University, who gave me valuable advice on this manuscript. Finally, I thank my husband, Mike, who helped more than anyone else, both during the four seasons in Oaxaca and in always giving his enthusiastic support—directly, in the field and at home, and indirectly, in keeping two small children at bay.

I wish also to acknowledge the generous support given by several bodies over the years 1966-70, without which help this work could not have been done: the Smithsonian Institution, in 1966; the National Science Foundation under Grant no. GS-1616 to the University of Maryland in 1967 and under Grant no. GS-2121 to the University of Michigan in 1968 and 1970; the Centre of Latin American Studies, University of Cambridge, England, for a fellowship during the academic year of 1967- and a Parry research grant for field work in 1968.

# I

# OBJECTIVES AND RESEARCH DESIGN

## INTRODUCTION

Land and water are the two most important natural resources in the Valley of Oaxaca. With the help of these resources, the Valley maintained its position as one of the five most powerful centres of cultural and economic activity in prehistoric Mesoamerica.[1] Today agricultural land and water are at the same time the most widespread and, in relation to the demand of the increasing population, the scarcest natural resources. This study looks at the ways in which land and water are used today and seeks to show, for peasant agriculture in this semiarid area, what aspects of the physical and cultural environment influence the ways in which agricultural resources are being used and how the resources are being exploited to their full potential. An understanding of these problems is a necessary starting point for any analysis of the economic basis of the great pre-Conquest civilisation that grew and flourished in the Valley, and is crucial to the future economic and social development of this part of the American tropics.

The Valley of Oaxaca is a landlocked region set in the middle of the southern highlands of Mexico and mainly surrounded by deeply incised valleys and precipitous forested slopes which discourage anything but small isolated settlements and shifting agriculture. Its great advantage over its neighbouring valleys is its large area of flat, cultivable land—about 700 square kilometers. The agricultural potential of this area is, however, partly offset by the semiarid climate which causes a moisture deficit during the growing season and the scarcity of irrigation water with which to supplement the inadequate rainfall. In addition, the agricultural productivity of the valley is dependent upon the population, which consists almost entirely of peasant agriculturalists who use traditional methods of cultivation and irrigation and have small and scattered holdings, low capital resources, and strong social and economic ties within the village.

Studies of peasant agriculture are not new; they have been undertaken by agriculturalists, economists, anthropologists and geographers. Much of the geographic work has been descriptive rather than analytic in approach and has been concerned with agricultural practices and techniques and relating their spatial distribution to rather generalised physical and cultural variables. Research by agriculturalists and economists has focused more on establishing the input-output costs of agricultural systems, the former in terms of productivity per unit area of land and the latter in terms of return from total investment. Both groups of researchers tend to view the present system in terms of its capacity for improvement in the future, given the appropriate additions of irrigation water, fertilizer, or credit facilities, without inquiring very deeply into the social structure and values that are an integral part of peasant agriculture.

The social aspects of traditional agriculture have been left principally to the anthropologist, who has done by far the most work on peasant systems of cultivation. The focus of most anthropological field studies of peasants has, however, been on understanding a particular social organisation and culture, of which agriculture is but one

---

[1] The other four areas were the Valley of Mexico, the Cholula-Puebla area, the Mixteca Alta and the area around Guatemala City (Palerm and Wolf, 1957:30).

aspect, rather than looking at agriculture itself as an expression of the degree to which resources are available and how and why they are used. Recent theories in economic anthropology are more concerned with the relationship between economic systems and social values, as will be discussed in the final chapter, and it is in this field that the data presented here probably can make the most direct contribution.

This research differs from most other studies of peasant agriculture not only in its focus on resource use rather than on economic or social systems, but also in the scale on which it is designed. Broadly, field anthropologists work on a micro-scale and economists work on a macro-scale. This research has been conducted on a meso-scale; that is, it covers an area of 3600 square kilometers and 256 settlements. This is closer in size to areas considered by economists, but much of the data presented are similar in detail and accuracy to those obtained by anthropologists. This coverage is made possible by obtaining data for individual fields and peasant cultivators from all parts of the Valley at points selected on the basis of the known total variability of physical resources and agricultural patterns within the Valley. In this way, the research was designed to avoid relying on published statistics which had been averaged over larger areas. These statistics, where they existed at all, were found to be unsatisfactory for the purposes of this study. It also avoided the collection of detailed information from one small part of the Valley which would be inadequate to give any idea of the total range of variation present or how individual results should be calibrated for the Valley as a whole.

At the micro-scale, the collection of data for anthropological studies is usually confined to a small social unit such as a family or a village. This is partly because such units can be clearly defined but more importantly because, for social systems in particular, the input required in fieldwork time and the output of complex information are both very large even for small units of study. Conversely, the economists rely more on averaged published statistics because they are dealing with larger areas for which data of the detail and accuracy that the anthropologist collects are simply not yet available. The type of data collected for this study and the methods of investigation stem from 1) the size of the study area, 2) the paucity of previously collected relevant information, and 3) the objective of understanding the internal variation within the Valley.

These factors in the design of the research are related to its position as an integral part of the Valley of Oaxaca Archaeological Project. The project, directed by Dr. Kent V. Flannery, has the general aim of understanding the adaptive processes that result in cultural change within early agricultural communities, particularly with reference to the evolution of centralised state organisations. To do this, the project aim is to study the present physical and social organisation of the Valley in as many aspects as possible as well as investigate its past history. The emphasis on understanding the internal variation of relevant factors within the Valley is important to the aim of the project because it is the presence of this variation which itself appears to have contributed to the cultural and economic development of the Valley from the earliest archaeological periods to the present day. This part of the project concentrates on present agriculture and irrigation in order to facilitate a better interpretation of past land and water use. It is closely related to two other parts of the project, both of which were designed and conducted on a similar meso-scale, aimed at identifying differences within the Valley. These are the research by Dr. Michael J. Kirkby (1973) into the physical environment and stratigraphic history of the Valley and the study of the social and political organisation of canal irrigation by Dr. Susan H. Lees (1973).

There were three main methods of investigation used. First, relevant measures of the physical environment and resource use for the whole Valley were mapped. These maps were based on field measurements at several hundred random points and interpolated between points by observation along field transects and by air photograph interpretation. Second, detailed field by field records of land use and input-output costs were made as well as time analyses for individual cultivators in areas selected after the total range of land and water use variation was known. Previous work by many anthropologists on individual villages provided valuable information on the range of economic and social organisation between communities. Finally, comparisons were made between the number and location of known archaeological sites and the settlements predicted for different times on the basis of conclusions reached from present agricultural productivity and resource use. In the past, we are dealing not with agricultural productivity directly but with evidence concerning the size, distribution and organisation of the labour force.

These data were analysed with two main objectives:

1) to establish what are the important aspects of the physical and cultural environment which influence the ways in which resources are used today and the degree to which they are fully exploited; and
2) to use this knowledge as a basis for interpreting the past history of the Valley, particularly with reference to the development of settled agricultural communities.

It is hoped that this study will not only add to our knowledge of the Valley of Oaxaca itself, but will serve as an example of peasant agriculture which will further understanding of how and why resources are used or not used in a more general context. Wolf (1966:6) has argued that it is not simply the existence of potential surpluses that stimulates development but also the presence of institutional means and imperatives within the organisational structure of society to mobilise them. This is an argument which will be returned to later because it holds important implications as to how cultural development has proceeded in the past, how far resources are exploited today, and how far planned agricultural and economic development can succeed in the future if it is not accompanied or preceded by fundamental changes in society.

## DEFINITIONS

Since some of the terms used in this work have been used elsewhere with slightly different meanings, they will be defined here for the purposes of this study.

*Peasant* is generally understood to mean an agricultural producer with a low level of technology and little land or capital resources, who grows food for his family and provides produce for sale in markets which support large centres of population. Redfield (1956:64) has defined peasants in terms of their common attitudes; namely, a reverent attitude toward the land, the idea that agricultural work is good and commerce is less good, and the principle that hard work is a virtue. These attitudes apply equally to many groups organised in tribes, and Wolf has stressed that the difference between peasants and other simple cultivators is that peasants do not form a complete society, but only one stratum of a larger state organisation. The agricultural suppliers of cities are therefore only peasants when they are part of a single state:

...only when the cultivator becomes subject to the demands and sanctions of power holders outside his social stratum can we talk of peasantry (Wolf, 1966:11).

Keeping in mind this idea of the link between peasant agriculturalists living in villages and state authority centred in cities, we can adopt Wolf's earlier definition of the peasant, which embodies the spirit of Redfield's definition. A peasant is an agricultural producer in effective control of his own land who practises agriculture as a means of livelihood, not as a business for profit (Wolf, 1957:1). In Oaxaca, therefore, peasant means a small-scale agricultural producer who grows some food for direct consumption by his family and also works to earn cash income by producing cash crops or other goods and services. A peasant household in Oaxaca is an economic unit for production and consumption.

In this paper a distinction is drawn between *subsistence* agriculture and *cash* agriculture. By subsistence I do not mean an economy which produces the bare minimum required to keep people alive or that *all* the needs of a household are provided directly by the subsistence agriculture. Nash has pointed out that in any human society subsistence includes a biological minimum requirement and an additional cultural component which can include the supplies for large feasts and elaborate ceremonies. Subsistence agriculture in

Oaxaca therefore means farming "in which production and consumption are more or less direct without intervening acts of exchange among producing units" (Nash, 1966:22), although some exchange will exist. A *milpa* is therefore regarded as part of subsistence cultivation not because it supplies all the caloric requirements of its owner, but because its produce is eaten directly by the owner's household. In the Valley of Oaxaca, subsistence agriculture must be combined with other sources of income because, by definition, it cannot provide cash for the household's other needs. When corn is grown in addition to the food needs of the producer and is aimed at the cash market, it becomes a cash crop.

In referring to the Valley of Oaxaca, two forms of the word valley are used (Valley:valley). Valley is used as an abbreviation for Valley of Oaxaca and includes the whole drainage basin up to the divides; valley and valley floor both mean the physiographic valley as distinct from the mountains and piedmont, and refer only to the area occupied by the high and low alluvium. The abbreviations used in the figures and tables are as follows: T and Tlac. refer to Tlacolula; E refers to San Pedro y San Pablo Etla, the administrative centre of the Etla Valley; Za refers to Zaachila; Zi refers to Zimatlan; and Oc refers to Ocotlán. All these are important towns and heads of *distritos*— the largest administrative unit within the valley into which *municipios* are grouped. All the place names mentioned in the text or illustrations are located on the map in Figure 1. All units used are metric and where tons are used they refer to metric tons. Costs are given in Mexican pesos which at the present rate of exchange are approximately 12.5 pesos to one U.S. dollar.

## METHODS

This research was planned and conducted as a field study to collect information which had not previously been obtained for the Valley of Oaxaca and only rarely obtained for other areas with a similar level of economic development. The material was collected over four field seasons between 1966 and 1970 during which a total of fifteen months was spent in the field. Although the data include that which is usually considered within the scope of geomorphology, economics, anthropology and archaeology, the approach is always geographic: that is, an analysis of the changing *spatial* distributions of land and water use.

The principal field methods used were direct mapping and measurement of data, and the obtaining of material indirectly through interviews with peasant cultivators and their families (hereafter called informants). Wherever possible, both methods were used on the same topic or area to provide as much internal cross-checking as possible. Field survey was carried out by jeep and on foot and concentrated on the valley floor and piedmont with relatively few transects through the mountains. As the survey proceeded, the distributions of collected data were drawn directly on to the 1:100,000 map of the Valley in the field. Field maps were produced of geology, topography, soils, hydrology, natural vegetation, agricultural crops and types of water use.

A map at 1:100,000 was also made of corn productivity (Fig. 25) after the results of 175 measurements of corn yield in 1967, 1968 and 1970 were analysed. These measurements were made in milpas throughout the Valley just before they were harvested in August and September and, wherever possible, were checked with informant data. For each milpa, its location in the Valley, physiographic zone, water availability and use, and degree of surface erosion were noted. Measurements were then taken of corn height, spacing between rows, spacing along rows, the number of corn plants per hectare, the length of corn cobs and average number of cobs per plant for a random sample of plants. The ratio of corn, beans and squash was also calculated. No sample had a population of less than 20 and few of more than 50. This method was found to be simple and quick in the field, and after the length of cob had been calibrated against weight of seed in the laboratory (Fig. 22), it provided measures of corn yield which were internally consistent and gave an index of spatial variation of yield over the valley floor. This direct measurement acted as a check on informant data and allowed a statistical analysis of the most important effects of the environment on corn yield (Chapter V).

After the survey and mapping of the whole valley had been completed, sample areas of 1-5 square kilometers were selected for detailed land use surveys at a scale of 1:7000. The locations of these sample areas are given in Figure 2. Within each area, physiographic variables such as geology, soils and hydrology were mapped in detail, and several fields were measured for corn yield. The prime purpose of the sample areas was to afford a field by field survey of land use which was repeated in each subsequent field season. These land-use data form the basis for the evidence of annual variations in corn area used in Chapters VI and VII. The collection of informant data on agricultural costs and decisions was also concentrated in these areas, since walking from field to field in order to map land use afforded opportunity to talk to peasant cultivators who were working in them.

Interviews with informants took the form of conversations without the name of the informant being taken (in most cases) or any notes made in his presence. No questionnaire was produced nor was any indication made that a series of questions was in mind. Most interviews covered the same topics, but these were introduced casually at appropriate moments and in different orders in each interview. Questions were made as specific as possible; for example, "What type of corn did you plant this year in this milpa?" Notes were made a few minutes after the interview, but out of sight of the informant. A local guide and interpreter was rarely used. The advantages of this method of interview were that:

1) It provided specific answers which could be checked by field measurement or observation because reference was made to a known field or area.
2) Time was saved by talking to men who were already in the fields rather than trying to arrange in a village to go out with a specific man on a certain day. In this way, up to six interviews were possible in a morning instead of one or none.
3) Men appeared to give answers more freely when the interview was unofficial and their names were not taken unless they offered them, so that they need fear neither official reprisals nor the leaking of their information to other men in their village.

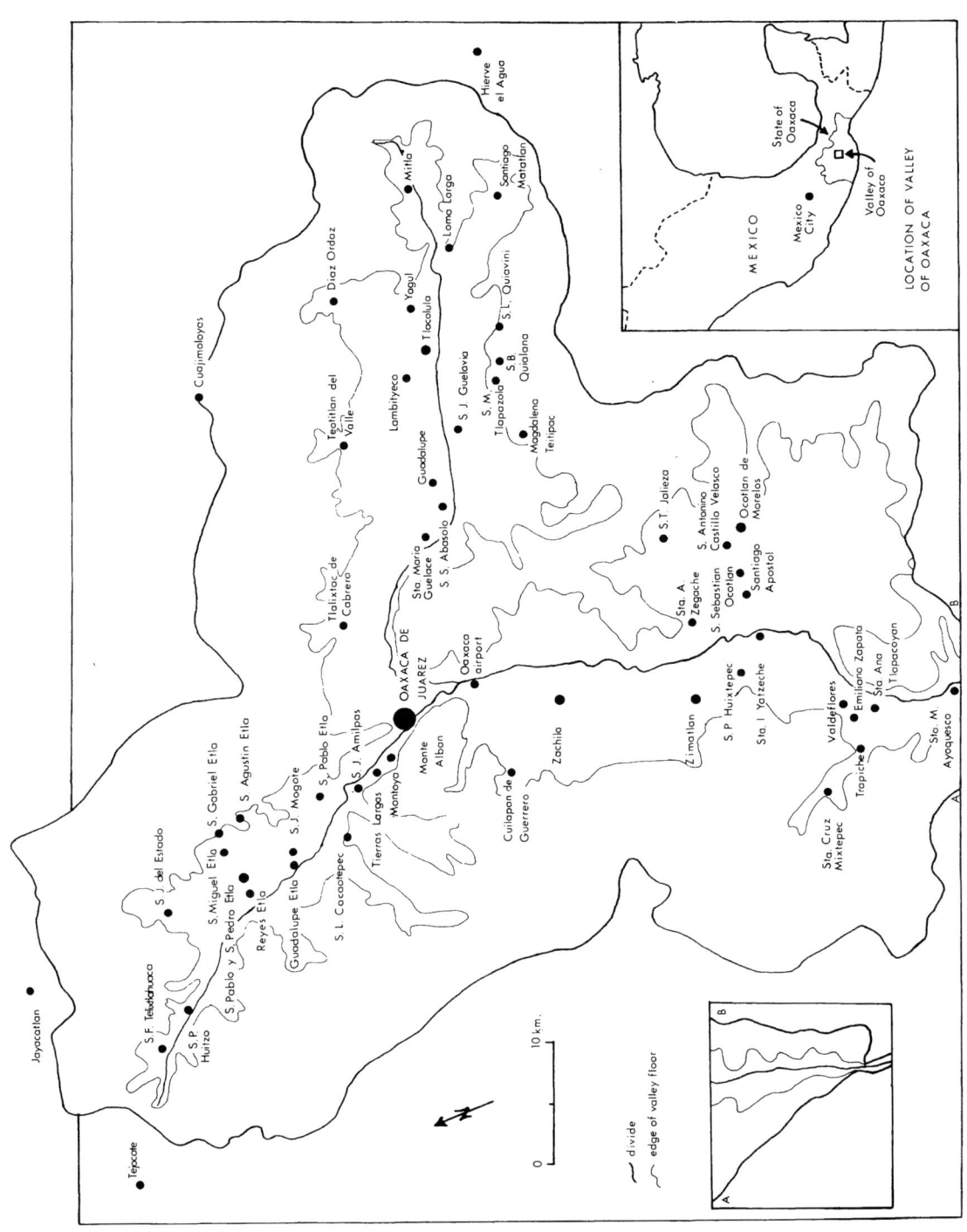

Fig. 1. Map of Valley of Oaxaca to show general features, location of all place names mentioned in text, and position of valley in southern Mexico.

## II

## AGRICULTURAL RESOURCES IN THE PHYSICAL ENVIRONMENT

### INTRODUCTION

The Valley of Oaxaca lies in the southern highlands of Mexico surrounded by country which is deeply dissected, heavily forested and sparsely populated (Fig. 1). In such an area, agriculture is limited to a few zones where the land is a little less steep, either along narrow valley bottoms or spur crests. Elsewhere crops are grown only in scattered fields cleared by slash and burn techniques and shifted every few years. In this mountain region are several important valleys where slopes are gentle and communications easier, and these valleys form the cultural and economic centres for the region. Of these valleys, the largest and most important is that of Oaxaca.

The Valley of Oaxaca is located between 16°40'-17°20' N and 96°15'-96°55' W with its floor lying at altitudes between 1420 and 1740 meters and surrounded by mountains rising to more than 3000 meters. It forms the upper drainage basin of the Río Atoyac with its southern (downstream) limit defined by the entry of the river into a gorge. At this point the wide alluvial bottomland that characterises the upper section disappears, and the river cuts southward through successive west-east trending ridges of the Sierra Madre del Sur to eventually join the Río Verde and flow into the Pacific Ocean. Above this gorge, the Atoyac and its main tributary, the Río Salado, flow through open valleys which join at the present city of Oaxaca de Juárez. The area called the Valley of Oaxaca has therefore three distinct arms which together form the shape of a Y. These three sections are the Etla Valley to the north, the Tlacolula (or Mitla) Valley to the east, and the Zaachila Valley to the south. The Zaachila Valley is considerably larger than the other two so that a distinction is sometimes drawn between the Ocotlán Valley (which is formed by a major ephemeral stream from the east) and the rest of the Zaachila arm (Fig. 2).

In comparison with the rest of the region, the major resource for agriculture afforded by the Valley of Oaxaca is flat land (Pl. 1). The surrounding mountains have higher rainfalls and the lower coastal zone has higher temperatures, but the highland valleys have large enough stretches of cultivable land to support towns and cities and the social and economic development that accompanies them. In its turn, it is this cultural progress that has made agricultural land one of the most scarce resources of the Valley because out-migration is ineffective in reducing the pressure on the land of a growing peasant population. The flat valley floor is therefore divided into thousands of small holdings, many of them only a quarter of a hectare in area.

If flat land is the major resource of the Valley for agriculture, water is its most critical resource. Temperatures never fall low enough to inhibit plant growth with a range of only 5°C above and below a mean monthly temperature of 20.6°C at Oaxaca de Juárez, the capital city. Temperature only becomes critical for a few frost sensitive crops which are excluded on the basis of altitude from all the mountain zone and the valley floor north of Oaxaca de Juárez, and from a few topographic depressions where cold air drainage produces ground frosts in winter. Water is scarce in the Valley because mean rainfall is less than potential evapotranspiration for every month of the year resulting in an annual moisture deficit (Fig. 7). There is thus a high demand for irrigation

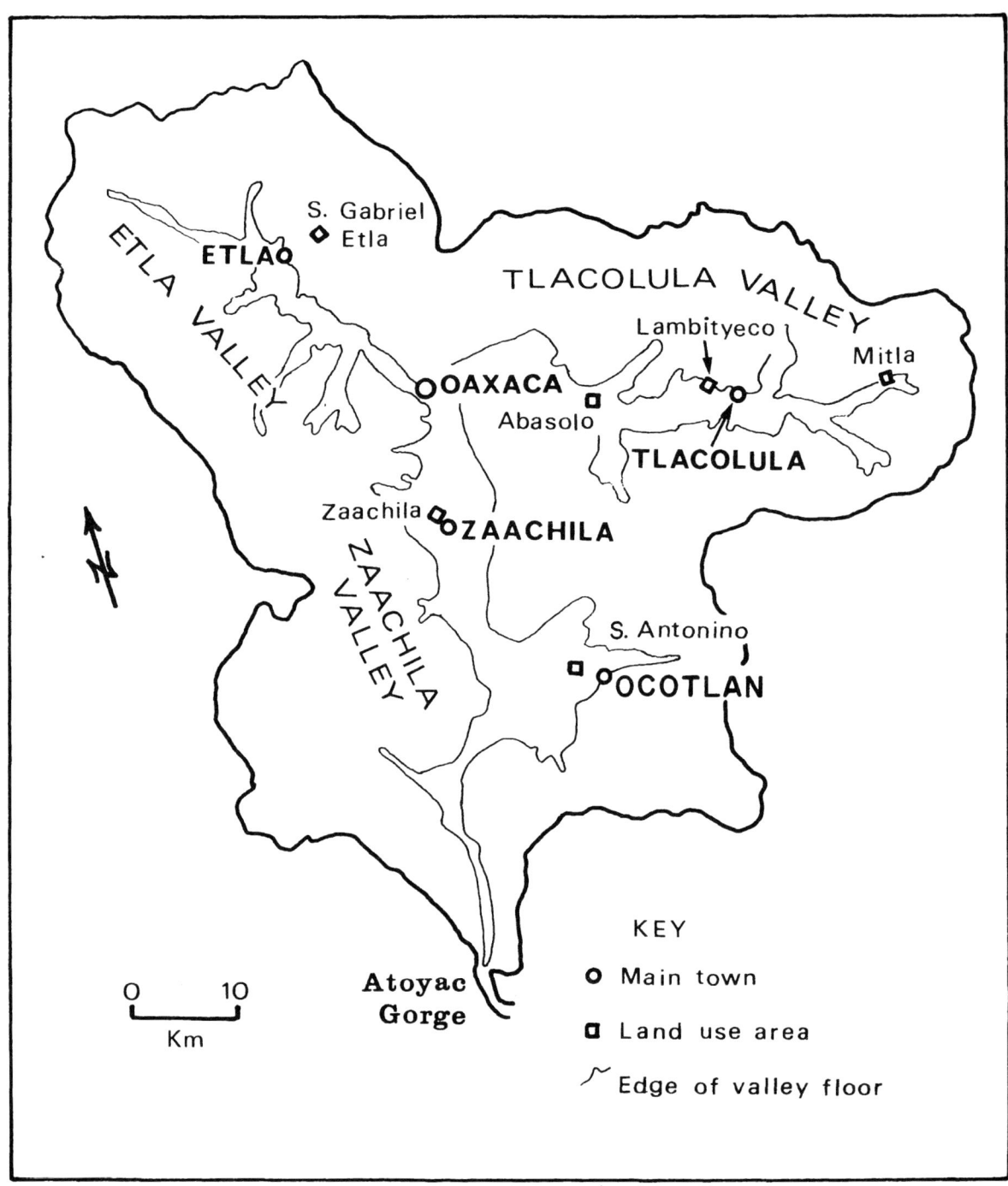

Fig. 2. Map of Valley of Oaxaca to show main towns and valleys and locations of sample land use areas.

TABLE 1
CLIMATIC VARIATION WITH ALTITUDE IN THE VALLEY OF OAXACA

| Station | Altitude (m) | Mean Annual Temperature (°C) | Mean Annual Precipitation (R) (mm) | Total Degree-days above 6°C (per annum) | Potential Evapo-transpiration (ET) (mm) | $\frac{R}{ET}$ (year) | $\frac{R}{ET}$ (3 summer months) | Frost-Free Period (months) | Natural Vegetation |
|---|---|---|---|---|---|---|---|---|---|
| Cuajimoloyas | 3100 | 8 | 1000 | 1000 | 340 | 2.9 | 6.9 | 0 | pine |
| Tejocotes | 2500 | 13 | 800 | 2500 | 720 | 1.1 | 3.0 | 0 | pine-oak |
| Ixtepeji | 2000 | 16 | 860 | 3600 | 1080 | 0.8 | 1.6 | 6.5 | oak |
| Oaxaca | 1540 | 21 | 630 | 5000 | 1890 | 0.34 | 0.81 | 12.0 | mesquite grassland |

water which cannot be supplied by the very low perennial stream flows alone, but requires recourse to several techniques tapping many small water sources.

## LAND

The most important criteria for distinguishing land for agriculture are gradient, altitude and soil. The type and density of natural vegetation were important in the past, but now the valley floor is continually under cultivation and clearing is only an important task in the mountains. On the basis of these criteria, the Valley can be divided into four physiographic zones: mountains, piedmont, high alluvium, and low alluvium (Fig. 3). The mountain zone is the least important agriculturally, with its lower temperatures and steep slopes. There are few villages, and these tend to be located on the divide where there is a larger area of land with gradients less than 30 degrees. Whatever the bedrock, soils in the mountains tend to be red in colour, very stony and variable in depth. Except near the villages, shifting agriculture is practised, and so far soil erosion is not a serious problem although terracing is not used, even on slopes steeper than 30 degrees. The mountains are used more as a collecting area for wood and wild fruits and making prepared charcoal than for cultivation. They are covered with high pine and oak forests which show a zonation of dominant species with increasing altitude from a broad-leafed oak woodland at 2,000 to 2,500 meters, to a mixed pine-oak forest at 2,500 to 2,700 meters, to a pine forest at altitudes above 2,700 meters.

This zonation of natural vegetation reflects the increase of rainfall and decrease of temperature[2] with altitude (Table 1). Mean annual temperature falls from 21°C (Oaxaca de Juárez, 1540 meters) on the valley floor to 8°C on the divide (Cuajimoloyas, 3100 meters). Associated with this decline in temperature is

1) a reduction in the growing season from 5000 degree-days per annum (that is, days × degrees C above 6°–this temperature being the approximate minimum for plant growth) at 1540 meters to only 1000 degree-days per annum at 3100 meters; and

2) a reduction in the length of the frost-free period from 12 months at 1540 meters to 0 at 3100 meters.

On the basis of temperature variation alone, therefore, the principal dry-farmed crops in the mountains must be increasingly frost resistant at higher elevations, and the number of crops it is possible to grow in a year declines from 3 on the valley floor to one on the divide. Within the elevation range of the mountains, the most significant altitude is 2100 to 2300 meters, which is about the height at which wheat and barley fields

---

[2] Temperature, precipitation and evaporation data used in this study come from the following sources:
1. Secretaría de Agricultura y Ganadera: records on file in Oaxaca de Juárez.
2. Secretaría de Recursos Hidráulicos: records on file in Oaxaca de Juárez.
3. Servicio Meteorológico Mexicano.
4. Cecil Welte: Oficina de Estudios de Humanidad del Valle de Oaxaca.
5. Records of rainfall gathered by members of the Valley of Oaxaca Project 1966-68.

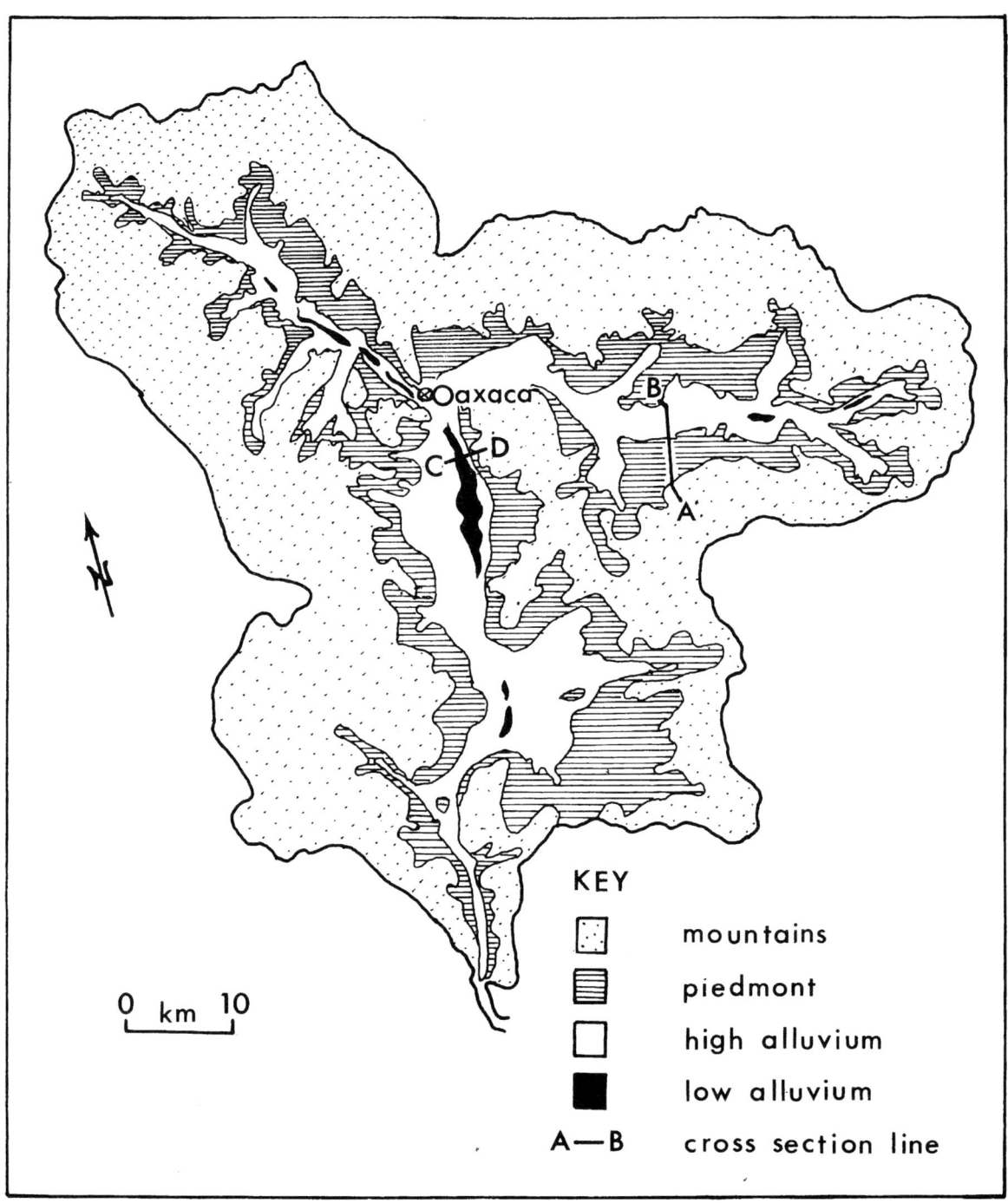

Fig. 3. Map of the Valley of Oaxaca to show main physiographic zones.

first become widespread in relation to the ubiquitous maize. At this elevation the frost-free period has just 2000 degree-days which is the approximate number required to grow one crop on the valley floor (Table 1).

Piedmont Zone

The piedmont zone is an area of transition across which slope gradients, depth of dissection, valley shape, and other features such as soil and vegetation grade from their characteristic forms in the mountains to those of the valley floor. It is the resource of water rather than land which has made parts of the piedmont very valuable for agriculture; the piedmont is the first point at which perennial streams flowing down from the mountains can be diverted to a gentle enough slope to provide irrigation. Without water the piedmont provides only marginal land for agriculture, since its slopes are steeper and soils poorer than those of the valley floor.

Originally the piedmont was formed as a series of coalescing fans which have since been dissected into a line of ridges and valleys delimiting the outer edge of the valley floor. The degree of dissection varies, being greatest in the narrow Etla Valley and much less in the Zaachila Valley. On the west side of the Zaachila arm, the piedmont (here developed on gravels derived from gneiss) is 3 to 5 kilometers wide and shows gentle dissection into a series of long, rounded spurs separated by shallow valleys so that the high alluvium grades up into the piedmont zone in a series of wide embayments. On the south side of the Tlacolula Valley the piedmont is also wide and forms a continuous surface with gullies cut 20 meters into it rather than a series of separate spurs. A characteristic cross section is shown in Figure 4a.

The average slope of the piedmont from mountain to alluvium is 1 to 2 degrees with later dissection producing side slopes with gradients up to 20 to 30 degrees. The soils developed on the piedmont are poor for agriculture, mainly because they are very stony; and where the surface is cut on bedrock, they are commonly thin with outcrops of rock scattered over the slopes. Soils are usually red-brown in colour, coarse textured and free draining. Typical mechanical compositions range between 5 and 15 percent gravel, and 40 to 90 percent sand with 10 to 30 percent of the ground surface covered by stones greater than 25 mm in diameter. In some areas, notably near Mitla in the Tlacolula Valley, where over 90 percent of the surface is covered by stones greater than 25 mm in diameter, surface stoniness makes agriculture impractical.

Despite its inferiority to the valley alluvium for agriculture, the piedmont is extensively cultivated and, even more important, grazed by domestic animals so that the natural vegetation is partly or wholly destroyed (Pl. 2). It is typically more open today than the natural vegetation of either the alluvium or the mountains; so the piedmont may have been one of the easiest areas of the Valley for early cultivators to clear. Between 1800 to 2000 meters, however, the open mesquite grassland does give way to a thorn forest which is almost impenetrable when well developed, with several species of cactus and *Agave*. Above 2000 meters, piedmont vegetation is again more open with the thorny species giving way to narrow- and broad-leafed oaks which are easy to clear and not as well developed as the oak zone in the mountains proper.

High Alluvium

The high alluvium forms the main part of the valley floor and is the most important zone for agriculture both in quantity and quality. It varies in total width from 1 kilometer just north of Oaxaca de Juárez to 17 kilometers near Ocotlán (Fig. 3). Within the high alluvium, the value of land for agriculture (apart from the consideration of water availability) varies with soil texture and with topography, principally in its effect on ground frost frequency.

In contrast with the mountain and piedmont zones, soils on the valley floor are always greater than 1 meter in depth, and soil thickness is nowhere a limiting factor for agriculture. Throughout the valley floor, soil profiles are poorly developed and retain their alluvial structure almost unaltered below the A horizon. Some salt accumulation is found in the B horizon, especially in the

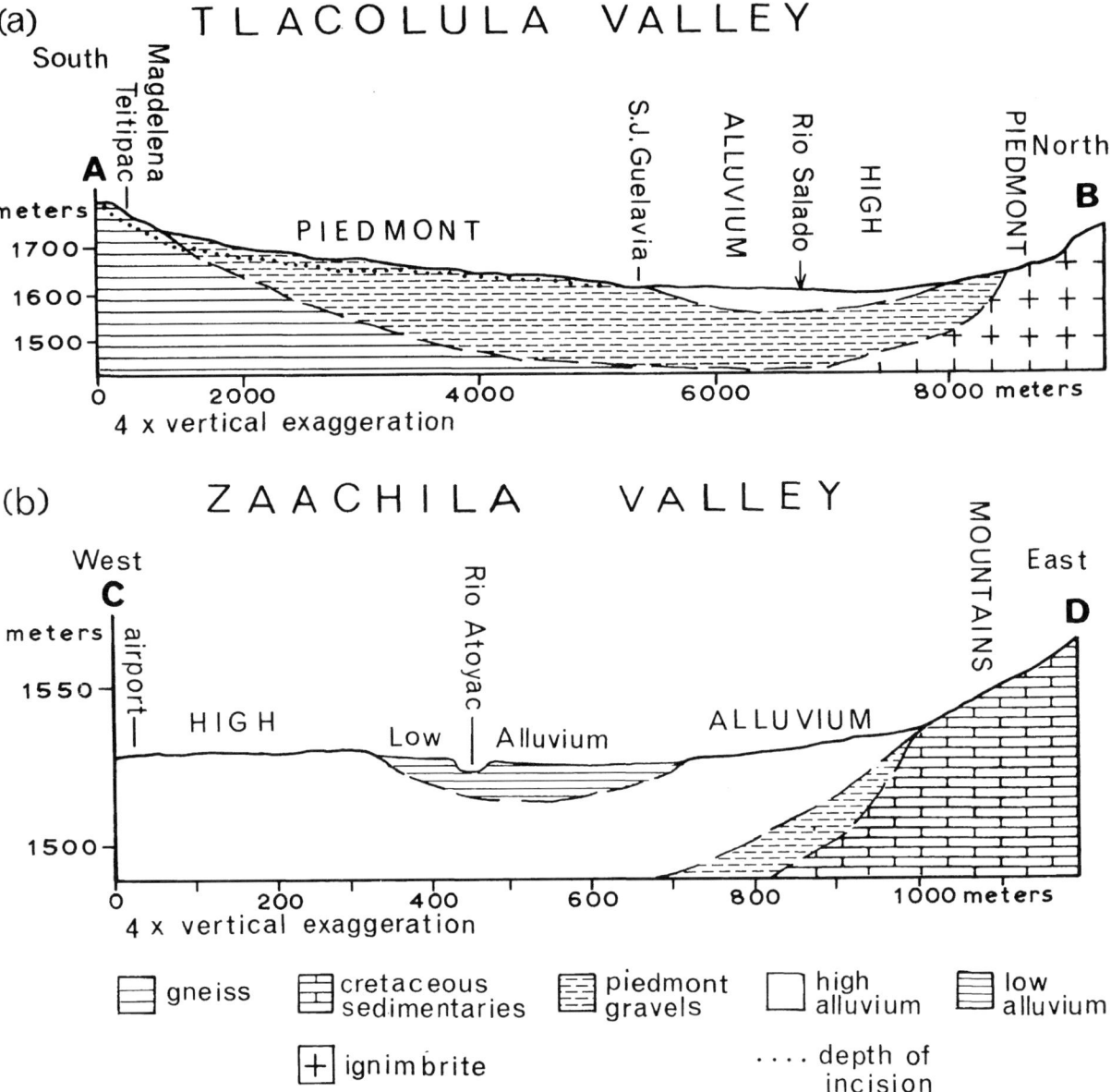

Fig. 4. (a) Cross section of Tlacolula Valley at San Juan Guelavía through seasonally flooded section of Río Salado. (b) Cross section of Zaachila Valley floor near Oaxaca airport showing the two levels of alluvium.

widest parts of the Valley where low gradients allow shallow depressions to contain standing water for several days or weeks after storms in the summer months. The alluvial soils are always alkaline (pH 8.0-8.7) and low in humus and nutrients. Soil color is generally brown and tends toward red-brown on the better drained gravels and grey-brown in the more arid parts of the Valley. The general uniformity of the young valley soils in thickness, chemical composition and profile development has emphasized the importance to agriculture of textural differences; grain size largely determines the water-holding characteristics of soil and therefore influences the amount of water available for crops from both groundwater and irrigation water.

The distribution of soil types by texture is shown in Figure 5.[3] Generally grain size increases from the outer edge of the floor to the main river courses. The transition from piedmont fan soil to high alluvium soil is therefore commonly marked by an abrupt change in soil texture from stony sand in the piedmont to fine clay in the alluvium, and in the valley centre the course of the Río Atoyac is outlined by a band of sand soils. In detail the pattern is more complicated because the larger distributaries, which rise in the mountains and cross the piedmont, deposit aprons of gravels and sands on the outer edge of the high alluvium. These deposits may be sufficiently extensive to produce a continuous band of sandy soil along the outer edge of the alluvium, as occurs, for example, on the western side of the valley near Zaachila.

In the central part of the Tlacolula Valley the high alluvium soils are entirely fine grained; the usual band of sandy soil following the river course is absent. This is caused by the unusual hydrology of the area. During most summers the Río Salado does not flow in a single channel to join the Atoyac, but spreads across a wide area between San Juan Guelavía and San Sebastián Abasolo in a complicated pattern of braided channels and slowly moving sheets of water, producing a seasonal swamp in which clays are deposited (Pl. 3). Silt soils are not widespread and occur in narrow discontinuous bands between the areas of sand and clay soils. Along major tributary valleys a characteristic sequence of decreasing grain size downstream is observed going from gravel soils to clay soils within distances of 10 to 15 kilometers. Cross-valley soil patterns are similar to that described for the main valley floor.

Gradients on the high alluvium are less than 1 degree, so that topography is an important factor for agriculture only in that the overall downwards gradient from north to south results in an altitudinal difference between the floors of the Etla and Tlacolula Valleys on the one hand and the Zaachila Valley on the other. Also, some areas in the valley centre form depressions into which cold air drains. These topographic differences affect crops in terms of frost frequency. Within the

[3]The compositions of sand, silt and clay soils as the terms are used in this paper are defined in Figure 5.

elevation range found on the valley floor (1500 to 1670 meters), two agriculturally distinct areas may be defined:

1) a higher, cooler zone including all of the Etla and Tlacolula Valleys, where absolute minimum temperatures recorded are $-8°C$. The probability of air frosts is once every 3 years, and ground frosts are likely every year so that the average length of the frost-free period is 10 months.

2) a lower, warmer zone including all of the Zaachila Valley, where absolute minimum temperatures are $+1°C$. The probability of air frosts is less than 1 in 20 to 40 years. Ground frosts are reported not to occur, and in any case their probability is so low that frost sensitive plants are not excluded; the average length of the frost-free period is therefore 12 months. Oaxaca de Juárez, at 1540 meters and with no air frosts in 40 years of records, lies close to the critical elevation that divides the valley floor into frost-free and non-frost-free areas.

The effect of elevation differences on temperature over the valley floor is summarized in Table 2.

The age of the high alluvium is important to this study because although its surface now consists almost entirely of abandoned floodplains of the main rivers, evidence has been found which dates the present surface to the archaeological period. The 3 to 6 meters of alluvium which separate the present high alluvium surface from the present river level have all been deposited since about 800 B.C.-200 B.C. By the time of the Spanish Conquest in the sixteenth century, the rivers had finished aggrading throughout most of the valley, and rapid downcutting was initiated which appears to be continuing today. This evidence and its implications for the causes of deposition and incision are discussed elsewhere (M. J. Kirkby, 1973).

Low Alluvium

The main rivers of the Valley are generally incised into the high alluvium to a depth of 1 to 3 meters, although below dams downcutting has reached 6 to 7 meters, and at this lower level a

14

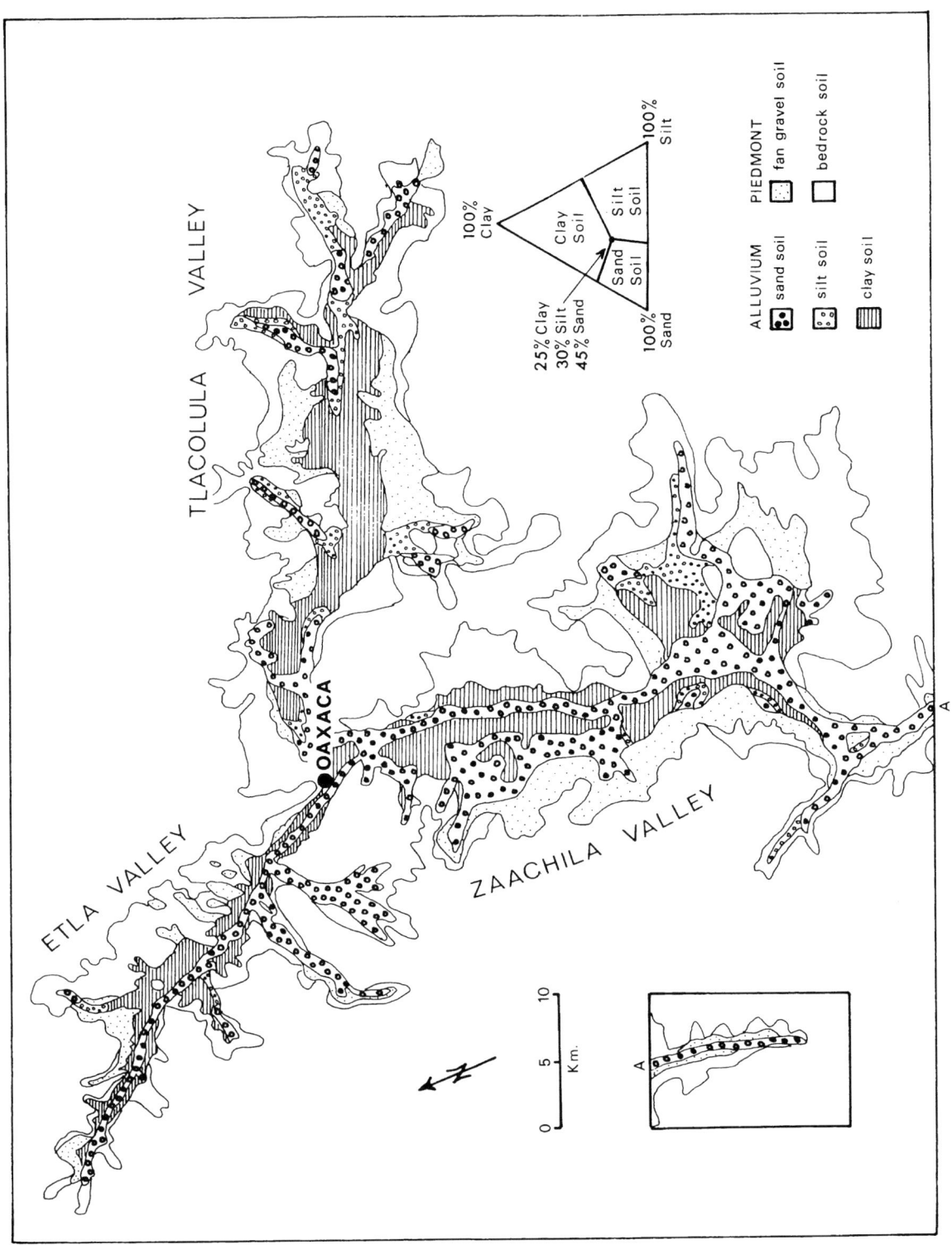

Fig. 5. Map of Valley of Oaxaca to show soils of the valley floor and piedmont.

TABLE 2
CLIMATIC VARIATION WITHIN THE VALLEY FLOOR

| Station | Altitude (m) | Mean Annual Temperature (°C) | Mean Annual Precipitation (R) (mm) | Total Degree-days above 6°C (per annum) | Potential Evapotranspiration (ET) (mm) | $\frac{R}{ET}$ (year) | $\frac{R}{ET}$ (3 summer months) | Frost-Free Period (months) | Natural Vegetation |
|---|---|---|---|---|---|---|---|---|---|
| Etla | 1660 | 19 | 650 | 5000 | 1670 | 0.39 | 0.92 | 10 | mesquite grassland |
| Tlacolula | 1620 | 18 | 550 | 4500 | 2020 | 0.26 | 0.5 | 10 | " |
| Oaxaca | 1540 | 21 | 630 | 5000 | 1890 | 0.34 | 0.81 | 12 | " |
| Ocotlán | 1520 | 20 | 740 | 5000 | 1900 | 0.39 | 0.93 | 12 | " |

new flood plain is presently forming. This flood plain, or low alluvium, is very restricted in area, occurring as a distinct geomorphic unit along less than 50 percent of the courses of the Río Atoyac and Río Salado, and attaining a maximum width of only 2.5 kilometers (in the Zaachila Valley). Incision leading to the formation of the low alluvium did not begin until after A.D. 1500 in the Zaachila Valley and as late as A.D. 1800 upstream in the Etla Valley near Huitzo. Throughout most of the period of agriculture, therefore, the low alluvium did not exist.

Where the rivers are incised and the low alluvium is absent, the channel bed is bordered by a steep, sometimes near-vertical bank cut in the deposits of the high alluvium. Where the low alluvium is present, the 1 to 3 meter high difference between the two levels is normally occupied by a gentle slope, degraded by natural slope processes and ploughing. A transect measured across the Río Atoyac near the Oaxaca airport shows the topographic relationship between the two surfaces at a point where the low alluvium is particularly well developed (Fig. 4b).

Soils of the low alluvium are similar to the sand soils of the high alluvium with pH of approximately 8.0 and little or no detectable profile development. Surface stoniness (greater than 25 mm diameter) increases towards the present river channels, and concentrations of gravel on or just below the surface indicate recent former positions of the bed. The river beds and most recent areas of deposition are usually pure sand and gravel and are locally excavated for these materials. The value of the low alluvium for agriculture depends primarily on its water resources rather than on its land characteristics since it is restricted in area, has poor soils, and is liable to crop damage from flooding during the summer growing season.

## WATER

Water for agriculture is obtained from three main sources: directly from rainfall, from streams, and from the water table.

### Rainfall

The need for irrigation in the Valley of Oaxaca is based on two critical aspects of the rainfall: moisture availability throughout the year and rainfall variability between years. Supplementary water is therefore needed to make up an annual water deficit and to remove the risk of drought at the time of planting.

The meteorological station at Oaxaca de Juárez has the longest period of observations and is representative of the valley floor climate. Figure 6 gives the mean monthly temperature, evaporation and rainfall, and one standard deviation above and below each mean value for Oaxaca de Juárez. The figure shows that it is rainfall rather than temperature or evaporation which is most variable both within and between years. Mean annual temperature is 20.6°C with a range of only 5°C between the hottest and coolest months (April-May and December respectively). Mean monthly evaporation follows the temperature curve with highest

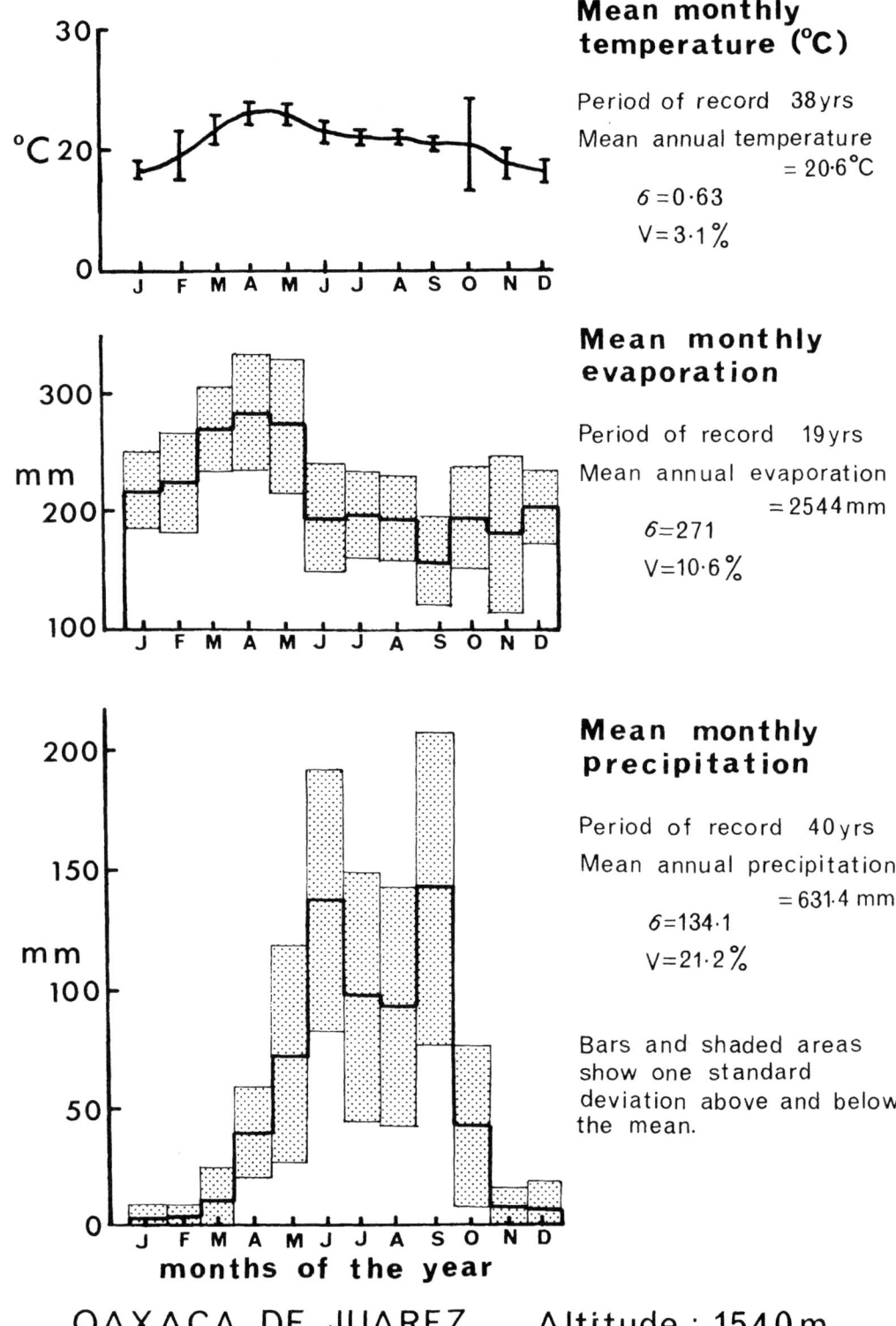

Fig. 6. Climatic data for Oaxaca de Juárez: mean monthly values and one standard deviation of temperature, evaporation and rainfall.

values in March, April and May; several months before maximum rainfall. The annual pattern of relative humidity is also less marked than that of the rainfall, with an annual mean of 63 percent, falling to 61 percent in January and rising to 69 percent in July.

The rainfall pattern shows a sharp distinction between the dry winter months from November to March whose mean monthly rainfalls are less than 10 mm, and the summer rainy season. This characteristically begins in late April to May but does not become well established until June with its mean rainfall of 137 mm. The rainy season has two peaks, one in June and a second in September (mean rainfall = 144 mm). By October mean rainfall has fallen to 44 mm, and the rainy season usually ends as abruptly as it began. From the records of rainfall and potential evaporation kept at Oaxaca de Juárez, a graph of the mean water deficit throughout the year can be constructed (Fig. 7). There is a deficit in every month ranging from about 100 mm in the growing season to almost 2000 mm at the end of the dry season in May. In this climate, dense and continuous stands of crops are not possible without irrigation or at least dry-farming techniques to concentrate water in the soil. Since such techniques are used and crops are sown so that they do not cover more than half the surface area, the curve for 0.5 (ET) − R is more relevant to the present farming situation (Fig. 7) and shows that between June and October there is, on average, just enough water to support agriculture.

Rainfall and the corresponding water deficit vary over the Valley chiefly with altitude but also with respect to topography and storm direction which produce characteristic rainshadow areas. Figure 8 shows a rainfall map for the Valley based on all available records, and Tables 1 and 2 give additional climatic data for selected stations to show variability with altitude and location on the valley floor.

Mean annual precipitation rises with increasing altitude from 630 mm on the valley floor (Oaxaca de Juárez) to 1000 mm+ on the divide. The decrease of potential evapotranspiration with increasing elevation (from 1890 mm at 1540 meters to 340 mm at 3100 meters) produces a large altitudinal variation in annual water deficit. In Table 1, available moisture is indicated by the ratio of rainfall to potential evapotranspiration (R:ET ratio) for the whole year and by the R:ET ratio for the three critical summer months, June, July and August. The R:ET ratio for the whole year varies from 0.34 on the valley floor to 2.9 at 3100 meters (Table 1). The R:ET ratio for the three summer months, which is the time most important to cereal production, ranges from 0.81 at 1540 meters to 6.9 at 3100 meters; above the elevation of the valley floor and low piedmont there is not a significant water deficit for summer crops.

On the valley floor, where almost all the Valley's agriculture is concentrated, the R:ET ratios are much more critical. The eastern Tlacolula Valley suffers from the most severe rainshadow effect. The station at Tlacolula has the lowest recorded mean rainfalls and the highest potential evapotranspiration rate (2020 mm per annum). Annual R:ET ratios are therefore lowest in the eastern Tlacolula Valley (less than or equal to 0.26), but they are below 0.40 everywhere on the valley floor. A R:ET ratio of 1.0 would mean that rainfall was sufficient to compensate for all potential evapotranspiration. When rainfall is insufficient and soil moisture falls below the ideal value (field capacity) actual evapotranspiration becomes less than the potential.

The exact mechanisms by which actual evapotranspiration declines as soil moisture conditions become less than field capacity are still unknown. Thornthwaite (1948, 1954) and Mather (1954) consider the decline to be a logarithmic function of soil suction whereas Veihmeyer and Hendrickson (1931) suggest that until plants are near wilting point and soil moisture is very low, actual evapotranspiration rates approximate potential rates. The work done by Chang (1965) and Holmes (1961) indicates rates of decline that lie between these two opposing views, with a continuous rapid decline in actual evapotranspiration (the Thornthwaite model) more nearly approached in sandy soils in arid conditions and the Veihmeyer and Hendrickson model applicable to heavy clay soils in humid areas (Barry, 1969:172-173).

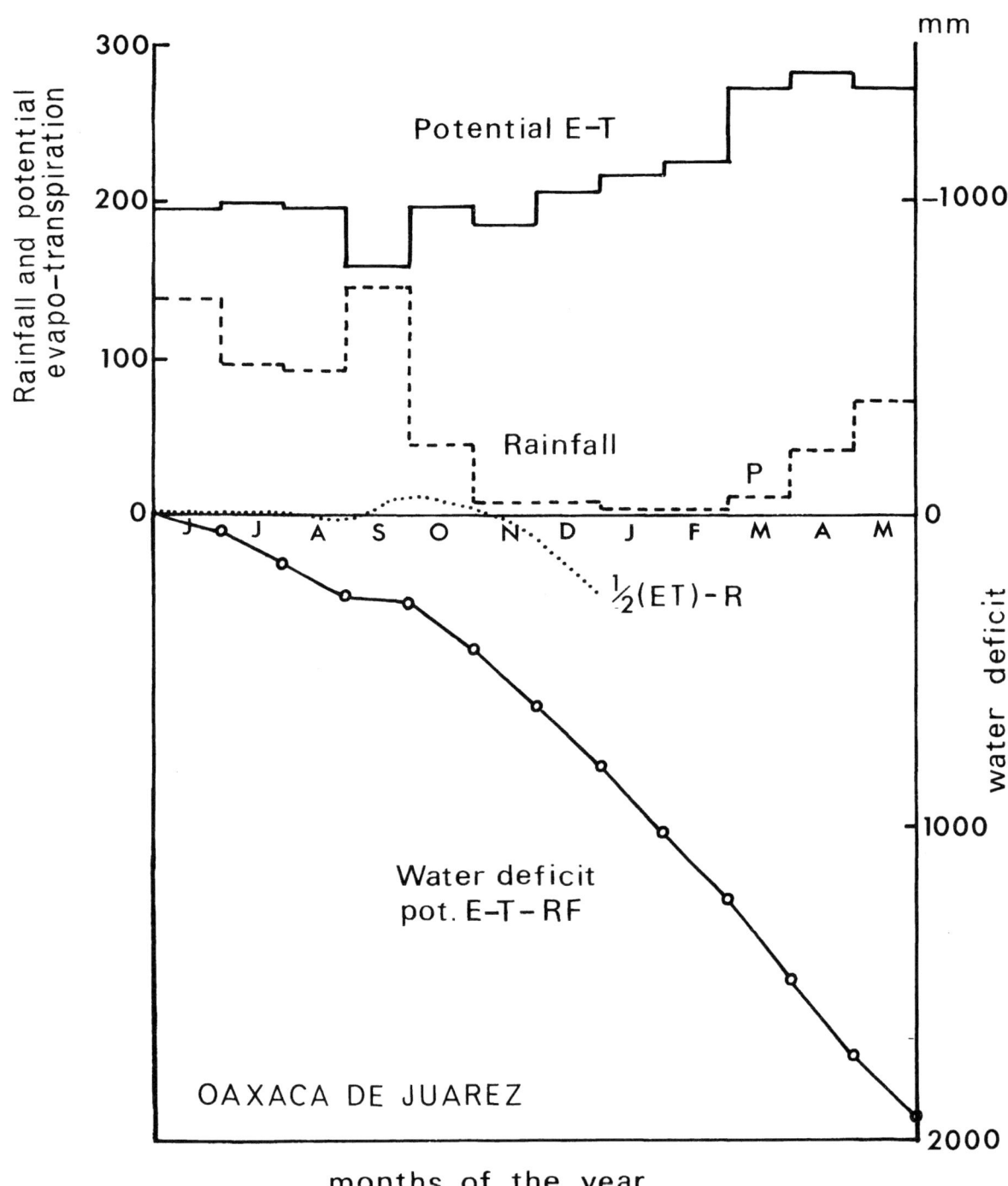

Fig. 7. Pattern of annual water deficit for Oaxaca de Juárez.

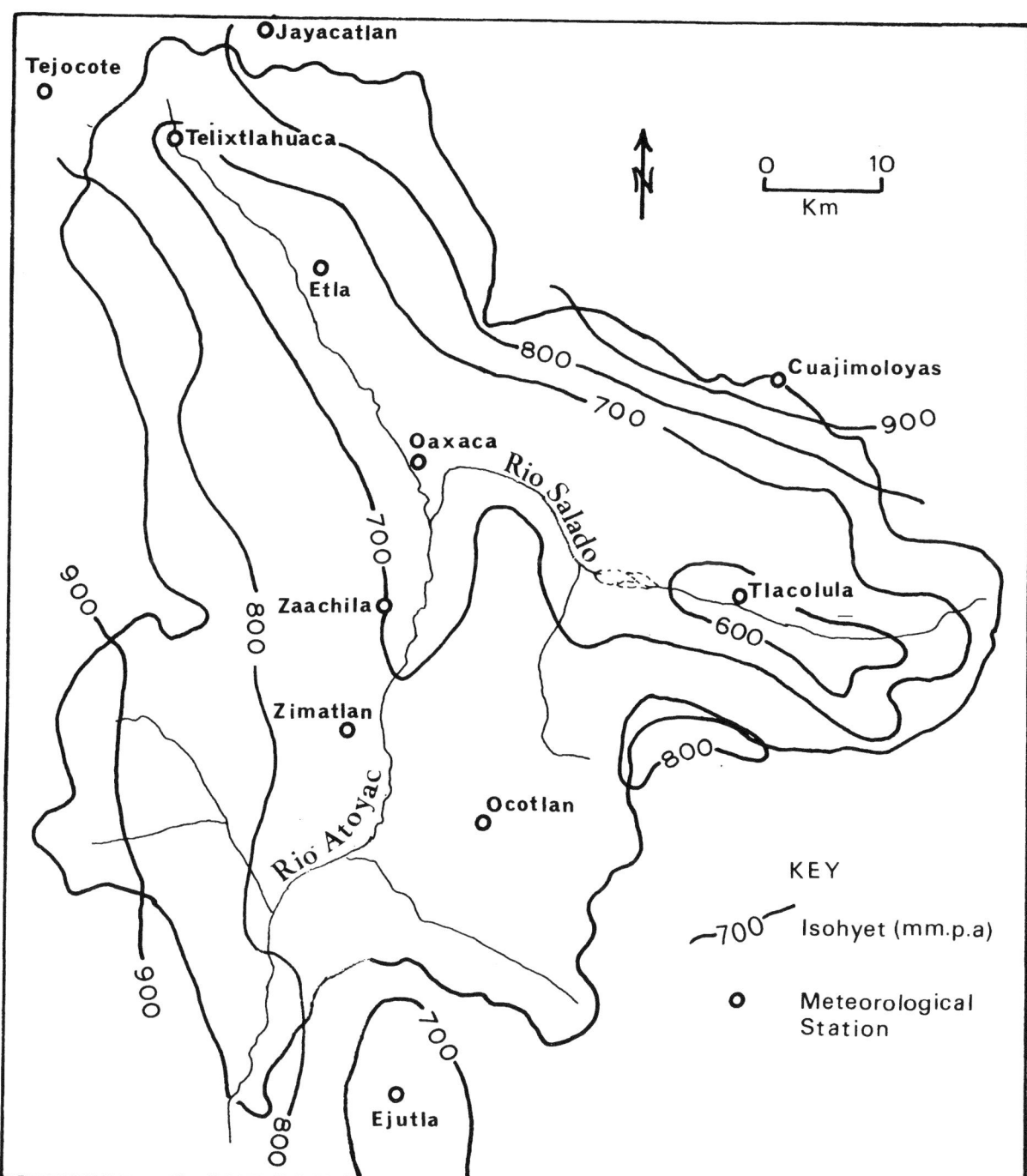

Fig. 8. Rainfall map of the Valley of Oaxaca based on all available records and interpolation with respect to altitude.

Whichever view is accepted for the relationship between actual and potential evapotranspiration, an average R:ET ratio of 0.40 or less for the year is not sufficient to support cereal production in the winter. Some perennial crops can *survive* a winter without irrigation, but no harvest will be produced. For the three summer months of June, July and August many parts of the valley floor have mean R:ET ratios of 0.80 or more (Table 2). This average ratio, combined with cultivation techniques which conserve moisture and the less than 100 percent ground cover by crops, leads to a reasonable expectation of one successful unirrigated crop during the rainy season. The exception to this is the eastern Tlacolula Valley which has a mean R:ET ratio of 0.5 or less for the three summer months. The greater frequency of low R:ET ratios for this area compared with Oaxaca de Juárez (Fig. 9) increases the risk of harvest failure and makes it the most marginal agricultural area in the Valley.

The problem of getting enough water for crops is basically one of inadequate mean annual rainfall, but it is aggravated by the variability of that rainfall from year to year, both in the amount of total rainfall and in the timing of the first major rains which, ideally, should coincide with planting. Variations in total rainfall for different years can be seen first in Figure 6 where the standard deviation for each month is superimposed on the

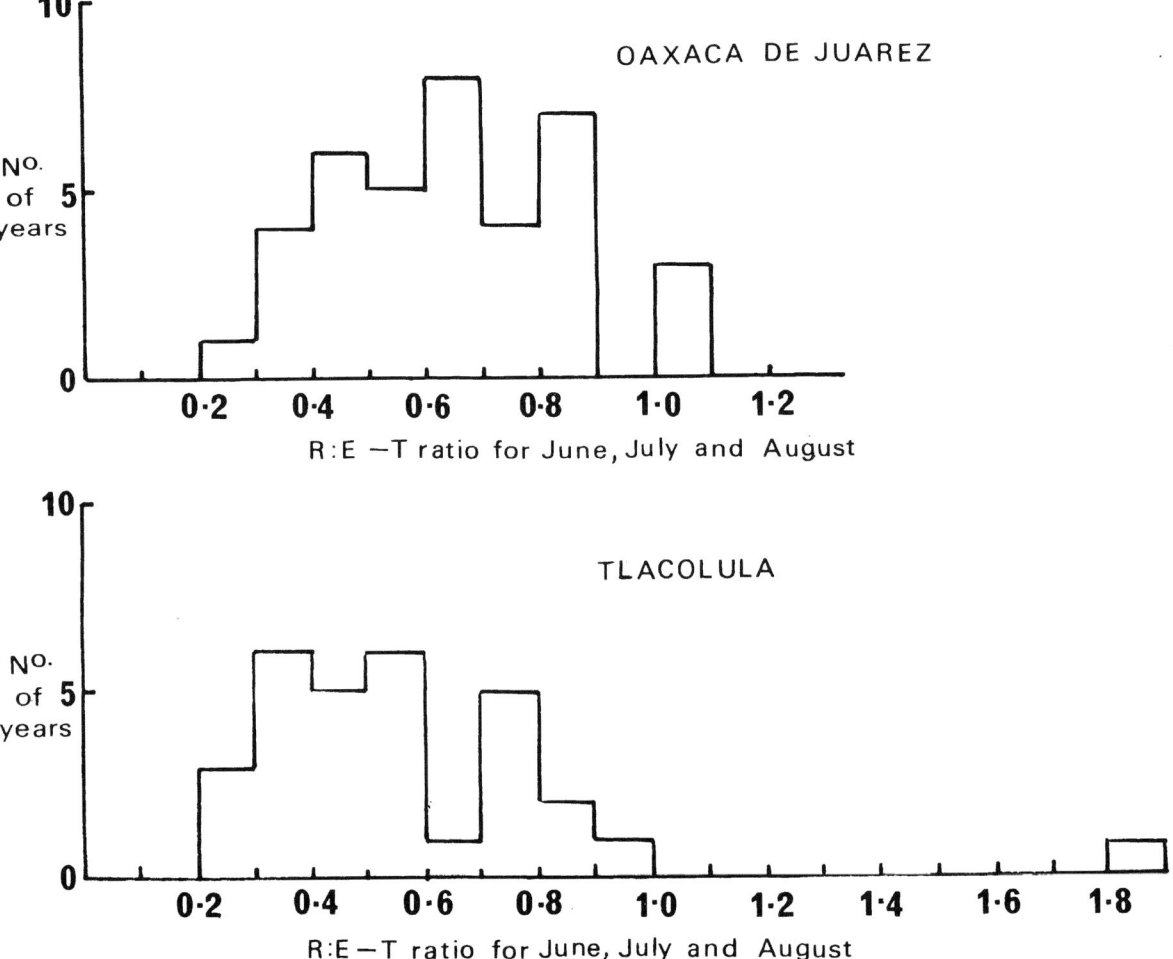

Fig. 9. Frequency distribution for Oaxaca de Juárez and Tlacolula of years with different R:ET ratios for June, July and August.

mean value. For example, in June, which is the most important single month for planting, mean monthly rainfall over 40 years of record is 137.4 mm with a standard deviation of 55.1 mm or 40.2 percent. Extreme values range from 12 mm in 1922 to 245 mm in 1957. The variability of total annual rainfall can also be seen in Figure 10$b$ which shows the frequency distribution of annual totals for Oaxaca de Juárez. Extreme values during the forty year period of record are 288 mm in 1922 and 925 mm in 1926.

The distribution of rain within a particular growing season is also critical to the success of crops, and in the Valley of Oaxaca it can vary considerably from the almost symmetrical double-peaked mean pattern illustrated in Figure 6. Two examples of rainfall years which are extreme in their distributions within the growing season rather than in their totals are shown in Figure 10$a$ (1933 and 1948). In the important planting months of May and June only 57 mm (7 percent of total) fell in 1933 compared to 302 mm (48 percent of total) in 1948. It is this variability, particularly during the planting period from April to June, that affects the time of planting, the location of crops, and the ultimate success of the harvest. Without irrigation, accurate judgment of the rainfall pattern is one prerequisite for the successful cultivator.

## Streams

Sources of stream water for irrigation fall into two categories: the mainstreams—Río Atoyac and Río Salado—and the perennial tributaries. It is because the mainstreams are not perennial and cannot provide a high proportion of the irrigation need that the small perennial tributaries are relatively so important. Dependence on these tributaries leads to dispersed rather than centralised water use. The more important sources of stream water for irrigation are shown in Figure 11 which is based on field survey and measurements of stream low flows at the end of the dry season.

The Río Atoyac and Río Salado remain dry for most of the year and along much of their lengths within the upper Atoyac drainage basin. The Río Atoyac only becomes a perennial stream capable of supplying irrigation canals below its confluence with the Río Mixtepec, by which point the area of land available for irrigation is very restricted. The perennial flow is not very large, being less than 0.5 cubic meters per second at the head of the gorge that defines the southern limit of the Valley. Above its confluence with the Río Mixtepec, the Río Atoyac flows intermittently with the period of flow depending on the frequency and amount of rainfall. In a wet year such as 1969 this may be sufficient to provide flows throughout most of the year, but usually flows are restricted to a few weeks during the rainy season.

The main streams, together with a few of their larger tributaries, provide large amounts of floodwater which, although temporary and erratic in occurrence, is a mainstay of agriculture throughout the valley, particularly in the Tlacolula Valley where other sources of water are less plentiful. The rivers have hydrographs typical of ephemeral streams in semiarid areas with discharges increasing rapidly from 0 to 50 cubic meters per second within 2 hours on the upper Río Salado (drainage area = 98 square kilometers) and in excess of 200 cubic meters per second within 8 to 10 hours on the Río Atoyac (drainage area = 2470 square kilometers). The time required for the falling stage may be from 1 to 4 days with low flows, which occupy only a fraction of the stream beds, continuing for several more days or even weeks.

These flood discharges are diverted out of the stream beds and onto fields by means of dams and canals. Where the floods are not so great as to destroy the diversion structures and lack of rain has led to a large water deficit in the soil, attempts are made to divert almost all the discharge and spread it over the high alluvium. On these larger streams floodwater is not usually stored, and fields are irrigated as the floodwater is diverted. Allowing for losses through seepage, effectively all of a flood discharge can be diverted. For example, in September 1967 a flood on the Río Salado of 10 cubic meters per second near Mitla was entirely diverted onto fields within 11 kilometers downstream by means of several take-off dams. Besides the two main streams, larger tributaries such as the Díaz Ordaz and Teotitlán del Valle streams also supply floodwater for large-scale irrigation.

A second and important source of streamwater

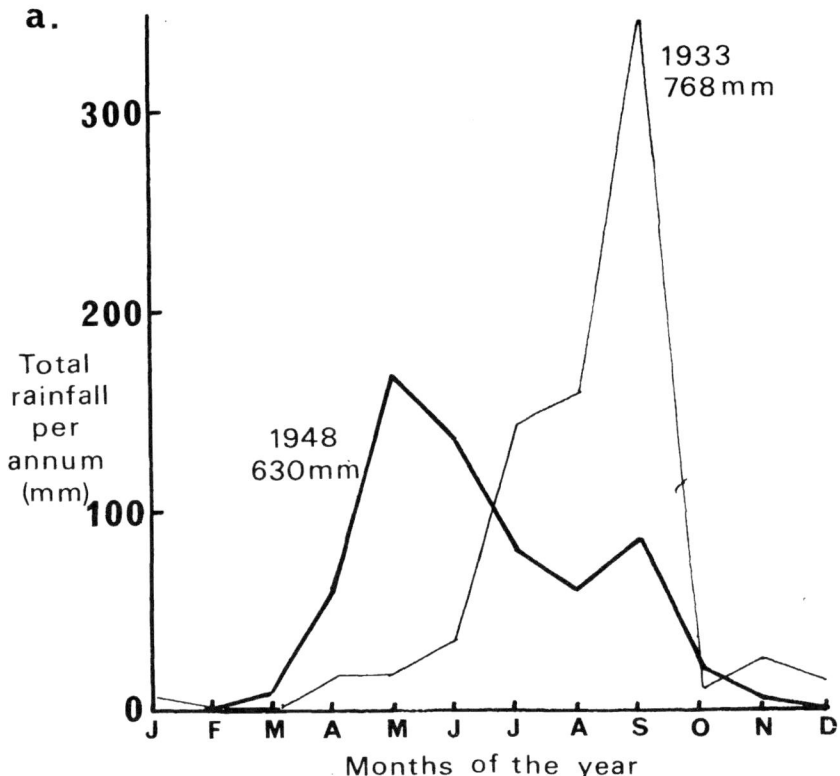
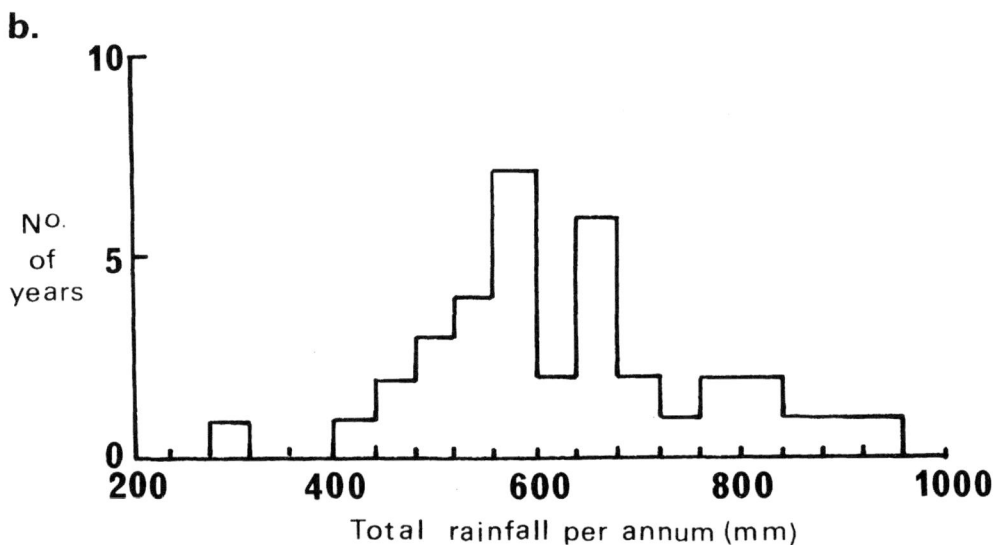

Fig. 10. (a) Monthly rainfall in Oaxaca de Juárez for 1933 and 1948 to illustrate variability of timing of rains. (b) Frequency distribution of total annual rainfalls for Oaxaca de Juárez to illustrate variability in amount of rainfall.

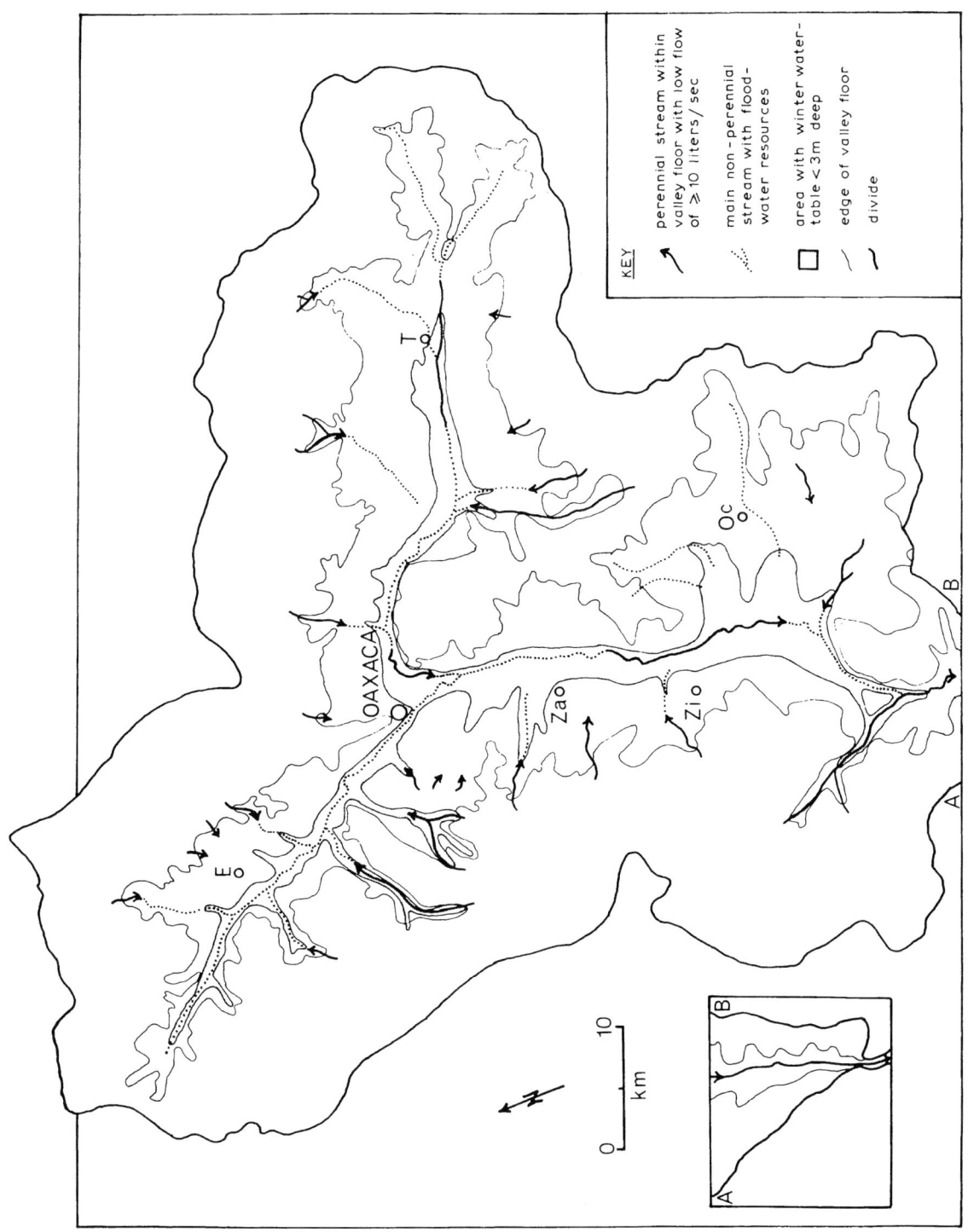

Fig. 11. Water resources of the Valley of Oaxaca for agriculture.

is the perennial tributaries. The drainage net of the Valley is not a wholly integrated system. Many tributaries crossing the wide area of high alluvium in the Zaachila Valley end their courses in deltas of their own debris which are deposited on the high alluvium before they reach the Río Atoyac. The lack of integration is even more marked in perennial streams because very few tributaries contain sufficient water to enable them to flow across the valley floor without losing their discharge through seepage into the alluvium. The perennial streams are therefore small mountain streams which decrease in discharge as they cross the piedmont and, more importantly, the high alluvium. One outcome of this hydrology has been the establishment of villages along the upper piedmont at the points of entry into the valley so that domestic and agricultural water consumption in the upper piedmont has aggravated the natural decrease of flows downstream.

Most of the perennial tributaries are small with low-flow discharges of 1 to 30 liters per second, although a few have low flows up to 60 liters per second. Many of the smaller streams, for example those along the southern edge of the eastern Tlacolula Valley, provide little water beyond domestic needs. Other streams, particularly along the eastern side of the Etla Valley from San Juan del Estado to San Pablo Etla, provide sufficient water for important canal irrigation schemes and even supply some of the needs of Oaxaca de Juárez. The most important perennial stream in the basin is the Río Mixtepec, which has a low-flow discharge of 222 liters per second and supplies water for canal irrigation over a wide area outside its own valley (which has little bottomland). The low flows of the perennial tributaries which support year-round canal irrigation are augmented in summer by floodwater which may also be diverted on to fields.

### Water Table

A third important source of water for agriculture is the high water table which is found in all three arms of the Valley, paralleling the main streams (Figure 11). The depths to water table shown in the figure were obtained by measuring water depth in more than 200 wells at the end of a dry season (April-May 1966). The overall slope of the water table in relation to the land surface, which results in increasing well depth from the centre of the valley towards the piedmont, is divided into three categories: high water table (0 to 3 meter depth), medium water table (3 to 6 meter depth), and low water table (greater than 6 meter depth).

The areas where water table is most important to agriculture are those in the centre of the valley where the water is within 3 meters of the surface during the dry season and may rise to within 1 to 2 meters during the summer growing season. The largest area where these conditions are found is in the Zaachila Valley; although in terms of the proportion of valley floor covered, the high water table is most important as a source of water in the narrow Etla Valley. The Tlacolula Valley suffers from the two disadvantages of a small area of usable high water table and a central section where the water table is at or near the surface, and conditions are too wet for cultivation.

Yields from the high water table area are low and most wells, even those being hand-drawn, cannot be used for more than 2 to 4 hours per day without drying up. In some areas, for example near San Sebastián Abasolo, coarser deposits of sand and gravel act as slightly higher yielding aquifers at shallow depths. Deep water-bearing deposits are being tapped by a few small-bore wells up to 60 meters deep which give yields of 80 to 100 liters per second, but so far these installations are exceptional and do not affect the general pattern of water use from the high water table zone.

### SUMMARY

The most important resources in the Valley of Oaxaca for agriculture are the extensive flat floor and the sources for irrigation water, although neither can meet present demands. Although the alluvial soils are deeper and finer textured than those in the piedmont and mountains, the major nonwater criterion determining that most of the agricultural land is concentrated on the valley floor is topographic. Within the area of the valley floor, finer distinctions can be drawn on the basis of altitude, which affects frost frequency and thus the types of crops which can be grown.

If the availability of flat land is the basis for the Valley being one of the most important agricultural regions within the southern highlands, the availability of water is the basis for distinguishing one part of the Valley from another. Rainfall is inadequate on the valley floor to provide a water surplus for plants, so that there is a need for irrigation to make up a year-round water deficit and to decrease the risk of crop loss through fluctuations in the arrival of major rains. Floodwaters from the Río Atoyac and Río Salado and perennial flows from small tributaries form the main sources of streamflow for irrigation water. On the valley floor a water table at depths of 1 to 6 meters and particularly at 2 to 4 meters forms a further source of water for agriculture, both directly through the soil and through surface application.

The pattern of resources for agriculture does not remain static through time, since it depends both on the physical environment and on man's technical and economic ability to exploit it. In the Valley of Oaxaca both these factors have changed, and the resulting history of water resources has been, and still is, one of increasing abstraction at the tips of the drainage network leading to a decrease in water availability downstream on the Río Atoyac itself. Through time, more water has been taken in canals from the perennial tributaries at their points of entry into the valley. Also, more water has been used upstream on the Río Atoyac in the Etla Valley by increasing the use of the high water table zone in both time and space, by extending and modernising canal schemes, and by increasing the number of wells with pumps. The acceleration of this trend in the last five years along with other changes in agriculture will soon destroy the traditional pattern of resources and resource use with which this paper is concerned; in the future more dependence will have to be placed on other sources of water such as deep wells and reservoirs.

# III

# SOCIAL ORGANISATION OF LAND, LABOUR AND PRODUCTION

## INTRODUCTION

The Valley of Oaxaca presents a paradox: on the one hand it is physically one of the least isolated areas of Mexico with good road, rail and air communications to Mexico City, the state capital of Oaxaca de Juárez, and several important archaeological sites. It is therefore a focal point of economic activity for regional administration and dollar-earning tourism. On the other hand, it remains one of the least developed areas of Mexico in economic and cultural terms, principally because Oaxaca de Juárez has no important industries to absorb a peasant labour force and provide a source of cash earnings, and because, so far, out-migration to other cities has been less than in many other areas (especially when compared with the neighbouring Valley of Nochixtlán). Forces acting toward change are present; their symptoms are the increased desire and ability to own consumer goods—transistor radios, bicycles and shoes—to eat wheat bread and processed food, or to buy new agricultural machinery such as irrigation pumps. The power of resistance is revealed in the continuance of peasant communities based on subsistence agriculture where incomes and social mobility are low and birth, death and illiteracy rates are high; where prestige is based on the holding of a religious office and where witchcraft sanctions are invoked against the social deviant. This power, however, is weakening.

Wolf (1957) has described such communities as "closed-corporate peasant communities" which share the following characteristics:

1) The community has communal rights to or jurisdiction over resources such as land and water.
2) The community is territorial rather than kinship based, so that membership depends on being born and raised within the community.
3) Restrictions are placed on outsiders entering the community and on members having links outside the community.
4) Membership in the community entails acceptance of its values even where these are in conflict with the ideal of personal advancement; the aims of the group transcend those of the individual. Community values include participation in religious rituals, the distribution of wealth or surplus within the community, and giving aid to other members and to the community as a whole.

These characteristics are shared, to a greater or lesser degree, by the peasant village populations of the Valley of Oaxaca. It is the purpose of this chapter to see how far the present structure of community organization affects those aspects of peasant life which are most closely related to agriculture—land, labour and production.

The communities under consideration are generally villages of less than 1 000 inhabitants, served by dirt roads along which transport is provided by buses, trucks, ox-carts and donkeys. Over 85 percent of the houses are *adobe* with an earth floor and a single room (1960 Oaxaca State Census), and are surrounded by a partially enclosed compound which serves as an extension of the house and in which animals, manure, harvested corn and tools are kept. Streets are generally unpaved, and, except in Oaxaca de Juárez, 90 percent of houses do not have private water supplies or any system for sewage disposal (1960 Oaxaca State Census). The Spanish-style church which dominates the village plaza does not usually have a resident priest, and resident doctors are even more rare. Health facilities are limited, with local herbal remedies and *curanderos* (folk healers) being resorted to before trained doctors and nurses, partly through superstition and partly because doctors are less available and more expensive. Most villages have a primary school and at least one schoolteacher, and children attend school for about 6 years after the age of 5 or 6, except when they are needed at home or in the fields. They are taught in Spanish, but in many villages Zapotec is the language spoken at home and between adults so that bilingualism is common and necessary. Despite great efforts by the state government to provide education in rural areas, illiteracy is about 50 percent over the Valley as a whole with higher rates in the smaller and more isolated communities (1960 Oaxaca State Census).

## LAND

Villages are nucleated and surrounded by the land belonging to them. The land of one village is divided from that of another by a specific boundary which is commonly marked on the ground by a series of cairns or single stones (*mojonera* = landmark) at strategic points or, in the mountains, by a swath cut through the forest. This land is not communally owned by the village, although parts of it may be, but the village authorities do have some jurisdiction over it. For example, they can refuse permission for a member to sell his land to a person from outside the village, even if he has to accept a lower price or wait for a buyer within his own community. Within villages, four types of land tenure are common: private, communal, rented and sharecropped. In addition, land is held as *haciendas* and *ejidos*, the latter organisation sometimes forming part of the traditional village structure and sometimes constituting its own community.

Most land in a village is privately owned, though the common practice of bilateral inheritance, in which all male heirs, at least, receive a portion of their father's estate, has produced a pattern of private ownership in which holdings are very small and scattered throughout the village territory. A man may own anything from 1 parcel of land to 20 or more. For a sample of 38 households in Díaz Ordaz, Downing has found a mean holding of 5 parcels per household (1970, personal communication) in a village where corn production forms the main source of cash income in addition to supplying subsistence needs.

The size of parcels depends on how much subdivision they have undergone and their initial size, which varies with the type of land. Holdings in poor, dry-farmed piedmont are characteristically larger than those in irrigated bottomland. Figure 12 shows the numbers of irrigated parcels of different sizes in three villages, based on data in Lees (1973). Although irrigated parcels are small because they can be more intensively cultivated and are more productive than unirrigated land, the figure shows that most parcels are extremely small, about 1 to 2 *almudes* or 0.25 to 0.5 hectares. Informant data from many areas of the Valley suggest that most holdings on the valley floor are 1.5 to 2.5 hectares in total.

Land may be rented at a fixed sum each year, but this type of tenure requires that the man renting the land can guarantee to pay that sum. Since harvest returns are variable and most peasants have no other source of capital to fall back on, renting is less common than sharecropping. In a sharecropping arrangement, the sharecropper provides the seed and the labour and the landowner provides the land and (rarely) any fertilizer or manure which might be applied. Each receives a fixed proportion of the harvest. In the Oaxaca Valley this is usually 50:50, but in other areas such as Chiapas the sharecropper may receive as little as 25 percent of the return. Under this system the sharecropper is guaranteed that he will not have to pay more than he has for the land since his rent varies with his return. The land owner receives an income from his investment without any outlay and has the mixed blessing that the land is being maintained (tilled). It is in the interests of the owner to secure as good a farmer as possible for his sharecropper, and once a satisfactory partnership has been reached it may continue for many years.

Sharecropping is a form of tenure that is used to increase a holding that is too small or to obtain land if a man is landless; in either case, it is

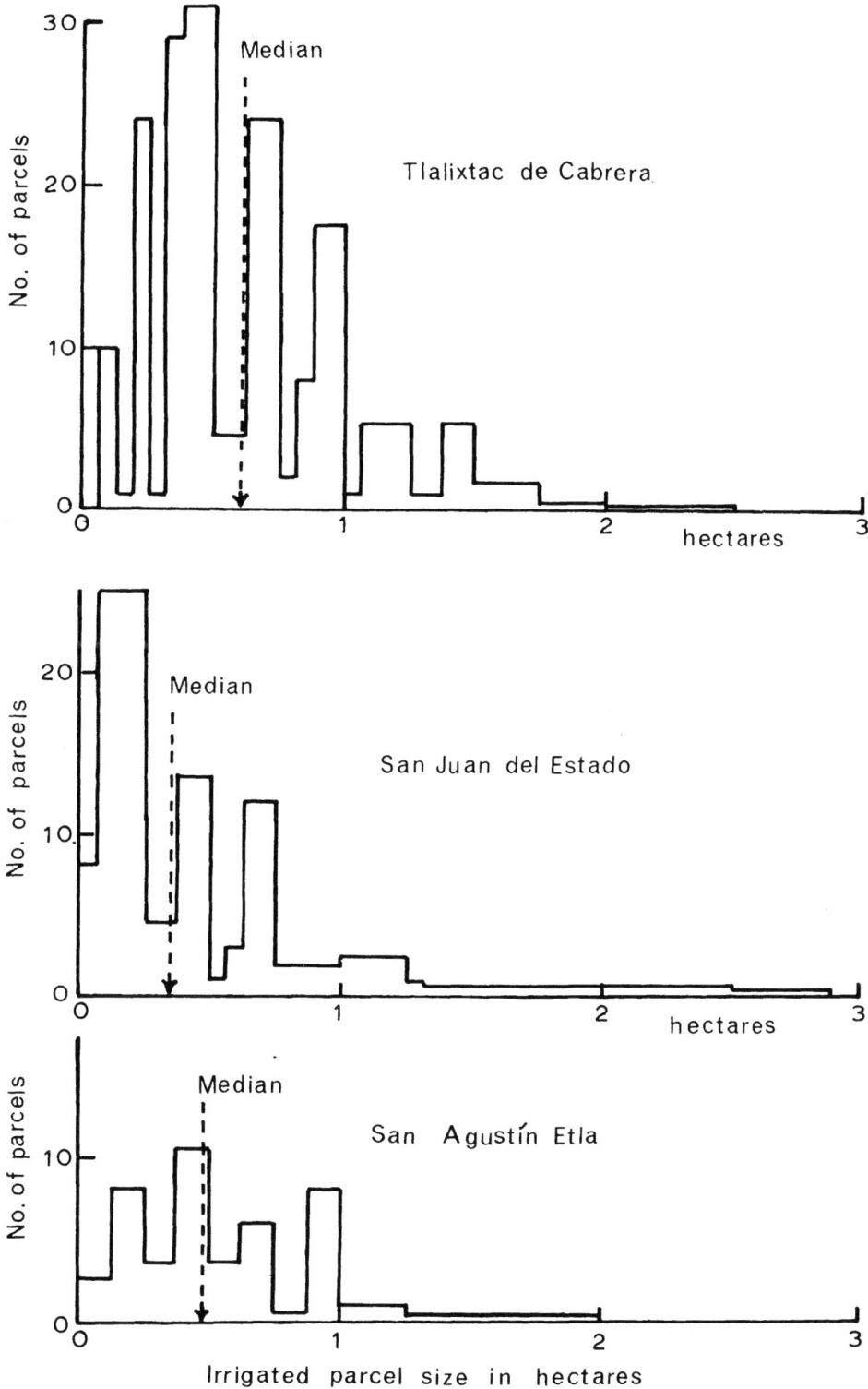

Fig. 12. Sizes of irrigated parcels of land in Tlalixtac de Cabrera, San Juan del Estado and San Agustín Etla (based on data in Lees, 1973).

considered preferable to working as a day-labourer. The proportion of land that is sharecropped is less than the proportion of land that is cultivated by the owner himself. According to Downing (1970, personal communication), in a 10 percent sample of parcels in Díaz Ordaz, 78 percent of the land was cultivated by the landowners, 17 percent by sharecroppers and 5 percent was uncultivated (as opposed to being in short-term fallow). In Tlalixtac, 64 percent of the men worked their own irrigated land, 13 percent were sharecroppers with no landholdings; sharecroppers with small landholdings constituted only 1 percent; and 12 percent were working the land as landless day-labourers. The remaining 10 percent were unaccounted for (Lees, 1973).

A proportion of the village territory is held as communal land and controlled by the village authorities, usually the *presidente*. Communal land is of two classes. One type can be grazed or cultivated by any member of the community upon application to the presidente, and the return belongs to the individual who has worked the land. This type of communal land is generally agriculturally poor and without water resources, and it is usually on fairly steep piedmont or mountain slopes. The second class of communal land is parcels which are worked communally by the community under the *tequio* system of obligatory labour on community projects, and whose produce goes towards the support of specific community services. Some parcels provide for general community expenses; others are reserved for the upkeep of the church, school and similar projects. This communal land is often some of the best in the village, especially the school plot, and the presidente has the power to convert some of the first type of communal land (that reserved for landless individuals) to tequio-worked land if additional funds, such as for the building of a new school, are necessary.

In addition, land in the Valley is held by *hacendados* and *ejiditarios*. Haciendas are small, privately owned estates, whose number is much reduced since the Mexican Revolution when many of the owners were killed or fled, and the lands were expropriated by nearby villages. The present haciendas are limited in size to 50 hectares of good irrigated land, but even so they account for much of the best land in the area south of Oaxaca de Juárez. They form small paternalist communities with many of the agricultural labourers and their families living in the hacienda. Some of the expropriated land was given to new communities called ejidos which were established by cooperative groups of men who received a land grant similar to the traditional village territory, and who then divided it equally among the members. Maximum individual holdings in an ejido should be 10 hectares of good irrigated or high water table land and 20 hectares of dry-farmed land (Editorial Porrua, *Código Agrario*, 1969:31). Most ejidal holdings in the Valley, however, are said to be much less than this, and seem to be similar in parcel size and number of parcels held to privately owned land.

While ejidos can form new communities or new towns, in the Valley of Oaxaca they are usually part of an established village community and are subject to its jurisdiction. Ejidal land, however, is controlled by the ejidal authorities, a hierarchy of offices similar to the civil ones in a village, and led by an elected presidente. Ejidos may apply directly to the national government for improvements to land such as irrigation dams and canals. Where these are granted, the use of such facilities is reserved exclusively for members of the cooperative, even though they are built on general village lands. Once an ejido has been established, new members must buy their way in. Rules of inheritance seem to vary, with some ejidos allowing land to be passed from father to son, whilst others require land to be rotated among the members so that an heir inherits a share in the cooperative but not a specific group of land parcels.

As far as the villages are concerned, water rights are related to land rights; that is, a village generally has jurisdiction over streamflow as long as it is within the village's lands. Upstream villages always have the physical advantage of being able to use the water first, and where this leads to disputes, the state authorities can intervene and act as judge. Water is a commodity which can be sold either by individuals or communities. Upstream villages used to sell more than they do today because now downstream users have rights to water that they once had to buy. Within communities, water rights are equally distributed among all adult males or heads of households independent of the size or location of their landholding. This means that landless men have water rights which they can sell and, more importantly, that water rights are dependent on being a member of a community (whether village or ejido) and are not related to the size of landholding (that is, wealth).

## LABOUR

Labour is organised on two levels, the household and the community. The household is an economic unit of production and consumption, and as soon as children are a few years old they are drafted into the household labour force, either to fetch and carry or to look after children a year or two younger than themselves. Within the household, labour is divided between the sexes, with the men and boys going out to the fields most days except Sunday and fiesta days, either to work or simply to check on them or to graze the animals. The women's and older girls' day is usually occupied in domestic duties such as looking after the house and younger children, preparing meals and making many *tortillas* over an open charcoal fire, washing clothes in a nearby pool or stream together with their friends, and making daily visits to the corn mill, local shops and neighbours. Into this pattern of time-consuming domestic and agricultural activity, most households fit the rearing of a few household animals (such as pigs and turkeys) and many also practise specialist crafts.

Both the rearing and selling of animals and the production of craft specialities are most commonly done by the women of the household. Women are usually the potters, although the men collect the clay and firewood and help to transport the finished pots to market. Weaving is practised by men and women; in Teotitlán del Valle (*sarapes*), Díaz Ordaz (sarapes), and Mitla (*rebozos*) the men usually weave, whereas in Santo Tomás Jalieza, the women weave the fine cotton belts. In villages where the men weave, the women generally help in preparing the wool by washing, carding, spinning and dyeing it. The labour for all stages of production can thus be found within one household, from raw material to the finished product in the market.

Until recently, when middlemen have increased in numbers and importance, households also produced their own marketing labour force. This task is also usually allotted to women who sell their products in local and regional markets and hawk them around neighbouring villages. The selling of sarapes, now a major tourist attraction, is only done by men, possibly because the cost involved per item is relatively high.

At the community level, labour organisation is directed toward communal labour and exchange of labour. Each adult male member of a community is required to give a certain number of days of free labour to work on village projects. These projects include the cultivation of communal plots, the maintenance of canals or roads, and any new constructions the village authorities may decide upon. Owners of ox-teams may also be required to loan them for free labour. A certain number of days a year are set aside as tequio days, on which all volunteers work at the same time. Usually the number of days of tequio work are less than 6 per year, and men may select the four or so that they must work. Sometimes a substitute may be hired to work in a man's place, but this is frowned upon. The tequio system is reputed to be pre-Conquest in origin and is organised primarily at a village level, although a few examples of intervillage tequios are known.

Exchange of labour is organised through a system of deferred reciprocity known as *guelaguetza,* in which labour received at one time must be returned at a later date. Guelaguetza exchange operates between households, never within them, and within communities, particularly between relatives, *compadres,* and friends. The principles of guelaguetza are that assistance must not be asked for unless the recipient knows he can return it when asked, and that both parts of the exchange must be equivalent in kind and in value. This is particularly important for the exchange of goods, which is also part of the guelaguetza system. Labour is most often exchanged through guelaguetza arrangements at planting and harvesting times, when it is more valuable to have a labour force of six men working together on each other's fields in turn than for each individual to work his own fields by himself. This mutual exchange of labour gives the peasant what he cannot afford to pay for—an economic working force at the time when he needs it.

## PRODUCTION

The surplus produced by peasant households is distributed in two ways: through the network of peasant markets in the Valley and through social institutions within the community. Markets in the Valley are organised as a regional sequence (Beals, 1967); each market town has its market on a specific day each week so that every day a market is being held somewhere in the region. The market is held at Ayoquesco on Mondays, Ejutla on Tuesdays, Etla and Zaachila on Wednesdays, Zimatlán on Thursdays, Ocotlán on Fridays, Oaxaca de Juárez on Saturdays, and Tlacolula on Sundays.

The centre of this system is the market at Oaxaca de Juárez. Three markets are held in the capital every day, but the main market day is Saturday when peasants come from all parts of the Valley and tourists from all parts of the world, to spread the market over several blocks in the centre of the city. The purpose of these peasant markets is to provide a means of exchange for local products of a much greater variety than could be found in any one village or held in any one store. Since most households are producing goods for exchange as well as requiring goods, many people present at the market will be selling as well as buying. Transactions are therefore made directly between producer and consumer, and the desire to maintain good personal relations influences the process of bargaining. Prices vary between markets and within the same market on the same day. Prices for fruits and vegetables tend to be higher in the main market in Oaxaca de Juárez than in the smaller ones, though the quality also is generally better.

The smaller satellite markets have a smaller range of goods and fewer middlemen doing the selling (Pl. 4). Many sellers, however, move from one market to the next following the regional cycle, and these may also be producers. The small markets are linked to the national economic network, but their primary purpose is to serve the needs of the peasant community. The large market at Oaxaca de Juárez not only serves the immediate needs of the local population, but also acts as a clearing house and redistribution centre for local products which are exported from the region and for imported goods coming in the opposite direction. Therefore, although many thousands of peasants buy and sell in Oaxaca market, the bulk of the trade is in the hands of relatively important merchants who own warehouse space for storing products and trucks to export them to other regions and markets. The market system is valuable to peasant communities not only because it provides a means of exchange between communities but because the present market structure allows peasants to sell small amounts of goods with minimum marketing losses. This is especially important to producers of fruit and vegetables who can pick their produce early on the day it is to be sold and avoid losses through spoilage.

Within the community, distribution of production that is surplus to subsistence needs is achieved through social institutions which are designed to take from the rich and give to the poor. Lees has described this system as "a way in which everyone can take turns at being wealthy while just about everyone remains equally poor" (1973). The principal instrument used to achieve this is the *cargo* system in which men proceed upward through a hierarchy of civil and religious offices which necessitate expenditures of time and wealth and provide the community with regular, communal celebrations. The civil hierarchy is theoretically distinct from the religious one; but election to civil office takes into account a man's religious career as well as his ability, and the religious officeholders are nominated by the civil leaders.

The civil hierarchy requires the expenditure of time rather than wealth, but the necessity of spending many hours on duty at the municipal offices acts as a brake on economic advancement for the officeholder. Civil offices are unpaid prestige appointments made by popular election every three years. The governing council of 5 men, called the *ayuntamiento* and headed by a presidente, have 5 stand-ins or *suplentes,* and among them, these 10 men man the municipal offices every day. In addition, there is a small justice department of 3 or 4 men, supported by a large village police force of 10 to 20 young men for whom this is commonly their first office. Since the holding of any of these offices takes a considerable amount of time and prevents the holder from working in the fields or earning money elsewhere, there is reluctance to take on the duties. Refusal to serve, however, is considered not only antisocial but criminal and can lead to fines or imprisonment.

The religious hierarchy of offices requires the expenditure of time and, more important, large amounts of wealth which are distributed among, and immediately consumed by, the community. Each town and village has a patron saint and several other saints whose days they observe with special masses and fiestas. The expenses for these observances are paid by *mayordomos* who are chosen by the civil authorities each year. The *mayordomías,* or celebrations of the saints' days, are ranked in importance, expense, and corresponding prestige for the mayordomo. In Santa María Guelacé, a village of about 100 households, 11 mayordomos are appointed each year. The annual expense to each mayordomo ranges from 1000-7000 pesos, and so much debt is incurred by the office holder that he cannot move up the next rung of the ladder and support the next mayordomía for 3 to 6 years. The metaphor of the ladder is a relevant one because the cargo hierarchy represents a man's career in a way which his daily task of farming does not. In Santa María Guelacé, it takes an average of 30 years from one's first minor mayordomía to reach the pinnacle of prestige, being mayordomo for San José. The tenure for these offices is not restricted to a small elite within the community, but is rotated among approximately 90 percent of the male heads of households living in the village (Webster, 1968).

Being a mayordomo involves the safekeeping of the saint's image and the wax for candles and other altar furniture; feting the civil authorities and the outgoing mayordomos in the municipal offices with mescal, cigarettes and music; paying for the saint's day mass and the priest's expenses; and giving a fiesta of several days' eating and drinking in one's own house. The means of paying for all this is the guelaguetza system which mobilises the stockpiled surplus from the network of friends' and relatives' households into one central household, that of the mayordomo. This surplus will be redistributed by him to the members of the guelaguetza network during the fiesta. It must also be repaid, for careful written records are usually kept of every item donated, and a similar item will be expected in return when the donor has to give a religious or family fiesta. In this way, a mayordomo is assured of instant wealth or surplus, which he must take the next few years to repay, and the donors are depositing their surplus in a credit account. The guelaguetza system of a community is thus a complicated network of credit and debit ties which are the peasants' principal form of insurance and whose protection against risk a man must forego if he leaves the community. Guelaguetza exchange is also used to provide family celebrations such as baptisms and marriages. The *fandango,* or marriage fiesta, is particularly lavish, and in communities where the cargo system is weakening, the fandango represents the biggest distribution of surplus and may take the bride's father many years to repay.

Besides rewarding the mayordomos and other fiesta givers with prestige, the community discourages the individual hoarding of wealth by negative sanctions, including witchcraft. Private wealth, where it is not accompanied by lavish entertainment and donation to civic projects, is regarded as antisocial and unnatural. Such men are often believed to have made a pact with the devil or his envoy and to have sold their souls in return for wealth. Unless a man can happily bear the suspicion and ostracism of his community, he is likely to accept its social values and enter into the cargo and fiesta systems.

To what extent the cargo system, supported by guelaguetza, is effective as a wealth leveler depends on its strength in any particular community and the degree to which personal wealth (usually based on land) is a major criterion for selecting candidates. Webster found that the higher echelons of the mayordomía system were available only to the richer men who could afford them and that the prestige they gained thereby made their wealth appear morally righteous (1968:31). This is a subject to which we will return in the final chapter.

# IV

# WATER USE TECHNIQUES AND THEIR DISTRIBUTION

## INTRODUCTION

In Chapter II it was shown that of the two most important resources in the Valley for agriculture—water and flat land—water is the more critical. The need for irrigation water is based on the inadequacy of the rainfall in compensating for the potential evapotranspiration losses from the surface of cultivated fields. The scarcity of irrigation water results from the absence of any major streamflows and the lack of traditional techniques, such as the Persian wheel, to lift water cheaply and easily to the surface. The combination of these factors has produced a situation in which a variety of techniques are practised, each of which is technically simple, small-scale and greatly adapted in order to make use of small amounts of water in a particular part of the physical environment. The effect of agricultural water use is to decrease the total amount of water leaving the basin at the point of the Atoyac gorge and to redistribute water within the basin. This redistribution is achieved mainly by spreading water more thinly over larger areas (though not for dry farming); redistribution through time by means of storage plays only a minor role.

## DRY FARMING

Dry-farmed fields are those watered only by the rain falling directly on them, and because mean rainfall is barely adequate to support even one crop during the summer, techniques to conserve water in the soil are adopted. All of these techniques are extremely simple. Transpiration is reduced by close attention to weeding. Evaporation losses from the soil surface are minimized by concentrating surface storage and encouraging infiltration immediately around plants, either by contour ploughing or, in the case of hoe and digging stick cultivation, by disturbing the surface as little as possible and confining cultivation to making shallow basins for each seed (Pl. 5). Contour ploughing also reduces overland flow and thus checks soil as well as soil moisture losses. This is relatively more important in the mountains where temperature rather than rainfall limits the growing season.

It might be expected that reducing overland flow by lowering the mean field gradient by terracing would also be practised, but today field terraces are rare in the Valley in dry-farming areas. Terraces are built for floodwater fields and are widespread outside the Valley. Within the Valley they were much more widespread in the past, with many abandoned field terraces in the piedmont dating from about A.D. 1300, which may imply that at that time there was a greater demand for agricultural land and consequently more of the soil erosion problems inherent in a reduction of length of fallow.

Despite the absence of widespread field terracing, efforts are made to hold back moisture and soil by building barriers across those parts of the slope where overland flow is likely to be concentrated (Pl. 6). In the construction of these barriers dry-farming techniques merge with those of floodwater farming, since the difference between a terrace holding back soil moisture resulting from direct rainfall only and a terrace storing overland flow is only one of degree and is often not distinguishable on the ground. These terraces will therefore be discussed collectively under floodwater farming, although it should be mentioned here that a common practice in the piedmont is to construct a series of walls along an ephemeral stream course and dry farm not the terraces themselves, which may be flooded too often, but the unterraced valley sideslopes. The terraces in the valley bottom check erosion of the valley sides and allow fields on slope gradients of 35 to 40 degrees to be cultivated without showing signs of accelerated erosion. The danger of erosion in these situations is not eliminated, however, and cultivation continued for several years in succession has led to complete stripping of the 30 cm deep soil in a few fields on gradients of 28 to 34 degrees and underlain by ignimbrite bedrock in the eastern Tlacolula Valley piedmont.

## FLOODWATER FARMING

Floodwater farming is the growing of crops by attempting to control temporary, natural water flows. In the Valley of Oaxaca most of these water flows come from summer flash floods lasting only a few hours or days along ephemeral streams. In a few areas the flood discharge of perennial streams may also be used for floodwater-farmed fields in addition to the base flow which is already directed to canal-irrigated fields. The principle of floodwater farming is the artificial spreading of floodwater over a larger area than it would naturally cover, and this involves the draining of low-lying fields as much as channeling water to fields farther away from the river. In practice, the floods on the Valley floor are often of sufficient magnitude that the fields nearest the river are abandoned to the floodwaters while all energy is expended on getting some water to fields farther away. This situation is illustrated in Plate 7, where fields near Teotitlán del Valle are first irrigated by floodwater and later inundated by at least a meter of water which destroy the crop.

Floodwater farming is the most widespread type of water use practised in the Valley and covers the greatest range of physical environments, scale, complexity, and frequency of use. It has already been shown that in their simplest forms floodwater techniques merge with those of dry farming. At the other end of the scale, floodwater distributary systems are similar to those of canal irrigation except in the temporary nature of their water supplies. A floodwater scheme may involve one farmer or many and may be in operation less than once every five years or as often as twice each year.

The distribution of floodwater farming is difficult to study because it is not until a flood actually occurs that the distributary network can be seen. Also, since the cleaning of field ditches takes place during the flood, their appearance of disuse belies their present importance. Once a floodwater system has been constructed, any other necessary labour is expended while the flood is in progress; dry-farming methods are used for the rest of the year. The success and importance of floodwater farming is dependent on the reliability, frequency, and magnitude of the flows involved. In the few areas where it is not only frequent enough, but also reliable enough, floodwater can support perennial crops such as alfalfa (for example, west of Tlacolula), but more commonly these crops are given supplemental irrigation from permanent water sources. Where possible, corn is floodwater farmed and fields receiving floodwater at least once a year, on an average, are so described. Where flood frequency is less than about once in three years, the main purpose of wall construction is to prevent flood damage and soil erosion, and the fields are considered to be dry farmed. Floodwater farming is therefore most important as a method of surface irrigation where the frequency of controllable floods is about once a year and where more reliable forms of water control are not possible.

### Floodwater Farming Without Canals

The general purpose of floodwater farming is to slow down and spread floods. In the American Southwest this was achieved with the minimum of artificial diversion by locating fields to be irrigated at arroyo mouths where the runoff of the entire drainage basin upstream spreads out naturally over an alluvial fan, called an *akchin* (Bryan, 1929; Hack, 1942). Today in the Valley of Oaxaca, floodwater schemes usually involve at least construction of low terraces which are designed to reduce velocity and spread water availability over time. One of the characteristic aspects of hillslopes

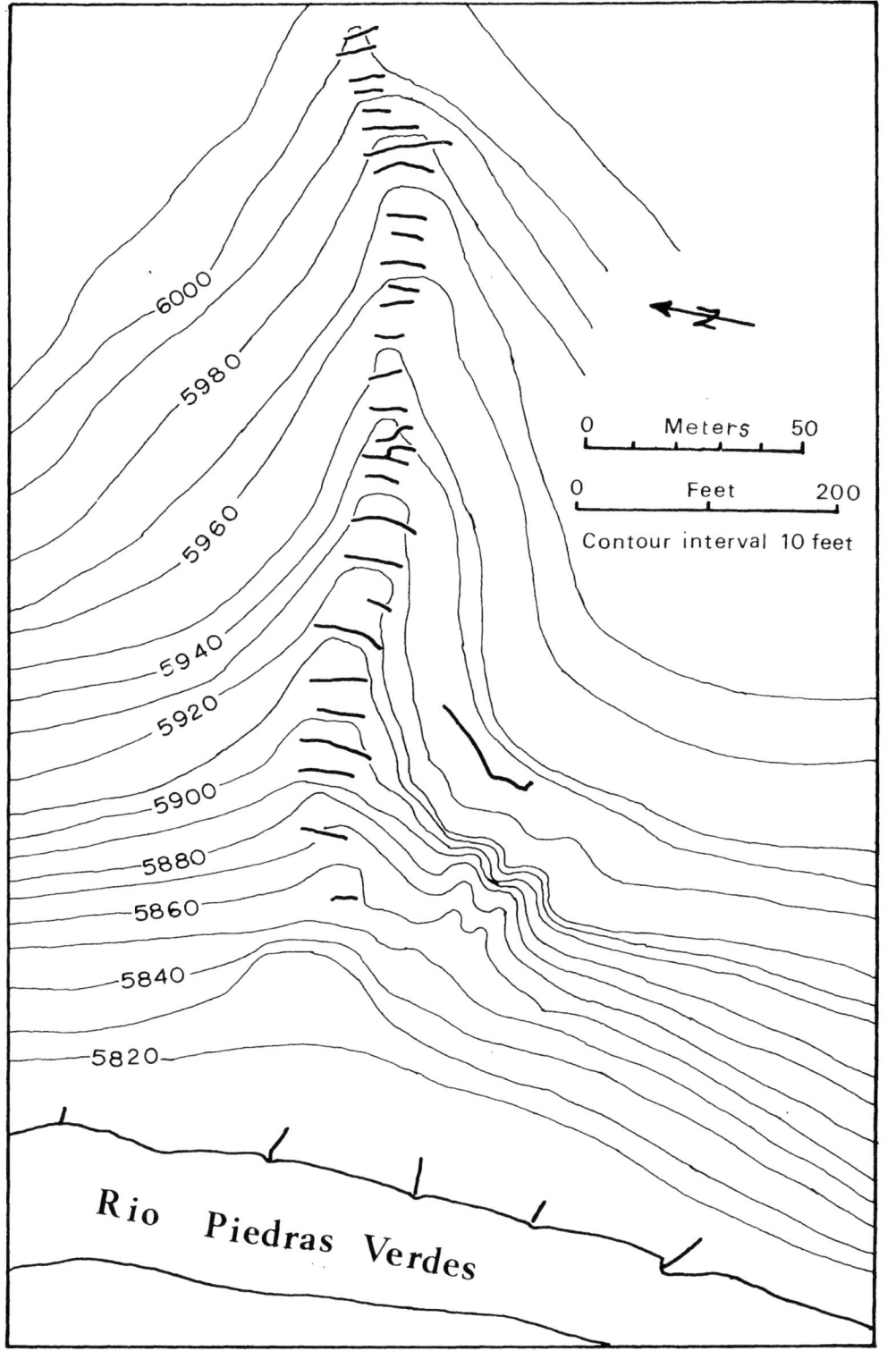

Fig. 13. Map of a series of trincheras along a small valley in Chihuahua, northern Mexico (from Herold, 1965: map 10).

around the Valley is the many small walls across stream beds, tiny valleys and barely perceptible depressions in the slopes. These walls, sometimes referred to locally as *muros*, are similar in design and purpose to the *trincheras* described in Chihuahua, northern Mexico (Herold, 1965). They are constructed of stone or a combination of earth and branches and are almost always less than 1 meter high, commonly less than half a meter. In length they range from 3 to 30 meters with most less than 10 meters long. In the mountains and piedmont they are characteristically found in groups, each group forming a series of steps down a depression or valley (Fig. 13) whereas on the valley floor they are usually built singly or in pairs.

Behind these walls, water-transported material accumulates to provide small flat areas of fine material which serve as reservoirs for moisture. This fine material is initially wetter than the surrounding slopes and keeps a high moisture content for a longer time. The terraces may be so moist that water seeps out from the base of the retaining wall. Farming these terraces is not without risk; the same concentration of water which makes them fertile can also be sufficient at times to destroy the crops. The result is that the pattern of cultivated terraces varies in time and space, with terraces being farmed in any year only if the expected magnitude and frequency of flows is compatible with crop survival. Some terraces are not used during the rainy season when the side slopes are dry farmed, but stored moisture allows them to support a winter bean crop.

On the gentle slopes of the valley floor, the walls may not necessarily be permanent structures, but are rebuilt each year after ploughing even if flooding has not occurred for ten years. Often the positioning of these barriers, which are usually of earth and branches, is the only indication of an ephemeral stream course which has been obliterated by ploughing. The construction of these barriers is worthwhile, as is shown by the example in Plate 8. This wall had not been used for ten years but served to trap 35 cm of sediment from a field with a gradient of 2 degrees during a single flood in May, 1966. The barrier in this example was less than half a meter in height and was built of loosely packed branches secured by wooden stakes to a low earth ridge.

### Floodwater Farming With Canals

Floodwater schemes without canals place great emphasis on soil erosion prevention, but the prime purpose of schemes *with* canals is to irrigate crops even where this seriously interferes with the natural distribution of stream erosion and deposition and initiates downcutting below dams and gullying of nearby fields. The success of many schemes relies on cooperation between cultivators and communities, and efficient floodwater control cannot be practised without this cooperation even where physical conditions are favourable. Likewise, water is not distributed indiscriminantly but only to those fields whose owners contribute to the cost and labour of maintenance.

Floodwater may be stored in reservoirs for a few days or weeks—this practice is most common in the Zaachila Valley—but generally the main purpose of dams is not storage but to raise the level of the streamflow to that of the fields. This is especially necessary along the Río Atoyac and Río Salado where the river beds lie as much as 7 to 10 meters below the level of the high alluvium. Several series of dams have been constructed across the Río Salado, many of which date from the nineteenth and early twentieth century and are still in use. These dams, which may be 11 meters high, are backed by sediment completely filling the former incised channel to a level with the high alluvium. Floodwater is drawn from the river through a canal immediately behind the dam at the high level, and excess water is allowed to pour over the dam and continue along the stream channel to the next dam and associated floodwater distributary system. The resulting long profile of the Río Salado is that of a series of steps marked by the locations of the dams, with accelerated downcutting below the dams and deposition of load up to the level of the high alluvium, above them. The plan of one small floodwater system on the Río Salado is given in Figure 14.

Participation in a floodwater scheme does not secure water for a cultivator's fields unless he actively directs the flow on to his land during the

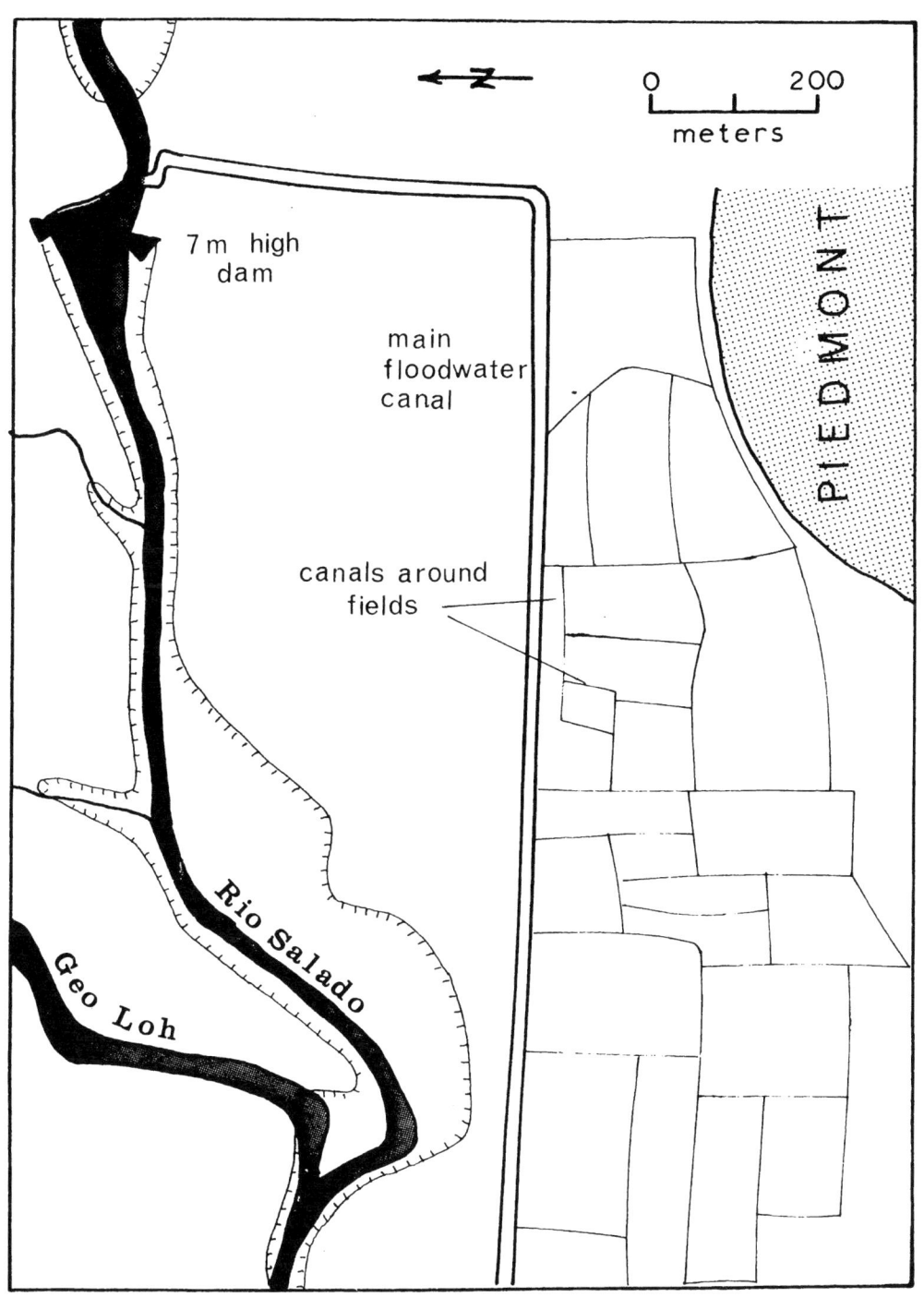

Fig. 14. Small group floodwater scheme on the Río Salado near Mitla.

period of flooding. Therefore the arrival of a flood in an area, whether during the day or at night, produces great activity in the fields with farmers ensuring that water passes from the main canals into the channels around and into their fields. The techniques involved are simple. To raise water out of the main canal into the smaller channels and on to the fields, piles of branches, *zacate,* or *maguey* leaves are put into the canal to form temporary dams. At the same time, ditches and canals are cleared of debris which has accumulated since the last flood and this is piled along the banks. Within the fields, floodwater is distributed along the furrows by men directing water from one furrow to the next by blocking off furrows with handfuls of earth (see section on well-and-furrow irrigation). When the field has received sufficient water the dams in the canals are removed or placed lower down the canal to raise water to fields farther away from the water source. At night these operations are especially difficult since the unseen wet ground becomes treacherous and the size of the flood is more difficult to estimate.

Streams are not the only source of floodwater used in canal schemes. Runoff from the high alluvium and piedmont after storms of high intensity is commonly channeled along dirt tracks that serve also as roads. Many fields, especially on the south side of the Tlacolula Valley, rely entirely on these tracks for additional water, and low earth ridges are built across the tracks to divert the flow into the fields through entrances screened by a lattice of thorny branches to obstruct debris. The diversion ridges are built singly or in pairs half a meter apart, and are 20-30 cm high so that travel along the roads in a vehicle is slow and uncomfortable though not entirely prevented. Track floodwater is an important source of irrigation in the area between Tlacolula and Guadalupe where the old road to Oaxaca, which is still partly cobbled, channels water from fields and the paved central area of Tlacolula itself. For part of its length, the road lies about a meter below the field level and low stone dams have been built to divert and raise the floodwater. In 1966, a flow along this road reached a depth of 1 to 1.5 meters and was combined with floodwater brought by canal from the Díaz Ordaz stream to water a large area (Fig. 15). The elevated position of this large floodwater canal, which supplies water at least once a year, also illustrates the amount of alluviation that has occurred in the 50 years since it was built.

Areas which flood naturally are subject to special problems, especially where water stands for most of the summer as it does near San Juan Guelavía in the Tlacolula Valley. Agriculture in these areas is restricted not only by the flooded

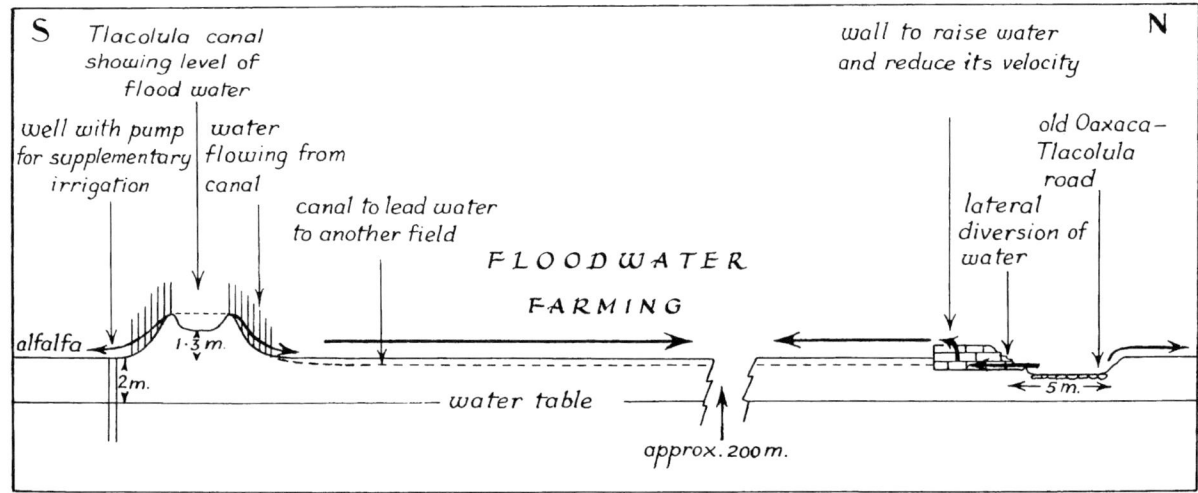

Fig. 15. Cross section of floodwater-farmed area near Tlacolula, irrigated from the Tlacolula floodwater canal and the old Oaxaca road.

zone itself, but also by the larger area of saline soils around it. Some attempt is made to dig drainage channels, but generally farming is restricted to the margins of the saline or waterlogged zones.

## WATER-TABLE FARMING

The presence of a high water table from 0.25 to 1.0 meters below the surface is the necessary condition for water-table farming. In its distribution, therefore, this method of water use is limited by the physical environment, and the area over which it is possible cannot be appreciably increased by man, although by lowering the water table he can decrease it.

The principle of water-table farming is that crops may abstract water continuously from the zone of high moisture content which lies above the water table itself due to capillary action. This land is locally described as *tierra* (or *terreno*) *de humedad*, and it is some of the most productive land in the Valley. The position of the water table is not static but fluctuates throughout the year, following the rainfall pattern, so that some land may become waterlogged and require draining by ditches during the summer growing season. The advantage of this type of land is that it usually has a high enough water table during the winter dry season to support crops. Where the mean position of the water table is lower, the land is most productive for crops during the summer rainy season. The area of highest productivity varies from year to year with annual fluctuations in rainfall patterns and also with flood frequency, since water-table farming is characteristically located on the low alluvium and near stream courses.

In the best tierra de humedad, the zone of moist soil extends to within a few centimeters of the surface, which is itself kept dry by evaporation. Irrigation water drawn from wells may be put on to the fields if the water table falls below the effective reach of the plant roots or in order to reduce the high temperatures of the ground surface during the day. This is done especially when young crops (particularly truck-farming crops) are planted. Alfalfa is an important water-table farmed crop because it is a phreatophyte which can abstract water from the water table itself, and is therefore able to produce strong growth which may be cut as many as ten to twelve times a year. The value of this type of land is reflected in the generally small land-holding units, which in Guadalupe Etla are only 0.25 to 0.75 hectare of bottomland per family, and also in the location of the most productive haciendas on tierra de humedad, especially south of Oaxaca.

Methods of cultivation on tierra de humedad differ little from those already described, except that the construction of adequate drainage ditches is necessary, and the favourable moisture conditions increase the problem and labour of weeding, which may be done three times for each crop. The most important aspect of water-table farming is its ability to produce crops throughout the year with two to three harvests per annum. Fallowing is rarely necessary, especially as any manure or fertilizer available is applied to tierra de humedad in preference to other fields. With fertilizers, two to three corn crops a year may be grown, but it is more usual to ensure the best possible yields for one summer corn crop by growing legumes such as chickpeas or beans during the winter. Wheat and alfalfa are also common crops.

The two most important characteristics of tierra de humedad are its limited distribution and its ability to produce high yields continuously. It is these aspects that make it highly valued today, and it was probably even more important as a method of water use in the past.

## WELL IRRIGATION

Irrigation from wells is practised throughout the valley floor wherever a high enough water table exists. Two main techniques are used today, pot irrigation (*riego a brazo*) and well-and-furrow irrigation. In the first method, the water distribution is done by the cultivator himself; in the second method, the furrow pattern is used to direct the water flow. A very few well-and-furrow schemes today are also dependent on human energy to draw the water, so that the distribution of these schemes is as dependent on depth to water table as is pot irrigation. But the majority of well-and-furrow schemes now use motor power for drawing water, and the introduction of pumps has changed both the spatial distribution and the amounts of water which may be applied. If well-and-furrow irrigation was practised in the past, its distribution and effectiveness were therefore more limited than they are today.

## Pot Irrigation

Pot irrigation (riego a brazo) is found today as isolated plots in many parts of the Valley, but its main area of distribution is in the flat alluvial zones where a relatively high water table—between 1 and 8 meters—may be easily tapped within each field. The yield of each well is low, but to compensate for this, several wells are dug from which the water is drawn by hand. Fields irrigated by this method are small, generally less than 0.1 hectares, because riego a brazo requires much labour. A cultivator will therefore have very little of his total land holding under pot irrigation, and even where they are most common in the Valley, pot-irrigated fields form only 2 to 10 percent of the arable land; the remaining area is usually dry farmed.

The method of pot irrigation is simple, if laborious, and has the advantage of enabling the entire irrigation scheme to be in the hands of each individual man. From 1 to 8 small unlined wells are dug within a field so that no part of the field is more than 10 meters from a well. The field is divided into rectangular beds whose dimensions are commonly somewhere between 1 by 5 meters and 10 by 15 meters. Between these beds are narrow earth paths. The beds are prepared by constructing the surface into circular hollows 30 to 50 cm in diameter, or into rectangular boxes, whose sides may be from 20 to 40 cm long and from 5 to 10 cm high (Figs. 16*a* and *b*). Occasionally this careful preparation of the surface is reduced to simply leveling it or making furrows, with a resulting loss in irrigation efficiency because a wall of soil around the plants helps to keep the irrigation water in and reduce evaporation losses (Fig. 16*c*). Several plants are grown within each earth hollow or box, each unit containing from 2 to 8 plants (Pl. 9).

To irrigate the field, an earthenware or metal pot or a metal bucket is lowered down a well on a rope, the other end of which may be attached around the man's waist. The man hauls up the water and carries the pot to each of the plant groups in turn, sometimes pouring the water through his fingers to lessen the force of flow on the soil (Pl. 10). He then returns to the nearest well and repeats the operation, which takes between 40 and 60 seconds to complete. In terms of optimum water use, this method of irrigation is very efficient because infiltration is concentrated around the plant roots and the retaining walls prevent water loss through runoff. Little water is wasted on the soil between earth boxes or plants, and the amount of water received by each plant can be adjusted by the farmer to suit the needs of individual plants.

In a typical example studied north of Zimatlán, a plot containing mainly *chile* measured 24 by 15 meters and contained 1800 earth boxes. The pot used would hold 10 liters of water which took the irrigator 45 seconds to take from the well and distribute to 4 boxes. He worked 5.5 hours every day during the growing season of three months so that he was putting approximately 4,500 liters per day on the plot which measured 360 square meters. The amount of water applied was therefore 1.25 cm per day over the whole area. Several other examples were measured and gave similar amounts of water applied. The plants grown under riego a brazo may require daily watering, especially when young, so that the amount of water applied must offset an evaporation deficit of 0.6 to 0.7 cm/day that exists on the valley floor on a dry day. Amounts of water applied vary from 0.6 to 1.4 cm/day which is just enough to offset the losses through evaporation and provide a little extra water for drainage of accumulating soluble salts from the root zone. This method of irrigation is therefore an extremely efficient one.

However, with so little extra water being applied to ensure adequate drainage of soluble salts there is a possibility of salinisation of the soil, and the common practice of frequent rotation of fields under riego a brazo may well be a response to this danger. In some areas, the majority of the fields are rotated every year, despite the labour involved in digging as many as 8 wells within 0.1

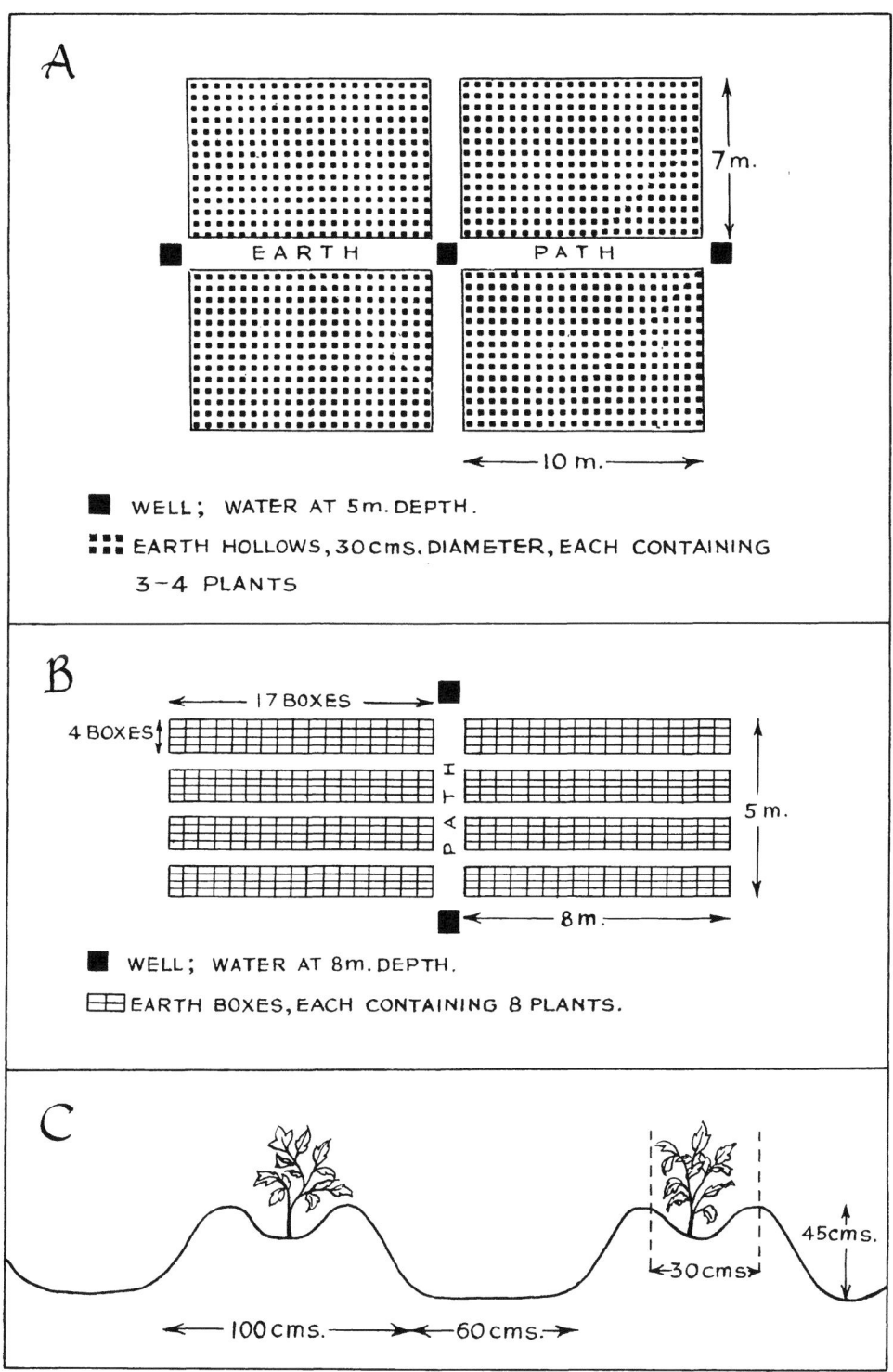

Fig. 16. Pot-irrigated fields: (*a*) circular basin pattern near San Pablo Huixtepec; (*b*) rectangular network near San Antonino Castillo Velasco; and (*c*) cross section of part of rectangular network containing tomato plants near Tlacochuaya.

hectare. In the formerly irrigated area, old wells are filled in and the field is ploughed for dry farming.

### Well-and-Furrow Irrigation

In well-and-furrow systems, furrows replace man as the distributary system and today pumps increasingly are replacing manpower for drawing water out of the wells. Both these factors combine to lower the density of wells to 1 per 1 to 100 hectares compared with 50 to 60 wells per hectare for riego a brazo. Likewise the wells may be deeper, and a very few tap aquifers as deep as 30 to 60 meters below the surface, although the majority are 4 to 15 meters deep. Correspondingly, field size—from 1 to 3 hectares without pumps—increases to 2 to 10 hectares with pumps. There is usually one well to each field, located either in the lowest or highest corner and ranging from a simple unlined hole to a lined well with storage tank and lined canal at the surface. If the well is in the lower part of the field, water from it is carried to the top of the field in a canal sloping opposite to the ground surface and supported on brick pillars or an artificial earthen ridge (Pl. 11).

The furrows forming the distributary network are made by normal ploughing, but up and down the slope instead of along the contour as in dry farming. A master furrow is ploughed along the top edge of the field at right angles to all the other furrows, and this furrow is connected to the well by a channel which may be lined for part of its length. Water is allowed into three or four of the furrows at a time by damming the master furrow with earth and twigs, just beyond the last furrow that is to be irrigated. As each group of furrows receives sufficient water, their entrances are blocked with earth and the dam in the master furrow is moved farther on. The whole field can be irrigated in this way with much less labour than by riego a brazo, but the uneven distribution of water from one end of the furrow to the other results in uneven crop yields and thus a less efficient use of water. Differences in corn yield from 150 to 300 kilos per hectare down to 0 kilos per hectare can be found within 10 meters distance along a single furrow.

Well-and-furrow irrigation involves slight differences in cultivation methods; for example, corn tends not to be hilled-up (earth piled round it so that it grows on the furrow ridge) but is left in the furrow channel to receive maximum water. Alfalfa fields are prepared by leveling the ground between furrows that are 1 to 2 meters apart or earth ridges that are 2 to 3 meters apart and 10 to 15 cm high. Ideally whole sections of the field are flooded to shallow depths of a few centimeters. It is perhaps worthwhile describing alfalfa cultivation a little at this point because, although it is extensively water-table farmed and canal irrigated, it is also the most important well-and-furrow irrigated crop.

Alfalfa has become widely distributed in the Valley since the Revolution and is a perennial plant which is grown for 5 to 10 years before being cleared out, usually by tractor-drawn machinery. Although it is a heavy water user in conditions of high available soil moisture, alfalfa receives the most variable amount of irrigation water because it will survive, though without producing enough growth to be harvested, with little or no additional water. Thus, when water is scarce it may be applied to annual crops like corn in order to save the harvest, while the alfalfa is left to fend for itself for several weeks or months. Alfalfa can be cropped continuously throughout its 10 years, but its production bears a close relation to the amount of water it receives. In areas where it is irrigated all day each 8 to 14 days, about 45 cm of growth can be harvested every 30 to 40 days, or 9 to 12 times per year. This yield declines to 20 cm growth harvested 1 to 2 times per year if irrigation is inadequate or the crop is relying on infrequent floodwater.

Well-and-furrow irrigation is ideally suited to be supplemental to other forms of water use, particularly floodwater and water-table farming, and it is therefore commonly found in areas where these other types of farming predominate. Not only will the same system of furrows distribute both well and floodwater, but the practice of having minimal pumping installations permanently at the well means that it is economical to dig a well even if it is used only rarely. The number of times a field is irrigated can therefore be adjusted to the frequency of flooding or the fluctuations in height of the water table. Where corn relies entirely on a well-and-furrow system, it is usually irrigated from 1 to 3 times during the 3 to 5 month growing season. Truck-farming crops may be irrigated as often as once a week.

Optimum applications of water by well-and-furrow irrigation in the Valley are best illustrated by an alfalfa-producing hacienda operating south of Oaxaca. Here water is drawn from a 60 meter deep small-bore well by a motor pump at a rate of 83 liters/sec, and 110 hectares of alfalfa are irrigated and cut 10 times a year. The water applied is at least 0.29 cm per day, or the equivalent of 1000 mm rainfall per year, which is able to offset the evaporation deficit of about 1300 mm per annum when it is added to the natural rainfall. However, other measurements of water application in well-and-furrow schemes indicated that in most cases the amount of water applied was inadequate to guarantee a crop during a dry year.

This inadequacy is especially apparent where water is drawn by hand and farmers using this method are applying only 0.013 cm/day, or about 10 percent of the mean annual evaporation deficit, even by working for 5 hours every day. In these circumstances the evaporation deficit during a dry year could not possibly be made up by irrigation, and alfalfa fields are likely to remain unirrigated for the entire year. Hand-drawn operations, therefore, can ensure crop success only during the wet years. With a pump, the water applied is greater, but even so measured amounts were commonly about 0.18 cm/day, which is equivalent to approximately 660 mm of rain per year or less than the potential evaporation in a dry year. To compensate for this deficit, the area adequately irrigated by well-and-furrow methods is decreased during dry months or dry years. The ability of alfalfa to survive (though not to produce harvestable growth) with little irrigation water for long periods and subsequently to revive suits that crop to this system of water use.

Informants attest to a recent increase in pump users, and this has expanded the area of well-and-furrow irrigation. It is difficult to estimate what the importance of traditional (hand-drawn) well-and-furrow irrigation might have been because today it scarcely seems a practicable method of water use, combining, as it does, a high labour input per unit of water with a relatively high wastage of water during distribution. On the one hand, riego a brazo would seem a more rational use of water, and many well-and-furrow fields simulate the detailed field layout and careful use of all water that characterizes pot irrigation; for example, by growing onions and garlic along the outer sides of canals and immediately around the head of the well. On the other hand, with larger fields and lower value crops, pumps would seem to be the only practicable method of drawing water. To achieve 10 cuttings of alfalfa a year, one farmer drawing water by hand must spend 3 to 4 days a week to irrigate 0.5 hectare whereas another with a pump can irrigate for one day a week over 5 hectares.

Pumps are either privately or, more usually, communally owned, and individual farmers may use them free or for a charge of about 75 pesos per day (1967). Gasoline to run the pump is quoted as costing 10 pesos per hour, and most pumps have an outlet pipe of 2 to 3 inches diameter which yields about 10 to 12 liters per second. Pumps are not usually left at the well heads but are taken home for safety.

## CANAL IRRIGATION

With the exception of the Río Mixtepec, perennial discharges in the Valley are low so that canal-irrigation schemes are generally small-scale and controlled by one village or by cooperation between two or three communities. Streams provide the water for all canal systems, and in almost all cases the water is abstracted and used directly without first being stored in a reservoir. The water is diverted by constructing a take-off (*toma*) which begins just behind a low dam. The take-off is simply the beginning of the main canal which juts out into the flow of the stream in order to divert part of the streamflow along it. The dam is designed to raise the level of the water and at the same time to allow part of the flow to pass over or through it. Dams are therefore constructed of boulders, branches, and earth rather than stone and cement, although solid constructions are also found.

Canal installations are simple, with the main canal being an earth channel whose sides are reinforced with boulders at points vulnerable to erosion. Occasionally the toma is concrete lined for the first few meters before continuing as an unlined channel. The water is passed to and round the fields along earth channels and applied to the crops along the furrows as has been described for well-and-furrow irrigation. The direction of water flow is usually controlled by wooden boards serving as sluice gates on the main canals, but throughout the rest of the distributary system, temporary dams of vegetation and earth similar to those described for floodwater farming are common.

As has been indicated before, except for the temporary versus permanent nature of the water source, the technologies of canal irrigation and floodwater farming are similar. However, the nature of the water source does influence the structure and degree of social organisation in the irrigating communities. For example, canal-irrigating villages are more likely to have an elected official or committee whose duties include organising water distribution and communal labour such as canal maintenance. They also represent the community's interests in periodic inspections of water-division installations and similar negotiations with representatives of other communities sharing water rights. The exact form this organisational structure takes and the degree to which the same hierarchy can be effective in organising other aspects of community life vary from one village to another (Lees, 1973). However, floodwater-farming villages do not have this same degree of organised water control; the distribution of water depends more on the active cooperation of all individuals who are present in their fields during a flood.

The decentralised nature of perennial surface water in the Valley, especially the absence of large, perennial main streams and the tendency of streams to lose their discharge into the valley alluvium before they can reach the main streams, has given canal irrigation two main characteristics—a large number of small-scale and independent systems instead of an integrated valley-wide organisation, and a high proportion of canal systems located in the less fertile piedmont and tributary valleys rather than on the main valley alluvium.

## Piedmont Canal Irrigation

Perennial streams that provide water for irrigation in the piedmont zone have low flows within the range 0.2 to 0.6 cubic meters per second. Water is abstracted from the stream a kilometer or more above the fields and villages, before the stream has left the mountains. Below the take-off point, the much-reduced flow continues down the channel through the dissected piedmont zone. The canal is contoured around the side of the valley (Pl. 12) so that when it reaches the piedmont, its level is that of the ridge crest, which is now the watershed for the natural stream below. The advantage of this translocation of water is twofold: There is a gravity feed of water to all fields since the main canal runs along the ridge crest, and the degree of piedmont dissection is such that areas with low gradients and/or more fertile fan gravel soils are less restricted on the ridge crests than on the valley bottoms, especially close to the mountains.

Irrigated fields are located on the crest and sides of the piedmont ridges, and in some cases the villages are also sited on the crests so that the main canal runs through the village beside the main street and supplies domestic water and even power for small flour mills (Fig. 17). Crops of the highest value and requiring the most water are therefore grown nearest the crest where they are close to the water supply and the supervision of the villagers. Even on ridges where a canal runs along the crest, only 20 to 40 percent of the area is canal irrigated, and main canal discharges are only 0.01 to 0.07 cubic meters per second during the latter part of the dry season. Despite the use of land with gradients of 20 degrees, the fields are not terraced for irrigation and overland flow is checked only by contour-ploughed furrows.

## Valley Floor Canal Irrigation

Canal schemes on the valley alluvium are similar in technology to those in the piedmont and in certain cases are even located lower down the same tributaries. The largest area of valley canal irrigation is supplied from one source, the Río

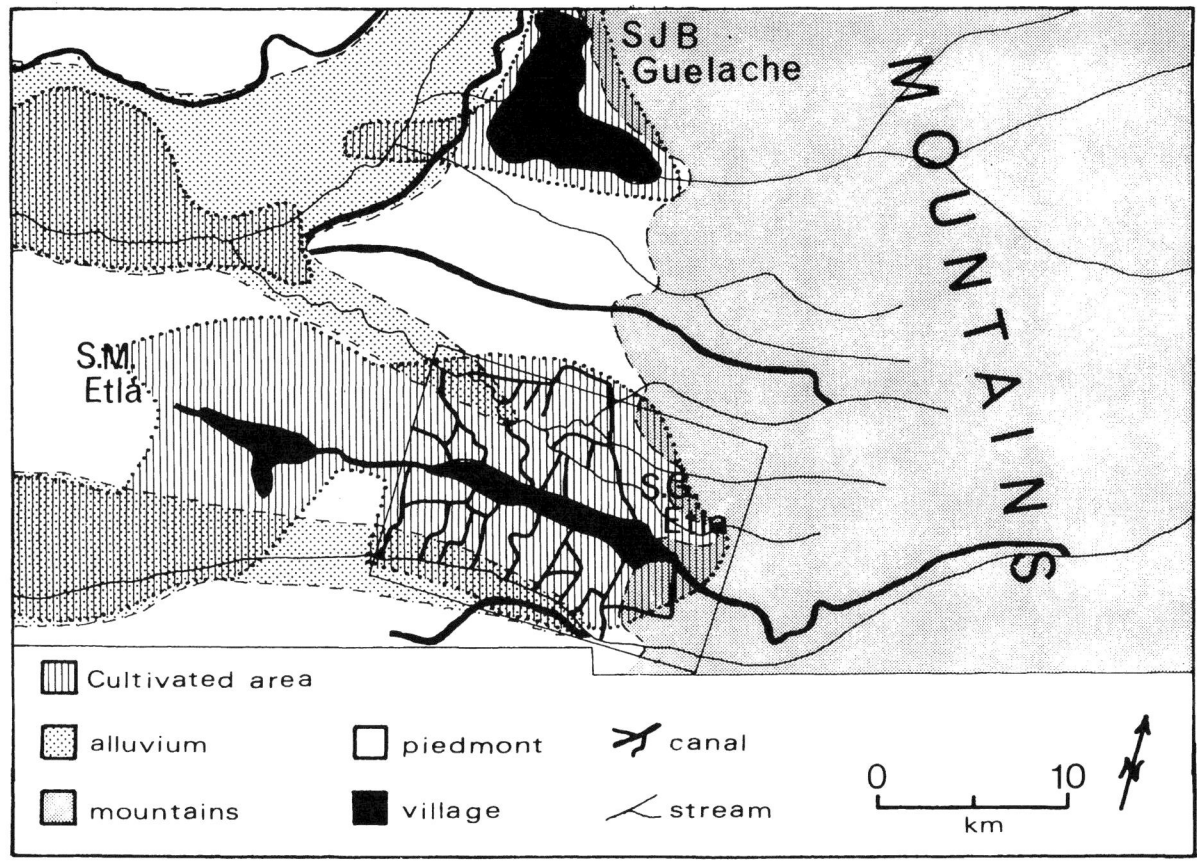

Fig. 17. Piedmont canal irrigation systems near San Gabriel Etla showing the main take-off canal and distributary canals within the sample land use area and their relation to villages and physiographic zones.

Mixtepec, which has a low flow discharge of 0.38 cubic meters per second just above its confluence with the Río Atoyac, even after irrigation water has been abstracted along the whole of the Mixtepec Valley. Discharge measurements at Santa Cruz Mixtepec and 3 kilometers farther downstream at Trapiche showed a reduction in discharge of 0.16 cubic meters per second downstream. The irrigated area between these two points is approximately 130 hectares, so that on an average the plants are receiving 0.45 cm/day of irrigation water. This is equivalent to 1600 mm of rain per year, or enough to offset potential evapotranspiration throughout even a dry year. More water is therefore applied to crops in this valley than elsewhere by any other method, except for pot irrigation of very small areas. The availability of water is also shown by the increased frequency of application, which is usually 3 times per growing season for corn, but may be up to 5 times (especially if fertilizer is being applied) despite a water table high enough to permit direct abstraction by plants. Alfalfa is grown widely in the Mixtepec Valley and responds particularly well to frequent irrigation (1 to 2 per fortnight) by producing a 60 to 70 cm growth 10 to 12 times a year.

## DISTRIBUTION OF WATER USE

The following discussion refers to the distribution of water use techniques shown in Figure 18. This map was made from field surveys in 1966, 1967, and 1968 combined with aerial photograph interpretation.

### Dry Farming

Maize yields in the Valley can be everywhere increased by the application of additional water,

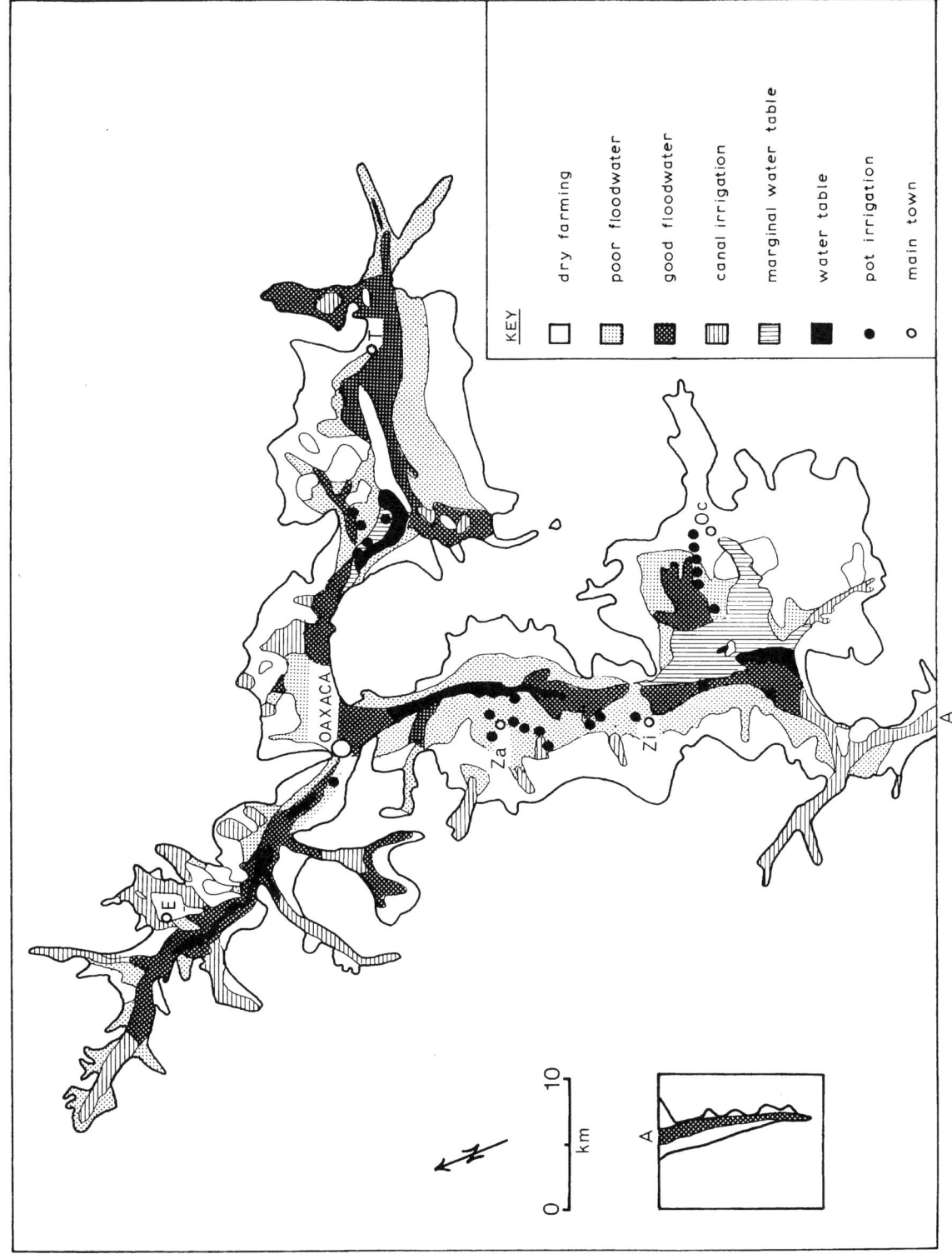

Fig. 18. Map of agricultural water use methods showing the main areas of canal irrigation, floodwater farming, pot irrigation, water-table farming and dry farming in the Valley.

so dry farming is practised only as a last resort where other types of water use are not possible. It is therefore found between the area of more intensive water use and the outer margin of cultivated land (defined here as land with greater than 25 percent of the area under crops in any one year). As would be expected, dry farming is typically a feature of the piedmont zone (which accounts for 80 percent of the whole dry-farmed area) and most of the remaining dry-farmed area is found on the floor of the Zaachila Valley. This valley contains the largest dry-farmed area both in total (319 square km) and as a proportion of its cultivated area (52 percent compared to 38 percent in each of the other two valleys; that is, 77 square km in Etla and 136 square km in Tlacolula).

The differences in the areas under dry farming in each of the three arms of the Valley are related to:

1) Rainfall distribution. Rainfall is highest in the Zaachila Valley and dry farming is therefore less unreliable, especially in the extreme south of the Valley. At the other end of the scale, dry farming in the eastern Tlacolula Valley on both the lower piedmont and valley floor is restricted by inadequate precipitation.

2) Land/water ratio. The dilemma of the Zaachila Valley is that it has a high ratio of cultivated land to a small amount of available water, particularly in contrast to the Etla Valley. This is a function of:

   a) size of the cultivated area—616 square km in the Zaachila Valley compared with 352 square km in Tlacolula and only 202 square km in Etla.

   b) characteristics of the tributary basins—those on both sides of the Etla Valley have higher altitude catchments and correspondingly higher stream flows. This is true only for the north side of the Tlacolula Valley and the west side of the Zaachila Valley. In particular, the mountains on the east side of the Zaachila Valley are very low and do not supply any perennial streams.

   c) location—the Etla and Tlacolula Valleys are upstream of the Zaachila Valley and therefore have first access to streamflows, which tend to be used up before entering the Zaachila Valley.

Floodwater Farming

As has been indicated earlier in this chapter, the term floodwater farming covers a considerable range of scale and reliability, so that in Figure 18 it has been divided into areas of good and poor floodwater farming. Good floodwater farming is always associated with distributary canal systems and provides at least one application of water every growing season. Poor floodwater farming may involve canals or simply trinchera-type walls to slow down and spread floodwater, but in either case its distinction is that it is not reliable; it occurs, on an average, less than once a year. In terms of area, good and poor floodwater farming together are the most important means of applying additional water for agriculture. They form the predominant method of water use in 22 percent of the Etla Valley (65 square km), 32 percent (146 square km) of the Zaachila Valley and 52 percent (182 square km) of the Tlacolula Valley. Floodwater farming's importance to agriculture in the Tlacolula Valley is evident in the greater attention given to exploiting any possible concentration of runoff, either by channeling water from tracks or by spreading it behind floodwater walls. Floodwater farming is most important in the Tlacolula Valley because of the low mean annual rainfall and the lack of other sources of water.

The most important floodwater-farming area of the Tlacolula Valley is located in the central area upstream of the seasonally flooded zone and contains some large-scale canal systems associated with well-constructed dams which raise the water to the level of the high alluvium. Floodwater farming is also commonly practised immediately downstream from permanent canal irrigation and receives any excess water, especially during peak flows. Although in the Tlacolula and Zaachila Valleys there are occasional examples of this relationship between canal and floodwater irrigation, it is characteristic in the Etla Valley where floodwater farming is practised along most of the length of the Río Atoyac and lower reaches of perennial tributaries in conjunction with marginal water-table farming.

The floodwater situation in the Zaachila Valley is the corollary of the distribution of dry farming: that is, floodwater farming is restricted because many of the flows of the Río Salado and Río Atoyac are used up on fields before they can reach the Zaachila Valley (except in the case of very large discharges or flows originating from storms within the Zaachila area); and flows from the tributaries within the Zaachila Valley are minimal when compared with the large area of cultivated alluvium. Good floodwater farming in the Zaachila Valley is mainly based on water from the Río Atoyac and is concentrated in areas served by several large, modern take-off canals behind concrete weirs. Beyond the limits of these new schemes, the larger part of the alluvium is inefficiently floodwater farmed by means of many small-scale systems.

### Canal Irrigation

Canal irrigation is concentrated in the Etla Valley because it contains most of those perennial streams which reach the valley floor. These higher surface flows in the Etla Valley are related to:

1) the characteristics of the tributary basins (most important being that they contain more land at higher elevation), and
2) the narrow width of the main valley floor, which reduces the amount of streamflow lost through seepage into the alluvium by minimising the distance to be crossed by tributaries and maximising the proportion of alluvium underlain by a high water table.

Although it serves only a small proportion (9 percent) of the total cultivated area in the Valley of Oaxaca, the distribution of canal irrigation among the three valleys is most important because of the preeminence it gives to the Etla Valley in terms of concentration of water use and hence agricultural productivity. Twenty-five percent (50 square km) of the cultivated area of the Etla Valley is canal irrigated compared with 7 percent (45 square km) in the Zaachila Valley and 3 percent (12 square km) in the Tlacolula arm. In the Zaachila Valley, the Río Mixtepec is exceptional in its high perennial discharge and the large irrigated area it serves.

### Water-Table Farming

Water-table farming is restricted to those areas underlain by a high water table—approximately 0.5 to 2.5 meter depth during the growing season. As the mean depth to water table increases, the amount of capillary water available to plants decreases, and water-table farming becomes more marginal and less productive. This continuous transition has been mapped in Figure 18 as two categories, water-table farming and marginal water-table farming, simply to indicate those areas of maximum water availability.

The main areas underlain by high water table are along the Río Atoyac where there is either a wide enough strip of low alluvium to grow crops (e.g., Fig. 4b) or where the usual 4 to 7 meter incision marked by a near vertical step between the two levels of alluvium is replaced by a lower and more gentle break of slope whose form is probably due to long-continued agriculture. Since incision appears to have first begun downstream (M. J. Kirkby, 1973), the Zaachila Valley contains the largest area of low alluvium and hence of water-table farming—22 square km or just over 50 percent of the total in the Valley of Oaxaca as a whole, although almost half of this area is marginal. In the Etla Valley, water-table farming can be practised on only 5 percent (10 square km) of the cultivated land, but this figure is really larger because some of the area mapped as floodwater farmed along the Río Atoyac can also be regarded as marginal water-table farmed land. The water table fed by the Río Salado in the Tlacolula Valley is considerably deeper, and the main area of high water table (5 percent of the cultivated zone) is related to the unusual hydrological conditions immediately downstream and around the margins of the flooded zone near San Juan Guelavia.

### Well Irrigation

Even where well-irrigated fields are concentrated, they still constitute a small proportion (less than 10 percent) of the cultivated area. This pattern may change with the increasing use of pumps, although at present pump irrigation is mainly supplemental and is practised at scattered points within areas predominantly irrigated by some other method. Well-and-furrow irrigation is therefore dispersed throughout the Valley, although it is most common in the Etla Valley. In Figure 18, concentrations of riego a brazo fields are given as points within areas dominated by other types of water use. Riego a brazo on isolated plots is widespread and is practised on garden plots in and around many villages even where the water table is as deep as 10 to 15 meters. Concentrations of pot-irrigation fields for truck farming are found mainly in the Zaachila Valley, around the towns of Zaachila, Zimatlán and Ocotlán. In the Etla Valley they are found immediately north of Oaxaca de Juárez, and in the Tlacolula Valley they are concentrated around San Sebastián Abasolo. Except for the last area, riego a brazo fields are not concentrated in areas of highest water table, but tend to be located in areas of poor floodwater farming where the water table in summer lies between 3 and 6 meters deep.

In conclusion, the general pattern of water use in the three valleys can be summarized as follows.

1) The Etla Valley contains the highest concentration of water use, with 50 percent of its cultivated area receiving water from perennial canals, reliable floodwater schemes and water-table farming, and high water use occurring on a significant proportion of the eastern piedmont zone.

2) The Zaachila Valley contains a higher amount of agricultural land, and its water resources are consequently spread more thinly. The general pattern is one of high water use concentrated in a narrow central band along the Río Atoyac and low water availability over much of the rest of the valley floor as well as the piedmont, resulting in 75 percent of the total cultivated area receiving little or no water.

3) In the Tlacolula Valley, low water resources combined with inadequate rainfall produce the least favourable agricultural conditions of all three arms of the Valley. Sixty-seven percent of the cultivated area is supplied with little or no additional water compared with 75 percent in the Zaachila Valley, but in the Tlacolula arm the situation is aggravated by the greater riskiness of dry farming. In addition, the central part of the Tlacolula alluvium is flooded for much of the growing season and is uncultivated, and the scarcity of perennial streams large enough to supply irrigation water means that most of the valley is dependent on floodwater.

# V

# CORN PRODUCTION AND ITS DISTRIBUTION

## INTRODUCTION

If water resources are the most critical factor of agriculture in the Valley, corn is by far the most important product. Most of the area of the valley floor is devoted to corn growing, and even in the irrigated areas of cash crop production corn is still a major crop, occupying between 30 and 50 percent of the agricultural land (see Appendix II). Corn is important not only in its areal dominance but because almost every peasant household in the towns and villages grows some corn to eat or to give to animals. Corn production is therefore not the concern of a few large landholders but is part of the life of every family.

Even for the families who do not farm their own land, corn is a staple part of the diet (together with beans) and is the focus of many beliefs and superstitions. Corn is not simply an agricultural crop; it is a means of life and God-given. A man regards his cornfield or *milpa* as a special place where he can do the work God has chosen for him and where he can find dignity in it. There is thus a very real bond between cultivators and their milpas in the Valley of Oaxaca. This bond has its roots in pre-Conquest times when, from the beginnings of agriculture in the area, corn played a major role. An understanding of the processes and distribution of corn production is therefore basic to any study of how peasants in the Valley use their agricultural resources today and of the changes in resource use in the past.

## TRADITIONAL CULTIVATION METHODS

On the steeper slopes and in the poorest farmers' fields (and the two often go together), hoes or digging sticks are still used to till the soil (Pl. 5), while on the most productive alluvium and in the richest farmers' fields tractors are increasingly being used. At one end of the scale, the fields are too small, steep or stony to make ox-ploughing practicable, with the limiting conditions being determined as much by socioeconomic as by physical factors but generally occurring somewhere between 20 degrees and 30 degrees gradient. At the other end of the scale, deep ploughing of alluvial soils more effectively clears weeds and increases yields, assuming that the farmer can afford the initial investment. Between these two extremes, the ox-plough is the main method of tillage on deep alluvial soils and thin, stony piedmont soils alike (Pl. 13). Ox-teams are characteristic features of the landscape of the Valley, pulling either the simple wooden plough which was introduced at the time of the Spanish Conquest or the local form of ox-cart (Pl. 14).

In order to maintain expected average yields above 200-250 kilos per hectare (which seems to be the lowest yield considered worth harvesting), fallowing of dry and floodwater-farmed milpas in the Valley is practised when possible. In contrast to the more humid lowlands of the Veracruz and Oaxaca coastal areas, fallowing in the Valley is a response to low soil mineral reserves and potential soil erosion rather than to severe weeding problems introduced by the production of secondary growth following clearing. The milpa cycle commonly begins with the necessity to clear vegetation from land which may have lain fallow for 1 year, 7 years or even more than 20 years in the piedmont and mountains. Where the natural vegetation is well established and includes trees, it may be removed by burning, with all except the largest trees having been previously chopped down with *machetes* and piled into heaps (Pl. 15). After burning, or where burning is unnecessary, the land is ploughed and the weeds removed by hand. A second ploughing follows in order to straighten the furrows.

The Spanish plough is wooden, but many today have steel tips. It is drawn by two oxen and controlled by one man walking behind it, although he may ride the plough by standing on it when it tends to jump out of the ground. Ploughing is shallow, about 25 cm deep, and furrows are 50 to 70 cm apart. Harrowing is occasionally a part of field preparation, more commonly for crops sown broadcast such as beans by themselves or alfalfa, and is done by dragging a raft of thorny branches behind the ox-team across the surface of the field. These preparatory stages usually take place during the dry season, between January and April.

Sometime between April and June most milpas are sown with varying proportions of maize, beans and squash; the time of sowing and the proportions of each crop depending mainly on expectations of rainfall (see below and Appendix I). Sowing is done by helpers—hired men or boys called *mozos*, or members of the family, both male and female. They follow close behind the plough, dropping seeds into the newly tilled furrow every 65 to 90 cm and covering the seeds up by moving soil sideways with their feet in a continuous shuffling action. A ploughman with one helper can plant about 0.5 hectares per working day. Beans may be sown later, but generally all crops to be grown in the milpa are sown together, and seeds are mixed in the desired proportions in a single bag. At each point along the furrow two to four seeds are dropped, and the proportions in the bag are such that two or three of the seeds are almost always corn.

During the growing season fields are usually weeded twice by hand (by pulling out by the roots or using a machete), once 2 to 4 weeks after planting and again 8 to 10 weeks after planting. At the same time, the soil surface may be broken by light tilling to increase percolation, and soil may be piled around the stems of the young corn plants to provide support against the wind. Weeds grow faster in the wetter and more fertile fields than in the drier piedmont, but weeding is nowhere in the Valley a limiting factor in cultivation. Three to five months after planting, depending on the type of maize and the rainfall conditions, the crops are harvested by hand, usually by several men with women and children helpers (Pl. 16). The cobs are gathered in large baskets carried on the back and are generally loaded into an ox-cart which has been brought to the field. If harvesting is delayed or rain likely so that there is danger of the ripe cobs rotting on the stalk, they may be bent over to shed water more easily. The stalks are usually taken out later and used for fodder (zacate) or manure, but they may be left in the field and be grazed as stubble. Transport from the field is usually on workers' backs or by mule or ox-cart; whereas in transporting crops to market, local buses and trucks are much more widely used.

Farmers are well aware of the benefits of fertilizers and manure, but little is applied to milpas because manure is scarce and fertilizers costly. When these are available, they are applied to irrigated crops of higher value. Dry-farmed milpas do receive manure in the form of dung and zacate mixed together, but the amount available each year covers only a portion of the field. The area covered is therefore rotated, leading to areal differences in corn yield within a field in any year. After the harvest, in September and October, the milpas may be sown with chickpeas (*garbanzo*) which, being leguminous, are able to mature during the dry season. More commonly they are left fallow until the following spring so that during the winter months the general impression of the Valley is of a dry, barren landscape which contrasts strongly with the dominant green colour of the summer.

## FACTORS AFFECTING PLANTING

The foregoing description of the sequence of events that takes place in a milpa during the corn-growing season belies the complexity of the task. Even if it is assumed, for simplicity's sake, that corn grown for direct consumption by the cultivator is not subject to the outside influences of market supply and demand, the remaining sources of choice and uncertainty make "simple" subsistence corn cultivation a difficult and risky process.

A peasant household in the Valley typically holds several pieces of land which are scattered across the village lands and are probably located in at least two physiographic zones as well. The parcels of land belonging to one family will, in any case, differ to some degree in physical characteristics such as slope, soil, and geology, which leads to differences in fertility. The domestic situation of the cultivator also affects fertility by determining how much of his holding can remain fallow and for how long, and whether any manure or fertilizer can be applied. In any year, an important determinant of crop success or failure is natural water conditions in each milpa; for most milpas these water conditions are the amount and timing of rainfall, but on the flood plains the size and frequency of floods are also factors.

The ultimate success of the harvest is, to a large extent, the result of correctly matching planting conditions with rainfall conditions. Probably most important to this is judging the time at which the first major rains will come in order to have prepared the appropriate peices of land by clearing and ploughing. The first major rains must be sufficient to make up the soil moisture deficit that has accumulated throughout the dry season and must provide enough moisture to support the young plants through the first three weeks or so, without additional rain or irrigation being necessary. Otherwise, cultivators are reluctant to risk sowing for fear of the plants being "burned up" before the next rains come. In order to guide their decisions about which fields to prepare and to help predict the pattern of rainfall in the growing season, the characteristics of the early spring rainfall are taken as good or bad indicators. Indeed, a relationship can be seen between early and later rainfall patterns in any one year for the 40 year period of meteorologic observations (see Appendix I).

In addition to judging the timing of effective rains, cultivators in the Valley have to decide how best to take advantage of the moisture conditions when they come. To do this, they have a choice of types of corn; a varying ratio of corn to safe, stand-by crops such as beans; and a range of possible densities of plants. A combination of these factors will enable them to make the best of particular dry or wet field conditions. If his present landholding distribution and these possible crop variations do not provide the cultivator with sufficient scope to obtain successful harvests, he has the further choice of changing the distribution of his milpas by long term or short term changes in his tenure. To give some idea of the complexity of the situation and the ways in which different planting factors interact, planting decisions can be drawn in the form of a flow diagram (Fig. 19).

At the beginning of each year there is a set of initial conditions which are known to the cultivator: the distribution of milpas held by him; the amount of seed available (that is, saved from the previous year or available locally for purchase); the crop yields from each milpa for known rainfall and flood patterns; and which fields should or must be fallowed that year. From the beginning of the year, there is a continual input of rainfall data on which planting policy is first based, and then continuously reassessed, until the fields are actually sown. In some fields, the decision may have effectively been made some time before planting takes place. For example, in milpas that are newly cleared and ploughed after a long period of fallow, the initial field preparation, which must take place before the rainfall pattern is well established, already represents a considerable investment of labour and capital so that planting is likely to occur even if moisture conditions augur low yields. At some point in the year, usually between March and June, the farmer assesses the ideal distribution of milpas for planting on the basis of his prediction of the rainfall pattern (for example, a predicted wet year might indicate expansion of corn in the piedmont), and then compares this optimum distribution with the land actually available to him.

If, as is likely, the distribution of his own milpas does not match the predicted ideal distribution, he may choose between two alternatives: to match his own situation as closely as possible to his predicted ideal or to change his initial set of conditions (see subroutine A, Fig. 20). This may be effected through long-term changes—by obtaining additional milpas by buying or sharecropping, or through making favourable social alliances such

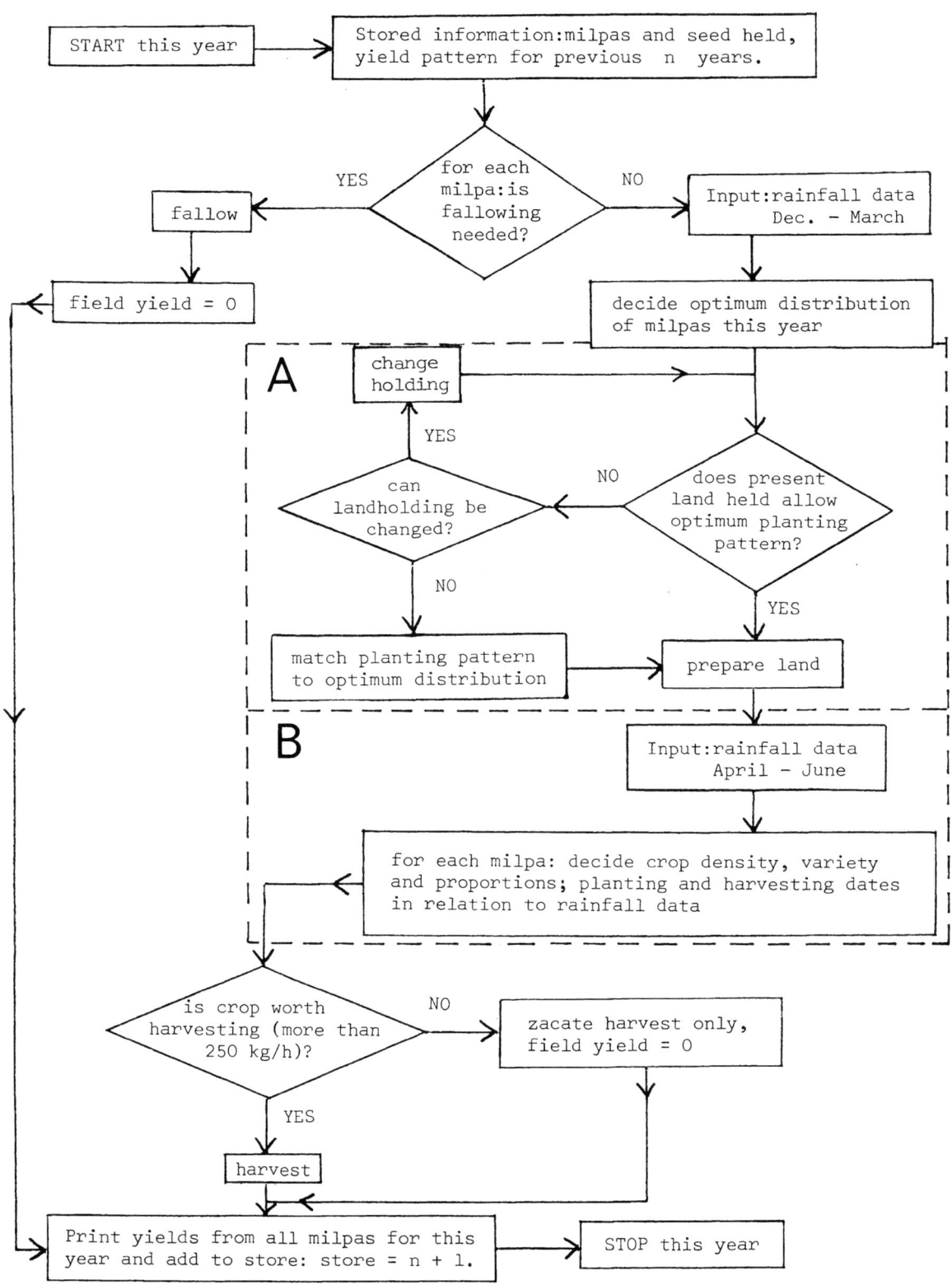

Fig. 19. Simplified flow diagram for corn-planting decisions in dry farming.

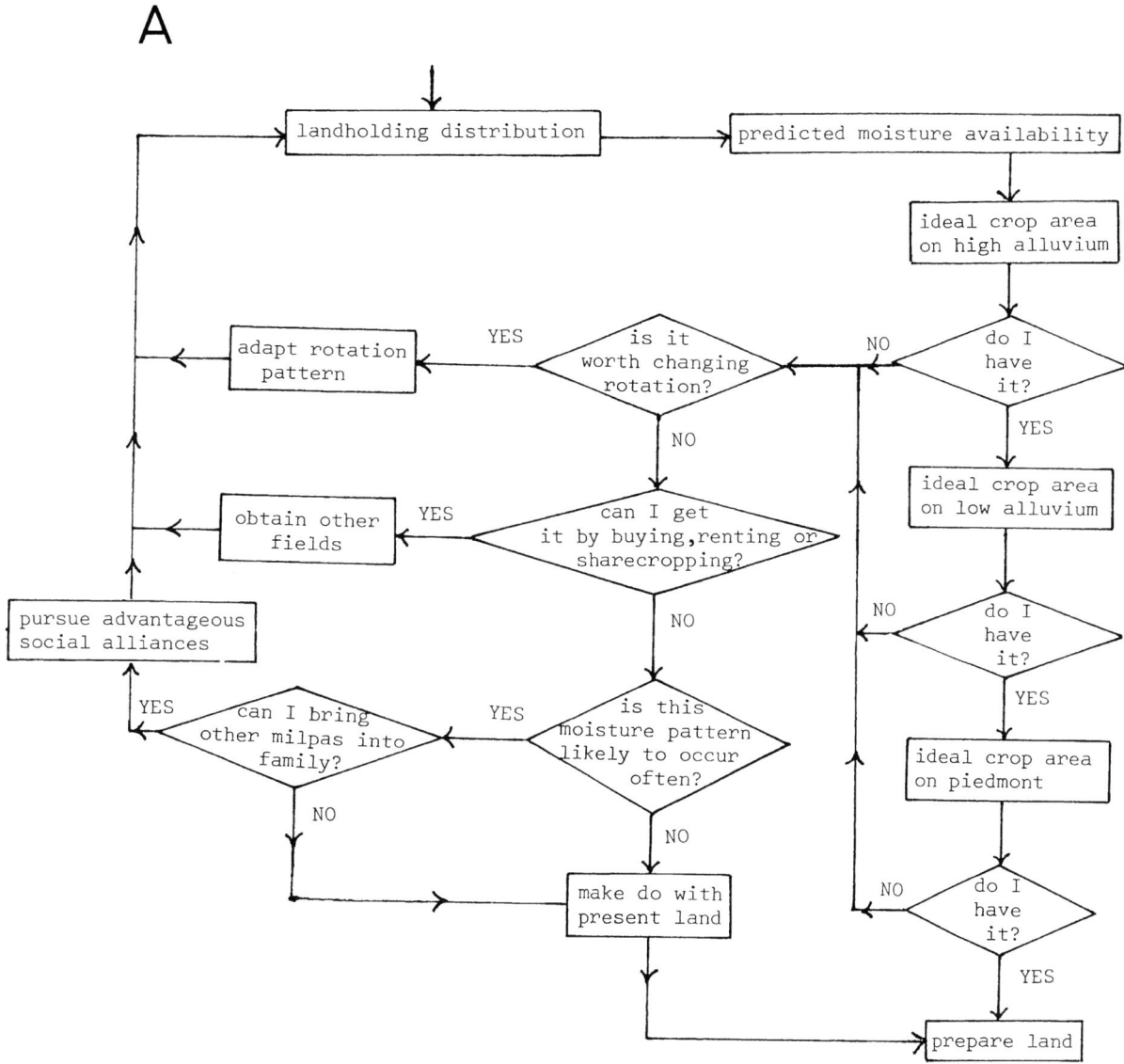

Fig. 20. Subroutine A: for matching spatial distribution of milpas to predicted moisture distribution (box A, Fig. 19).

as marriage. On a shorter-term basis, it may also be achieved by extending or decreasing the length of fallow. Once these distributions are chosen and the selected milpas prepared, two further choices remain—when to plant and what to plant—and both depend on rainfall prediction. The choice of what to plant covers several variables, such as type and density of corn plants and the relative proportions of corn, beans and squash. These alternative planting strategies, which are discussed below, are shown diagramatically in Figure 21 as a subroutine of the more generalized flow diagram in Figure 19.

Corn can be classified into four main groups in the Valley of Oaxaca: 3-month (*violento*) indian corn, 4 to 5-month (*tardón*) indian corn, 6-month *cajeta* indian corn, and 6-month hybrid varieties. Within these groups there are local varieties, and corn in each area is so specialized that it is said that seed from the Etla Valley cannot be grown successfully in the Tlacolula Valley. The short growing season of the 3-month corn is advan-

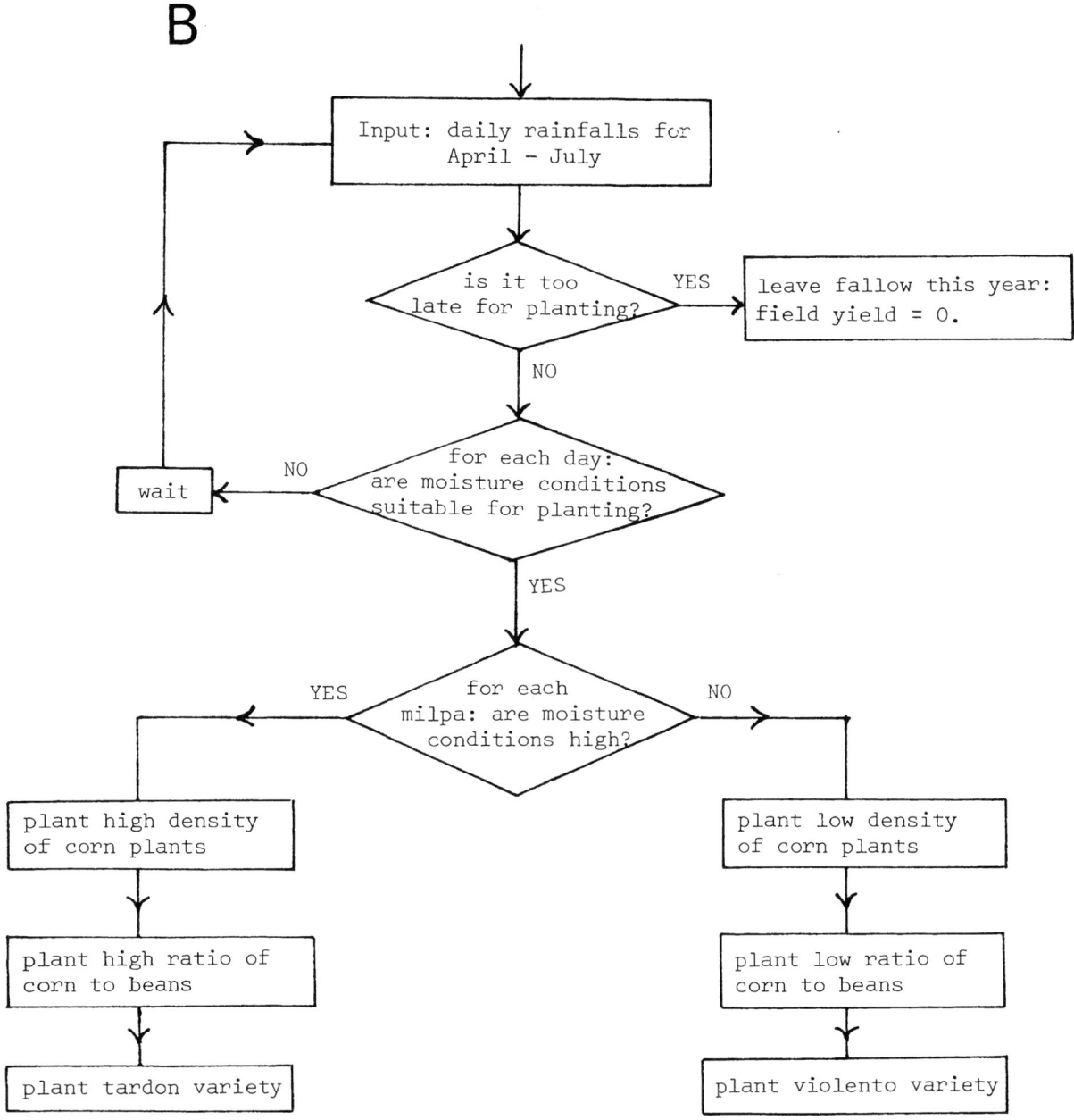

Fig. 21. Subroutine B: for planting and timing decisions within each milpa (box B, Fig. 19).

tageous in dry conditions (where the danger from drought is increased rather than decreased by a longer time in the ground) and in areas where all-year-round cropping is possible. Its disadvantage is its low yield compared to tardón and hybrid varieties when moisture conditions are good. Conversely, tardón corn's higher yields under good conditions are offset by greater risk of failure when conditions are less favourable, and by the longer time it occupies the ground when two or three crops per year are grown. Cajeta corn has a long growing season and is adapted to colder conditions so that in the Oaxaca Valley it is found only high up in the mountains. Hybrid varieties of corn have the advantage of much higher yields if moisture and mineral conditions are favourable, but they require more water and fertilizer than are generally available, and without these, yields may fall below those of the indian corns. Furthermore, hybrid corn is sterile and new seed must be bought each year, whereas the indian varieties can be sown from seed saved from the previous year's harvest. Within the alluvium and piedmont zones of the Valley, the choice of type for most farmers is between the violento and tardón varieties.

The amount of corn to be sown in each milpa must also be decided, and considerable range has been found. The density of maize plants sown per hectare ranges from less than 9000 to more than 80,000 throughout the Valley as a whole; and even in fields with similar moisture conditions and similar yields, ranges from 30,000 to 80,000 plants per hectare have been measured by the author. Cultivators see their alternative strategies in the following terms: high plant densities are preferred in fields with optimum moisture conditions to get the maximum possible yield of cobs; as moisture conditions become less favourable, optimum plant density decreases. However, in the worst situations they report a reverse strategy, that of maximising the amount of stalks (zacate) produced for fodder, even if (or because) the yield of cobs is likely to be so low that it is not worth harvesting them. In these situations, which are commonest in the piedmont and in the Mitla end of the Tlacolula Valley, plant density is said to be increased.

Testing to see of these strategies were actually followed, it was found that in the sample of 166 milpas there was a slight, although not significant, trend to increasing plant density with increasing yield (which reflects better moisture conditions), but the reverse trend when moisture conditions, and hence yield, were very low was not apparent. The data show that in a wet year little distinction is made in plant density between the milpas on the high alluvium and those with optimum average moisture conditions (high water table), but a relatively larger proportion of seed is expended in the piedmont. This perhaps lends weight to a conclusion of the next chapter, i.e., that in this most marginal agricultural area, gambling decisions are given the greatest scope. Conversely, in the sample of 166 milpas it was found that when moisture conditions are poor and the risk of no-return is highest, the highest plant densities are sown on the high alluvium or "safest-bet" zone.

Another planting strategy is to change the proportions of corn, beans and squash in each field to match the predicted moisture conditions. Milpas may contain all corn, all beans or occasionally all squash, but the majority lie somewhere between 80 and 100 percent corn, the preferred and staple crop. Beans are said to be more reliable than corn in the poorest conditions, and squash grows best in moist though not the wettest situations. Cultivators have the alternative of increasing the proportion of beans where moisture conditions are expected to be poor and the reverse, so that beanfields tend to be increased in the high piedmont and mountains and in dry years. Measurements of the proportions of corn, beans and squash in 109 milpas (excluding those containing only beans) showed significant differences among the physiographic zones. The mean percentages of corn in milpas were 93.0 percent in the mountains, 96.0 percent in the piedmont, and 98.6 percent in the high alluvium, thus confirming the strategy the farmers said they were following.

The flow diagram in Figure 19 illustrates the sequence of some of the decisions confronting subsistence farmers each year. The same diagram, repeated many times, can be seen as a simulation of the development of an agricultural tradition, which, in its simplest terms, is the accumulation of annual information on yield patterns in relation to actual and predicted moisture conditions. Thus, at the beginning of the year, the stored information on yield patterns is for $n$ years and at the end of the year, it becomes $n + 1$. The traditional decisions current at any time are a function of the length of time represented by $n$ and the weight given to any particular value of $n$, that is, the weight given to the yield pattern of any particular year; and both of these depend on the memory and environmental perception of the individual and the community.

## FACTORS AFFECTING YIELDS

During 1967 and 1968, samples of milpas (numbering 57 the first year and 109 fields the

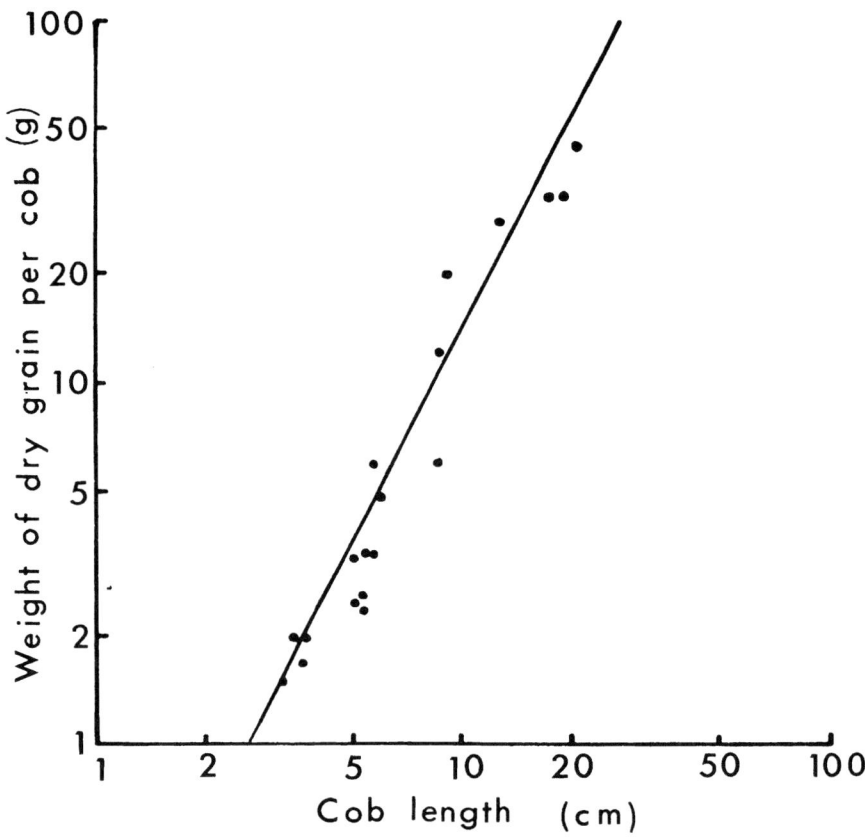

Fig. 22. Relation between cob length and weight of dry grain per cob for modern maize in the Valley of Oaxaca.

second) from all parts of the Valley were taken just before they were harvested in August and September. In each, milpa crop and environmental variables were measured. Crop variables included corn height, spacing between rows, spacing between plants within rows, average cob length and ratio of numbers of corn, bean and squash plants. Environmental variables included location within the Valley, physiographic zone, water availability and use, slope angle, soil type, and degree of surface erosion. From the measurements of spacing of corn plants within and between rows, the density of corn plants per hectare was calculated. A sample of cobs was measured and weighed to show the consistent relationship between cob length and weight of dry seed (Fig. 22). On the basis of Figure 22, for each milpa in the sample the mean cob length was converted to mean dried weight of seed and multiplied by the number of corn plants per hectare to give corn yield per hectare.

A series of two-way analyses of variance were run for the logarithm of corn yields. Corn yields obtained from the measured milpas were analysed in terms of area of the Valley, physiographic zone, type of water use, and soil texture. For each analysis of variance one factor was held constant and two varied; in this way five values were obtained for each subclass in all the analyses. Area of the Valley was selected to reflect broad differences in rainfall from a minimum in the Tlacolula Valley to a maximum in the southern Zaachila Valley. The central area, where all three valleys come together around Oaxaca de Juárez, has a mean annual rainfall between that of the Etla and Zaachila Valleys.

The differences between physiographic zones that most affect agriculture are:

TABLE 3

EFFECTS OF LOCATION AND PHYSIOGRAPHIC ZONE ON DRY FARMING
CORN YIELDS AS SHOWN BY 2-WAY ANALYSIS OF VARIANCE

| Source of Variation | Mean Yield Metric Tons/Hectare | Area/Zone Mean Yield / Overall Mean Yield | Variance Ratio = F | Signif. Level |
|---|---|---|---|---|
| Total | 0.78 | | | |
| Area: Etla | 0.70 | 0.90 | | |
| Central | 0.98 | 1.24 | 5.38 | 1% |
| Zaachila | 1.54 | 1.97 | | |
| Tlacolula | 0.38 | 0.45 | | |
| Physiographic Zone: | | | | |
| Piedmont | 0.48 | 0.62 | 12.59 | 1% |
| High Alluvium | 1.26 | 1.60 | | |
| Interaction | – | | 0.42 | not sig. |

1) those between the high and low alluvium—depth to water table and soil texture. The low alluvium has a higher mean water table and coarser mean soil texture.
2) those between high alluvium and piedmont—slope gradient, soil texture and thickness, and depth to water table. The piedmont zone has steeper slopes, generally coarser and thinner soils, and a deeper water table. For a typical unirrigated piedmont field see Plate 17.

Type of water use reflects the amount of water available for corn and, for the purposes of handling the analyses, was divided into dry farming, floodwater farming and irrigated (including canal, well and water-table farmed) representing low, medium and high water consumption. Soil texture is analysed in terms of sand, silt, and clay ignoring surface stoniness.

Tables 3 to 7 summarise the results of five analyses of variance which together indicate the most important factors influencing corn yields today. The simplest case, dry farming, is shown in Table 3. Both factors (area of the Valley and physiographic zone) were found to be significant (1 percent level), with no significant interaction, and the effects of both factors can be interpreted in terms of water availability. It has already been shown that different areas of the Valley receive different amounts of rain, and likewise the differ-

TABLE 4

EFFECTS OF LOCATION AND PHYSIOGRAPHIC
ZONE ON IRRIGATED CORN YIELDS AS
SHOWN BY 2-WAY ANALYSIS OF VARIANCE

| Source of Variation | Mean Yield Metric Tons /Hectare | Variance Ratio = F | Signif. Level |
|---|---|---|---|
| Total | 1.90 | | |
| Area of Valley | | 2.95 | nearly 5% |
| Physiographic Zone (High and Low Alluvium) | | 1.69 | not sig. |
| Interaction | | 0.82 | not sig. |

TABLE 5

EFFECTS OF SOIL TEXTURE AND WATER USE
ON HIGH AND LOW ALLUVIUM CORN YIELDS
IN ALL AREAS OF THE VALLEY AS SHOWN
BY 2-WAY ANALYSIS OF VARIANCE

| Source of Variation | Mean Yield Metric Tons /Hectare | Variance Ratio = F | Signif. Level |
|---|---|---|---|
| Total | 1.37 | | |
| Soil Texture | | 0.54 | not sig. |
| Water Use (Dry, Floodwater and Irrigated) | | 1.30 | not sig. |
| Interaction | | 0.43 | not sig. |

TABLE 6

EFFECTS OF LOCATION AND WATER USE ON HIGH ALLUVIUM CORN YIELDS
AS SHOWN BY 2-WAY ANALYSIS OF VARIANCE

| Source of Variation | Area/Water Mean Yield / Overall Mean Yield | Mean Yield Metric Tons/Hectare | Variance Ratio = F | Signif. Level |
|---|---|---|---|---|
| Total | | 1.90 | | |
| Area: Etla | 1.02 | 1.94 | | |
| Central | 1.07 | 2.18 | 3.42 | 5% |
| Zaachila | 1.66 | 3.16 | | |
| Tlacolula | 0.52 | 1.0 | | |
| Water Use: | | | | |
| Dry Farming | 0.67 | 1.28 | 9.38 | 1% |
| Irrigated | 1.49 | 2.84 | | |
| Interaction | − | − | 1.04 | not sig. |

TABLE 7

EFFECTS OF SOIL TEXTURE AND PHYSIOGRAPHIC ZONE ON DRY AND IRRIGATED
CORN YIELDS IN ALL AREAS EXCEPT ZAACHILA VALLEY
AS SHOWN BY 2-WAY ANALYSIS OF VARIANCE

| Source of Variation | Mean Yield Metric Tons/Hectare | Variance Ratio = F | Signif. Level |
|---|---|---|---|
| Total | 0.79 | | |
| Soil Texture | | 1.54 | not sig. |
| Physiographic Zone (All 3) | | 0.33 | not sig. |
| Interaction | | 0.34 | not sig. |

ence is between physiographic zones with the greatest significance for corn yield are those of water availability.

This is supported by Table 4, which analyses the effect of area of the Valley and physiographic zone on irrigated corn yields, where neither factor is found to be significant. Since the only difference between the two analyses is in the amount of water applied, it can be inferred that the two factors affect dry-farmed corn yields through their influence on natural differences in water availability and that these differences are in effect obliterated by the application of additional water.

It was considered possible that the effect of physiographic zone on corn yield was also through differences in soil texture; farmers state preferences for fine-textured soils, and the high and low alluviums do have significantly different textures. However, in an analysis of variance run for high and low alluvium yields (Table 5) and for all corn yields (Table 7) soil texture was found not to be significant. The importance of water availability is also shown in Table 6 where the effects of (a) area of the Valley and (b) type of water use are analysed for all high-alluvium corn yields. Both are found to be significant—5 percent and 1 percent level respectively. Therefore, on the high alluvium where most milpas are located, the most important factors influencing corn yields are water use and rainfall. The mean yields for dry and irrigated fields are 1.28 metric tons per hectare and 2.84 metric tons per hectare respectively (Table 6).

At this point, the effect of slope angle on yield should be considered, since mean gradient is different for the piedmont and alluvial zones and may therefore be a contributory factor in the

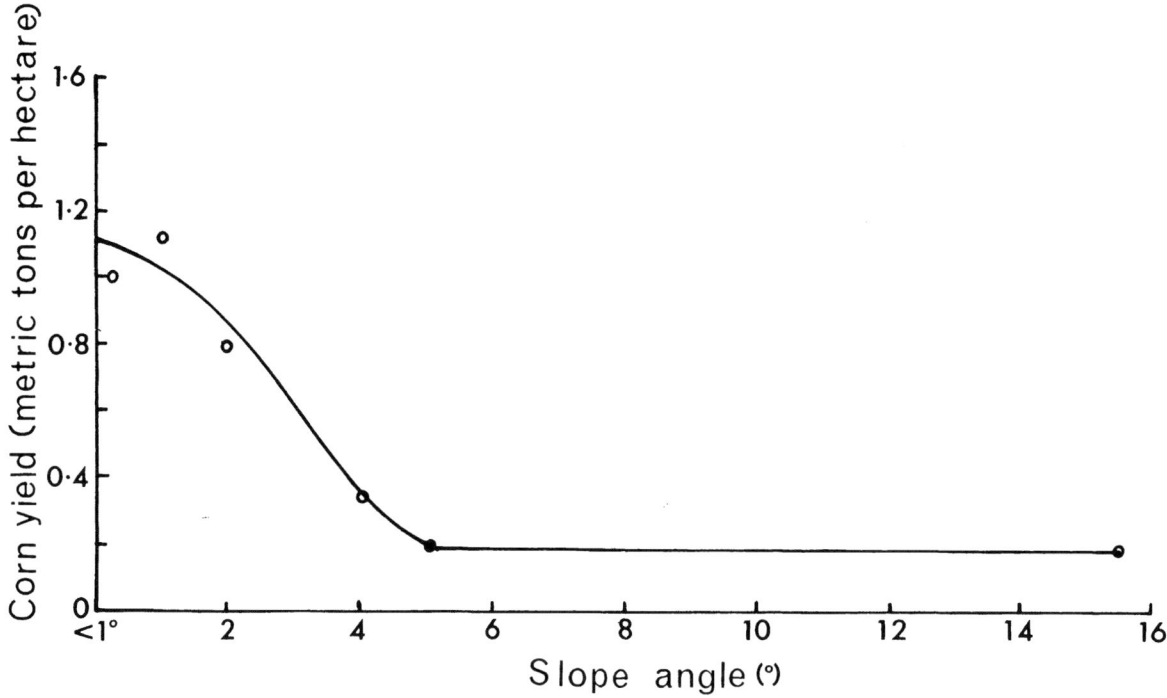

Fig. 23. Relationship between slope angle and corn yield for dry farming in the Etla and Tlacolula Valleys.

significant yield differences between zones (Table 3). Figure 23 shows the relationship between slope angle and corn yield for dry farming in the Etla and Tlacolula Valleys. Only at gradients lower than 5 degrees is increasing slope angle related to decreasing corn yields; above this angle no effect could be detected. The way in which slope angle influences corn yield is probably through its effect on soil thickness and rate of soil and (more importantly) water movement downslope, both of which cause steep slopes to provide a drier environment for plants.

The analyses of variance strongly indicate that, of the factors chosen, differences in water availability are the most important for corn yields, whether through differences in natural rainfall or through inequalities in the amounts of water applied artificially. Furthermore, given sufficient irrigation water, similar yields (approximately 2 to 3 metric tons per hectare) can be obtained from any area of the Valley, in any physiographic zone, on any slope within the range measured (0 to 16 degrees), and on soil of any texture (clay, silt, sand). Such conclusions have far-reaching implications for the importance of water use and water rights now and in the past and for future planning and development. They are supported by other data on measured corn yields obtained from the land use areas selected for detailed study.

For each of these areas, a mean figure was obtained for total water consumption, which can be assumed to be equivalent to the amount of water available to all crops within the area considered because availability is always less than potential water consumption. This figure was calculated by measuring by field survey the proportions of land under:

1) crops dependent on water additional to rainfall, such as alfalfa and sugar cane
2) corn receiving additional water
3) dry-farmed corn and other crops
4) fallow and uncultivated land

and multiplying these areas by appropriate factors for water consumption (assumed to be equivalent to potential evapotranspiration for the total growth period of each crop). The result is shown in Figure 24a which gives the significant (0.1

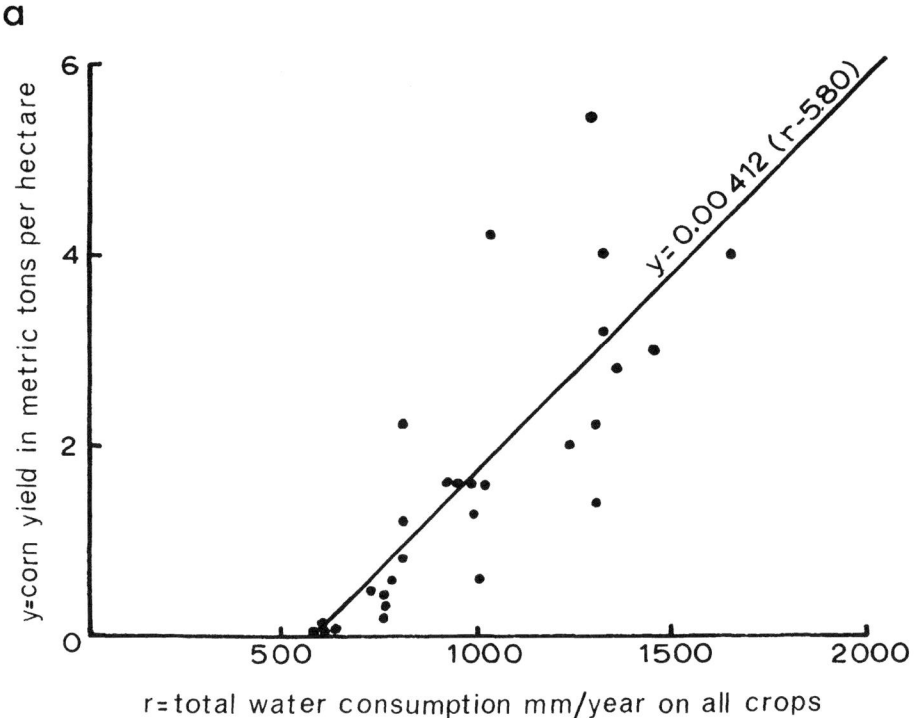

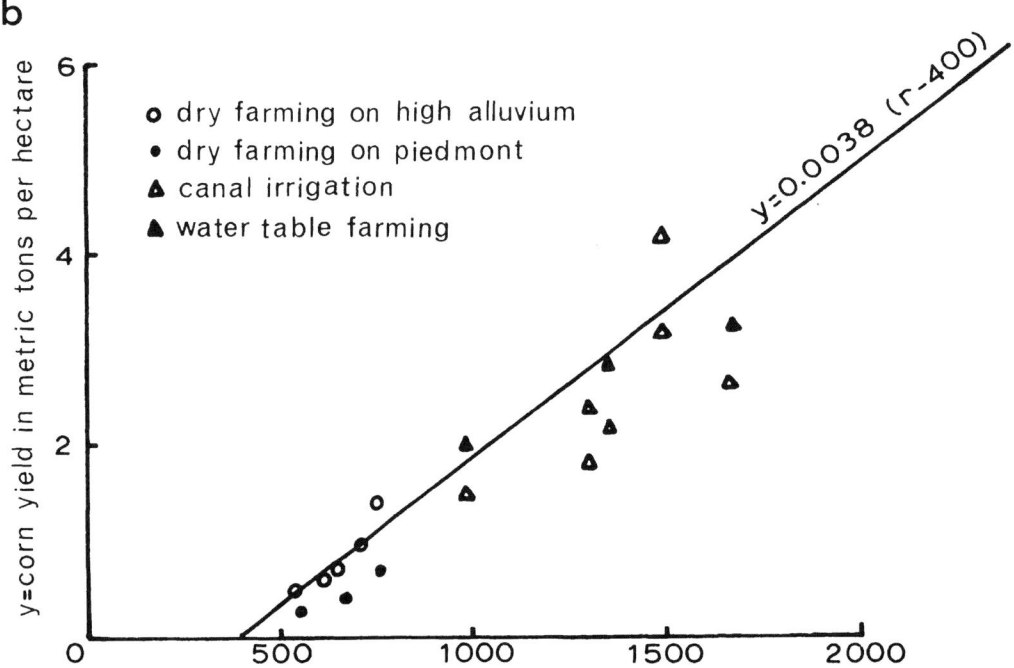

Fig. 24. Relationship between measured corn yield and water consumption: (*a*) using data from mapped sample land use areas, and (*b*) using averages of all measured yields (166) for different types of water use.

percent level) relationship between total water consumption and corn yield.

The data correlating proportions of land in classes 1 to 4 in the land use areas with a figure for total water consumption were used as a basis for converting aerial photograph interpretation of crop proportions into total water consumptions throughout the whole Valley. This air photograph interpretation was supported by visual field checking at 100 sample points across the Valley, and the relationship between the total water consumption obtained in this way and all measured corn yields is given in Figure 24b. Despite the indirect method of obtaining total water consumption, both graphs show significant and similar correlations between corn yield and water consumed, thus confirming the analyses of variance in that, of the many factors involved, the prime determinant of corn yield in the Valley today is the availability and hence consumption of water.

## AREAL VARIATIONS IN CORN YIELD AND WATER CONSUMPTION

At this point it will be useful to specify the stages of this analysis of land and water use since several important relationships are being established. In earlier chapters, the present physical environment and agricultural technology were discussed and given spatial dimension; specifically, the distribution of water use techniques has been related to the distribution of physical environmental factors. In the immediately preceding section, the extent of the dependence of corn yield on water consumption has been shown. This should now be set in a spatial context in order to:

1) give a more complete picture of land and water use around the valley, and
2) provide a basis for comparing areal variations in corn yield with population density. In a later chapter it will be shown that the present distribution of population is significantly related to differences in local mean corn yields and hence to differences in water resources.

The distributions of corn yield and water consumption are presented as two maps (Figs. 25 and 26) which can be compared with the previous map of the distribution of water use methods since all three present different aspects of a single pattern. The distribution map of corn yield is based on:

1) the known relationship between corn yield and proportion of land under each of the four land use categories obtained from the land use areas
2) all measured corn yields (166 points)
3) air photograph interpretation of crop proportion in the land use categories based on field measurement in the 24 land use areas studied in detail, combined with visual field checking at more than 100 points across the valley.

Figure 26, water consumption in excess of rainfall, is a reinterpretation of the same data, using Figure 24a to justify the relation between corn yield and water consumption and subtracting the rainfall for different parts of the Valley. Comparison of the maps shows the close association between high water consumption, high mean corn yield, watertable farming and canal irrigation on the one hand and between low water consumption, low corn yield, dry and floodwater farming on the other. The map data are presented as histograms in Figures 27 and 28 in order to bring out the differences among the three arms of the Valley.

In Figure 27, corn yield per hectare is plotted against area, and the proportion of each yield class receiving different types of water use is indicated. Since least water is available in the Tlacolula Valley, it represents the most nearly natural situation with the largest amount of its land (30 percent of the area of 113 square kilometers) falling into the lowest category of corn yield and successively smaller amount of land able to produce higher mean yields. The large proportion of land producing only 0.2 to 0.4 metric tons per hectare reflects the low rainfall of the Valley, particularly at its eastern end where yields are this low even on the high alluvium and where the piedmont is uncultivated. Likewise, the very small area of land producing more than 2 metric tons per hectare reflects the small water resources for applying additional water in the Tlacolula Valley.

This trend of a decreasing area which is capable of producing each successively higher yield is also seen in the Zaachila Valley, with one exception.

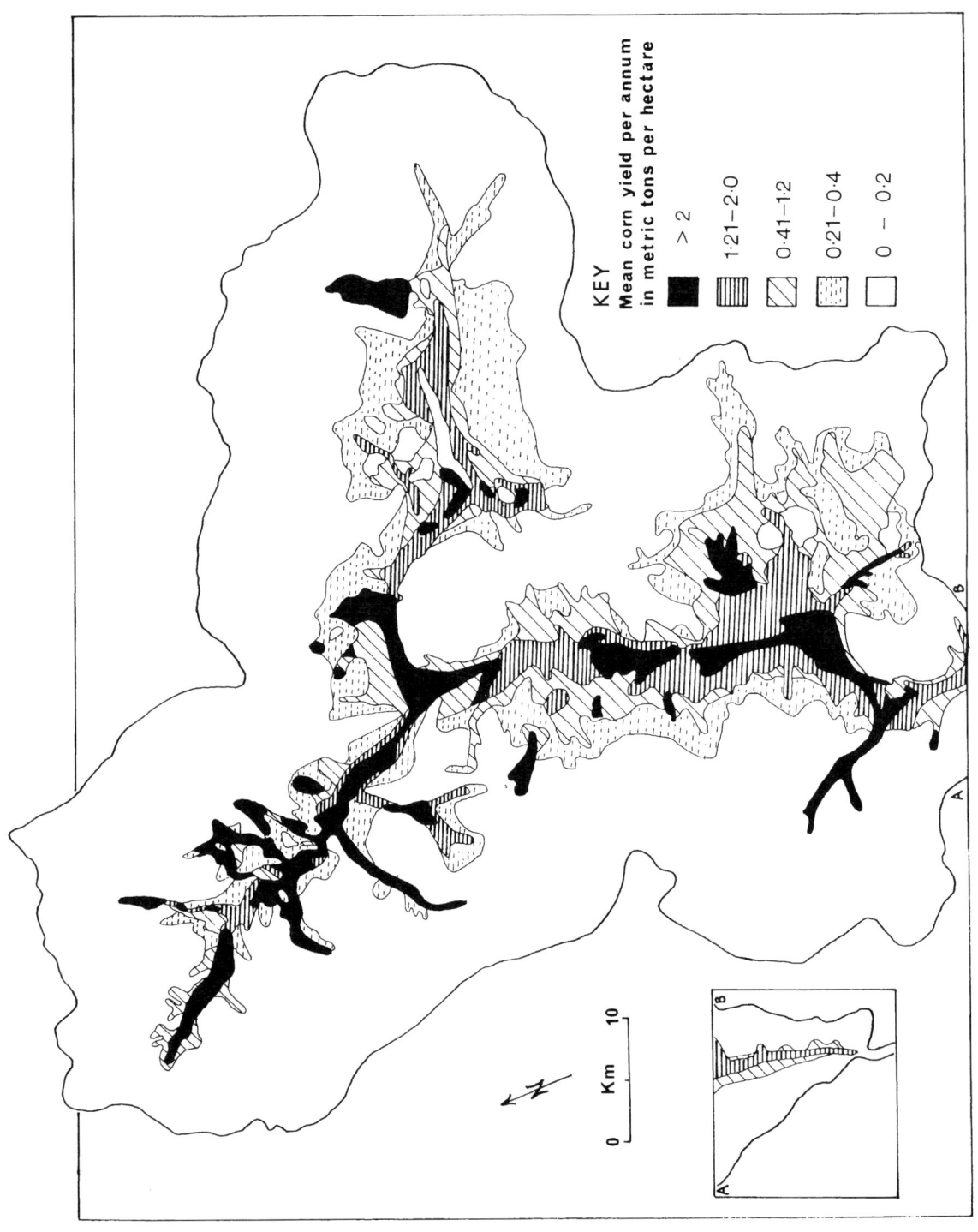

Fig. 25. Distribution of present mean corn yield per hectare for the Valley of Oaxaca.

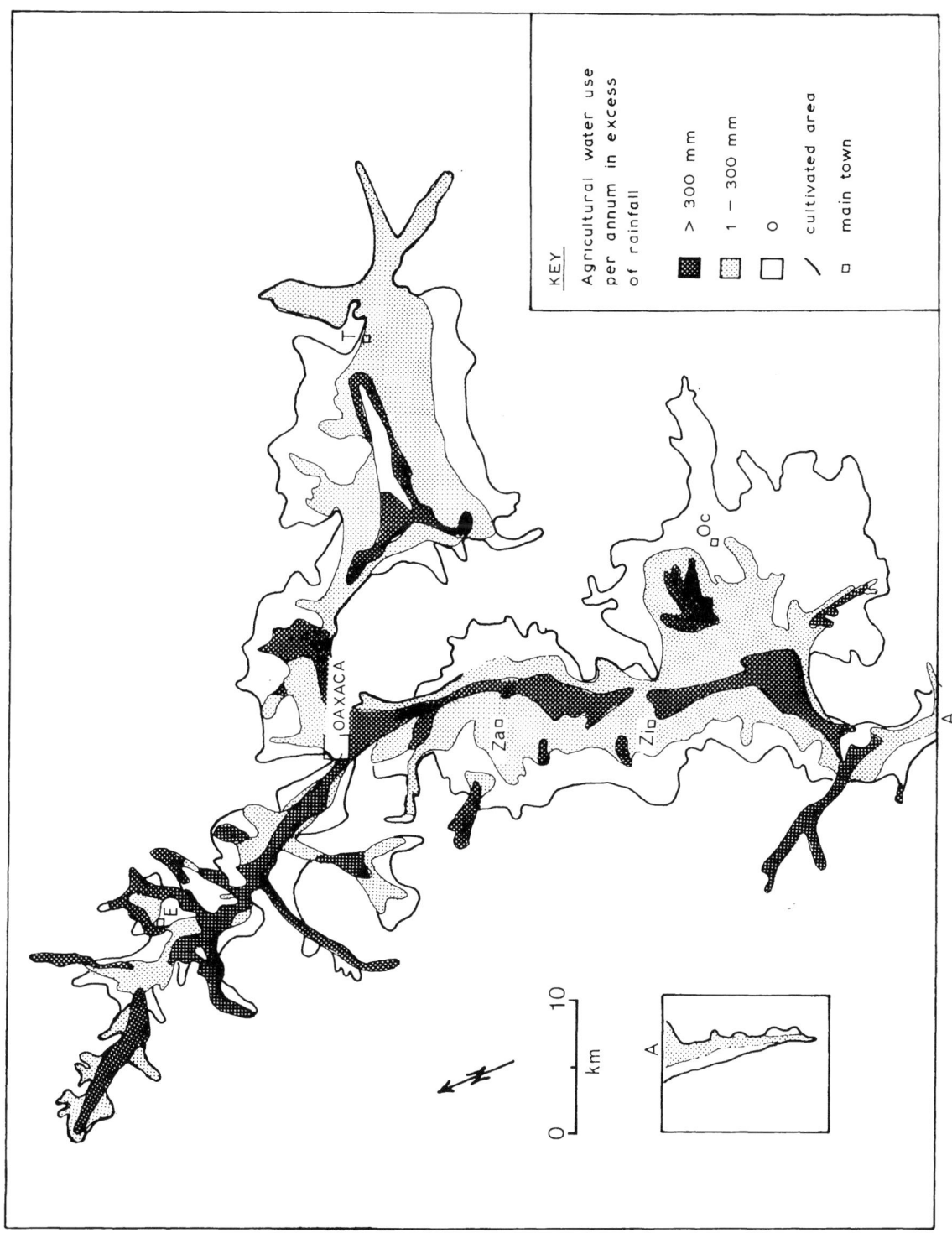

Fig. 26. Distribution of agricultural water consumption in excess of rainfall for the Valley of Oaxaca.

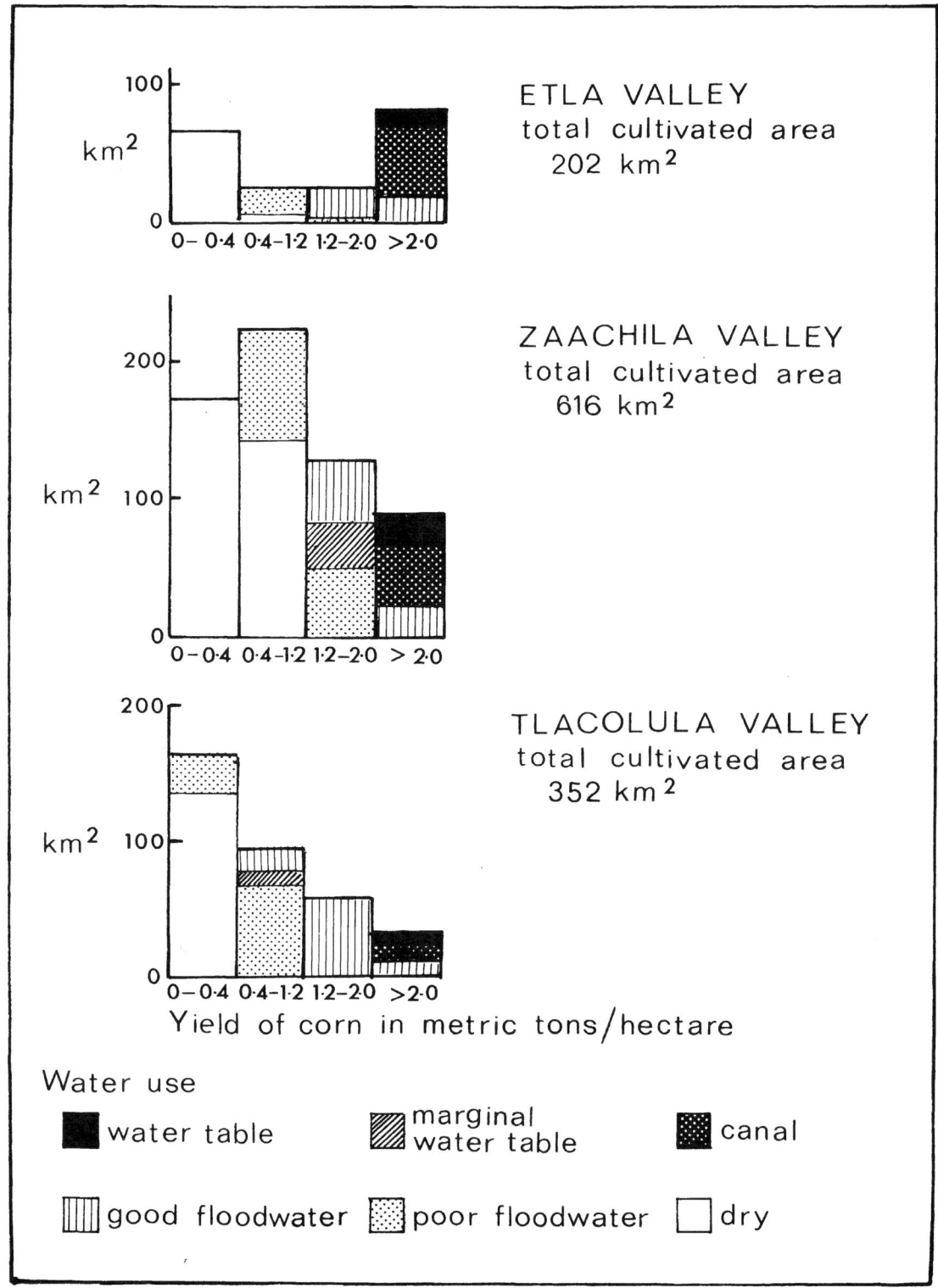

Fig. 27. Area of each arm of the Valley giving different mean corn yields per hectare.

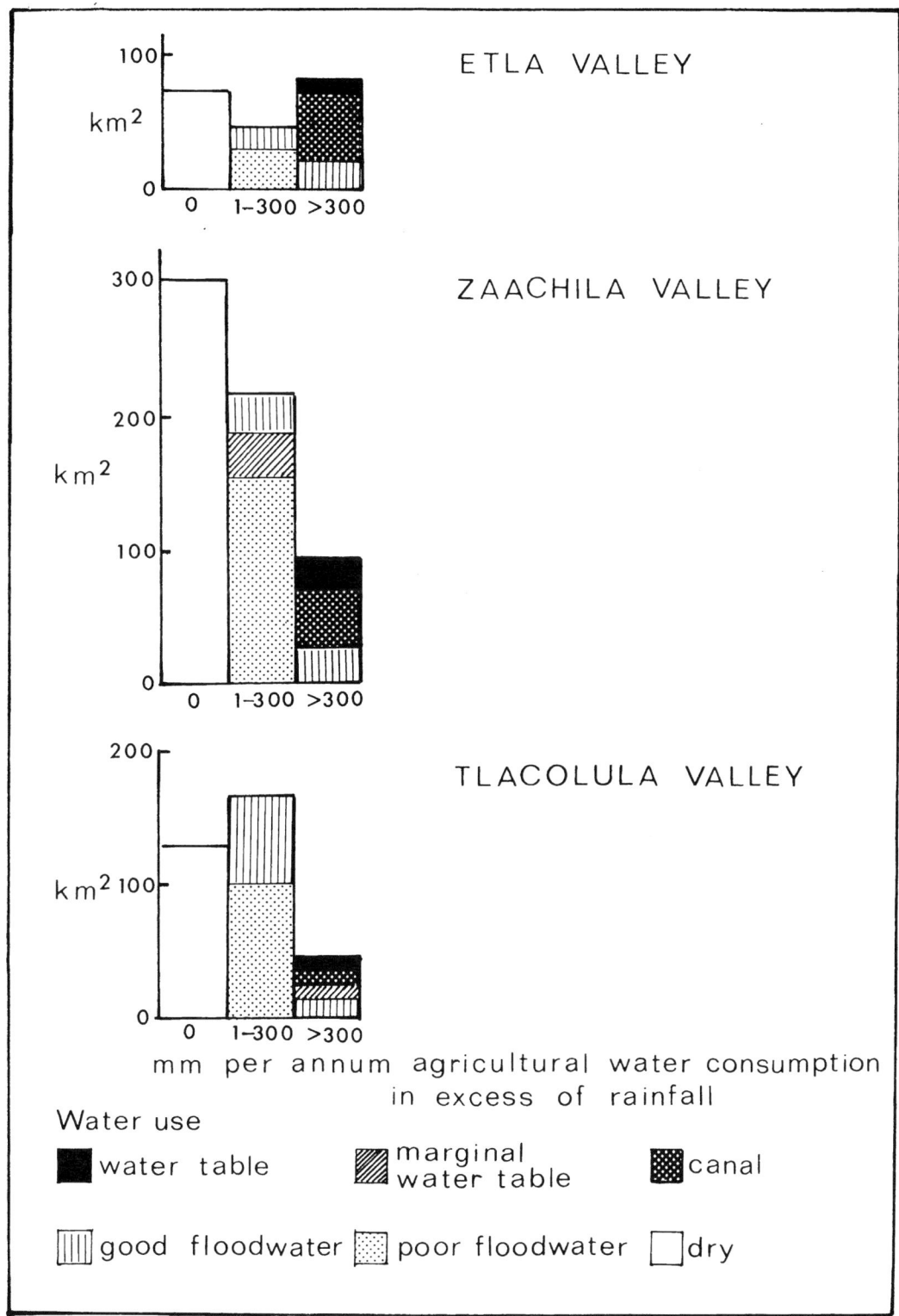

Fig. 28. Area of each arm of the Valley on which different amounts of agricultural water in excess of rainfall are applied.

The proportion of land in this valley producing 0.41 to 1.2 metric tons per hectare (224 square kilometers) is higher than the figure for the 0 to 0.4 category because the mean rainfall is higher here and dry farming produces higher yields in the Zaachila arm than anywhere else in the Valley. The effect of rainfall differences on local mean corn yields is well illustrated by comparing the yields produced under dry-farming and floodwater-farming methods in the Tlacolula and Zaachila Valleys. In the Tlacolula area, rainfall is so low that even some floodwater-farmed land can produce only 0.21 to 0.4 metric tons per hectare, whereas in the southern arm 140 square kilometers receive sufficient rainfall to produce yields of up to 1.2 metric tons per hectare by dry farming alone.

The Etla Valley stands out as the most productive agriculturally because, although it has the smallest amount of total cultivated area (202 square kilometers), a proportion (82 square kilometers) of that area falls into the highest yield category (more than 1 metric ton per hectare) than into any other (Fig. 27). The distribution is bimodal with little land in the two intermediate yield categories and a large proportion (68 square kilometers) still in the lowest yield group. This distribution reflects a combination of the high water resources, which enable even piedmont fields to receive canal irrigation, and the relatively low rainfall which dictates that, beyond the limits of irrigation schemes, dry-farming yields are low.

In all three arms of the Valley, the ranking of water-use methods with regard to mean corn yields is similar and is what would be expected: that is, in order of increasing yield, dry farming, floodwater farming, marginal water-table farming, canal irrigation, and water-table farming. A similar ranking of water-use methods is seen in Figure 28, which is derived from Figure 26 and gives, for each valley, histograms of millimeters of water in excess of rainfall against area (in square kilometers). The same contrast in agricultural productivity between the Tlacolula and Zaachila Valleys is seen in the effect of natural rainfall. In Zaachila, the largest proportion of land receives no additional water, whereas in the Tlacolula arm the largest area of land necessarily receives 0 to 300 mm additional water per year in order to make corn production a feasible proposition at all. The Etla Valley again stands out by having the highest proportion of land falling into the highest category of additional agricultural water (more than 300 mm per annum).

These figures serve to reemphasize the important regional differences within the Valley of Oaxaca:

1) the relatively low rainfall and small area but high water resources of the Etla Valley, resulting in high agricultural productivity and intense water use;
2) the even lower rainfall but larger area combined with minimal water resources in the Tlacolula Valley resulting in low agricultural productivity and least intensive water use (the marginality of dry farming in this area produces a tendency to spread available water resources even more thinly than elsewhere);
3) the intermediate conditions in the Zaachila Valley—since its water resources and area are greater than the Tlacolula Valley and rainfall is sufficiently high in its southern part to make dry farming fairly reliable, there is less tendency to spread available water thinly over large areas. The pattern is more one of high water use and high corn yield in selected areas in contrast to much larger zones of dry farming and medium corn yields.

# VI

# SUBSISTENCE FARMING ON UNIRRIGATED LAND

## INTRODUCTION

In the previous chapter, corn production was viewed in terms of its efficiency and value per unit area of land. This was seen to be related to the distribution of resources in the physical environment, particularly the distribution and use of water. But this is necessarily only half the story. Although physical resources may determine the average productivity per hectare around the Valley, the organisation of human resources affects the year-to-year productivity per man or per landholding unit. It is this aspect of corn production that will be considered here.

The data are drawn mainly from the sample areas in which land use was studied in detail, because for these areas annual changes in actual corn area planted can be related to different rainfall conditions. One sample area, that near Mitla (a detailed ethnographic study of Mitla is provided by Parsons, 1936), was selected because it is located in one of the most marginal agricultural regions and includes three physiographic zones with very different moisture characteristics. It is used as a case study to examine the effect of local variation in physical resources on the overall trend of agricultural aims and strategies found throughout the Valley. The choice of environmental settings found in Mitla are treated as a simple game situation to see if peasant agriculturalists follow maximising or minimaxing strategies in deciding which fields to plant in one of the few areas of the Valley where they have a choice within their own landholdings of putting, or not putting, all their eggs in one basket. One aspect of the exercise in game theory is to show the low degree of correspondence between the theoretical (game theory) range of possible strategies and the actual freedom of choice as it exists in Mitla.

The majority of the data used here are derived from interviews with cultivators in their fields, and these again were concentrated in the sample land use areas. The tables of production costs and profits are not based on single interviews but give the best average figures the author feels are valid for the Valley since individual figures vary considerably from village to village and from year to year, as will be apparent in the text.

In this chapter and the next, the terms "satisfaction" and "satisfaction level" are used. These do not indicate that a cultivator has satisfied all his subsistence or other needs; nor should they be confused with Simon's concept of "satisficing" (1957:200-05), in which a goal of economic maximising is replaced by one which is "good enough" because the ability of men to remember and compute is limited. A satisfaction level in corn, as used here, is simply an amount grown by a cultivator which is defined not by the limits of his landholding or his labour, or even of his family's needs, but is a response to the amount he *wants* to grow and the time he wishes to expend in relation to his other work and leisure activities. In some cases, as will be shown, this satisfaction level fulfills a psychological as much as an economic need, and peasants will grow a ton of corn a year principally to fulfill their desired role as a literal breadwinner and to use their land rather than let it lay idle.

# EVIDENCE OF FIXED GOALS IN CORN PRODUCTION

## Comparisons of Production Using Different Tillage Techniques

Although almost all corn grown in the Valley is produced by means of the ox-plough introduced at the Spanish Conquest, there are today two alternative methods; one is using the pre-Conquest traditional digging stick, the *coa,* and the other is by means of the newly introduced tractor and mechanical plough, which are gradually becoming available to peasant agriculturalists in the Valley. It will be useful to compare the traditional and tractor methods, since the comparison will show why it is advantageous for large landowners with sufficient capital to invest in mechanisation even when agricultural wage levels are low. The comparison will also serve to illustrate some of the prevailing attitudes toward and difficulties of organising farming as opposed to other forms of cooperatives among the peasants.

A first analysis considers the comparative costs of working one hectare of land by each method of tillage. The second examines the cost and profit per man's labour, assuming the hypothetical situation of unlimited land. The third analysis looks at the costs and profits for the present real situation of limited landholdings and assumes a median holding of 2.5 hectares of good land, giving an average corn yield of 1.5 metric tons per annum; this is considered a reasonable typical figure for the Valley today.

First let us consider the costs of corn production per hectare using an ox-plough. These costs are set out in Table 8 and are given as average amounts for the Valley today since in individual cases the costs vary considerably. The cost of seed corn varies from 1.50 to 1.80 pesos per kilo, but the greatest source of variability as well as the greatest cost is in the price of ox-teams per hectare. Lewis found only 57 percent of land-owning households in Azteca also owned oxen (1964:540), and in Oaxaca the figure is probably considerably lower. Prices of ox-teams or *yuntas* for one day's work (six hours) vary from village to village, depending mainly on their comparative scarcity in relation to demand. This, in turn, is partly dependent on the amount of fodder, especially alfalfa and corn, which can be raised locally to feed them. Highest prices quoted are for Mitla (80 pesos per day) where alfalfa is very scarce, and lowest (20 pesos) from San Sebastián Abasolo and Díaz Ordaz where alfalfa and (in the case of Díaz Ordaz) corn are relatively plentiful. In villages without irrigated land (e.g., San Sebastián, Ocotlán and Santiago Matatlán), 50 pesos is a common daily charge.

In addition to this spatial variability, prices also rise from March (low season rates) to July and August (high season rates); for the purposes of calculation in Table 8, the low season rate is given as 30 pesos per yunta-day (price includes the ox-team and ploughman), and the high season rate

TABLE 8

COSTS OF CORN PRODUCTION PER HECTARE USING AN OX-PLOUGH
(in pesos)

|  | Yunta | | Mozos | | |
| --- | --- | --- | --- | --- | --- |
|  | Days | Cost/Day | Days | Cost/Day | Total |
| Seed (at 1.50 pesos/kilo) | ... | | ... | | 20 |
| First Ploughing | 4 | 30 | ... | | 120 |
| Second Ploughing | 4 | 30 | ... | | 120 |
| Third Ploughing/Sowing | 4 | 40 | 4 | 10 | 200 |
| Fourth and Fifth Ploughings (to hill-up and weed) | 10 | 40 | 6 | 10 | 460 |
| Harvesting | ... | | 10 | 10 | 100 |
| Carting (2 ox-cart trips) | ... | | ... | | 40 |
| Total | | | | | 1060 |

as 40 pesos per day. The amount of land an ox-team can work in one day also varies, depending on the quality of the animals, the terrain and soil conditions and the stage of cultivation. The first ploughing takes the longest time, especially if the field has been long-fallowed, and the fourth ploughing takes the shortest because on one of the stages of hilling up only every second furrow is ploughed and the work proceeds twice as quickly. The time required to plough one hectare of land, therefore, can vary from two days to ten days with four days, or one quarter of a hectare per day, an average figure. The cost of a mozo or agricultural labourer also varies a little but is generally about 10 pesos a day with food.

If the relative costs of corn production per hectare using coa, ox-team and tractor cultivation are compared (Table 9), the cost for coa is only 160 pesos (this being mainly the cost of labour for harvesting). On the other hand, costs for ox-plough and tractor cultivation are very much higher and fall much closer together (1060 and 820 pesos respectively). The calculations made in Table 9 assume that the peasant landholder gives his labour free. In Table 10, the analysis is taken one step farther and shows the cash cost and profit per peasant agriculturalist, assuming that his landholding allowed him to farm as much area as he could, given the limitations of the method he used.

The first difference among the three methods

TABLE 9

COSTS OF CORN PRODUCTION PER HECTARE USING COA, OX-TEAM AND TRACTOR CULTIVATION*
(in pesos)

|  | Cost | | |
|---|---|---|---|
|  | Coa | Ox-Team | Tractor |
| Seed | 20 | 20 | 20 |
| 2 Ploughings to Prepare Land | ... | 240 | 200 |
| Ploughing and Sowing | ... | 200 | 200 (yunta) |
| Hilling-up and Weeding | ... | 460 | 260 |
| Harvesting | 100 | 100 | 100 |
| Carting (2 trips) | 40 | 40 | 40 |
| Total | 160 | 1060 | 820 |

*Excludes cost of owner's labour.

TABLE 10

COSTS AND CASH PROFIT PER PEASANT AGRICULTURALIST FOR CORN PRODUCTION USING COA, OX-PLOUGH AND TRACTOR CULTIVATION
(in pesos)

|  | Coa | Ox-Team | Tractor |
|---|---|---|---|
| Number of Hectares One Man Can Cultivate | 2 | 8 | 50 |
| Cost/Hectare | 160 | 1060 | 820 |
| Cash Yield/Hectare | 2900 | 2900 | 2900 |
| Cash Profit/Hectare | 2740 | 1840 | 2080 |
| Total Cost per Man's Labour | 320 | 8480 | 41000 |
| Total Cash Profit per Man's Labour | 5480 | 14720 | 104000 |

of tillage is in the number of hectares one man could farm at any one time, increasing from 2 with a coa to 8 with an ox-plough and 50 with a tractor. In Table 9, the costs of production per hectare are given and by multiplying these figures by the number of hectares one man can work, the total cost for each maximum work unit can be obtained; that is, 320 pesos for coa cultivation, 8,480 for ox-plough tillage, and 41,000 for tractor tillage (Table 10). Table 11 gives the cash yield of one hectare of good land producing 1.5 metric tons of corn. Assuming a constant corn yield of 1.5 metric tons gives a cash yield of 2900 pesos, the total cash profit per one man's labour can be calculated using coa (5,480 pesos), ox-plough (14,720 pesos) and tractor (104,000 pesos). Thus, although the net profit per hectare is highest for coa cultivation, because of the much larger amounts of land one man can work with the other

TABLE 11

CASH YIELD FROM ONE HECTARE OF LAND*
(in pesos)

| Product | Yield |
|---|---|
| 1.5 Metric Tons of Cobs (1.00 peso/kilo) | 1500 |
| Stalks and Leaves (zacate) | 1200 |
| Flowers (espigas) | 200 |
| Total | 2900 |

*Assuming 1.5 metric tons of corn.

forms of tillage, the total profit from one man's labour would be highest for tractor cultivation.

In a situation of unlimited land and sufficient capital, the least labour-intensive method, that of tractor cultivation, would give the highest net return. Within each community there is a sliding scale of increasing capital input and size of landholding, leading to increased mechanisation and increased net return, and the position of each household along this scale is primarily dependent on the capital it can raise. It is not difficult to see why the largest landowners with holdings of an economic size and sufficiently consolidated for tractor cultivation are beginning to buy tractors as soon as they can raise the necessary capital.

What is more relevant to peasant agriculture is why there is not a similar spread of households in each community at the other end of the scale; that is, why more peasants in the Valley today do not use the coa when the amount of capital available to them would indicate that this method of tillage is the most "economic" solution in the Western sense. The average Oaxacan peasant is not labour-limited but land-limited; median landholdings in many communities are about 2-3 hectares. Although the maximum allocation of land per individual in an ejido is 10 hectares of irrigated or tierra de humedad and 20 hectares of temporal land (Editorial Porrua, *Código Agrario*, 1969:Art. 76), either through inadequate area expropriated when the ejidos were originally formed or through subdivision through inheritance since, most ejidal holdings are also small (less than 5 hectares).

Table 12 gives the cash cost and profit not per man but per landholding, which for the purposes of analysis is assumed to be 2.5 hectares of good land, giving an average corn yield of 1.5 metric tons per hectare. For a landholding of this size, one man (with help at harvest) could work it by himself with either an ox-plough or a tractor but would require help with one half of a hectare if he used only a coa. It is likely that this help could be obtained from within his household and so would not involve capital outlay on wages. But even if this were set as a labour cost against his profit, the small landowner who farms with a coa secures a larger cash profit at the end of the year than would his neighbours who used either ox-teams or tractors (6640 pesos as against 4600 pesos and 5200 pesos respectively, see Table 12). This difference of 2040 pesos between coa and ox-plough cultivation profits is a significant amount; it covers the minimum living expenses for a family of four for a year and is equivalent to the wages of about 200 days manual labour.

Although tractors cost a little less than ox-ploughs per hectare if the land is in large enough units, they are not a feasible alternative for most peasants for several reasons.

1) Many landholdings are in parcels which are widely separated, and each parcel is too small to be practical to plough with a tractor.
2) A tractor is commonly hired by the day and can plough about 3.5 hectares so that the landholding must be at least this size to be worth the cost of a day's hire charge.
3) The cost of buying a tractor is prohibitive for small peasant landowners so they must hire one by the day, and tractors available for hire are scarce.

The formation of cooperatives of small landowners might help to combat several of these difficulties by buying communal tractors and agreeing to plough several adjacent parcels of land as one tractor unit. But this type of cooperation is almost impossible to achieve at present even when a communal tractor or cooperative organisation already exists. A cooperatively owned tractor stands unused in one village because no organisational structure has been formed to apportion its use or exact levies for its maintenance (Lees, personal communication), and this in a community where

TABLE 12

CASH COST AND PROFIT PER PEASANT LANDHOLDING FOR CORN PRODUCTION USING COA, OX-PLOUGH AND TRACTOR CULTIVATION*
(in pesos)

|  | Coa | Ox-Team | Tractor |
|---|---|---|---|
| Total Cost | 460 | 2650 | 2050 |
| Cost of Excess Labour | 150 | . . . | . . . |
| Cash Yield | 7250 | 7250 | 7250 |
| Cash Profit | 6640 | 4600 | 5200 |

*Assuming 2.5 hectares of good land per holding.

land is lying fallow because ox-teams are not available to do the work. Likewise, peasants who own land within the same *tramo* (group of adjacent parcels of land which may receive collectively one unit of a community's irrigation supply) who already have the social organisation to divide water among their landholdings, are unable to cooperate to form a single working unit for the hire of a tractor—mainly because of disagreement about the best time to plant corn in relation to the rains.

For most peasant landowners, the alternative methods of production are therefore coa and ox-plough, and from Table 12 it can be seen that the average profits from a small coa-worked holding would be almost 30 percent greater than from one worked by ox-team. Despite this difference in profit, almost all peasant landowners choose the alternative of tillage by ox-plough. Although they are by circumstance land-limited, they also impose, by choice, a further limitation on themselves and their incomes, that of least-work. This preference for least-work as far as corn production is concerned is openly revealed in conversation and is also shown in the common choice of letting land lie fallow if they cannot afford the capital investment of 1060 pesos per hectare needed to work it with an ox-plough, rather than working it by coa themselves. In this way, Oaxacan peasant agriculturalists have fixed goals with regard to effort expended in corn production and are not maximising their gains even within the scope available to them. This is not to say that their attitude is an irrational one within the present structure of their society and economy—a point which will be discussed later.

## Annual Variations in Corn Area as a Function of Rainfall Expectation

Depending on the type of land and the size of the family, 2.5 to 5 hectares of corn are said to be necessary to support a family which has no source of income other than agriculture and the selling of animals on a small scale. Since one man can work up to 8 hectares with an ox-team, it might be expected that in landholdings comprising less than 5 hectares, the needs of the family would be met by planting as much land as possible under corn every year. However, even allowing for the land requirements of any cash crops grown and the need to fallow, most peasant landholdings do not show a maximum corn area each year. This can be seen in the transitional matrices for land use change given in Tables 14 (Mitla), 18 (San Gabriel Etla and Zaachila), and Table 24 in Appendix III (Lambityeco), which show that the area of corn in each sample area of physiographic unit varies more from year to year than the spatial requirements of cash crops or fallowing demand.

In the areas where cash crops are also grown, the annual variation in corn area is likely to be partly a function of market supply and demand for cash crops and the increasing commitment of peasant cultivators to cash-crop specialisation. However, over and above these economic trends, annual variation in corn area can be closely related to annual variation in rainfall. In Appendix I, the importance of rainfall in the month of June is shown for unirrigated agriculture, both from the point of view of its relative reliability (compared with other indicators) as a predictor of rainfall during the growing season, and its believed importance in the minds of Oaxacan peasant agriculturalists. When corn area is plotted for each land-use area against different proportions of the total rainfall for each year (Fig. 29), the best-fit relationship is with the rainfall for June rather than any other period. The lines in Figure 29 are for nine sample land units in which corn area is given as a ratio of corn area to corn plus fallow areas.

That corn area should be related to June rainfall is not in itself surprising (although a variable corn area is not a maximisation process), but the way in which it was found to be related was unexpected. When June rainfall is heaviest and the chances of a larger harvest are best, the area under corn is reduced rather than expanded. This inverse relationship holds for all unit areas sampled except the Mitla piedmont, which will be discussed later in this chapter. The relationship therefore holds for a wide variety of physical settings and water availabilities, ranging from marginal dry farming on the high alluvium east of Mitla to tierra de humedad in San Sebastián Abasolo and even canal-irrigated land in San Gabriel Etla. This wide

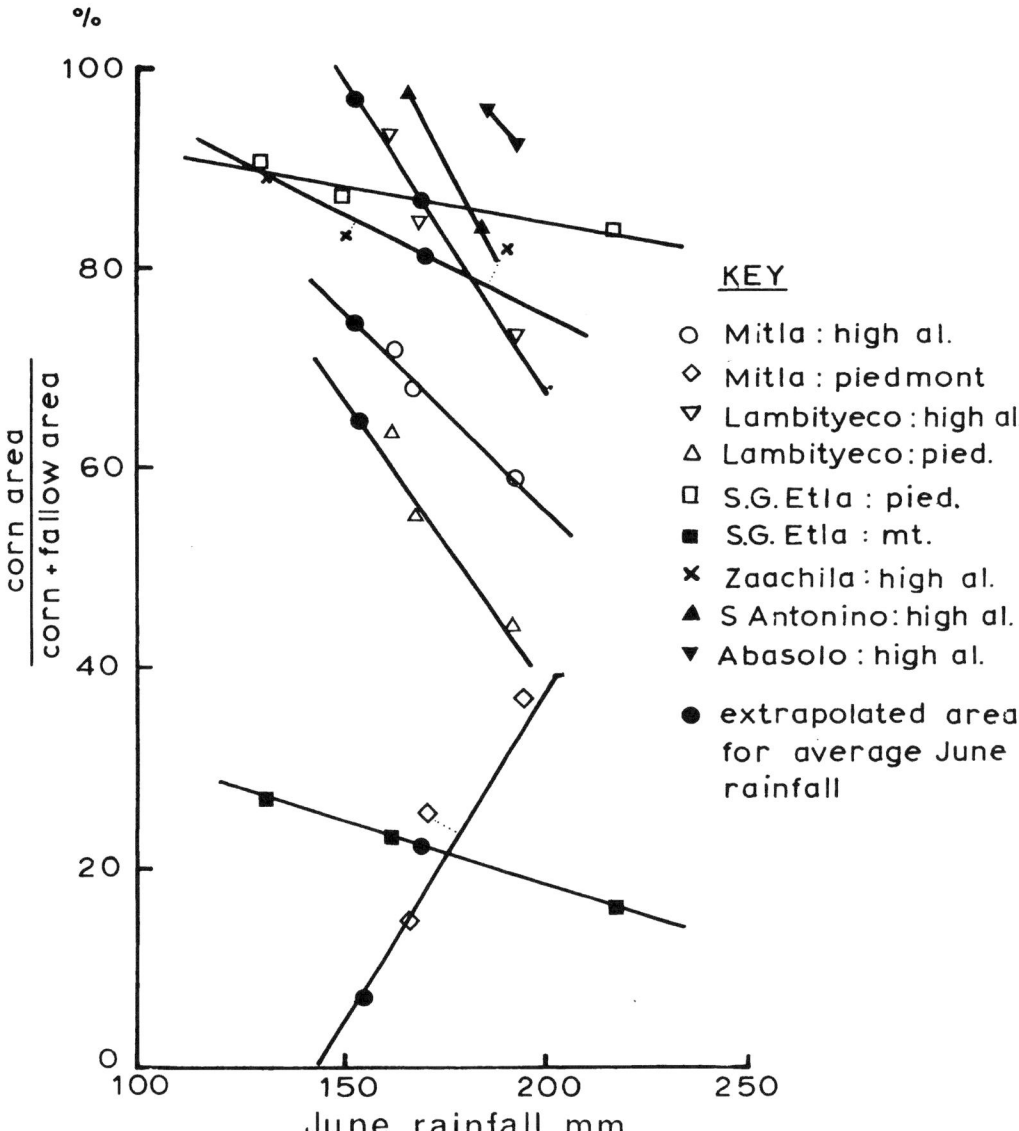

Fig. 29. Relationship between area under corn and June rainfall for nine sample areas, 1966 to 1968.

variety of physical settings negates one possible reason for this—that increased June rainfall produces sufficient waterlogging of fields to prevent planting. While this control could operate in parts of the valley, for example in the low-lying areas sampled near San Sebastián Abasolo and Lambityeco, it could not be equally true in the well-drained slopes of San Gabriel Etla or the drier areas of the Tlacolula Valley.

The evidence of areas planted in corn in several localities of the Valley, therefore, strongly leads to the conclusion that in corn production, as well as in method of tillage, some satisfaction process is taking place, and that the fixed-goal target is reached along the route of least work. Thus, if the rainfall in June (the main planting month) augurs good corn yields, fewer parcels of land are worked (and fewer parcels have capital invested) since the family can expect to get by with the produce of a smaller proportion of their total possible corn area.

# EFFECT OF LOCAL VARIABILITY ON THE ACHIEVEMENT OF FIXED GOALS: AN EXAMPLE FROM THE MARGINAL DRY FARMING AREA OF MITLA

## Introduction to the Mitla Sample Area

The Mitla sample area is located in the eastern end of the Tlacolula Valley where rainfall averages 550 mm per annum; it is one of the most marginal areas for dry farming to be found within the Valley of Oaxaca (Pl. 2). The particular area sampled is also unusual in that it cuts across three distinct physiographic zones. The valley is so narrow at this point that there exists a real choice for peasant agriculturalists in terms of which physiographic or ecological area they wish to farm each year. The marginality of the land for agriculture also means that a smaller proportion of it is in the hands of a few large landowners although even here much of the bottomland can be traced to a few families. However, if we wish to see how far and in what way corn production is varied among different physical environments, the Mitla land use area is the best unit for which data are available. Elsewhere in the Valley, the width of alluvium is commonly so great that the landholdings of one family do not necessarily encompass as great a range of physical environment and are certainly more difficult to sample.

Figure 30 shows the land use and physiographic zones of the Mitla area for 1968. The area studied includes the three important geologic and topographic units in the valley; the piedmont slope, the high alluvium, and present flood plain or low alluvium. Topographically, the piedmont grades into the high alluvium, but the break of slope between the two levels is sharp and consists of a 5 to 7 meter, near-vertical cliff. The piedmont is underlain by volcanic ignimbrite (Williams and Heizer, 1965), which generally lies within 20 cm of the surface and forms slopes of 3 to 20 degrees. Soils on the high alluvium are thicker, increasing from less than 1 meter near the boundary with the piedmont to more than 7 meters at the cliff formed with the low alluvium, and in the same direction mean gradient declines from 3 degrees to less than 1 degree. The gradient of the low alluvium is less than 1 degree, and soils are generally several meters thick.

Soils are everywhere derived from the ignimbrite bedrock and are therefore similar in all three physiographic zones, being generally neutral (pH 7), fairly stony (gravel = 5-10 percent) and sandy (sand = 50-85 percent of total after removal of gravel). All the soils (except for a few finer-grained patches along the outer margin of the flood plains) are free draining and offer dry environments for plants. Differences in moisture availability are therefore mainly a function of soil thickness (which is greatest on the high alluvium) and depth to water table. On the piedmont and high alluvium, depth to the water table is greater than 6 meters. Only on the low alluvium is water available to plants from the water table, which is sometimes within 1 or 2 meters of the surface during the summer. Floodwater is also most available to fields on the low alluvium. There is therefore a gradient of increasing water availability from the piedmont to the low alluvium which is not offset by any other factor in the physical environment. Although for the purposes of analysis this spatial variability is treated in terms of three distinct units, it is closer to a continuous gradient with the only discontinuity occurring at the break of slope between the high and low alluvium.

This gradient in water availability is reflected in the land use pattern, particularly in the proportion of land under fallow, which in 1966 varied from 67 percent in the piedmont to 20 percent in the high alluvium and only 7 percent on the low alluvium (Table 13). The crop pattern is a simple one of corn (with beans and squash) and *maguey azul* (the local Agave which is cultivated mainly for distilling *mezcal,* a drink similar to the better known *tequila*). Corn is the most important crop in all three zones and is grown in the maguey fields between the rows of maguey as well as in the milpas proper. Maguey is a long-term (7 to 10 years) crop which is planted in rows several meters apart to allow for later growth. In the early years, several rows of corn can be grown between the rows of maguey. Land use patterns for 1966-68 and 1970 are given as proportions of each physiographic zone in Table 13.

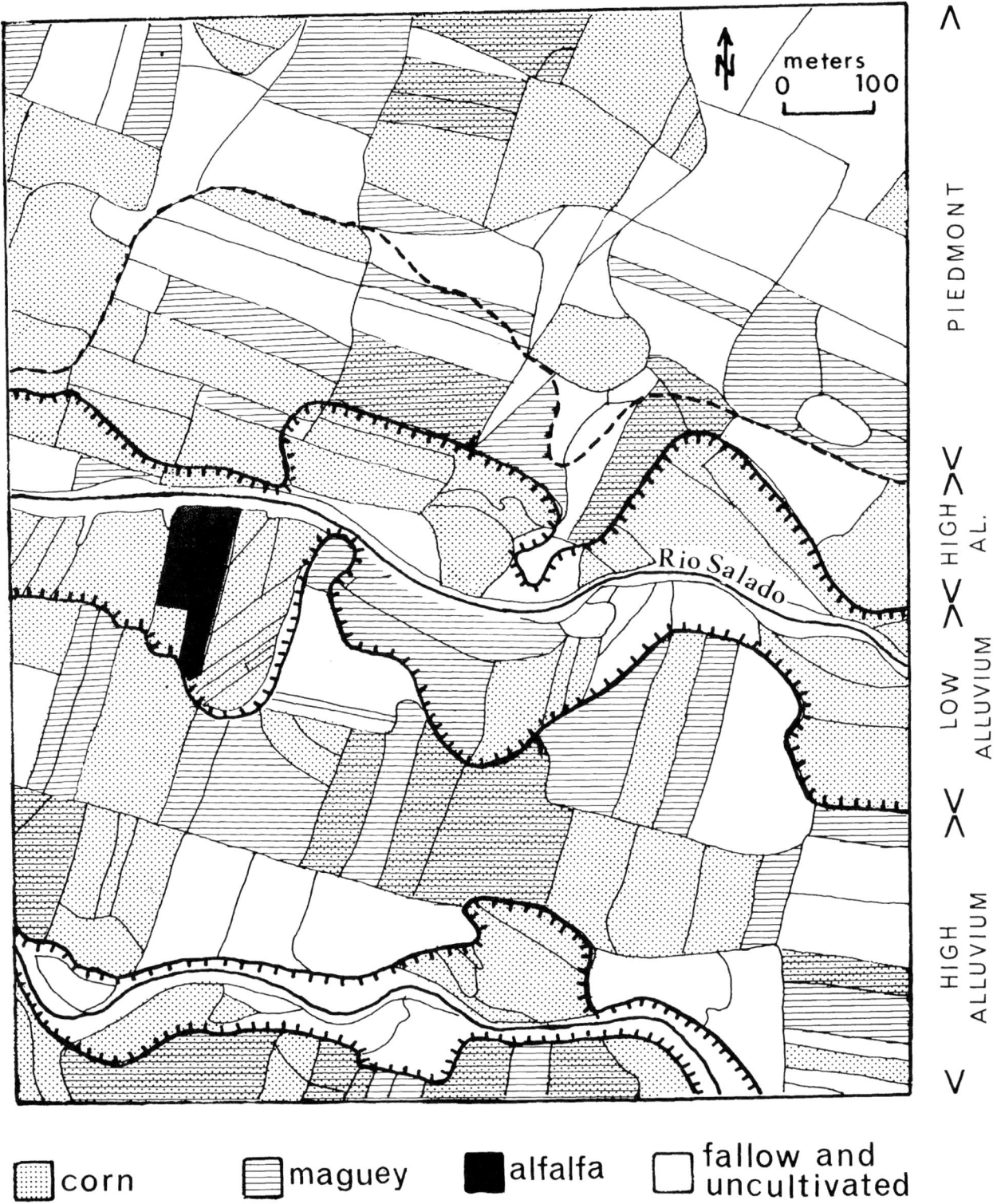

Fig. 30. Land use and physiographic zones of part of the Mitla sample area in 1968.

TABLE 13

LAND USE OF THE MITLA SAMPLE AREA, 1966-1968, 1970*

| Use | 1966 | | | 1967 | | | 1968 | | | 1970 | | |
|---|---|---|---|---|---|---|---|---|---|---|---|---|
| | P | HA | LA | P | HA | LA | P | HA | LA | P | HA | LA |
| Corn | 12 | 50 | 53 | 21 | 50 | 42 | 31 | 41 | 46 | 30 | 50 | 40 |
| Maguey | 12 | 18 | 3 | 10 | 15 | 3 | 8 | 18 | 3 | 7 | 14 | 5 |
| Alfalfa | 0 | 0 | 3 | 0 | 0 | 3 | 0 | 0 | 4 | 0 | 0 | 3 |
| Fallow | 67 | 20 | 7 | 60 | 23 | 18 | 52 | 29 | 13 | 54 | 24 | 18 |
| Uncultivated | 9 | 12 | 34 | 9 | 12 | 34 | 9 | 12 | 34 | 9 | 12 | 34 |

*Numbers given are percent of land under the given use for that area (P = piedmont, HA = high alluvium, LA = low alluvium) for that year.

Annual Land Use Changes

Land use in the Mitla area differs not only spatially between physiographic zones but also within the same physiographic zone from year to year. These annual land use changes are greater than are necessary to sustain fallowing and cash-crop rotations and lead to significant changes in the overall spatial pattern of land use between physiographic zones. However, the total amount of change effected by year to year variations in land use is still much less than the spatial variation from one part of the Valley to another. In other words, the principal variations to be found in the Valley are spatial, and what we are looking at here are no more than small deviations about this basic pattern. The importance of these annual changes, therefore, lies not in their intention to materially alter the distribution of corn production throughout the Valley but in what they can indicate about the cultivators' aims and decisions.

From the field mapping of land use in each of the four years 1966-68 and 1970, four annual maps were made from which the total area under each crop was measured for each of the three physiographic zones (Table 13). These proportions are given as the top three matrices for all physiographic zones in Table 14. In order to determine the amount and direction of land-use change, the area changing from one crop to another has been put in matrix form, and these data are given as the transitional matrices in the middle line of Table 14. These matrices show the *measured* amount of land-use change between the years 1966-67 and 1967-68, such that

$P_{ij}$ = p (changing from crop $i$ to crop $j$)

These transitional matrices for each physiographic zone land use were treated as first-order Markov chains, and the equilibrium distributions of crops were calculated for each of these chains; that is,

$$\underline{x}' \cdot P = \underline{x}'$$

where x is the equilibrium proportion of different crops after the same rotation is repeated indefinitely. Thus for each physiographic zone we can compare

1) actual land use patterns in each of the three years,
2) the amount and direction of land use change from year to year, and
3) the pattern that would result if the measured annual land use change were the same each year.

An examination of Tables 13 and 14, which show the differences in land use between physiographic zones and between years, raises several interesting points:

1. In the sample area as a whole, the amount of corn area planted each year remains almost constant. This fact distinguishes the Mitla sample area from all the others considered which show a decrease of corn area with increasing June rainfall (Fig. 29). We must therefore consider whether Mitla peasants differ from those in other parts of the Valley in that they do not have fixed goals in corn area planted, but are achieving satisfaction in some other way, or are following some other aim such as maximising returns.

## TABLE 14
### LAND USE CHANGE MATRICES FOR MITLA SAMPLE AREA, 1966 TO 1968

#### MITLA PIEDMONT ZONE

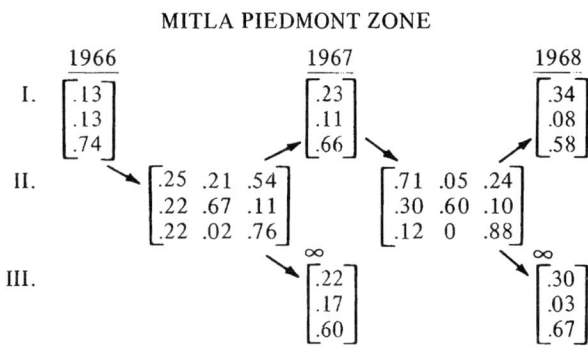

#### MITLA HIGH ALLUVIUM ZONE

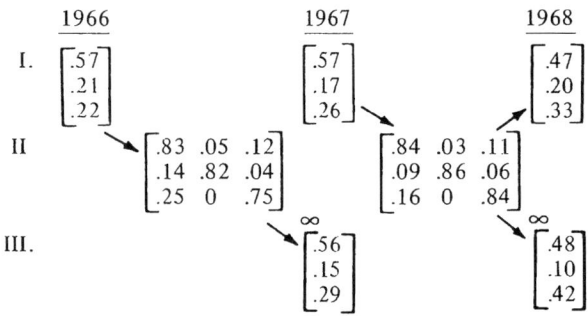

#### MITLA LOW ALLUVIUM ZONE

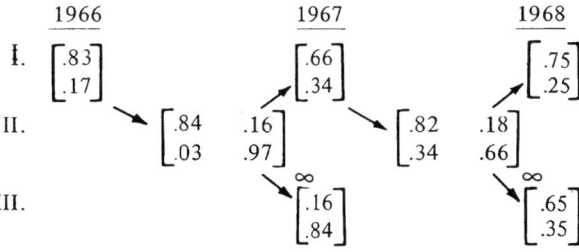

I. measured land use pattern for each year
II. transition matrices for land use change between years
III. equilibrium land use pattern resulting from similar changes repeated indefinitely

$P_{ij}$ = p(changing from crop i to crop j)

For piedmont and high alluvium:
    i,j = 1. corn
            2. maguey
            3. fallow

For low alluvium:
    i,j = 1. corn
            2. maguey, fallow and alfalfa

2. Variability in corn area occurs between physiographic zones such that corn area shifts from one zone to another in different years. Between 1966 and 1968 the area under corn in the piedmont increased from 13 to 34 percent while during the same three year period corn area on the high alluvium declined from 83 to 75 percent. As corn area increased in one area, a corresponding amount of fallow declined and vice versa. These shifts of corn area between physiographic zones can be followed in the top matrices in Table 14 and in Table 13. They imply that if satisfaction in corn area is being achieved, it is in a more complicated form than considered hitherto. One possibility is that the source of this complication is the presence of environmental choice.

3. The transition matrices are significantly different from each other. Since both transition matrices are based on independent field measurement rather than derived from each other, the difference between them shows that the land use change is not of the form of a first-order Markov chain, an assumption which might be made if only two years' records were available. Likewise, although without the data for 1969 it cannot be proved, the data from 1970 indicate that the land use change is not a second-order Markov chain either. Similar differences between transitional matrices for measured land use change can also be seen for other sample areas (see the Lambityeco area, Appendix III). Peasant subsistence agricultural rotation and change patterns are therefore based on a longer cycle than has been recorded here over five years, and were similar data available over time for other peasant communities, this might well be shown to be a general pattern.

4. The amount of change that occurs in any one year is generally large enough to alter significantly the land use pattern within a very few years. This is shown by the diagonal elements in the transitional matrices (Table 14) which are relatively small and are nearly always less than 0.9. In the first transitional matrix for the Mitla piedmont (1966-7), the first element is unusually low (.25) because in 1967 almost all the increase in corn area took place in newly cleared milpas.

Because the diagonal elements are small, the transitional matrices will rapidly approach the equilibrium patterns shown below them, within a few years of similar land use changes. This is also evident from the general similarities between the equilibrium matrices in Table 14 and the actual pattern for the second year of each pair of years considered. If the amount of change that occurs is indeed so great (involving 10 to 20 percent of the total area each year), why are these annual changes not altering the spatial pattern of land use around the Valley? This is because the annual changes of land use are not unidirectional; that is, corn area is not moving from one environmental zone to another but is fluctuating annually between zones. It is the process and implications of these fluctuations which will be considered in the next section.

## The Process of Substitution Among Environmental Zones

In this attempt to see what effect a choice of environmental zones has upon agricultural aims and strategies in the Mitla area, we shall first consider how close the shifting of corn area between zones comes to a maximising or minimaxing strategy in classic game theory terms, or if the constraints of the real decision situation in Mitla even allow purely game-theoretic choices to be made. Since land use changes are the direct result of annual planting decisions such as those discussed in Chapter V, it will be useful to an understanding of the aims of these changes to consider them in terms of two very simplified decision models—game theory and event matching. The situations described by such models are always gross oversimplifications, so that some of the discrepancies between the real world from which the data were obtained and the model world into which they are being fitted should be considered.

### Constraints on Decisions

The set of decisions being made each year in the Mitla area is that concerned with the redistribution of corn area, or planted milpas, among the three physiographic zones. This is already a simplification since it can be argued that each milpa represents a unique set of physical conditions and that therefore the range of choice is as large as the number of milpas available to the decision maker. However, for the purposes of analysis this range of choices can be grouped into the three physiographic zones: wetter low alluvium, medium high alluvium and drier piedmont. The choice can be illustrated in a triangular diagram with each vertex representing 100 percent concentration of corn area in one physiographic zone (Fig. 31). Assuming the initial constraint of constant area under corn, Figure 31 shows how far the actual choice situation in Mitla is restricted in comparison to the theoretical situation.

The theoretical (unconstrained) choice of corn distribution is represented by the total area of the triangle; the sets of lines show the effects of three constraints in the real situation:

1) limit of total land available in each zone, which is such that within the sample area only one pure strategy is possible—that of planting all corn on the high alluvium
2) the limit of land available in any year after taking into account the land under long-term cash crops (mainly maguey)
3) the limit of land available after fallow land has been accounted for. In general terms, the need to fallow land is greatest in the piedmont and least on the low alluvium, but in detail the positions of these constraint lines are variable since the amount of fallow land in any year is usually the result rather than the cause of planting decisions. The lines drawn in Figure 31 are the mean fallow areas for 1966 to 1968, but since these were expected to be greater-than-mean rainfall years, the amount of fallow on the low alluvium is probably greater than the average for that zone.

The combined effects of these constraints is to reduce the freedom of corn distribution among zones from the total triangle area to the unshaded area, and to dictate that only mixed strategies are available to cultivators since there is insufficient area within any one physiographic zone to grow all the corn they desire. In Figure 31 it can be seen that actual planting strategies in 1964, 1966 to 1968, and 1970 do conform to these conditions and all fall within the unshaded area. The additional data for 1964 were obtained from an air

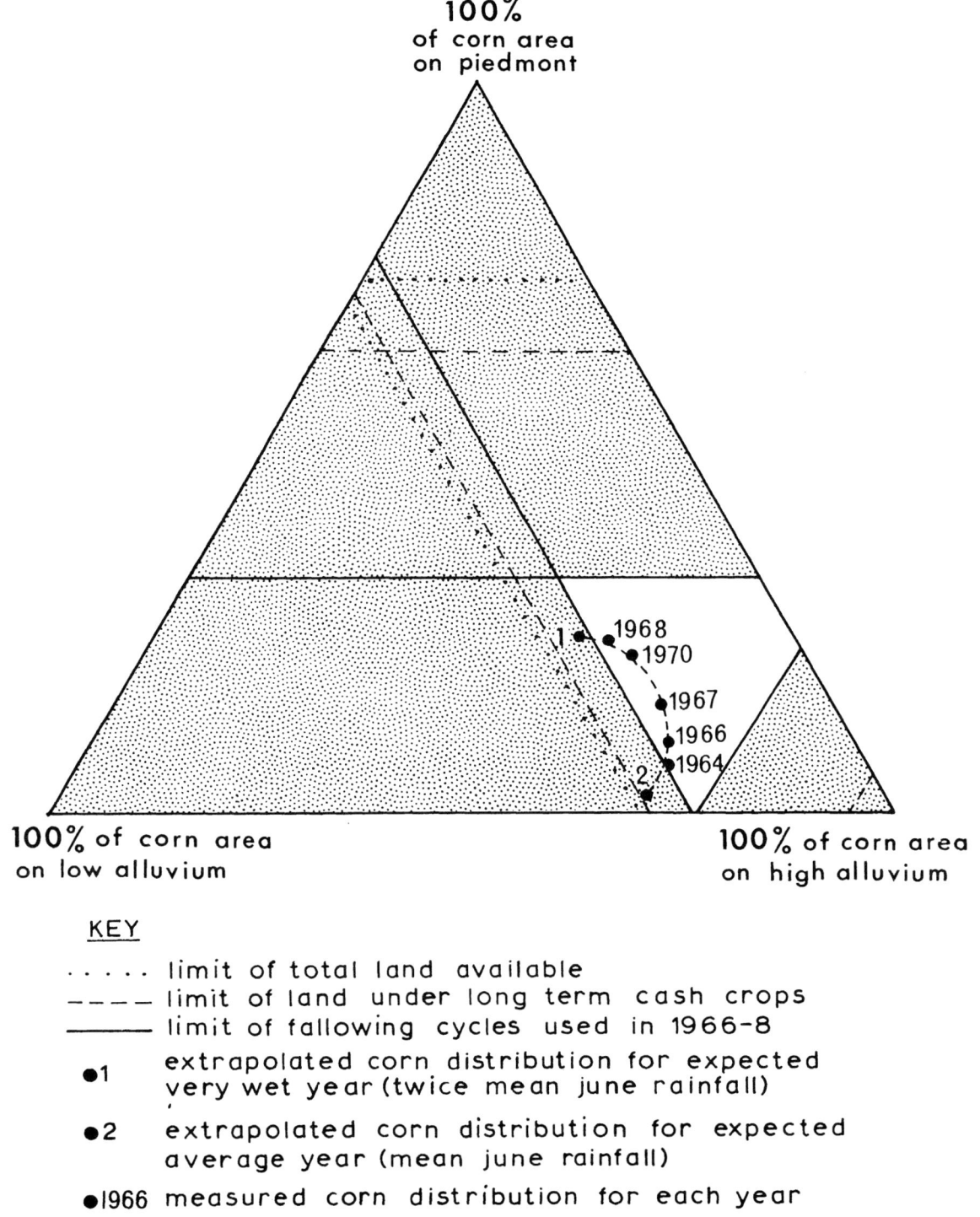

Fig. 31. Triangular diagram to show theoretical and actual (unshaded area) freedom of planting strategies in the Mitla sample area and measured and extrapolated corn distributions between physiographic zones.

photograph made in that year for archaeological purposes. On its scale of 1:7250, the land use was clear enough for interpretation.

### Game-Theory Model

Game-theory models are of particular interest because they are being increasingly used to describe decision-making in the face of uncertainty about the physical environment. In such situations they may provide a rationale for choices where the frequency distribution of a variable is known but not its next value (or strategy); for example, the distribution of annual rainfalls may be known but not the rainfall that will occur next year. If nothing is known or presumed about the rainfall of a particular year, game-theory describes two rational policies: a maximin and an optimising strategy.

The maximin or minimax is the most important solution of game-theory and is that strategy which maximises the payoff in the worst possible years; that is, guarantees a certain yield. This solution may therefore apply to the strategies of traditional near-subsistence agriculturalists whose resources are so limited that they cannot survive a year of crop failure; they accept lower returns on average if their risk of no-return is also lower. An optimising solution requires considerable resources to survive successive lean years in order to achieve higher gains in the long run. Assuming that the physical environment does not itself change during the period of time considered, both these solutions result in the best strategies being invariable since the maximin and optimum points are fixed.

From Figure 31 it can be seen that the planting patterns in the Mitla sample area are not fixed but lie along a curve within the area representing the peasants' real freedom of choice. On the same curve are plotted extrapolated planting distributions for years with twice the mean June rainfall (expected very wet years) and for years with mean June rainfall (expected average years). It is the

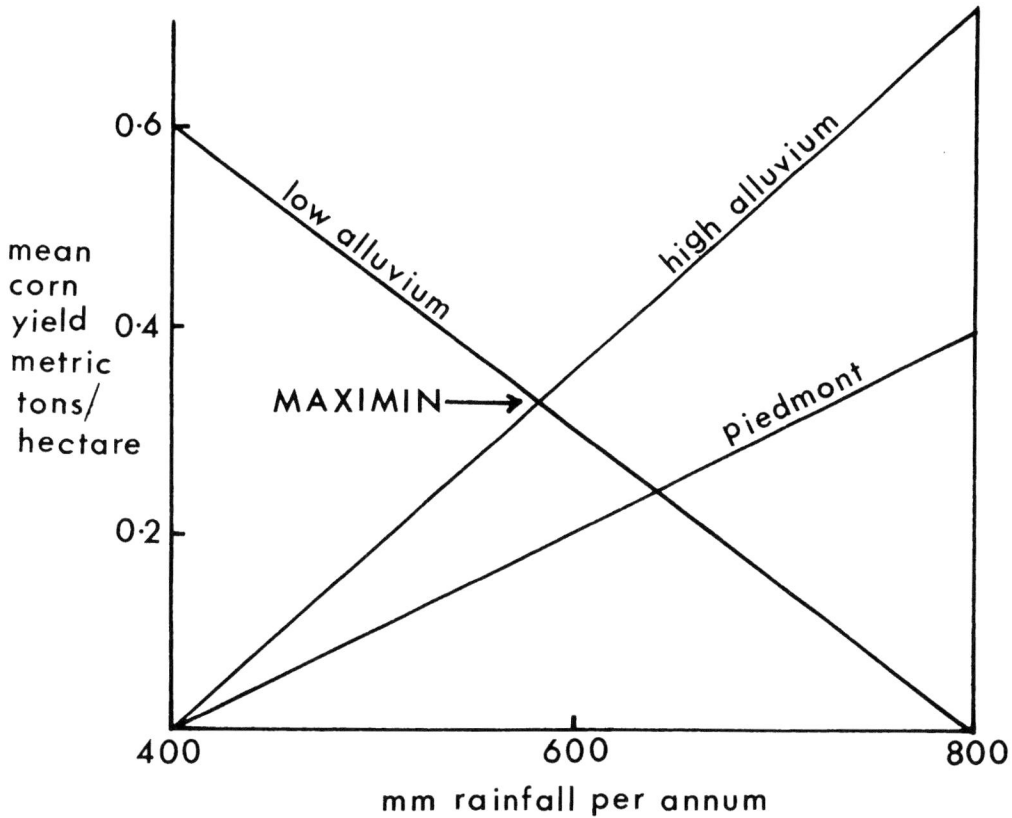

Fig. 32. Maximin solution for corn distribution among physiographic zones in the Mitla sample area.

restriction of real as opposed to theoretical choice that also limits the power of game theory to describe these choices. Figure 32 shows graphically the simplified maximin solution for corn distribution among the three physiographic zones of the Mitla area, based on measured corn-yield data used in the analyses of variance. Measured corn yields and informant data show that mean yield increases directly with rainfall in the piedmont and high alluvium and inversely in the low alluvium (although for the purposes of analysis this decline has been simplified from a curve to a straight line in Figure 32). Since high-alluvium mean yield is always greater than piedmont mean yield, the maximin solution is a combination of low and high alluvium zones only, in the proportions of 54 percent to 46 percent; the maximin yield is 0.32 metric tons per hectare.

If the information in Figure 32 is replotted on a triangular diagram similar to that in Figure 31, showing lines of worst-possible yields resulting from various proportions of corn in each physiographic zone, the maximin, or highest worst-possible yield distribution (point C) falls outside the range of choice open to Mitla peasants simply because there is not enough land available on the low alluvium (Fig. 33). The nearest corn distributions to the maximin that cultivators can plant are represented by the line A-B. A similar diagram can be constructed to show mean yields resulting from various combinations of corn area in the three zones. This is here simplified by ignoring the effect on yield of underfallowing, something that concentration in any one zone necessarily involves (Fig. 34).

Again, the unconstrained solution—this time the highest mean yield or optimum—falls outside the range of possible distributions since it requires all corn to be grown on the low alluvium (point F). The best optimum Mitla peasants can achieve is at point A which lies at one end of the constrained maximin line A-B. In this case, therefore, the effect of ability to sustain increased risk (by moving rational planting strategy from the maximin to the optimum through a series of satisfising solutions) becomes irrelevant because in the constrained game which corresponds to the real situation the maximin and optimum coincide.

From the corn distributions of the four years shown in Figure 31 it can be seen that the actual planting strategies lie almost along the constrained maximin line. This suggests a general tendency towards maximining, since the risk of total failure and the yields of a poor (very dry) year remain the same for all corn distributions along that line (A-B). On the other hand, *average* yields increase from B to A, that is, towards the optimum. In a good year yields do not remain constant for all distributions along the maximin line, but are higher and higher as the optimum is approached. This model shows therefore that in changing their planting patterns close to the maximin line, Mitla peasants are following an extremely safe strategy.

The model does not, however, explain why their strategy should be to move along this line in the first place, since the best policy is to adopt an invariable planting distribution corresponding to the optimum (point A). The implication is that either the Mitla peasants are irrationally trying to beat the odds or that they know, or believe they know, what their opponent's next move (that is, annual rainfall) will be. In neither case is a simple game-theory model, with its assumption of complete ignorance of the next event, adequate to completely explain the variable planting patterns observed.

Event-Matching or Gambling Models

Gambling models describe ways of trying to improve on the returns from the best fixed point, whatever criteria are used to define that point (optimum or minimax). They do not result in an invariable strategy because they are based on an assessment of recent experience in order to know or predict the value of the next event, and they assume a knowledge of the frequency distribution of a large population of events. Two factors suggest that a gambling model may be applicable to corn distributions in Mitla:

1) corn distributions do vary from year to year, and
2) farmers express belief in the regularity and predictability of annual rainfall (Appendix I).

The discussion of rainfall perception in Appendix I provides several rationales for planting

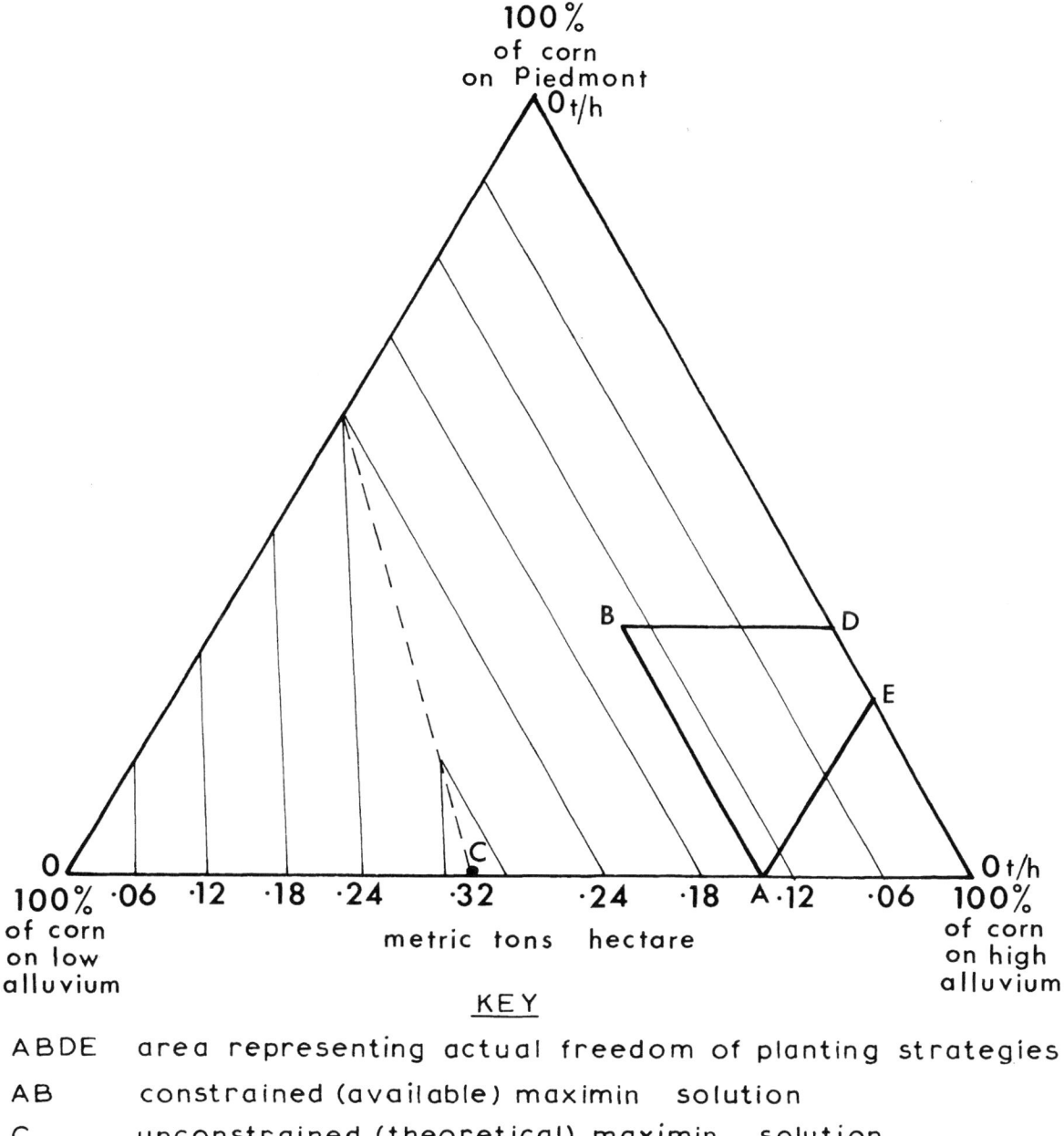

Fig. 33. Worst-possible corn yields for dry farming in the Mitla area for different proportions of corn in the piedmont and high and low alluvium zones.

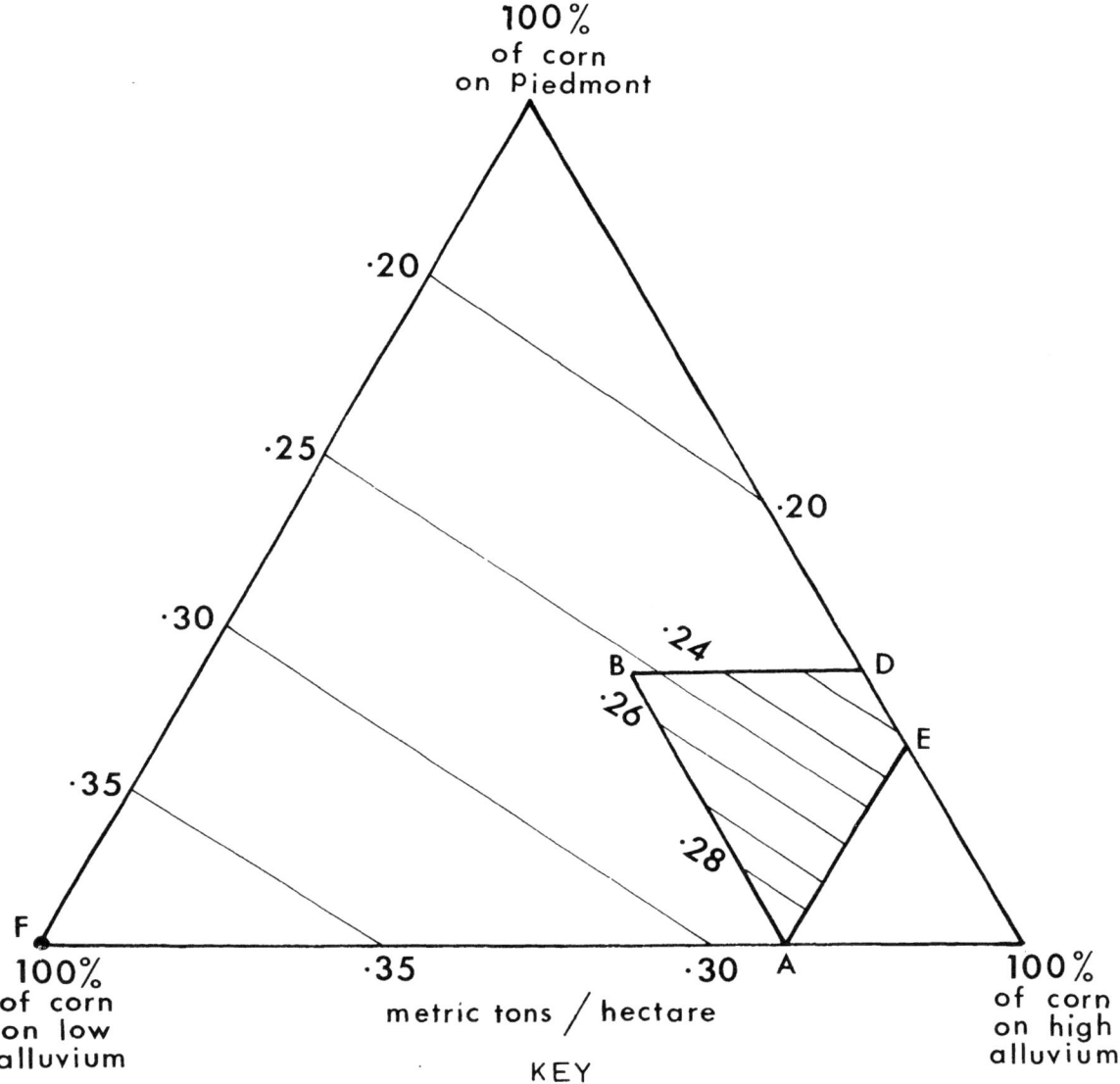

Fig. 34. Mean corn yield for dry farming in the Mitla area for different proportions of corn in the piedmont and high and low alluvium zones.

strategies. These are divided into two groups, those using a rainfall of a previous year as a predictor and those using part of the same year's rainfall. In Appendix I it is also shown that expressed beliefs in the first group are not supported by the evidence of meteorological records for the Valley and that, of the second group, June rainfall is found to be the most reliable (though not very) predictor of rainfall during the growing season. In the Mitla sample area, this comparison between the perceived and real environment can be carried one step further; it can test the relationship, if any, between *expressed* beliefs about rainfall and *measured* agricultural strategies intended to derive maximum benefit from rainfall variation. By such an analysis, the specific aspect of the environment will be defined to which the annual movement of corn area is a response, and to gain some insight into the more general problem of the ways and means of environmental perception.

Table 15 sets out the rainfall patterns that would have been predicted for the growing seasons in 1966 to 1968 by each of seven methods of prediction that are suggested by Oaxacan peasants (Appendix I). For example, if a peasant believed annual rainfall followed a three year cycle, and three years before 1966 (that is, 1963) was a wet year, he would expect 1966 also to be a wet year. This is shown in the table by a positive sign (greater than average rainfall expected). In the same table, the actual June to September rainfalls (shown as higher than, lower than, or close to average for forty years of records) for each of the three years are contrasted with the planting strategies (that is, patterns of corn distribution suitable for wet or dry years) that were actually followed. From Table 15 we can see that although some peasants express belief (at least to an inquisitive stranger) in rainfall cycles encompassing several years and in autocorrelation between years, there is no evidence in the Mitla area that a significant proportion of peasants are unwise enough to base their planting decisions on such beliefs.

While there is no statistical rationale on the basis of forty years of meteorological records for using one year's rainfall to predict another, there is some basis for making planting decisions in response to the pattern of early rainfall in the same year. Early rainfall serves two functions:

1) to help predict rainfall in the second half of the year, and
2) to provide definite information on soil moisture conditions throughout the first half of the year, up to the moment of planting.

On the basis of the Tlacolula rainfall records since 1926, early rainfall is seen to be a poor, rather than a reliable, predictor, especially for dry years (Appendix I). However, if April rainfall is more than 50 mm, the June to September rainfall has a 60 percent chance of being heavier than average (that is, greater than 400 mm). By June, reliability has increased so that if June rainfall is more than 150 mm then the June to September rainfall has an 85 percent chance of being above average. Since the reliability of early rainfall increases through time both as a predictor of later rainfall and in providing soil moisture data, the obvious planting strategy is to defer decisions as late as possible.

However, there are also factors operating in the opposite direction, tending towards an earlier planting date.

1) Field preparation takes time and labour, particularly when operations involve clearing scrub or forest vegetation from a long-fallowed field, so not all the milpas belonging to one family can be left until the last minute.
2) To obtain maximum infiltration and so build up an adequate store of soil moisture for early plant growth, the first ploughing should ideally anticipate the first main storms.
3) With the increased demand for ox-teams as the end of June approaches, the cost of hiring them rises steeply between April and June.

TABLE 15

COMPARISON OF RAINFALL-PREDICTING METHODS WITH ACTUAL RAINFALLS AND PLANTING STRATEGIES FOR MITLA SAMPLE AREA, 1966 TO 1968

| Prediction of June-September Rainfall* Based on Belief in: | 1966 | 1967 | 1968 |
|---|---|---|---|
| 3-Year Rainfall Cycle | + | − | − |
| 4-Year Rainfall Cycle | − | − | − |
| Autocorrelation with Previous Year | − | + | − |
| Jan-April Rainfall of Same Year | + | ++ | − − |
| Jan-May Rainfall of Same Year | ++ | = | = |
| Jan-June Rainfall of Same Year | ++ | = | + |
| June Rainfall of Same Year | + | + | ++ |
| Actual June-September Rainfall Recorded | + | − | − |
| Observed Corn Distribution Strategy | + | + | ++ |

*(+) = above average
(=) = average
(−) = below average

If rainfalls for progressively larger parts of the first half of the year are compared with total rainfall for the same year and with the planting strategies employed in Mitla (Table 15) we find that: (1) early rainfall is not related to total rainfall at any stage, and (2) early rainfall is related to planting strategy only for June rainfall, a relationship which has already been established for all the other land use areas. Since it is also known from field observation that most planting in the Mitla area takes place during June, it would appear that the constraints working against a late planting date are not effective on average. Evidence from the farmers themselves suggests that the constraints against June planting operate for most farmers on only a portion of their milpas where they are willing to take a bigger risk, and especially on those milpas in the piedmont, where constraints (1) and (2) apply most. The portion of milpas involved in the higher risk of early planting tends to be greater for poorer farmers since they tend to have a higher proportion of their land holding in the piedmont and mountains, and constraint (3) is most effective on them. Poorer farmers are therefore involved in greater risk and tend to remain poorer.

From the above discussion of environmental zone substitution, we can arrive at certain conclusions about agricultural strategies in Mitla and about the power of game-theory as an analytical tool when applied to such problems. Thus, the maximin solution of the simple game-theory model used here does describe the general pattern of corn distribution—observed distributions lie close to a line defined as a constrained minimax.

However, this study also shows that the power of game-theory as a model to describe agricultural strategies in real situations is limited because:

1) the degree of freedom in real choice situations can be so restricted that minimising and optimising solutions lie outside the realm of possibility;
2) with the addition of these restrictions, the constrained minimax and optimum solutions may be very close or coincide, so that neither strategy can be distinguished;
3) as shown by mapping of milpa distributions over several years, there were annual variations in planted corn area. These cannot be explained by simple game-theory because its solutions are fixed, but they can be explained by gambling or event matching on an annual basis.

As might be expected, therefore, the general pattern of land use in Mitla is aimed at minimising the worst possible outcome. But within that pattern, changes in corn distribution between zones in different years is an event-matching procedure which tries to match land use to growing-season rainfall on the basis of June rainfall. The data from Mitla can be fitted in the general concept of a satisfactory level of corn production per household that has been shown for other areas of the Valley (and which is certainly valid for Mitla in terms of satisfaction of ox-plough tillage over coa) using the argument that in having a constant input (planted corn area) rather than aiming for a constant output (corn harvest) Mitla peasants are aiming for satisfaction in terms of work rather than in quantity of corn desired. However, the important point about this overall constancy of corn area is that it is made up of *two* components:

1) the alluvial zones in which corn area *decreases* with increasing June rainfall in exactly the same way as that described for other sample areas around the Valley and illustrated in Figure 29 and
2) the piedmont zone in which corn area follows the opposite trend—it is *increased* in expected wetter years.

On the one hand, therefore, it seems as though Mitla peasants are aiming for a satisfactory corn production level in a way similar to those elsewhere in the Valley. On the other, it seems as if they are trying to maximise their gains by literally gambling on getting any returns from the piedmont. The effect of environmental choice on the overall pattern of satisfaction would appear to be the addition of a new category of land, one in which event matching with the aim to maximise takes the place of aiming for a fixed expected return. Unfortunately, no other area sampled is as poor agriculturally as the Mitla piedmont so there are no other land use change data for a comparable area. However, on the basis of general informant data from cultivators in all parts of the Valley, it does seem that the Mitla piedmont is not a unique area but represents a whole category of land which is so marginal for agriculture that corn cannot be grown there successfully in most years and not continuously year after year. It is an area of sporadic corn production both in time and space in which corn area increases in expected wet years.

There are at least two main reasons why Mitla peasants expand the corn area in the piedmont in expected wet years. For one, the Mitla area as a whole is so marginal for agriculture that there comes a time when, given adequate rainfall in both areas, yields on long-fallowed piedmont will be as great or greater in any one year than yields on underfallowed alluvium. A wet year (as predicted by a wet June) provides the only opportunity to take advantage of higher yields resulting from long fallowing on the piedmont and at the same time allows the alluvium to be fallowed, since in all other years the piedmont environment is too dry to give sufficient corn yield (greater than 250 kilos per hectare).

Another reason for expanded piedmont use is that much land in the low piedmont zone is privately owned. Despite its general marginality for agriculture, it constitutes "an extension of the peasant" in the same way that land elsewhere does (Chapter II), and owners feel they should cultivate it when they can. The local peasant view of land is epitomised by one Mitla man in the statement, "If a man owns a milpa he shouldn't let it stand idle all the time because it was not given to him for that purpose, but he should plant it when God gives him the rain."

In the Mitla area, expansion of corn planting on the piedmont in wet years fulfills a functional purpose in enabling fields elsewhere to be fallowed. This functional relationship between poorer and better land seems to be related to the marginality of the Mitla area as a whole. Elsewhere in the Valley a gambling attitude to marginal land was said not to be directly linked to a desire to fallow part of the better land. Sporadic corn planting in poor land, besides obtaining satisfaction for peasants in terms of being able to use all their land units, may also provide other psychological benefits in allowing them to try to beat the odds by following a safe gambling strategy rather than resigning themselves to always receiving the same low returns.

To summarise the role of environmental variability and choice in peasant agricultural strategies, we can conclude that the main effect demonstrated here is to provide another type of agricultural setting which is formed from areas which are so marginal for agriculture that they cannot be planted every year and so constitute areas of opportunism rather than satisfaction. If peasant agriculturalists have an effective range of environmental choice which covers both types of land, it seems likely that they will have two distinct aims and attitudes toward the two types of land. However, the desire not to do too much work or invest too much capital (satisfaction in terms of labour) will operate in defining the total amount of opportunism (expansion of corn area) that takes place. In the Mitla area, the constancy of overall corn area indicates that the desire not to increase the total amount of work expended even in wet years and the desire for the chance of higher returns, operate as effective mechanisms to dampen opportunism.

## SOCIOECONOMIC INFLUENCES ON LEVELS OF SATISFACTION IN CORN

The level of satisfaction, the amount of corn a peasant agriculturalist is aiming for, varies principally (1) between individuals, as their socioeconomic status and attitudes vary, (2) between communities with different social frameworks and different economic activities, and (3) within the same household or community through time.

An average family of five persons eats about one metric ton of corn a year at an absolute minimum. In addition, many other foods are needed, of which beans, chile and irrigated vegetables such as tomatoes, garlic and onions are important elements. In terms of monetary value, corn probably constitutes only some 50 percent of the family's total food needs. A typical size of peasant landholding in the Valley is 2.5 hectares. With a holding of this size, subsistence corn needs of a family could probably be secured except in bad years. However, money or goods to exchange for all other needs must come from some other source; the most common one is the sale of animals raised mainly by the women of the households.

Livestock rearing is practised by almost all peasant families on a small scale, and besides achieving a division of labour between men and women, it provides a necessary source of income. Thus animals kept around the *solar* such as chickens, turkeys and pigs, in addition to goats and sheep, which are pastured farther afield, are reared so that when money is required to buy food or other necessities, an animal of appropriate value can be sold. Likewise, when there is money to invest, a similar animal can be bought for rearing. This buying and selling of animals provides a form of investment and income which can be realised throughout the year. In addition, most households earn money by producing cash crops or by having a craft specialisation as well as tending animals and growing subsistence crops. From the scant evidence available, we might however, postulate a satisfaction level of about 2 to 3 metric tons of corn per household per annum for subsistence—the amount the family will actually consume plus enough for consumption at fiestas, for their animals, and to exchange for other foodstuffs. In addition, money for clothes, etc., would probably come from animal rearing and selling.

Although there are differences between individual families in the amounts of corn they are aiming to produce, it is perhaps more relevant to the present study to look at differences between villages or areas of the Valley in the hope that this will enable us to make some generalisations about the main controlling factors. Individual family levels of satisfaction in corn production are related to the amount of money that can be earned from other sources, including craft specialisation or cash-crop production. Peasant craft specialisation and (as far as the Valley is concerned) peasant cash-crop production tend to be a community rather than an individual household activity. Thus, in the same way that whole villages can be classified as pottery-making villages or weaving villages or even truck-farming villages, levels of satisfaction in corn production can be defined which are also characteristic of whole communities. As a general rule, as the proportion of income obtained from other sources increases, the level of satisfaction in corn decreases.

In pot-irrigating communities where each family tends to have one irrigated plot during the corn growing season and the truck-farming produce from this plot provides an average daily income of 15 pesos per household, the level of satisfaction in corn is about 2 metric tons per family (see Chapter VII for San Sebastián Abasolo, San Antonino Castillo Velásco and Zaachila land-use areas). In a palm-weaving village such as Zachio (located in the mountains between the Valley of Oaxaca and the neighbouring Valley of Nochixtlán) with an estimated daily income of 5 pesos per family from palm weaving alone (wheat and *alpiste* [canary seed] are also grown for cash), informants gave 3 tons of corn per annum as a desired goal.

What is particularly interesting from the point of view of peasant attitudes is that when we look at the other end of the scale, where households could completely support themselves by their cash-earning specialisations, the level of satisfaction in subsistence corn does not decline to zero but rests at a lower limit of about one metric ton per annum per family. Mitla is one example of such a community. Households receive a large proportion of their income from weaving, tourist trade, and mezcal distribution, but on the evidence of the sample land-use area and data from informants, it has a characteristic satisfaction level of one metric ton per peasant household. This was described to me as a minimum amount which it was desirable for every man to provide for his family from his own lands and/or by his own labours, even if he could afford to buy the corn with cash derived from some other source.

This attitude can be ascribed to the peasant's close identification of himself with his land. It is also a form of minimaxing, reducing the risk of total loss by providing at least some food should the bottom suddenly drop out of the weaving market or similar disaster befall the family's alternative source of income. Since craft specialisations are characteristically followed by women more than by men (presumably first because the men were occupied in the fields), men continue to work in the fields to avoid the socially undesirable situation of the women being the main breadwinners. Men express desires to have milpas to work in order to have a reason to leave the house, as well as feeling some symbiotic relationship with the act of growing food on their own land. It should be mentioned here that differences between communities which have relevance to satisfaction levels in corn are not only economic but appear also to be a function of the degree of traditionalism or progressiveness of a village, as shown by the relative importance of community fiestas, the cargo system and such practices as guelaguetza. These attitudes are discussed in the final chapter.

Levels of satisfaction in corn also vary through time as the economic development that is affecting Mexico as a whole makes itself felt to a greater or lesser degree on each peasant community and each peasant family. Increasing social mobility and the growing proportion of wage earners results in each household being more directly involved in the overall economic and monetary system of the country, and agricultural development for peasants generally means an increasing proportion of one's effort expended in producing cash crops which may be sold to supply subsistence needs. The decline of subsistence agriculture that accompanies this present economic development is proceeding at a fast enough rate to have affected land-use patterns measured during the period 1966 to 1970.

Figure 35 shows the proportion of land under corn, cash crops and fallow for all measured sample areas from 1966 to 1970. There are two main directions of land-use change (with the exception of the Mitla piedmont which has been discussed above), from corn to cash crops and from corn to fallow. Both land use changes are movements away from subsistence agriculture. On the better land former milpas of subsistence corn are being planted in cash crops, especially alfalfa, and on the worst land where subsistence corn production is most precarious, fields are abandoned as their owners leave the villages to become wage earners in the cities, especially Mexico City and Puebla.

The trend away from subsistence agriculture is also a trend of declining levels of satisfaction in corn production since each household is obtaining more income from other sources to buy corn rather than grow it. If we take one village where specialisation has expanded rapidly over the period of study, we can see how the declining importance of subsistence crops can also be translated into a decreasing characteristic level of satisfaction for the whole community. San Gabriel Etla is a canal-irrigating community which, since about 1956, has increasingly turned over more of its corn area to alfalfa production in order to feed a growing population of dairy cattle whose milk is sold to another village to make cheese. It will be discussed more fully in a later chapter with reference to canal irrigation, but here attention can be given to the decrease in corn area that occurred in the sample land-use area located near the village between 1957 and 1968. This sample area (Fig. 36) represents approximately sixty family holdings. Table 16 gives the measured number of hectares under subsistence corn for 1957 (data from air photograph) and 1966 to 1968. On the basis of measured corn yields and informant data, the local average yield per hectare is 1.5 metric tons. From this figure the total number of tons produced by the sixty households in the area can be calculated (Table 16). As the area under corn and therefore the total tonnage declines through the period 1957 to 1968, so also does the level of subsistence corn production per household. Corn production can be roughly equated with desired production in this case because the availability of irrigation water reduces

TABLE 16

VARIATION OF SATISFACTION LEVEL IN CORN PRODUCTION THROUGH TIME WITH INCREASING CASH-CROP SPECIALISATION: SAN GABRIEL ETLA

| Year | Amount of Land under Corn (hectares) | Total Corn Production (metric tons) | Mean Corn Production/ Family (metric tons) | % Land under Alfalfa |
|---|---|---|---|---|
| 1957 | 87 | 130 | 2.6 | 28 |
| 1966 | 81 | 120 | 2.4 | 35 |
| 1967 | 69 | 104 | 2.1 | 43 |
| 1968 | 60 | 90 | 1.8 | 49 |

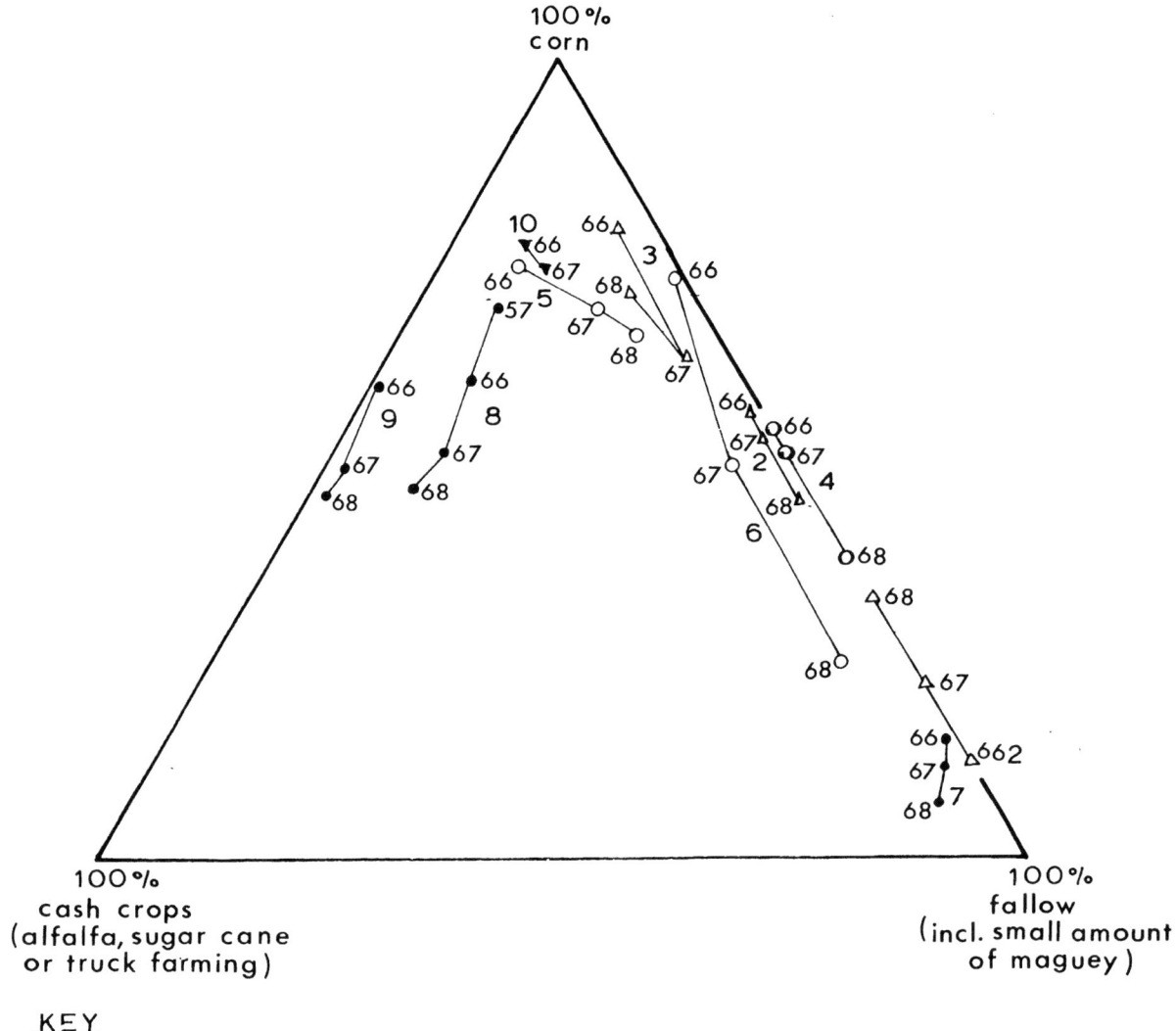

Fig. 35. Changing proportions of land under corn, cash crops and fallow for 10 sample areas between 1966 and 1968.

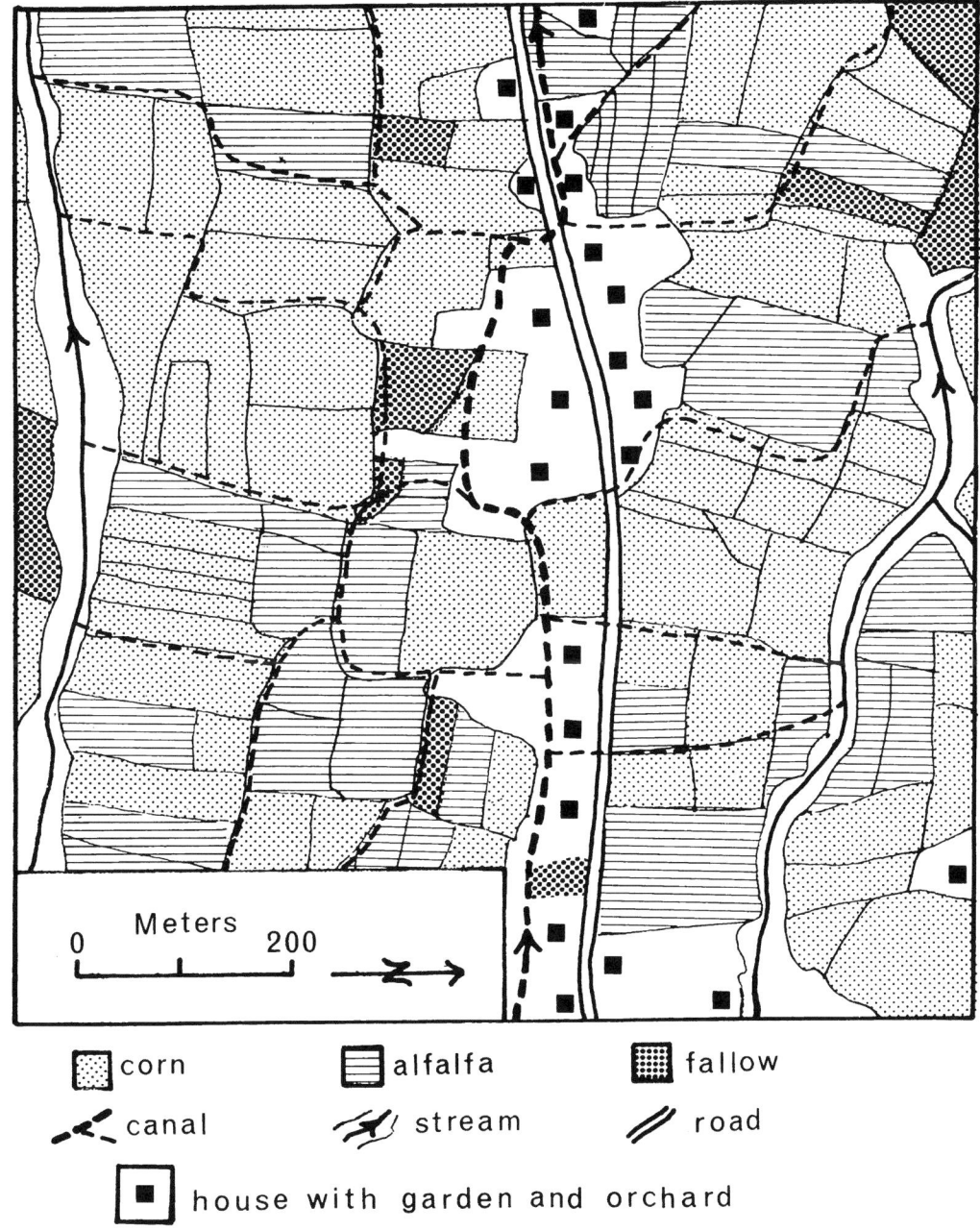

Fig. 36. Canal system, land use and physiographic zones of part of the San Gabriel Etla sample area in 1970.

the discrepancy between desired and achieved yields.

In 1957 corn production per household was 2.6 metric tons, falling to 2.4 metric tons in 1966 and to 1.8 metric tons in 1968. At the same time, the area under alfalfa increased from 28 percent to 49 percent of the total land area sampled, accompanied by a corresponding increase in the number of dairy cows. Levels of satisfaction in corn production can, therefore, not only be defined as characteristic for whole communities, but over a period of a decade these characteristic levels can be seen to change. It should be added, however, that such longer-term economic trends overlie annual changes in corn area that, even for a cash-earning agricultural community such as San Gabriel Etla, appear to be responding to annual variations in June rainfall, as will be seen later.

## SUMMARY

Most peasant landholdings in the Valley are small (less than 5 hectares), and for a typical landholding of 2.5 hectares of good land, comparative costs of corn production by coa, ox-plough and tractor methods show that cultivation by coa gives the highest cash return. Despite a 30 percent higher profit per hectare for work with a coa, almost all peasants in the Valley choose the less profitable alternative of working with an ox-team. This preference for the less work and lower profit of ox-team cultivation can be seen to be effective in actually preventing planting from taking place if the 1060 pesos per hectare necessary to work the land with oxen are not available.

A desire not to work more than necessary to produce a fixed, "satisfactory" amount of corn is also evidenced by the variable corn areas planted each year. Data from nine sample land units from various parts of the Valley and environmental settings indicate that the area of corn planted in any year is related to the June rainfall of that year in such a way that as June rainfall increases, the area planted decreases. Thus, as expectation of higher yields per hectare increases, the number of hectares planted decreases, apparently providing a more or less stable and satisfactory amount of expected corn yield.

One sample land use unit near Mitla, which was chosen to test the effect of a range of environmental settings within a small area, showed that corn area shifted among three physiographic zones from year to year. By comparing actual planting patterns with theoretical minimax and optimum solutions of a simple game theory model, it was shown that the constraints of the real situation in Mitla made these theoretical solutions impossible to achieve. Instead, the average corn distribution in Mitla can be related to a "constrained minimax" which is defined as the closest solution to a theoretical minimax solution that can be obtained in the real situation.

Although the average corn distribution among zones approximates a minimax solution, the planted distributions changed from year to year, and so a game theory model is felt to be inadequate to describe them. Planted corn distributions for each year can be related to June rainfall in each year; with increasing June rainfall, corn area in the alluvial zones decreases and in the piedmont increases. The main effect of environmental choice on a strategy aimed at satisfaction is therefore to provide a new type of agricultural land. This is a zone of marginal land, in which sporadic planting takes place, around a permanently cultivated area.

This marginal land provides an area in which opportunism or gambling on wet years takes place; the process of gambling consisting of matching planting distributions to wet Junes. Where this marginal land lies alongside permanently cultivated land that is also marginal, as in Mitla, the expansion of corn area on it that occurs in expected wet years serves a functional purpose in allowing tired alluvial land to be fallowed. This substitution between permanently cultivated and marginal agriculture zones is not necessarily a functional relationship. Elsewhere in the Valley the marginal land appears to be a land of opportunism divorced from any need to fallow the better land.

In addition to differences between individuals, characteristic levels of satisfaction can be defined for whole communities. These appear to be related to the strength of traditional institutions such as the cargo system and the proportion of income derived from other economic activities for that village. This characteristic satisfaction level does not decline to zero for villages able to support themselves completely from other sources; there appears to be a minimum level of one metric ton per family which again can be understood in terms of peasant culture and also as a minimaxing strategy. Characteristic levels of satisfaction vary not only between villages but also within a single village through time. Thus, in one village the characteristic corn production level in 1957 was 2.4 metric tons per family per year and a decade later it had declined to 1.8 metric tons.

# VII

# CASH FARMING ON IRRIGATED LAND

## INTRODUCTION

Irrigated land together with water-table-farmed fields is the most productive land in the Valley. It is not, however, separated areally from land that is dry farmed for subsistence crops because everywhere irrigated fields are interspersed with dry-farmed milpas. Peasants who irrigate land therefore also farm much of their holding without irrigation; whatever agricultural strategies exist that are specific to or arise from the practice of irrigation are in addition to the goal of fixed returns found in subsistence farming.

This analysis considers the two main forms of irrigation practised traditionally in the Valley, canal irrigation from surface streams and pot irrigation from wells. Floodwater farming covers a wide range of effectiveness and scale, and although it will not be discussed as a separate topic here, much of the following discussion of canal systems applies also to good floodwater schemes with canal distributary systems. Likewise, much of the previous analysis of unirrigated land applies also to land which receives floodwater irregularly without canals to distribute it.

In this chapter, four main questions are posed and evidence is brought forward in an attempt to answer them.

1) Since the ability to irrigate crops is ultimately dependent on the distribution of water sources, to what extent does the physical environment influence the practice and location of canal and well irrigation?
2) Irrigated land constitutes the best land in the Valley and is more or less synonymous with cash-crop production. It might be expected therefore that satisfaction strategies which were predominant in unirrigated subsistence agriculture might be minimised where production for a market is concerned and might even be superseded by an optimising strategy aimed at maximum profit. The following discussion will therefore consider whether peasants have two agricultural aims—one of satisfaction for poorer land and subsistence production and one of profit maximisation for irrigated land and cash crop production—or, alternatively, if cash-earning agriculture is also aimed at satisfaction of noneconomic goals.
3) It has often been argued that the nature of a canal distribution system, in requiring that irrigators share a single water source, provides constraints on the way the water is used and on the social institutions that accompany it. By examining the land use in canal- and pot-irrigating communities, we can test how far the form of the land use is related to the nature of the water source and how far it is a symptom of peasant culture in the Valley.
4) In Chapter V it was shown how closely linked water availability and agriculture are today, and since this paper is also concerned with land use in the past, we will consider what can be inferred from the present forms of canal and well irrigation about the role of irrigation in pre-Conquest times.

These last two questions are particularly relevant to the problem of the association between the emergence and development of statehood and centralised government in this or any area and the growth of canal irrigation (see Wittfogel, 1957, for a detailed examination of this thesis). They also apply directly to the archaeology of the Valley of Oaxaca, since canal and well irrigation have probably been known since about 400-300 B.C. and the growth of irrigation practices was contemporaneous with the development of a state authority encompassing at least the whole Valley (Flannery, personal communication). However, the links between statehood and irrigation control are not the primary concern here nor is there sufficient evidence to do more than indicate a few possibilities about the social institutions that accompanied irrigation.

The main purpose here is to examine the relationships between the form of irrigation and land use, rather than social structure, although the two cannot entirely be separated. First, the physical settings and land use patterns of the four sample areas used in the analysis will be described. Pot irrigation was studied intensively in three areas since it is not restricted to any one environmental setting. These areas are near Zaachila and San Antonino Castillo Velasco in the Zaachila Valley, and near San Sebastián Abasolo in the Tlacolula Valley. The canal-irrigated land studied is in the piedmont of the Etla Valley near San Gabriel Etla (Fig. 1).

## SAMPLE LAND USE AREAS

### San Gabriel Etla

The village of San Gabriel Etla is located at the upper edge of the crest of a piedmont spur on the eastern side of the Etla Valley (Figs. 2 and 17). It is in an area where the piedmont has been eroded by streams rising in the Sierra Juarez to the east into a series of ridges and valleys, exposing the gneiss bedrock. The piedmont gravels remain principally as residuals capping the spur crests and give rise to very stony agricultural soils. The sample area is located in and around the village and includes the main street and the main canal which parallels it (Fig. 36). Topographically, this area is the most interesting of all the sample areas since it cuts across the rolling terrain characteristic of the junction between the mountain zone proper and the more gentle piedmont. The area sampled includes some of the mountain zone and a little of the piedmont valley alluvium, but it is mainly a piedmont area (Pl. 18). These physiographic zones have less direct effect on agriculture than on water availability which in this case varies with distance from the main canals.

Since the main canal runs along the crest of the ridge rather than along the valley alluvium, the direction of increasing agricultural productivity and land values is from the bottomland up towards the hill crest—that is, the reverse of the common pattern. The method of diverting the river flow by erecting a brush toma and canalizing the water on to the ridge crest was described and mapped in Chapter IV (Fig. 17). From the main canal, water is taken off in lateral canals to fields down the two sides of the ridge. These fields may vary from 5 to 20 degrees in gradient and are usually not terraced. The soils are everywhere very stony, but the gravel and sand are contained in a clay matrix which improves their water-holding properties. Mountain soils are similar but tend to be even thinner and poorer so that the soil characteristics, together with steep gradients from 20 degrees up to 70 degrees, combine to make this an area of discontinuous subsistence agriculture similar to the Mitla piedmont. Land use in San Gabriel Etla is shown in Figure 36 for 1970, and its composition is tabulated in Table 17 for all years (1966 to 1968 and 1970).

### Zaachila

The study area is located half a kilometer west of the present town and archaeological site of Zaachila and lies on both sides of the paved highway from Oaxaca to Zaachila (Fig. 2). It is situated entirely within the high alluvium zone which is here 6.5 kilometers wide on the western bank of the Río Atoyac. Gradients are therefore extremely low, less than 1 degree, and soils are everywhere at least 3 to 4 meters deep and probably very much deeper. One major ephemeral stream crosses the area, after rising in the mountains to the west, near San Lucas Tlanichico, and ends in a delta immediately outside the eastern edge of the study area without reaching the Atoyac. This stream has brought considerable quantities of sand into the area especially along its banks and in its delta. Within the area considered,

TABLE 17
LAND USE OF SAMPLE POT-IRRIGATED AND CANAL-IRRIGATED AREAS
BY PERCENTAGE OF TOTAL AREA SAMPLED

| Sample Area | Land Use | Percent of Total Area | | | |
|---|---|---|---|---|---|
| | | 1966 | 1967 | 1968 | 1970 |
| **Pot Irrigation** | | | | | |
| Zaachila | Corn | 71 | 66 | 68 | 57 |
| (high alluvium) | Pot Irrigated Crops | 3 | 3 | 3 | 6 |
| | Alfalfa | 6 | 7 | 5 | 4 |
| | Peanuts | 15 | 16 | 10 | 17 |
| | Fallow | 5 | 8 | 14 | 16 |
| San Antonino | Corn | | 86 | 72 | 71 |
| Castillo Velasco | Pot Irrigated Crops | | 9 | 6 | 6 |
| (high alluvium) | Alfalfa | | 1 | 1 | 1 |
| | Castor Bean | | 1 | 1 | 7 |
| | Fallow | | 3 | 20 | 15 |
| San Sebastián | Corn | | | 54 | 60 |
| Abasolo | Pot Irrigated Crops | | | 2 | 5 |
| (high alluvium) | Alfalfa | | | 41 | 32 |
| | Fallow | | | 3 | 3 |
| **Canal Irrigation** | | | | | |
| San Gabriel | Corn | 41 | 36 | 32 | 44 |
| Etla | Alfalfa | 22 | 26 | 29 | 24 |
| (piedmont) | Maguey | 2 | 2 | 2 | 3 |
| | Orchards | 31 | 31 | 31 | 22 |
| | Fallow | 4 | 5 | 6 | 7 |

the stream is presently incised 0.5 to 2 meters, and the water table is within 2 to 4 meters of the surface with a downward trend away from the stream (Fig. 37). Well yields are more related to the presence of a stringer of sand or gravel to act as an aquifer than to differences in water table or surface soil. Differences in surface soil define an area of sand soils generally to the south and along the present and former stream courses and clay soils generally in the north with a narrow band of silt soils in between the two (Fig. 37). Differences in land use among these three soil types are not significant. The land use has been analysed for the area as a whole in Table 17, and part of it is shown in Figure 37.

Corn is the most widely grown crop, occupying 57 to 71 percent of the land, followed by peanuts (10 to 17 percent). The two are often grown in the same field or alternated in different years. Alfalfa is a minority crop which may be pot irrigated but usually relies on the water table directly. It occupies 4 to 7 percent of the area and this proportion is decreasing. The amount of area left fallow is between 5 and 16 percent, with pot irrigation occupying the smallest amount of land, only 3 to 6 percent. The principal pot-irrigated crops are *jicama* (a farinaceous root; *Bumelia solscifolia*), tomatoes and *miltomates*, and green beans (*frijol de carrizo*). Also grown in much smaller quantities are flowers, chile, cabbage, and corn (for corn on the cob). Most of these pot-irrigation fields are rotated every year despite the labour of field preparation and well digging.

San Antonino Castillo Velasco

The study area forms part of the lands of three villages—San Antonino Castillo Velasco, San Sebastián Ocotlán and Santiago Ocotlán—and most of pot-irrigated area lies within the land of San Antonino. It is located entirely on high alluvium between the Río Atoyac, 6 kilometers to the west, and the main town and market centre of Ocotlán on the piedmont edge, 3 kilometers to the east (Fig. 2). The area lacks any surface water and does not

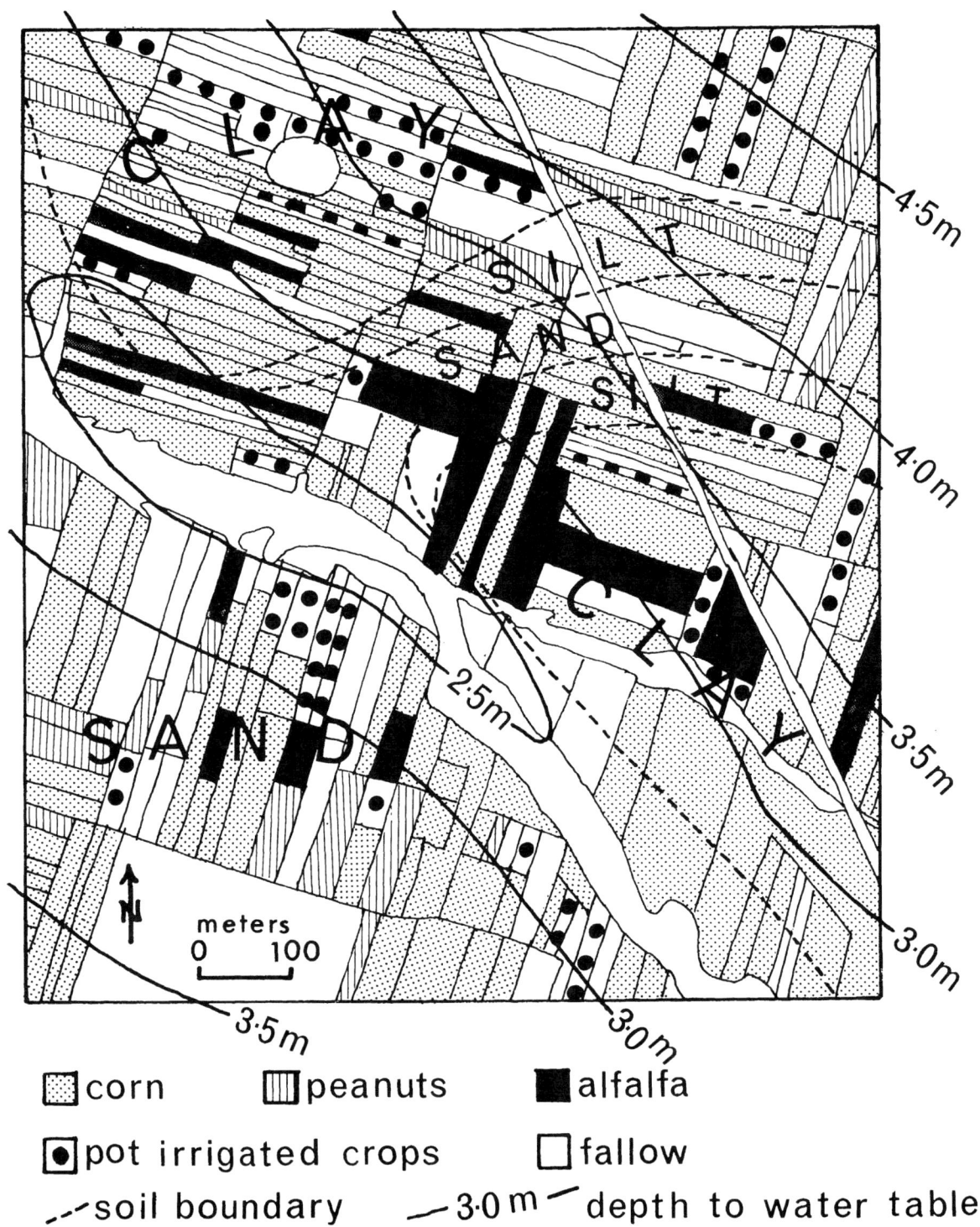

Fig. 37. Land use, depth to water table and soil texture of part of the Zaachila sample area in 1970.

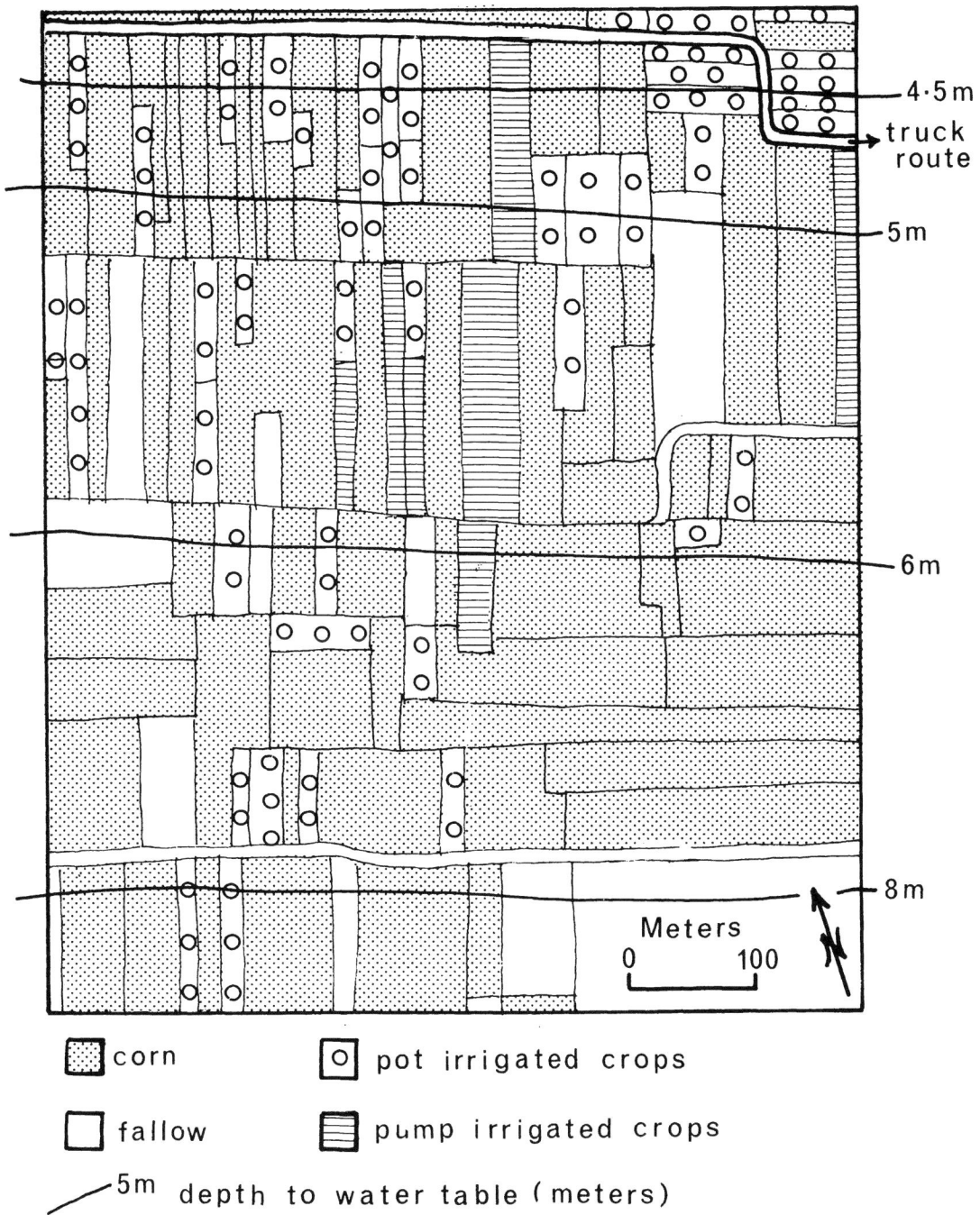

Fig. 38. Land use and depth to water table of part of the San Antonino Castillo Velasco land use area in 1967.

include any major ephemeral stream courses, although incised tracks act as ditches to carry off storm drainage. Throughout the area the soils are very sandy and free draining and gradients are everywhere less than 1 degree. The major physical distinction within the area is depth to water table, which increases from 4 meters in the north to 8 meters in the south (Fig. 38). The main transport route is in the north and consists of a dirt road passable to trucks.

The land use of part of the San Antonino sample area for 1967 is given in Figure 38 and in table form in Table 17. It is mostly devoted to dry-farmed corn production which varies in area between years from 71 to 86 percent. Pot-irrigated crops are next in importance, occupying from 6 to 9 percent of the area in different years. The main pot-irrigated crops are flowers for cutting and onions and garlic. Irrigated fields are rotated every one or two years. Out of 57 plots irrigated in 1967, only 14 were irrigated the following year, but because the wells are deeper than in Zaachila and tend, therefore, to be better constructed, they are kept open even if dry-farmed crops are planted in the field. Alfalfa accounts for only 1 percent of the area and is irrigated from a well with a pump. Castor bean is the other cash crop, and until 1970 it covered only 1 percent of the area but increased to 7 percent in 1970 and was expected to be greater still in 1971. Castor beans are sold for light machine oil and the stalks and husks can be ploughed back into the land for fertilizer. Although castor bean is a perennial, it is often pulled out after 1 or 2 years when it is already 3 meters high, because if left for longer it is difficult to remove. Fallow land varies from 3 to 15 percent of the area, depending on how much is under corn in any year. About 30 percent of the land changes use each year.

### San Sebastián Abasolo

The study area lies immediately to the southwest of the village of San Sebastián Abasolo in the centre of the Tlacolula Valley (Pl. 19) and is important archaeologically for the Early Formative (San José phase) site dating from 1000 B.C. discovered within the area at the bottom of pot-irrigation wells. The area adjoins the built-up zone of the village and is the closest of the three pot-irrigating areas to habitation. It lies within the high alluvial zone of the Río Salado just 4 kilometers downstream from a braided section through the seasonally flooded zone near San Juan Guelavía (Fig. 2). The water table is within 3.5 meters of surface throughout the sample area, but is highest in the northwest where it is within 1 meter of the surface. Most of the area is underlain by heavy clay soils although in the southeast sand has been deposited by the ephemeral stream from Teotitlán del Valle. As in the other pot-irrigated areas, gradients are everywhere very low. The Abasolo area is crossed by the single railway line which runs from Oaxaca to Tlacolula, and buses and trucks can enter the village as far as the northeast section of the sample area.

The land use of part of the sample area is given in Figure 39 for 1970, and the proportions of land occupied by different crops for all years are shown in Table 17. The high water table enables a large proportion of the land to be water-table farmed for alfalfa and also corn. These are the two main crops, occupying 32 to 41 percent and 54 to 60 percent of the land respectively. Apart from alfalfa and the pot-irrigated crops, no other cash crops such as peanuts or castor bean are grown, and the area left fallow is very small (3 percent). Pot irrigation is practised on 2 to 5 percent of land in summer and about double this amount in winter. Of the 17 pot-irrigation plots in 1968 only one was still irrigated in 1970. The general policy is to rotate them every 2 to 3 years. Some wells are ploughed in while others are left. Because half of the land is under perennial alfalfa, annual land use changes involve only 10 percent of the total area. The Abasolo area specializes in the production of chile, tomatoes and garlic by pot irrigation and manages to support enough dairy cows on its alfalfa to produce a little cheese locally.

### Summary of the Characteristics of Pot Irrigation in the Sample Areas

The principal characteristic of pot irrigation is that it is distributed as small, scattered plots throughout a larger area mainly devoted to unirrigated subsistence corn production. Analysis of land use changes through time (the next section) shows that location of pot-irrigation plots changes regularly from year to year or every 2 to 3 years. Thus, pot irrigation can be described as a form of shifting cultivation, where the irrigated land moves within the general area of unirrigated land. Within areas where pot irrigation is practised, corn grown for subsistence is the main crop and occupies 54 to 86 percent of the land. The area under pot irrigation in any one year is always small (less than 10 percent although this varies between areas,

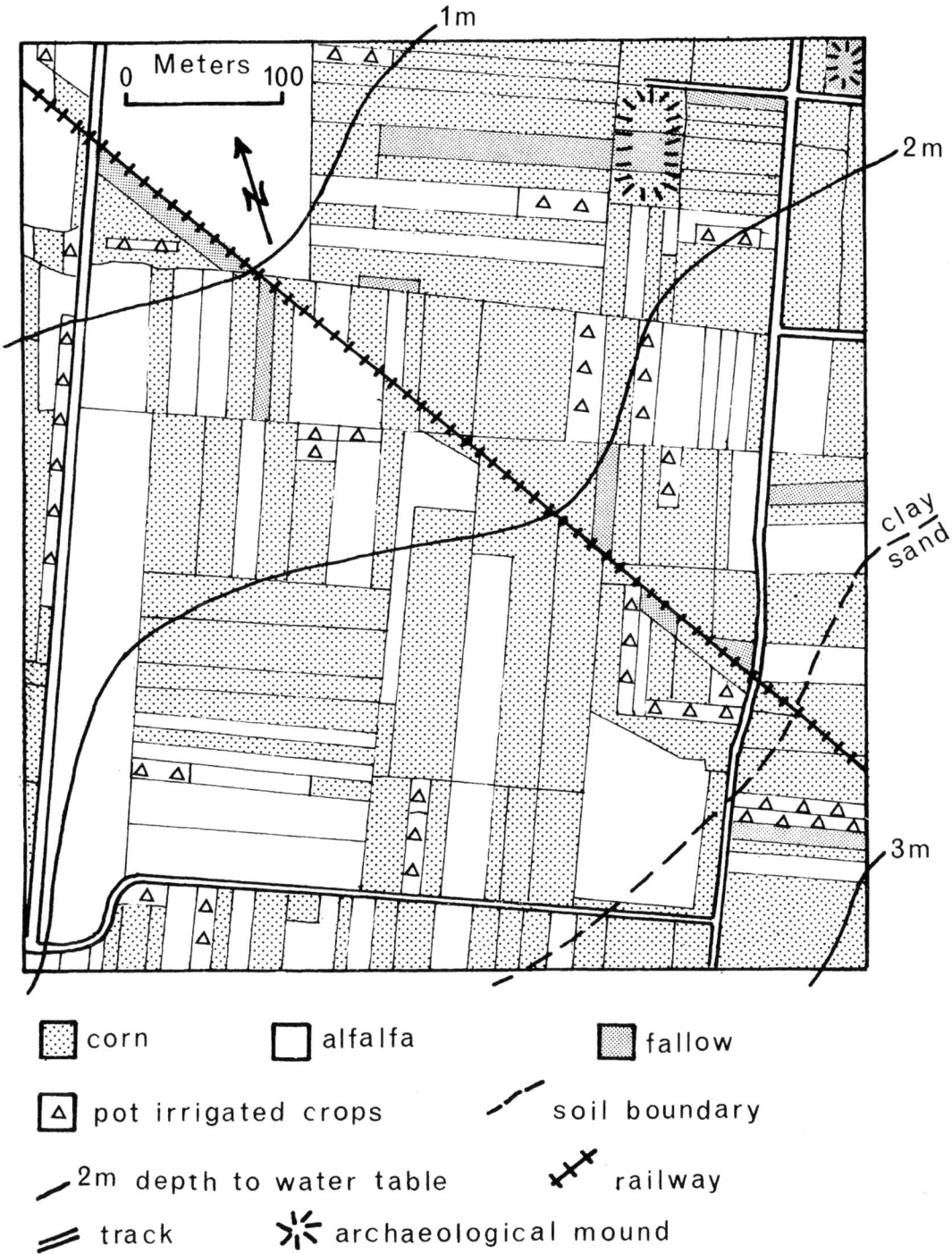

Fig. 39. Land use, depth to water table and soil texture of part of the San Sebastián Abasolo sample area in 1970.

between years and between seasons, ranging from 2 percent in summer in 1968 in Abasolo to 9 percent in autumn in 1967 in San Antonino. The area under pot irrigation generally increases in the winter when corn is not grown and more labour is available. Pot irrigation is used for cash crops only, principally flowers and vegetables, and there may also be minor areas devoted to other unirrigated cash crops such as castor bean. The area under alfalfa varies from 1 percent in San Antonino to 41 percent in Abasolo depending on the depth to the water table and whether it can grow as a phreatophyte or needs pump irrigation.

Changes Through Time in Irrigated Land Use

From the field mapping of land use in 1966 to 1968 and 1970 on which the data in Table 17 are based, land use change matrices were constructed to show the area changing from one crop to another between years. These transitional matrices have already been described for the Mitla area, and those for Zaachila and San Gabriel Etla are shown in Table 18. In the Mitla area, the total amount of corn planted remained more or less constant while the proportion of planted corn in each physiographic zone changed annually. In the pot-irrigation and canal-irrigation areas considered here, physical distinctions *within* the sample areas are less important, and the areas are considered as part of single physiographic zones. The area planted with corn for the total sample unit changes from year to year. This fluctuating corn area has already been related to annual variability in June rainfall at the time of planting (Fig. 29). Here land use changes in Zaachila and San Gabriel Etla will be considered in more detail.

Over the five year period 1966 to 1970, land use changes in the Zaachila area have resulted in only one trend which has lasted for more than two years, and that is a movement from corn to fallow land. Corn area in 1966 was 71 percent of the total sampled and this has steadily declined to 57 percent. Fallow land has risen from 5 percent to 16 percent during the same period. Corn remains the most important crop in terms of area, and in the transition matrices the corn to corn elements are the highest in both matrices, showing that corn fields tend to stay as corn fields. The last diagonal elements are also fairly high in each matrix, indicating that some fallow land is rarely used. The reasons for this are probably social rather than physical since fallow fields are interspersed with cultivated ones and are no more subject to damaging floods or poor soil than the land immediately around them. On the other hand, this area is one of intense sharecropping and absentee landlords so that land may lie untilled because the owner does not wish to work it himself and does not want or cannot find suitable sharecroppers to work it for him.

Except for the first and last diagonal elements in the transition matrices, the rest are small, indicating that land use of individual fields, under peanuts and pot irrigation particularly, changes almost annually. The high changeover in pot-irrigation fields is of most interest since it involves the filling in and redigging of wells each year in the Zaachila area (although in the San Antonino area wells are left open when a pot-irrigation field is rotated with dry-farmed corn). For example, of the 28 plots pot irrigated in 1966, only 4 remained under pot irrigation in 1967. Of the other 24 fields, the wells were covered in and most (14) were put down to corn. Although this shifting of land from irrigated to dry farmed produces a varying land use pattern on the ground, its effect on the overall land use trend is less because of the small amount of land (less than 10 percent) which is under pot irrigation in any one year.

In contrast to the Mitla area, the transition matrices for Zaachila and San Gabriel Etla are not significantly different from each other, thus suggesting a stable trend in land use change over the five year period. Since irrigation in both areas is applied mainly to cash crops, economic trends are likely to affect land use changes. However, for San Gabriel Etla the reversal of the trend to increasing alfalfa production in 1970 suggests that factors other than economic ones are important. For San Gabriel Etla, and less so for Zaachila, the relationship between June rainfall and corn area already discussed in Chapter VI is supported by the data for 1966 to 1970.

The transition matrices for San Gabriel Etla (Table 18) show large diagonal elements indicating

TABLE 18

LAND USE CHANGE MATRICES FOR THE ZAACHILA AND
SAN GABRIEL ETLA SAMPLE AREAS, 1966 TO 1968

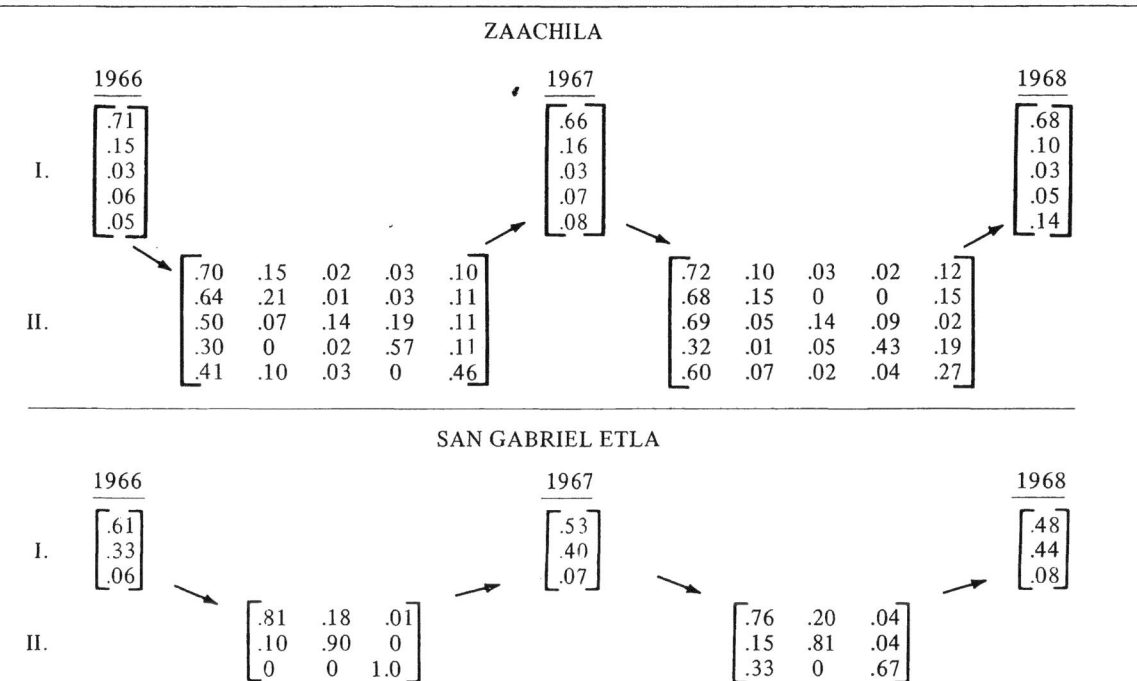

I. measured land use pattern for each year
II. transition matrices for land use change between years

$p_{ij}$ = p (changing from crop i to crop j)

For Zaachila (high alluvium)

i,j = 1. corn
2. peanuts
3. pot irrigated crops
4. alfalfa
5. fallow

For San Gabriel Etla (piedmont and alluvium)

i,j = 1. corn
2. alfalfa
3. fallow

that over a period of a few years most fields do not change their land use. Where an alfalfa field is ploughed out, it is planted with corn rather than allowed to lie fallow so that the corn crop will benefit from the high nitrogen content of the soil. Likewise, no fallow field is put immediately under alfalfa without first being planted with corn for a year or two so that the corn may benefit from the fallowed soil. The transitional matrices thus reflect the evidence of peasants in the area who insist that despite the high proportion of their land under alfalfa which supports a rapidly expanding dairy industry in the village, corn remains the most important crop because it is their most valuable and desired food.

## EFFECT OF THE PHYSICAL ENVIRONMENT ON IRRIGATED LAND USE

### Canal Irrigation

Except for a very few cases of underground *galerias* (similar in principle to Persian *qanats*), canal irrigation schemes are dependent on the presence of surface streams. Perennial streams in the Valley are small and widely distributed (Fig. 11) so that the outcome has been the establishment of many small-scale irrigation schemes. Ultimately, therefore, the distribution of canal irrigation is dependent on the distribution of suitable streams, and today the flow of all such streams is directed to a greater or lesser degree into canal systems. However, although the source of canal flows is more or less fixed by the circumstances of the physical environment, neither the take-off point nor the area on which the water is applied are similarly determined but can vary from stream to stream and through time on the same stream.

The location of the take-off point feeding the San Gabriel Etla system and its relationship to the irrigated area are shown in Figure 17. Here a toma is situated several kilometers into the mountain zone, and a main canal leads water from the bottom of a precipitous mountain valley out on to the crest of the piedmont spur to water its upper surface and sides (Pl. 12). This situation is characteristic of a whole group of canal systems which are called here "piedmont-ridge canal schemes" and which are particularly common in the Etla Valley. The area irrigated by these schemes is not, however, determined by the physical environment since water could be abstracted below the present toma (in fact, there is also a lower take-off point) and could be used, within the limitations of evaporation and seepage losses en route, on any area chosen by the irrigators. The present day systems are aimed at using the water as high up as possible, principally in order to guarantee the users control of the streams. Thus the toma is located so that the canal is at the ridge crest at the point at which the slope first becomes gentle enough to allow irrigation without terracing—that is, at the junction between the mountain and piedmont zones. The present areas irrigated by these schemes are essentially determined by the political consideration of water rights and control and are not necessarily the optimum use of the natural resource for total production. In fact, in terms of matching the best land to the water, the present distribution of irrigated land is not an optimum one.

Despite the important influence of social and political considerations, the constraint of distance can produce structuring of land use within an irrigated area with the result that crops requiring most water are grown closest to the source (in this case, the main canal) and others less demanding are located farther away. In Figure 40 the distributions of orchards, alfalfa and corn fields are given in terms of distance from the main canal in San Gabriel Etla. The median distance for orchards and gardens is 60 meters compared to 150 meters for alfalfa fields receiving regular irrigation and 210 meters for corn fields receiving an average of only one irrigation per crop. The main canal is also the source of domestic water so that houses are situated along it and the gardens and orchards are located close to the houses. This arrangement allows the fruit trees to receive water from the canal and waste domestic water, and at the same time they can be guarded by the inhabitants of the houses and provide them and their animals with shade. This stratification of land use based on intensity of water use is typical of many canal-irrigating schemes in the Valley, although deviations from the ideal location pattern arise through differences in land tenure and water rights, which will be discussed later.

Well Irrigation

Since well irrigation is dependent for its water supply on the water table, the most important effect of the physical environment might be expected to be depth to water table and the rate at which wells can yield water without drying up. Pot irrigation uses water from aquifers at shallow depths located in the coarser alluvial deposits, and these everywhere have low yields that are more suited to hand-drawing than mechanical pumps. The drawing of water from a well by hand will therefore minimise the importance of differences between well yields since most wells can supply water for the few hours that a man can draw it, but will accentuate differences between well depths since every extra meter of depth requires that much more effort. Depth to the water table will ultimately act as a limit on the practice of pot irrigation since (1) if the water is close to the surface irrigation will be unnecessary, and (2) at

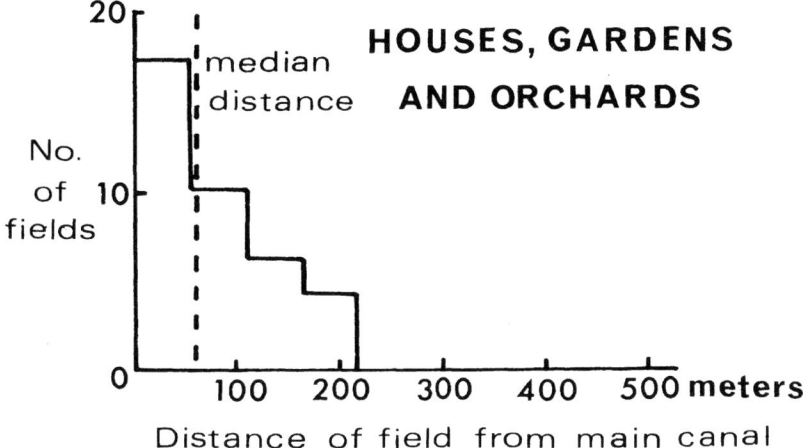
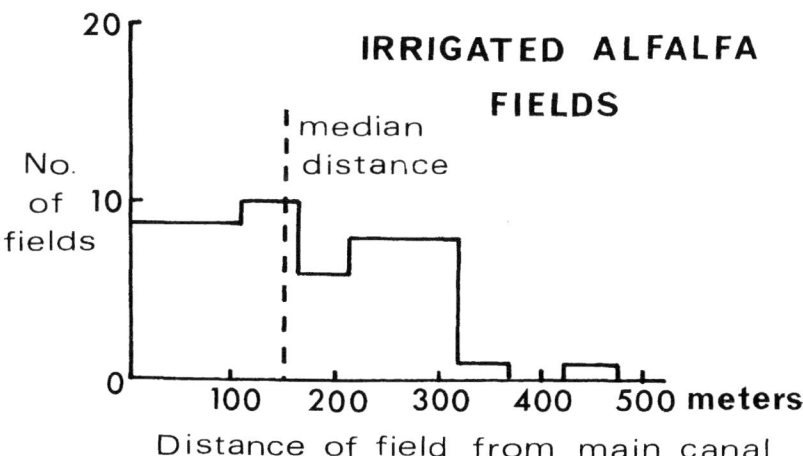
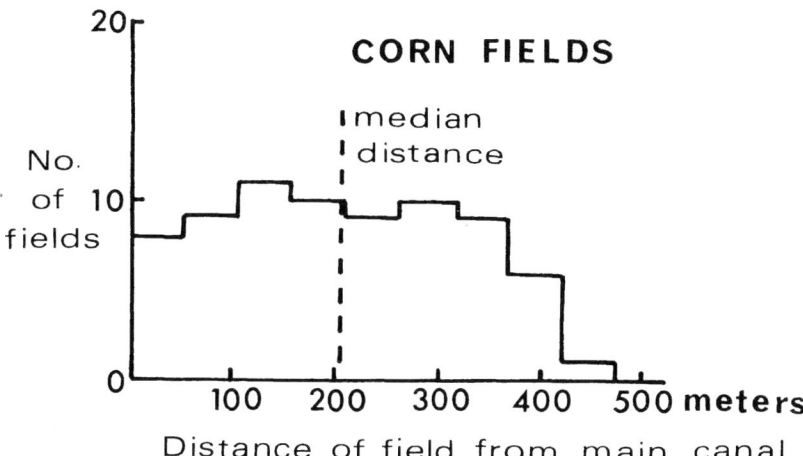

Fig. 40. Distribution of orchards, alfalfa and corn fields in relation to distance from the main irrigation canal, San Gabriel Etla.

the other end of the scale the water table will eventually become so deep that pot irrigation is not practicable.

However, the range between these two limiting cases is wide and pot irrigation is not characterised by any one depth to water table. In the three areas studied intensively, the mean depth varies from 2 to 3 meters in Abasolo, from 3 to 4 meters in Zaachila and from 5 to 8 meters in San Antonino. If pot irrigation can be practised in areas with a 2 to 8 meter depth to the water table, many more sites are available than are being used today because much of the high alluvium is underlain by a water table at depths within these limits. Indeed, in areas of 2 to 8 meters depth to water table there appears to be no *simple* relationship between depth to water table and intensity of pot irrigation such as might be expected from an examination only of the physical environment.

For example, the area with the highest mean intensity of pot irrigation, near San Antonino, has the lowest water table combined with the most permeable soils in contrast to the Abasolo area which has the highest water table and finest-grained soils and has the lowest proportion of pot-irrigated land (Table 17). If the intensity of pot irrigation with depth to water table *within* each sample area is compared for two of the areas, there is no clear relationship (Fig. 41).

The exception is the San Antonino area where the number of pot-irrigation fields decreases with increasing depth to water table. But here the relationship may be coincidental because the direction of increasing depth to water is also the direction of increasing distance from a transport route and includes differences in village ownership of land. However, water is deepest in this area, and it may equally be that depth to water table only becomes critical after a certain depth has been exceeded. In the Abasolo area, where the water table is higher on average, the opposite trend is seen, with well intensity increasing with increasing depth to water table. In the Zaachila area, which has a water table intermediate in depth between the other two samples, no consistent trend is seen (Fig. 41). The graph also shows that at the 4.5 meter depth to water table, irrigation in the Zaachila area has fallen to less than 0.1 fields per

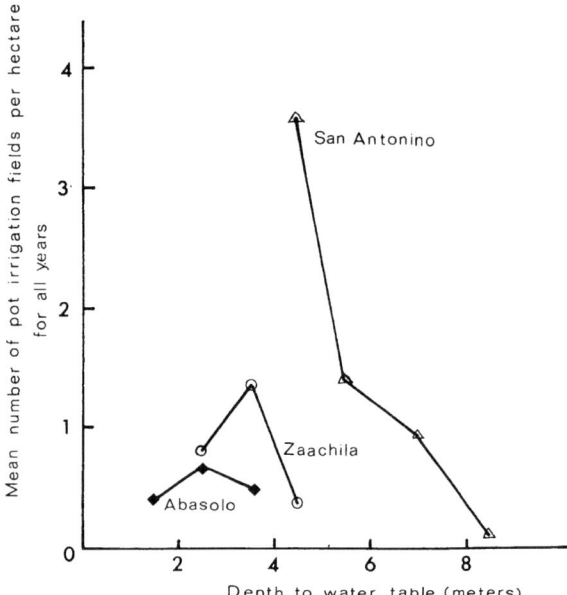

Fig. 41. Mean distribution of pot-irrigation fields in relation to depth to water table for four years in Zaachila, San Antonino and San Sebastián Abasolo sample areas.

hectare, whereas at the same depth in the San Antonino area it reaches a maximum value of 3.8 fields per hectare. Within the large area of high and medium water table on the high alluvium (3 to 9 meters below the surface), depth to water is not the only determinant of pot-irrigated fields nor is it solely critical for the distribution of pot-irrigated *fields* within pot irrigation areas. Some other factors must therefore also be operating to determine the specific location of pot irrigation over and above the generalised effect of physical conditions.

Pot irrigation is almost entirely used for the production of truck-farming crops which require rapid transportation to market and require frequent irrigation while they are in the ground. It might be expected therefore that the constraint of distance would operate in two directions: first to minimise distance to consumers, which under the present economic situation means markets as much as large towns, and second, to minimise distance from the source of labour—that is, the village. On the first count, pot-irrigated areas are characteristically located close to markets (or vice versa). Abasolo is located fairly close to Tlacolula market; San Antonino is close to Ocotlán market; the Zaachila sample area is within a few minutes walk of the Zaachila market. Likewise, a fourth important pot irrigation area, near Montoya in the southern Etla Valley, is located close to the Oaxaca market. This association of pot-irrigation areas with markets may, however, be a little misleading since the main market for Abasolo and Zaachila is not their local markets but Oaxaca itself, and the main market for San Antonino in terms of cash value would seem to be Mexico City rather than nearby Ocotlán. At the same time, all areas supply some crops to many if not all of the local markets in the Valley.

The close identification of pot-irrigating areas with markets is therefore not a simple functional one for the present marketing system, and were distance to market the most important factor in their location, one of two patterns would be expected:

1) a pot-irrigating area around each market or each village, producing crops for local consumption—in other words, many more pot-irrigating areas than there are today;
2) a large concentration of truck farming around the city of Oaxaca which contains the highest concentration of consumers and is the site of the largest market directly serving the region and acting as a distribution centre for crops and goods produced in the Valley and exported elsewhere. Such land use, with decreasing intensity away from the main centre of population, would resemble that developed in Germany in the last century by von Thunen in his classic model of agricultural location, in which the spatial distribution of different types of land use was entirely a function of distance from a central place and lines of communication to it.

The distribution of pot irrigation fits neither of these patterns. A simple distance to market function does not hold, primarily because it is distorted by cultural factors—the organisation of the peasant economy into an integrated regional system of markets and the tendency of villages to follow community rather than individual specialisations. If distance to market is not a primary locational factor for the truck-farming areas as a whole, neither is distance from irrigators' homes a primary factor in the location of plots within those areas. Although all pot-irrigation plots are located within half an hour to one hour's walk from a village, they tend to be randomly scattered with regard to distance within the general area. No consistent relationship can be found for all three sample areas between the number of irrigated fields per hectare and distance from a transport route (which can be equated with village). Figure 42 shows the mean number of pot-irrigated fields per hectare for all years, and it can be seen that whereas the number of irrigated fields per hectare declines sharply with distance from a road or village in San Antonino, it does so less sharply in Zaachila and not at all in Abasolo.

Although depth to water table does limit the distribution of pot irrigation in the Valley, there remains a large area of the valley floor which, were depth to water table the only criterion for the location of this type of irrigation, could be pot irrigated, but is not. Likewise, it is felt that distances from owners' homes and to market are inadequate to explain completely the distribution of pot irrigation, and that some of this unexplained variation may lie in the history of pot irrigation in the Valley. This is a point which will be returned to later.

EFFECT OF THE CULTURAL ENVIRONMENT

Canal Irrigation

The relationships between the physical and cultural environment of an area through the medium of canal irrigation have long been debated in the fields of anthropology and geography, and much literature has been associated with this debate stemming from the classic work by Wittfogel, (1957). Here attention is confined to two main points: the problem of matching the best land to the water and the effects on the land use pattern of the sharing of a single water flow.

In an earlier part of this chapter the idea was introduced that the present distribution of areas irrigated from canals is not dictated by the physical environment nor is it necessarily an

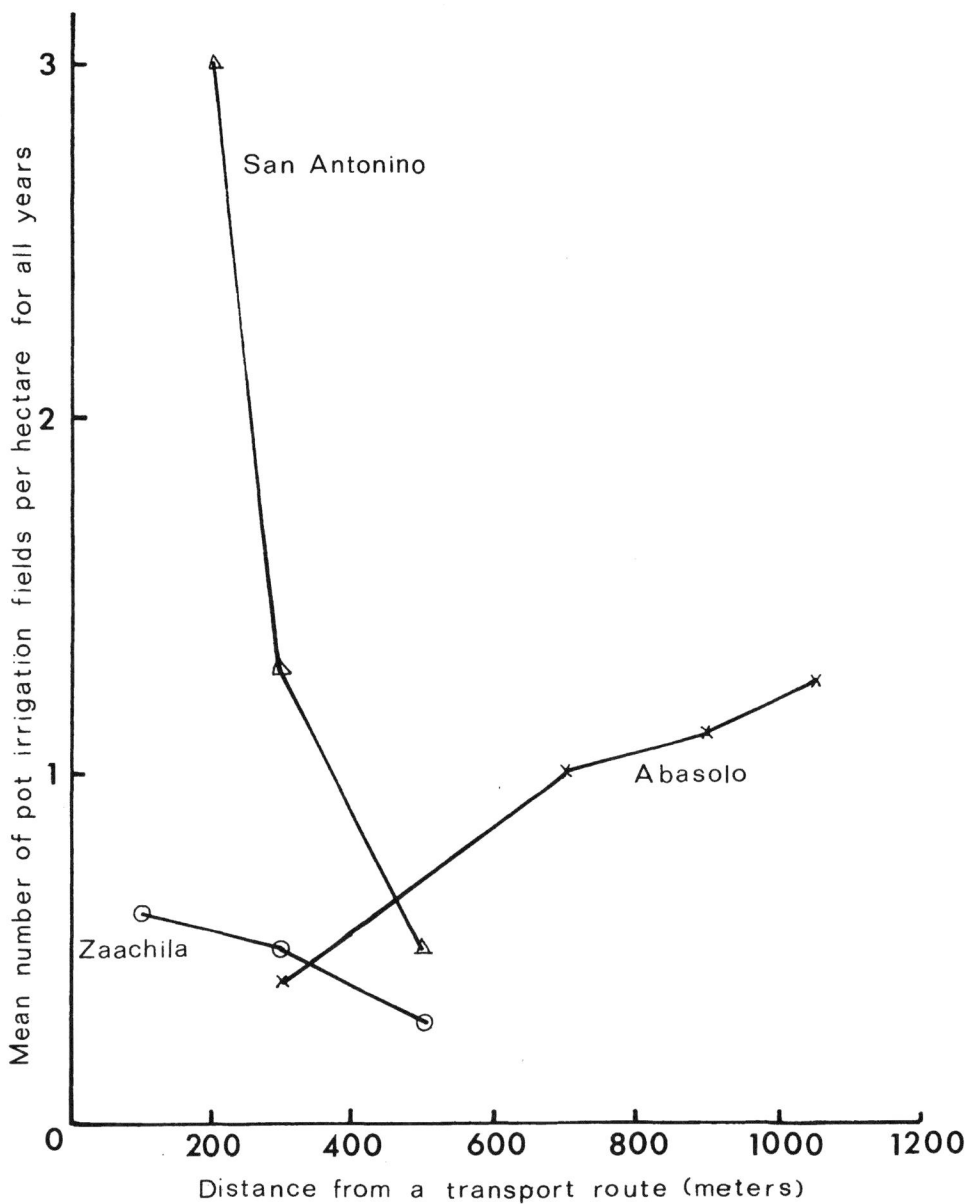

Fig. 42. Mean distribution of pot-irrigation fields in relation to distance from a transport route for four years in Zaachila, San Antonino and San Sebastián Abasolo sample areas.

optimum one in terms of total production. If we consider a stream issuing from the mountains and crossing the piedmont zone to join the main stream on the Valley floor, it is possible to imagine several alternative distributions of irrigation water. If both the piedmont and alluvial land were in the control of a single authority which aimed for the maximum total production and if the irrigation water available were only sufficient for part of that area, the increased yields provided by irrigation would be highest if the water were applied to the alluvium rather than the piedmont. This can be seen by reference to the analyses of variance on corn yields discussed in Chapter V (Tables 3 and 6) which show that without irrigation the mean yields on the piedmont are 0.48 metric tons per hectare and on the high alluvium are 1.26 metric tons per hectare. With irrigation, piedmont yields can be increased, on average, to 1.5 metric tons per hectare and alluvium yields rise to 2.84 metric tons per hectare. Taking both areas together, highest total corn production theoretically would be achieved by irrigating the valley floor first and irrigating farther out in the piedmont only if the amount of water permitted it. In reality, the piedmont is irrigated rather than the alluvium.

If authority were centred on the valley floor because the increased marginal benefit from irrigation is highest there, it is possible that for a long time the piedmont would be left largely unoccupied. When occupation and cultivation of the piedmont occurred, however, the physical advantage of its upstream position in controlling water would probably soon have been realised. It is likely that such a sequence of events took place at about 500 B.C.[1] when sites in the piedmont expanded following an earlier settlement pattern concentrated on the valley floor (Flannery, personal communication). The history of irrigation in the Valley may therefore be one of expansion outward from the valley floor to the valley margins. This is discussed more fully in the next chapter.

If the area of irrigation did move to the piedmont in the Monte Albán I period, it did not remain there until today. Since the Conquest, and probably also before, it has been moved around depending on which community or local lord (*cacique*) owned or shared the water rights and to which areas water was sold at various times (Taylor, 1969). Throughout fluctuations in the centres of political power, however, the upstream village on a stream or canal system always has the physical advantage. This can be seen today in the differences in amounts of irrigated land belonging to San Gabriel and San Miguel Etla. Both communities theoretically receive equal shares of water from the canal which passes along the ridge crest and through both villages (Fig. 17). The basis of sharing is that each village should receive the entire discharge of the canal on alternate weeks, but measurements of the total area irrigated and of the canal discharge that reaches each village during its turn indicate that the upstream community uses more water, even taking into account the higher seepage losses, etc., for the downstream village's supply.

This discrepancy may be due to San Gabriel taking advantage of its upstream position to abstract more water or it may be due to San Miguel not fully utilizing its share or distributing it among fewer parcels of land. Lees reports a general attitude of resignation among downstream villages in the Valley to receiving less water than upstream ones and unwillingness to take any action over a suspicion of cheating by the upstream communities (1973). In any case, the actual pattern of irrigated area that results from the water rights enjoyed by the piedmont villages is very different from what would be the theoretical optimum were maximum productivity more important than community and individual water rights.

The effect of water rights being shared between two or more villages is to spread the irrigated area, since if all the water rights were owned by one village, the irrigated area would tend to be confined to that village's lands. Where more than two villages share water, the irrigated area becomes even more diffuse, and there is a tendency to spread the water more thinly over the fields. The two largest perennial tributaries, the Río Mixtepec (Fig. 43) and the San Agustín Etla stream are both shared by several villages. The result of so much water being taken from the Río Mixtepec is that by the time it reaches Santa Ana Tlapacoyan its flow is so greatly reduced that villagers do not feel that the amount of water is sufficient to warrant a system for water allocation within the village.

The distribution of water within communities is generally to each adult male or household requiring it. Lists of irrigators are drawn up by elected officials who also allocate the amount and time for each individual's turn. The form that water allocation and authority take in 26 villages in the Valley has been examined by Lees (1973), and here the effect of this egalitarian division of water on the land use will be examined.

The main effect of water allocation within

---

[1] The trend actually began before 800 B.C., but is most noticeable after 500 B.C.

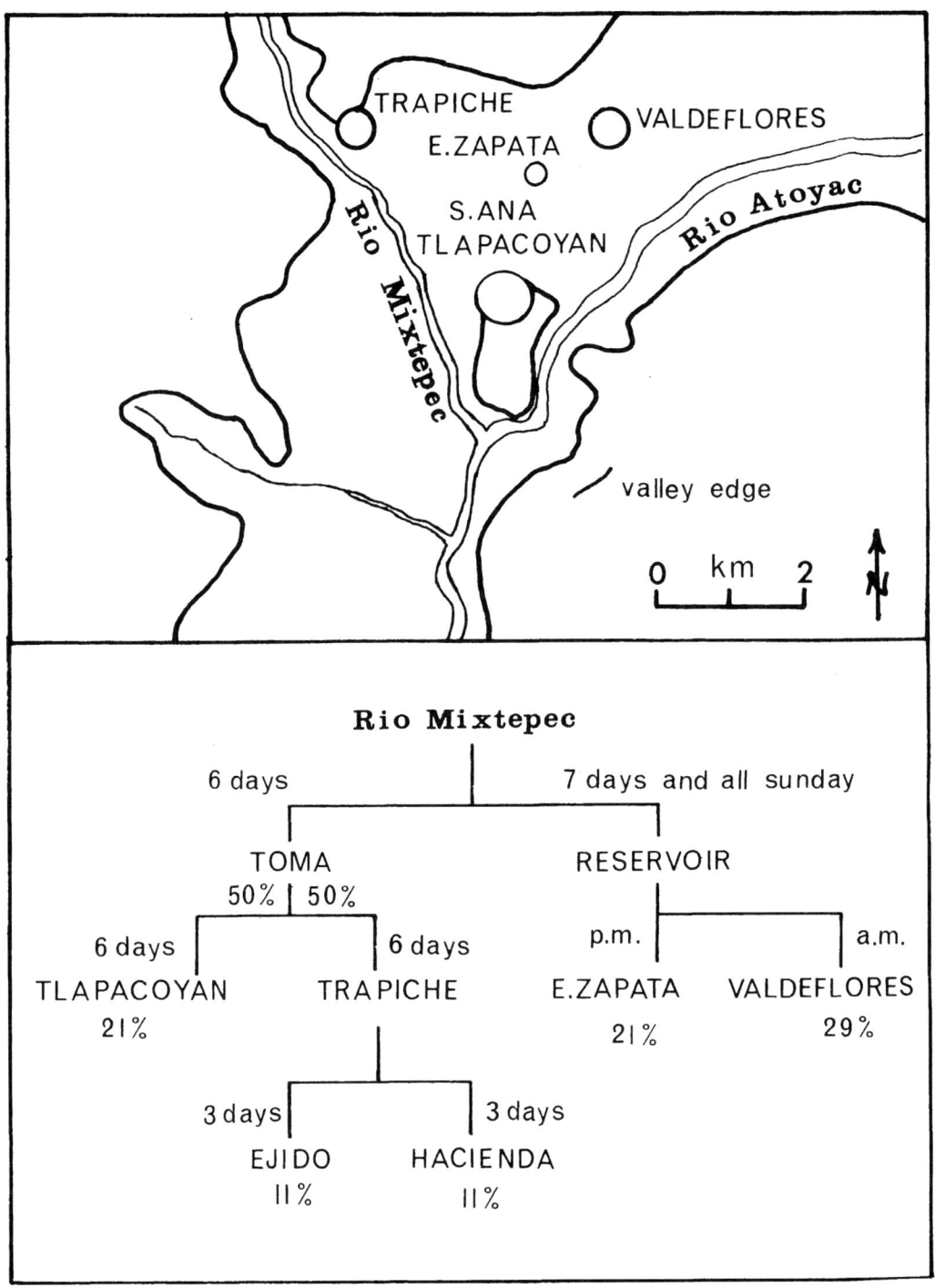

Fig. 43. Division of water among five communities on the lower Río Mixtepec.

villages is to multiply the effect of sharing water between villages, that is, to make the irrigated area even more diffuse. This is because landholdings are small and fragmented and an area of about 200 hectares will typically be held by 50 to 150 families. If an area of comparable size were held by one owner and the available water could irrigate half of that area, a rational division of the landholding into two zones, irrigated and non-irrigated, would be possible on the basis of matching the land most likely to be productive with irrigation to the water (Fig. 44a). However, in a situation of many small scattered landholdings, each with one share of water, the water is applied in an equally fragmented pattern which will not necessarily result in all the best land being irrigated and all the worst being dry farmed, because some families will own water rights but none of the best land (Fig. 44b).

These observations are very simplified, but they demonstrate the point that we are not dealing here with an optimising single authority (who might approximate Economic Man) but with peasant cultivators organised in many small communities who do not appear to be aiming for the maximum productivity they could achieve. Thus, in the same way that peasant subsistence agriculture can be described as inefficient in terms of gaining maximum total productivity for the Valley, the fact that each individual in a peasant community has a right to a share of the community's water supply produces a matching of land and water that is less than optimal. Thus, the effect of the present organisation of canal irrigation water control, both between communities and within them, has been to *reinforce* the trend toward diffusion of irrigated areas. In other words, the present dispersed spatial organisation of canal irrigation can be related to the social distribution of water rights and water use as well as to the physical distribution of perennial streams.

A second and related question is what effect sharing of canal water among many individuals has on land use patterns. The sharing of a single water flow necessitates some cooperation among individuals or subjection to some overall authority. The concentration of water in a flow gives rise to the possibility of a person or group physically controlling the supply of many individuals. It is these two aspects of water flow, plus the often vital need for irrigation in arid areas, that led Wittfogel and his followers to claim that the sharing of canal water and the organisation of states were causally linked. For the Valley of Oaxaca, however, Lees

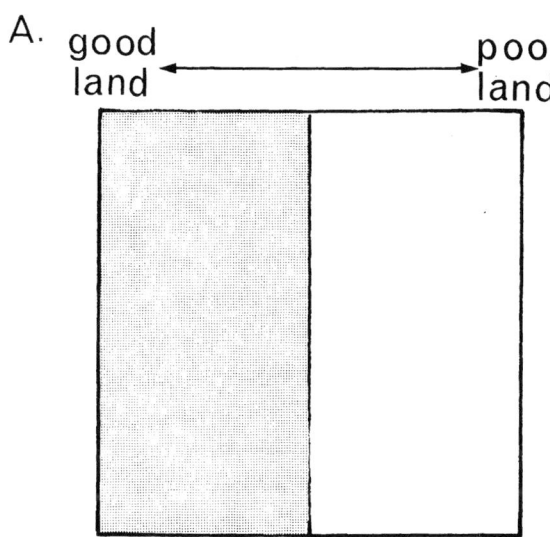

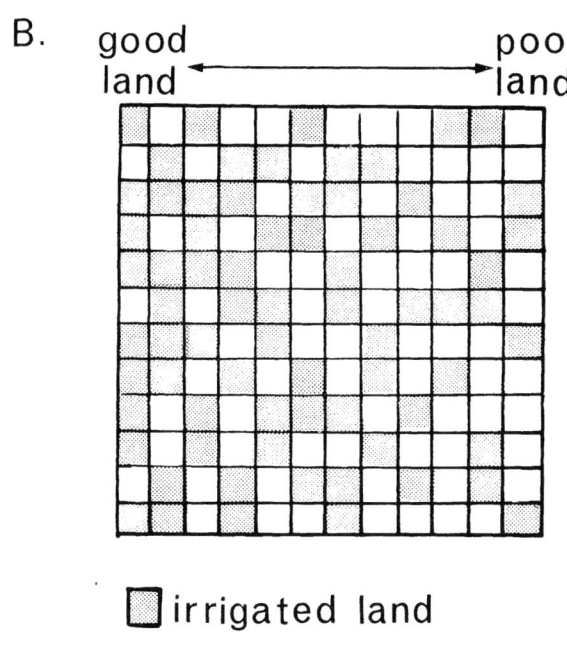

Fig. 44. Hypothetical distribution of irrigation water over an area of variable agricultural quality under conditions of (a) single ownership or control and (b) community ownership with individual water rights.

(1973) argues that because the (1) distribution of water rights within communities is egalitarian, (2) water control forms an integral part of village organisation, and (3) water control is associated with time-consuming and unpaid official posts, water is a minimal source of political power today.

This egalitarian distribution of water among many individuals and several communities does, by the process of division itself, produce definite constraints on the ways in which the water can be used. A water flow can be divided either by physically splitting the flow into several components or by temporally allocating the total flow. A canal distributary scheme is thus a system for subdividing flow into individual field irrigation units as well as a means of transporting the water from source to field. Since water sources in the Valley are generally small and need to be divided into many components, both systems of division are used. Division between villages may be on the basis of a proportion of the flow or the entire flow for a proportion of the time. In the lower Mixtepec system, where five communities share the water, the flow is physically divided at one point and the rest is allocated on a time basis (Fig. 43). The Trapiche ejido, for example, receives 11 percent of the total flow, a proportion which is achieved by first dividing the flow into two equal parts at the toma, and then allocating three day units of twelve hours each of one half of the flow to the ejido (Fig. 43).

Division within communities is necessary because the amount of water available at any one time is inadequate to supply more than a fraction of the fields requiring irrigation; generally division is achieved on the basis of time units. The allocation of water is arranged and supervised by an elected official whose exact status and title varies between communities. Irrigators who wish to use water ask to have their names put on a list, and from this list the official allocates the amount of timing of each irrigator's turn. Once all the names on the list have had their turn or have declined it (or, in other cases, once the time for that irrigation list—usually 20 to 40 days—has expired), a new list is drawn up. Those irrigators who, for various reasons, did not receive water in the last list tend to have priority in the new list. Lees (1970) has found that this system operates fairly, and there is a general consensus that justice is done; conflict rarely goes beyond a mild dispute that can be quickly settled by the water controller.

If we look at a sample land use area again, it can be seen how this egalitarian division of water affects the land use pattern. San Gabriel Etla receives the entire flow (mean base flow of 50 liters per second) of its stream for 7 days out of 14. At any one time the flow can irrigate about 3 hectares of land, which is divided into 12 fragmented parcels called *tareas*. (Tarea is a word generally used as a unit of work—for example, one day—but it is also used in the Valley to refer to a unit of land and, by extension, the amount of water needed to irrigate that land, the exact size of both units being variable depending on how long it takes to till the land.) Tareas in San Gabriel Etla, in addition to being a unit of land of just under half a hectare, are also the *amount of water* required to irrigate 0.3 to 0.4 hectare (here called land tarea). This amount of water (water tarea) could be applied in a shorter period of time if the streamflow were not subdivided and consequently takes longer to apply as the number of simultaneous users increases. In San Gabriel Etla, the system of water allocation is done on a time basis between the two villages (San Gabriel and San Miguel), and between their individual irrigators. Therefore water is used by San Gabriel irrigators on alternate weeks only; and water tareas received by individuals are the equivalent of 1/63 of the main canal discharge for a period of twelve hours. Since water tareas are taken both day and night, this means that each week there is enough water to irrigate 63 × 2 = 126 land tareas. These 126 fragmented parcels of land constitute about 42 hectares in all, which can be irrigated each week.

Irrigators petition the water controller for the number of tareas they require and designate which of their parcels of land they wish to irrigate, and the official organises the timetable. From the point of view of each irrigator, he receives a certain number of water units once every two weeks, but these must all come within the week water is alloted to his village. He must therefore grow crops which need not be irrigated more than once every 14 days or so, unless he provides his own storage for water. If, for example, one irrigator wished to grow flowers or chiles, which yield best with irrigation every two days, the constraints inherent in the sharing of water would not allow him to do so unless both communities were to agree on a new basis for water allocation which would enable all irrigators to receive a little water every other day. The only way an individual can break away from the community rhythm of irrigation is to provide his own water storage and become his own water allocator. Almost all irrigators in San Gabriel choose the first alternative, that is, to accept the frequency of irrigations supplied by the community authority without recourse to individual allocation. Only one example is known in San Gabriel of a small storage tank used to irrigate flowers during the week that irrigation water passes to San Miguel.

The land use pattern resulting from this acceptance of irrigation once every two weeks is a very uniform one of corn and alfalfa (Fig. 36), with corn being dry farmed or receiving just one irrigation a few weeks after planting if it is a dry season, and alfalfa receiving water every 14 to 28 days. This pattern is characteristic not only of San Gabriel but of many canal-irrigating areas, and it can be seen as a natural outcome of the division of water by time units. It is not, however, a *necessary* outcome, since individuals could build storage tanks from which they could pot-irrigate crops if they wished or the whole community could change the frequency of irrigations.

It had been previously thought that the constraints inherent in the water allocation system were the most important factor in this uniformity of land use and community specialisation in a single cash crop (A. V. Kirkby, 1969:209-212). In other words, that alfalfa is the cash crop grown in canal-irrigating communities because all irrigators received water at a community–determined frequency. In the pot-irrigating villages considered now, we can begin to see how far such a hypothesis holds for the Valley, because in a pot-irrigating village, the frequency of irrigation is controlled by the individual irrigator and without the constraints imposed by a canal system. At first, the comparison seems to support the hypothesis since pot irrigation is used for a variety of crops: chiles, tomatoes, miltomatoes, garlic, onions, cabbages, green beans, jícama and flowers. But on closer examination, it can be seen that the entire range is not grown in any one village; each pot-irrigating village also specializes in the production of one or two cash crops. For example, Abasolo grows tomatoes and chiles in the summer and garlic in the winter; San Antonino grows flowers in the winter and garlic in the summer; and Zaachila specialises in jícama and green beans. Thus, despite the freedom for each irrigator to grow exactly what he pleases, 80 to 90 percent of pot irrigators grow the same crops as all their neighbours.

Not only is pot irrigation a community rather than an individual pursuit, but the particular cash crops grown are also community specialisations just as are weaving or potting. The incentives to conformity within a community, or rather the disincentives to individualism, were introduced in Chapter III and will be discussed further in Chapter IX. There are also strong economic reasons why a village should specialise in one or two crops. Group production has the potential to reduce marketing costs and provides a pool of skill and information. This potential power of cooperation is only just beginning to be realised by Oaxaca peasants, but already the buying of produce by the truckload by Oaxaca middlemen is breaking down the traditional marketing pattern of producer selling directly to consumer in a market, or from door to door, and is reinforcing and polarising the crop specialisation of these villages.

The important point here is that in the Valley of Oaxaca there is no evidence that uniformity of land use and crop specialisation is a direct consequence of sharing water in a canal system; even in the absence of such constraints, irrigating communities specialise in a few cash crops. We must, therefore, look not to the specific characteristics of canal irrigation but to the general cultural environment for the causes of specialisation by groups rather than by individuals in peasant villages.

## Well Irrigation

In contrast to canal irrigation, the amount of water available to plants in a system of pot irrigation from wells is dependent on the decisions of the individual irrigator. Thus, within the limits imposed by his labour, he can irrigate as many plants or as often as he likes, independent of community control. It has been shown how this independence results in conformity on a village scale as to *what* crops he grows, and now we will examine how far he uses his independence in terms of how *many* plants he grows. In other words, are pot irrigators aiming for a satisfaction level similar to, or complementary to, that for subsistence corn production in their cash crop production? Or, do they have two agricultural aims—one of satisfaction for subsistence and one of profit maximisation for cash farming?

First the profitability of pot irrigating vegetables will be compared with that of dry-farmed corn production in terms of cash and labour inputs to determine how much land a peasant could pot irrigate and how much he should, if his aim were to obtain maximum profit. Table 19a gives the cash costs and yields of one crop of pot-irrigated garlic from a parcel 0.125 hectare in size. Seed costs for garlic are high compared with other vegetables (700 pesos compared with only 5 pesos for chile seed) and form the main production expense. Manure is a necessary cost of pot irrigation, since without regular application of either manure or chemical fertilizer, yields decline sharply and make pot irrigation unprofitable. It is almost impossible to cost manure itself since it is never purchased but is produced by the household's animals directly for the household's plots or exchanged between households. Therefore only cartage costs are quoted. Since the beneficial effects of manure last for several years, it is only applied once every 3 to 4 years at the rate of 20 *carretones* per 0.125 hectare. Chemical fertilizer costs about 150 pesos per hectare, but it must be applied for each crop, or 3 times a year if 3 crops are produced. Formerly clay pots were used for irrigation (Pl. 10), but today metal ones have almost completely replaced them, and these last up to 3 years so that the cost per crop is only 4 pesos.

The total cost therefore is 774 pesos excluding any labour charges, which must be set against a total yield of 3300 pesos if the entire field is sold to one middleman who brings his truck to the village and assumes all further transport and marketing costs and losses. Where the produce is not sold to a middleman but taken to market by the members of the household, the sale price of about half the crop is higher than the middleman's price, but this part of the crop must be of high quality to be accepted in Oaxaca market. The poorer, somewhat damaged or blemished half of the crop is sold in other local markets and hawked around the villages for a lower price than the middleman's so that the cash yield per crop, taking into consideration marketing costs and losses, is about the same or probably a little less than bulk selling to a middle-man. Field measurements of yields and the values of the yields quoted are almost all within the range 2500 to 3500 pesos per 0.125 hectare.

If pot irrigation costs and cash yields are compared with those for one hectare of dry-farmed corn cultivated with an ox-plough, cash profit is found to be highest for pot irrigation of 0.125 hectare: 2526 pesos against 1840 pesos

TABLE 19

COMPARATIVE CASH PRODUCTION COSTS AND YIELDS FOR POT IRRIGATING AND DRY FARMING

*a.* Costs and Yields for 0.125 Hectare Pot-Irrigated Garlic

| Item | Cost (pesos) |
| --- | --- |
| Seed (14 almudes, 50 pesos/almud) | 700 |
| Manure Cartage (0.12 of 20 loads at 30 pesos/load) | 70 |
| Irrigation Pot (0.2 of 1 pot at 20 pesos) | 4 |
| Total Cost | 774 |
| Total Cash Yield of Field (Wholesale) | 3300 |

*b.* Comparative Costs and Yields: Pot-Irrigated Garlic and Dry-Farmed Corn*
(in pesos)

| | 0.125 Hectare Garlic | 1 Hectare Corn |
| --- | --- | --- |
| Total Cost | 774 | 1060 |
| Total Yield | 3300 | 2900 |
| Cash Profit | 2526 | 1840 |

*Excluding cost of owner's labour.

TABLE 20

COMPARATIVE LABOUR REQUIREMENTS FOR POT IRRIGATION OF 0.125 HECTARE
AND ONE HECTARE OF DRY-FARMED CORN USING AN OX-PLOUGH

|  | Man-Days Labour | | | |
|---|---|---|---|---|
|  | 0.125 Hectare Pot Irrigated | Oxteam Driver's Labour | Additional Labour | Total Labour Required* |
|  |  | 1 Hectare of Dry Farmed Corn | | |
| Field Preparation | 5 | 8 | 0 | 8 |
| Sowing/Transplanting | 6 | 4 | 4 | 8 |
| Hilling up and Weeding | 30 | 10 | 6 | 16 |
| Irrigating: Av. of 0.5 Day Every 2 Days | 25 | 0 | 0 | 0 |
| Harvesting and Carting | 5 | 6 | 5 | 11 |
| Total Labour Requirement | 71 | 28 | 15 | 43 |
| Total Labour Available Per Man | 120 | 120 | 120 | 120 |

*The landowner can be either the oxteam driver or may supply the additional labour, according to whether he owns an oxteam himself or not. In either case the total labour required is the sum of the oxteam driver's time plus the additional labour.

(Table 19b). When these profits are compared on a per hectare basis, the differential is even greater— 20,208 pesos per hectare for pot irrigation against 1840 pesos for dry-farmed corn. Since it has already been shown in the last chapter that in a situation of small landholdings, the most profitable form of production *per unit area* is the one which will give each household the highest income, it follows that the most profitable strategy is to pot irrigate as much of the landholdings as possible.

The problem is that although pot irrigation is extremely profitable in terms of cash it also has very high labour requirements. Table 20 gives comparative labour inputs for 0.125 hectare of pot irrigation and 1 hectare of dry-farmed corn using an ox-plough. Although the total number of man-days labour required to cultivate 1 hectare of corn is 43, because more than one person is needed in the field at one time (especially for sowing), the number of man-days the owner can provide himself is only 15 or 28 depending on whether or not he hires an ox-plough—that is, depending on whether he, himself, is the ploughman. Since most people hire ox-ploughs, 15 days of the owner's time for 1 hectare of corn can be set against 17 days of his time if he supplied all the labour for a pot irrigation plot (Table 20). The total number of days available is about 120 for a 4-month growing season so that the maximum number of pot irrigation plots 1 man can work is 2, Since there are usually at least 2 male members of a household capable of doing field work, the maximum number of plots an average household can operate is 4, or 0.5 hectare, assuming no additional labour is hired from outside the family.

The total profits for different combinations of areas under dry-farmed corn and pot irrigation during the summer growing season are given in Figure 45. Also shown are the lines of labour limitation for a household owning an ox-team and a household hiring one, for different proportions of their holding in pot irrigation and dry farming. The other variable is the size of the landholding, and for the purposes of analysis, the most profitable combinations for just two sizes of holdings are considered, again assuming that no additional labour is hired except an ox-team. These sizes are 1.5 hectares and 2.5 hectares, both of which are common sizes of holding among the pot-irrigating households providing data.

If the most profitable distributions of land between pot irrigation and dry farming are considered for the four cases illustrated in Fig. 45, we find that:

1) for a household hiring an ox-team and having a 2.5 hectare holding, the most profitable solution is to pot irrigate 0.25 hectare or 2 plots;
2) for a household hiring an ox-team and having a

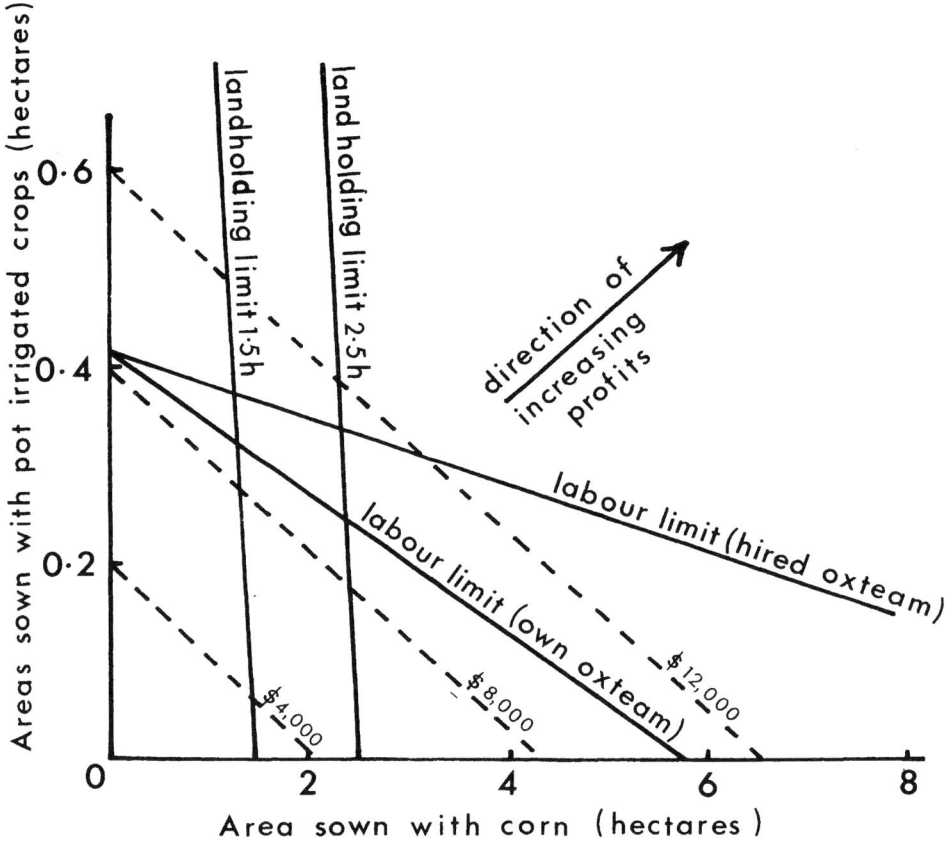

Fig. 45. Total cash profit in pesos for different proportions of landholding area under pot irrigation of cash crops and under dry farming of corn.

holding of 1.5 hectares, it is to irrigate 0.25 hectare or 2 plots;
3) for a household owning an ox-team and having a 2.5 hectare holding, the most profitable solution is to irrigate 0.38 hectare or 3 plots; and
4) for a household owning an ox-team with a 1.5 hectare holding, it is to irrigate 0.33 hectare or 2.5 plots.

Comparing these profit-optimising distribution figures with the number of plots actually pot irrigated per household in the 3 land use areas during the summer growing season, most families have 0 to 1 plot and during the winter most families have 2 to 3 plots, whereas they have sufficient labour and land resources to irrigate 4 plots. These households are therefore not adopting the most profitable strategy (in Abasolo it was said that no one irrigated more than 2 plots in the summer whatever the size of their holding), but they are accepting less cash return for less labour input. This attitude is also shown in conversations with pot irrigators who admit they could irrigate more (especially since they could also hire mozos to work for them and still receive more profit) but prefer not to because it is very hard work and *one eats corn rather than all those chiles anyway*. That the area actually irrigated is less than they could manage is also apparent from the variable areas under pot irrigation from year to year. This variation between years (Table 17) indicates a tendency for pot irrigation to increase and decrease at the same time as subsistence corn area. Both types of agriculture appear to be guided by a similar strategy rather than there being a trade-off between the two types of production.

The evidence from this analysis of pot irrigation, therefore, indicates that in cash-crop production, as well as subsistence corn production, peasant agriculturalists are aiming for satisfaction rather than for maximum profits. The way in which they are achieving satisfaction is to use all their landholding but not all their labour. The desire to use all their land has already been ascribed to the peasant's perception of the land as an extension of himself. This, combined with his desire to grow his own subsistence food, is effective in making a satisfactory solution one in which most of the landholding is under corn and enough is under pot irrigation to provide cash to supply noncorn subsistence needs. Thus, even in a situation where labour inputs would be the same, such as 0.125 hectare (1 plot) under pot irrigation and 1.75 hectares under corn compared with 0.25 hectare (2 plots) under pot irrigation only, the solution which uses more of the land and grows corn is the preferred one. Even where cash-crop production is in the hands of individual households, peasant agriculturalists appear to achieve satisfaction in a similar manner to the way in which they achieved it in their subsistence agriculture—by underutilising their labour resources rather than their land resources. However, the increasing commercialism of some irrigators indicates that these attitudes are undergoing change at the present time.

## PRE-CONQUEST IRRIGATION IN THE VALLEY

### Archaeological Evidence

Canal irrigation was widely known in Mesoamerica before the Conquest (see, for example, the spectacular system of Tetzcutzingo near Mexico City described by Wolf and Palerm, 1955). It has been practised in Oaxaca at least since early Monte Albán I times. During this period (450 to 200 B.C.) for the first time many villages were located in the piedmont zone in sites where they could have controlled water coming from the perennial mountain streams that are used for irrigation today. Indeed, the principal advantage of many of these village sites seems to be their ability to control water since they are not related to good agricultural land or to known mineral resources.

More direct evidence of canal irrigation comes from Hierve el Agua, a site located just outside the Atoyac drainage basin 20 kilometers east of Mitla. The site contains a well-integrated canal distributary system served by spring water with a high content of calcium carbonate and magnesium. The deposition of travertine over the canal network has preserved the entire system including canals, agricultural terraces and tanks that were probably used to store and/or settle the water. The earliest use of the system appears to have been from $420 \pm 140$ to $310 \pm 150$ B.C. according to radiocarbon dates obtained from the terraces (Flannery, personal communication). Hierve el Agua is the most complete early terraced irrigation site known so far in Mesoamerica. It is located in a spectacular position on the upper part of a cliff 30 meters high and with a gradient of 70 degrees.

It is of particular interest to this discussion because along many of the lateral canals supplying individual terraces are steep-sided circular basins cut into the bed of the canal and spaced at roughly regular intervals of 3.25 meters (Fig. 46). Although their original dimensions were probably larger, to judge from the deposition of travertine within them, their present dimensions average 17 cm in diameter and 10 cm deep. The purpose of these circular basins or *pocitos* is not known (Neely, 1967), but it is considered likely by the present author that they were used for pot irrigation. This view is supported by ethnographic evidence of a similar practice in the Valley today. In one example seen in the Zaachila Valley, the water was distributed through the field in an E-shaped canal system; and along each arm of the system, spaced 3 to 4 meters apart, were basins (cut into the earth canals) which were 50 cm in diameter and 30 to 40 cm deep. The rest of the field was laid out in circular hollows, each of which contained one tomato plant. When the canals were filled, water was taken from the nearest canal basin in a pot to each plant in the same way that has been described for pot irrigation (Chapter IV). This laborious method was used only when the plants were young and most vulnerable to drought. Later the field layout was converted to furrows and irrigation was effected along them.

Such a sequence of water use might have been practised at Hierve el Agua. The use of pot

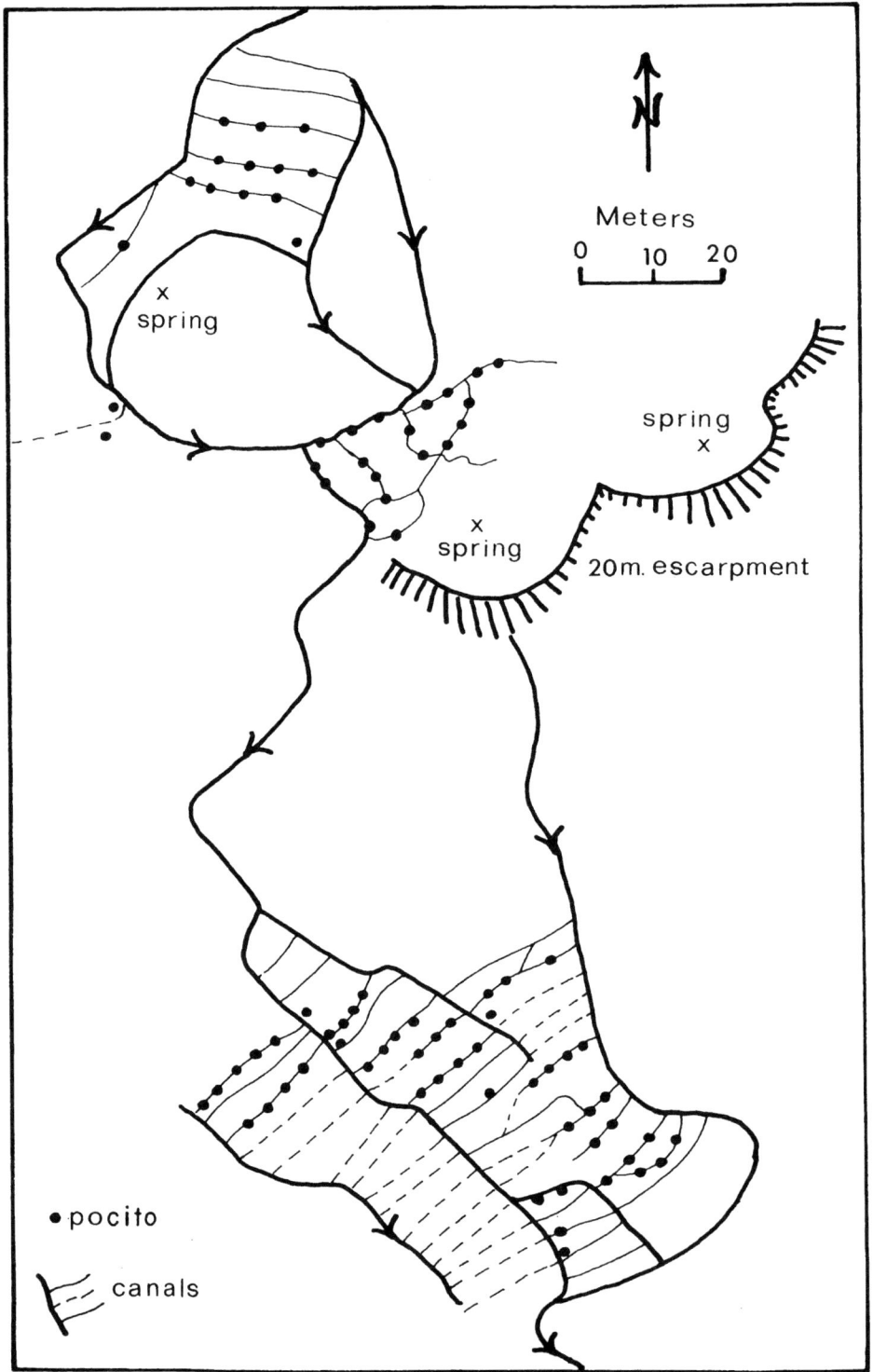

Fig. 46. Map of part of archaeological canal system at Hierve el Agua showing distribution of pocitos, possible pot irrigation basins.

irrigation at all stages of plant growth would have had advantages in economy of applied water. This may have been critical at Hierve el Agua because present indications suggest that water supply there has always been small. Present water supply for the uppermost terraced area of about 1 hectare is only 2 liters per second during the summer months. In addition, pot irrigation directly on to each plant would be more efficient with water, and perhaps more likely, than either basin flooding (which requires more water) or row irrigation which requires furrows. These furrows would have to have been specially made since coa cultivation in the Valley today results in a pock-marked surface rather than furrows (Pl. 5), and ploughs are unknown for the pre-Conquest period (Weatherwax, 1954:18, Figs. 5, 6).

Hierve el Agua represents the best evidence we have for pre-Conquest canal irrigation and, the author thinks, for canal and pot irrigation. More definite evidence of the use of wells is known from Mitla where a well was exposed in a river bank dating from the late Guadalupe phase (500 B.C.) (Orlandini, 1967). Wells have also been discovered in the San José phase site excavated at San Sebastián Abasolo and dating from 900 B.C. (Flannery, 1969:70-78). The evidence from these sites shows only that wells were used as a means of obtaining water, not necessarily that the water was used for irrigation. It is known, however, that both well and pot irrigation could have been practised by 400 B.C., and it is likely that irrigation has formed an integral part of agriculture and settlement expansion since the Formative period.

## Present Land Use Evidence

From the description of techniques in Chapter IV it is clear that canal irrigation, as practised today, does not depend on anything more than the simplest technology. All of the perennial streams can be diverted by means of a brush and earth toma which can be built each year in one day of collective labour. Canals are invariably made of earth and are unlined; once built they require less than a week of collective village labour (tequio), involving only 20 to 50 men, to maintain them. The technology and degree of organisation required to canal irrigate on the present-day scale are both within the reach of small sedentary agricultural groups living in communities of 200-500 people. There is no technological or manpower reason why present day canal irrigation schemes could not have been operated in the Formative period.

Although the principal canal-irrigated crops in post-Conquest and modern times—wheat and alfalfa—were not available before the Conquest, the basic pattern of land use was not necessarily different from today. No new techniques are practised, and water is distributed in uneconomic small units to individuals with several fragmented parcels. Fields are generally unterraced and surrounded by simple earth ditches, and control is held at a community level. The canal-irrigated areas around the margins of the valley floor complement the high water table land in the centre and could have formed a second important corn-producing zone of the Valley to support the pre-Conquest cities. Since the form of water control today and its relationship to state authority, together with its implications for social organisation in the past, are discussed for the Valley of Oaxaca by Lees (1973), this discussion concentrates on evaluating the present pattern of pot irrigation in terms of its feasibility in the past (see also Sanders, 1968, and Steward, 1955, for more general discussions).

Pot irrigation today demands high labour and high manure input. The general level of nutrients in the desert soils of the valley floor is so low that manure is critical to the production of vegetables such as tomatoes, garlic and chile. Today oxen and dairy cows provide the bulk of this manure, and almost all pot-irrigating households either own or have access to manure-producing animals or can afford to buy fertilizer. One cow produces 3 kilos of manure per day, or 1 ton per year, which is enough to manure about 0.063 hectare for pot irrigation. Thus, each plot of 0.125 hectares requires the manure from 2 cows or oxen. Since the preferred diet for these animals includes a high proportion of alfalfa, there is generally a rough correspondence between the amount of alfalfa that can be grown (this means the amount of canal- or pump-irrigated or de humedad land) and the number of animals kept: 1 hectare of alfalfa to support 2 cows. Where alfalfa can be produced, as in Abasolo, because of the high water table, manure rather than bought chemical fertilizer is used. In San Antonino and Zaachila where the areas under alfalfa are 1 percent and less than 7 percent respectively, chemical fertilizer is more widely used.

If we consider the situation in pre-Conquest times when large, manure-producing animals did not exist, the area that could have been pot irrigated in any one village must have been much smaller since the amount of manure that would have been available would have been only that produced by the human population itself. Assuming, for the purposes of analysis, that human manure (night soil) was used, the maximum area that could have produced intensively grown vegetables per head of population during the pre-Conquest period can be delimited. From the distribution of household compositions today, and assuming that manure productivity is related to food intake (such that women represent 0.7 of an adult male unit, and children under 14 years represent 0.5) an average household's manure productivity can be approximated at 1.5 kilos per day or 0.5 metric tons per year. On this basis, one family could provide sufficient manure for 0.04 hectare or 400 square meters, or between an eighth and a quarter of what they pot irrigate today. This is assuming that the beneficial properties of night soil roughly correspond with cow manure and that household composition and manure productivity were approximately the same in pre-Conquest times as now—all of which assumptions provide sources of error. The benefits of manuring soil were known however in the pre-Conquest period; this was practised on the *chinampas* or floating gardens in the Valley of Mexico, and bat guano from Oaxacan caves was applied to tomato fields until recently (Flannery, personal communication).

The land use pattern that would have resulted from this manure limitation would almost certainly have been much more dispersed throughout the Valley than it is today unless human manure was moved from one settlement to another, a practice which is extremely unlikely. The more likely pattern is that each community, and probably even each household, was using its own night soil to grow vegetables. The pattern is therefore one of horticulture or gardens close to the house which were characteristic of each village and each household. Such a land use pattern would mean that high value crops were manured easily by people living in the house, could be harvested over several weeks according to the household's needs, and could be irrigated from the well supplying domestic water and also from domestic waste water. Pot irrigation as a means of intensive vegetable production is therefore seen as beginning as a form of gardening with each village essentially supplying its own needs. The present production of vegetables is very far from this pattern because a very few villages supply all the others, and vegetables are rarely grown by households in their solar.

It is possible therefore that the present concentration of vegetable production and pot irrigation has evolved from a pre-Conquest pattern that was widely dispersed throughout the valley floor. If this concentration is seen as a continuous process through time, it must have been speeded up after the Conquest when animal manure first became available; but increased specialisation may also have been a feature of pre-Conquest pot irrigating villages. One household today could produce more than its own vegetable needs from 400 square meters under continuous pot irrigation so that villages more advantageously situated would probably have begun to produce vegetables for sale outside the village. Those villages specialising in pot irrigation would have been those located on or close to the alluvium where the water table was high, assuming that this was a more important location factor in the absence of present-day marketing and trucking arrangements.

The problem is to see how the likely pre-Conquest pattern of dispersed garden plots evolved into the present concentration of truck farming in a few areas. In the absence of direct evidence, it can only be speculated that such an evolution was a continuous process through pre- and post-Conquest times, and probably operated along the following two directions.

1) From a pattern of self-sufficiency in vegetable production for most villages on the valley floor to a specialist occupation for less than ten villages. This trend probably occurred at the same time as the development of a peasant market network and is but one aspect of the total cultural evolution of the Valley. At first the valley floor villages probably supplied themselves and had sufficient surplus to export to the mountain villages, but by late pre-Conquest times pot irrigation could have become sufficiently concentrated for one village in every three or four to specialise in it.

2) A movement of pot irrigation out of the confines of the solar or house-plot into the village fields. As each household increased its pot irrigation plot to the maximum it could provide manure for, hauling the amount of water needed would have required more effort than the transport of manure out to the fields. Therefore a rationalisation of land use would have been to move the plot to where the water was most easily available; since most houses are built on piedmont to avoid a high water table, this would mean going to the alluvial fields surrounding the village site. Such a relocation of high value garden plots beyond the protection afforded by proximity to houses would require some measure of guarantee against losses through theft and vandalism, and implies at least a village authority and probably even a supravillage or intervillage guarantee of protection of rights. Under this system, one would expect an infield-outfield pattern to emerge with high-value pot-irrigation crops grown close to the village and dry-farmed corn grown farther away.

The two land use patterns for pre-Conquest times and for today differ in two respects—the dispersion of the earlier pattern throughout many villages and the earlier infield-outfield structure. The greater concentration today can be explained in terms of greater concentration of manure and chemical fertilizer, but it is difficult to see why today's plots should be so scattered (rather than infield-outfield) unless pot irrigation today is not necessarily a very old form of land use. In other words, pot irrigation and its association with intensive vegetable production may have cultural continuity for the Valley but not *necessarily* for individual communities.

If we take as one example Zaachila, which is almost a type example of a pot-irrigating village focused on a market centre, there are several anomalies about the land use pattern. It is not particularly related to differences in depth to water table, distance to roads, or soil texture—any one of which might be expected to be a factor in plot location. Today it is hard to avoid exaggerating the areal importance of pot irrigation because the well-laid-out plots and their picturesque method of irrigation tend to dominate the landscape out of all proportion to their real percentage of the area. Yet the *Relación* of Zaachila for 1580, in answer to the specific question concerning the existence of any irrigation, reports that there was none, only dry farming, at the same time commenting on a water table high enough to form a swamp in some localities (Paso y Troncoso, 1905:191). Despite the problems associated with the use of old documents for geographical description, it seems unlikely, if pot irrigation was a specialist occupation of Zaachila at that time, that it would not have been mentioned. It is reasonable to conclude that either pot irrigation was so common (that is, in almost every village) that it was not considered special enough to comment on, or it was not practised in Zaachila at that time. That there was, in any case, a break in pot irrigation at Zaachila is shown by the fact that a sugar-cane-producing hacienda occupied the area now pot irrigated until about 1940—the old irrigation ditches can still be seen. In this one area, therefore, there is reason to believe that the anomalous scattered and shifting pot-irrigation pattern is a function of it being *locally* a new form of land use. Likewise, the present *concentration* of pot irrigation in San Antonino (though not its origin) is said to date from about 1930 when, under the leadership of one family, the village began to specialise in flowers for export to Mexico City.

If the scattered distribution of irrigated plots is a function of the short time they have existed in their present areas, a pattern of concentration should emerge as land tenure distribution is rationalised through the process of inheritance, to adjust to the new land use which creates its own patterns of desirable and less desirable land. Since in San Antonino land is said to be inherited through sale by the father during his lifetime rather than as a gift only to his sons on his death, this rationalisation process might take place more quickly there. As far as the author knows, no studies have been made in these types of communities of the time required for inheritance to rationalise a sudden imbalance in agricultural land values created by, for example, a new irrigation project or new road. We can, however, conclude here that there is evidence to show that the present pattern of pot irrigation and vegetable production is more concentrated than was possible in pre-Conquest times and that the villages practising it today are not necessarily those that practised it during the pre-Conquest period. The *Relaciónes* of 1579-1581 provide some supporting evidence in that they mention vegetables as being grown in more villages than they are today (Paso y Troncoso, 1905). There is thus some reason to be wary of simply translating present patterns of land use into the past, however traditional the agricultural practices may appear.

# VIII

# PREHISTORIC AGRICULTURE AND POPULATION

## INTRODUCTION

In the absence of direct evidence for prehistoric agriculture and population in the Valley such as contemporary records and maps, indirect methods must be used. This study incorporates two such methods to estimate prehistoric population patterns: the evidence of archaeological sites that remain today and the projection of present population and agriculture back into the past. Both methods involve difficulties in obtaining data and in data interpretation. The purpose of this chapter is to present both sets of evidence and to compare them. Since the projected populations and settlement patterns are based on the present, the difference between the projected and the archaeological evidence is taken as some indication of how far population and agriculture in the past differed from those of today. Ultimately the question we are trying to answer here is, "If the Valley of Oaxaca, in terms of its land and labour resources, is being underused today, how far was the Valley an underused agricultural resource in the past?"

The problems of the survey and interpretation of archaeological sites will not be fully discussed here since the archaeological data are not the author's own. In this chapter, we will be using data on 274 archaeological sites recovered by Dr. Ignacio Bernal (personal communication), added to and partly re-surveyed by Flannery. These sites will ultimately be added to and published by Bernal, Richard Blanton, Dudley Varner, Flannery, and others. Briefly, the problems of archaeological survey which affect the interpretation for population densities and distribution are:

1) The proportion of the total number of sites that are being recovered in a survey. Any approach to the total number of remaining sites will require an intensive survey taking many man-hours to walk every field such as that carried out by Parsons in the Valley of Texcoco near Mexico City (1968). Such a survey has been started for the Valley of Oaxaca by Richard Blanton and Dudley Varner, but will take years to complete. In the meantime, Flannery has supervised intensive surveys in selected sample areas to determine the proportions of total sites that may have been recovered by Dr. Bernal's more extensive methods. His results so far suggest it is very unlikely that Dr. Bernal overlooked any large sites, although some small sites may have been missed (Flannery, personal communication).

2) Areal differences in the effectiveness of a survey, that is, in the proportion of the total population of sites that is discovered. In the Valley of Oaxaca these differences arise principally through differences in the amount of later alluviation; in the type of terrain (hilltop sites being particularly conspicuous from a distance); in land use, especially the planting of tall or dense crops (such as corn, sugar cane or alfalfa); and in the intensity of later cultural activity such as house-building. In addition there are problems associated with the practical survey itself, such as the difficulties of walking through fields at certain times—after rain or irrigation or when the plants are mature. Likewise the degree to which sherds can be seen varies from site to site on the same site from week to week as ground conditions change.

3) The criteria used for the designation of a site and an estimation of its size. The date and size of a site is determined from an analysis of the surface material recovered by the survey, but since fields or temporarily occupied huts may also be represented by sherd scatters, some criteria must be used to distinguish a permanent settlement. Standard procedures for this have now been worked out by Blanton and Varner, and will be reported in the future.
4) The interpretation of a site in terms of population at any period in time. This is an extremely difficult problem which can only be solved numerically by excavation to determine the number of houses per unit area as has been done by Flannery and Winter in the Valley of Oaxaca (1969).

Although these problems all apply to the archaeological data for the Valley of Oaxaca, by the use of intensive sample surveys and associated excavation Flannery has tried to minimise them, and for the two earliest periods with which this paper is concerned (1300 and 1000 B.C.) special attention has been given to areal differences in survey efficiency and to determining the number of households per unit area of surface site. For the purposes of this chapter, therefore, and keeping the problems of archaeological data in mind, Dr. Ignacio Bernal's survey will be used, and the number of sites he or Flannery recovered for each period in the Valley will be considered to *approximate the pattern* of the real number of former settlements.

## LAND USE MODEL OF PREHISTORIC AGRICULTURE AND SETTLEMENT

The independent approach to the study of *past* population and agriculture which will be described here in detail is based on the study of *present* land use which has formed the basis of this paper. In earlier chapters it was shown that agriculture in the Valley is first and foremost the cultivation of corn for subsistence, and that in terms of yield per unit area, corn productivity is primarily a function of water availability. A further relationship can also be established, that between corn production for different parts of the valley and local present population density (Fig. 47). The existence of such a degree of correspondence between corn yield and population is surprising today with the increasing effects of outside markets, commerce and industry. It serves to show that the traditional pattern of subsistence agriculture based on a village-centered society is still one of the main determinants of where people live in the Valley. On the evidence of Figure 47 it is also reasonable to assume that the degree of interference from external factors was no greater in the past than in the present so that in prehistoric periods local population density can be assumed to have been related to local agricultural production.

A second reason why reconstruction of prehistoric agriculture and settlement patterns is considered feasible for the Valley is the data available on pre-Conquest corn cob sizes from the neighbouring Valley of Tehuacán and from dry caves near Mitla. The corn cobs recovered during archaeological excavations by members of the Tehuacán Project directed by Dr. Richard S. MacNeish are particularly valuable since they provide a record of increasing cob size, and hence increasing corn yield per plant, from circa 4000 B.C. (Mangelsdorf, MacNeish and Galinat, 1964; 1967:178-200). From the data they present, a curve of increasing cob size at different archaeological periods can be drawn (Fig. 48a). Present corn yields from different types of land and from different parts of the valley are calibrated on the basis of this curve to determine what corn yields would have been at various times in the past (assuming little or no difference in early corn races between Tehuacán and Oaxaca). The relationship between cob length and yield of seed established by the author for present corn cobs is shown in Figure 48b.

The expansion of agricultural land use and settlement over time is examined at five periods: 1300 B.C. (Tierras Largas phase), 1000 B.C. (San José phase), 300-1 B.C. (Monte Albán I); A.D. 900 (Monte Albán IIIB-IV) and A.D. 1970 or the present. The area of agricultural land and the density of population for each period, together with the distribution of archaeological sites, are shown in Figures 49 to 53. The construction of these maps involved four main steps:

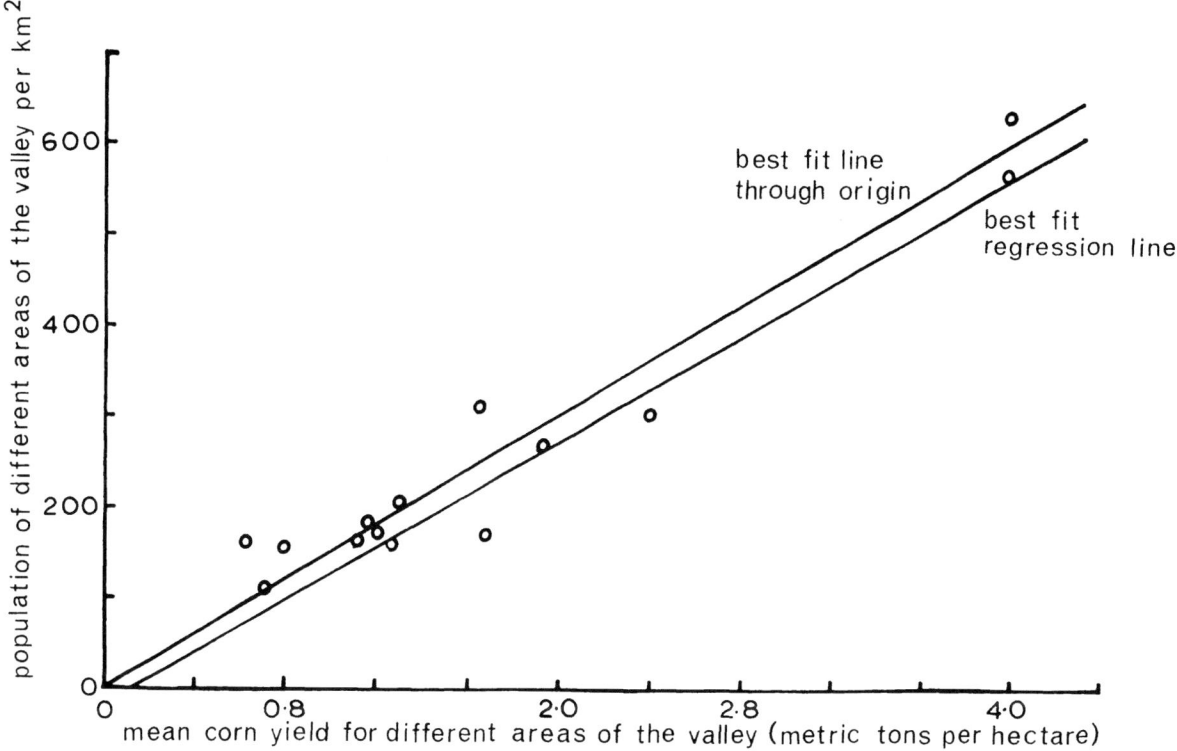

Fig. 47. Relationship between present mean corn yield per hectare and population in 1960 for different parts of the Valley.

1) Areal differences in present corn yield have been established by field measurement and are shown in Figure 25. These present yields are calibrated by means of Figure 48a to give the yields that would have been obtained in that area at each of the time periods considered. Where the calibrated yield falls below 200 kilos per hectare, the area is considered to have been uncultivated at that time. For each period, therefore, the agricultural land is assumed to have been the area which would have yielded at least 200 kilos per hectare at that time.

2) For each area of the Valley (n = 12) the total corn yield from the agricultural land (as defined above) is calculated for each time period. This total figure is used to determine the population which could have been supported in each area of the valley at different times.

3) On the basis of the graph in Figure 47, the relationship of present population to present corn yield is 3 persons to 2 metric tons per annum. When the present population of Oaxaca de Juárez is included, the number of persons supported by 2 metric tons is increased to 4.2. The figure of 4.2 persons to 2 metric tons per annum is therefore taken as the basis for calculating the population of areas of the Valley at different times.

4) Present mean settlement size on the basis of the 1960 Oaxaca State Census is 1000 population, so that one dot on the maps has been drawn to represent one settlement or 1000 people for the purposes of comparison. (This arbitrary figure is, of course, much higher than the actual populations of the Early Formative sites as revealed by excavation.) The number of dots is determined as described in 3) above and their location within each area is determined by the locations of optimum sites available in relation to the most productive agricultural land at each period. It is obviously easier by this method to determine the prime agricultural locations which would be likely to have been first occupied than to decide which of a number of second-best sites would have been selected at later times.

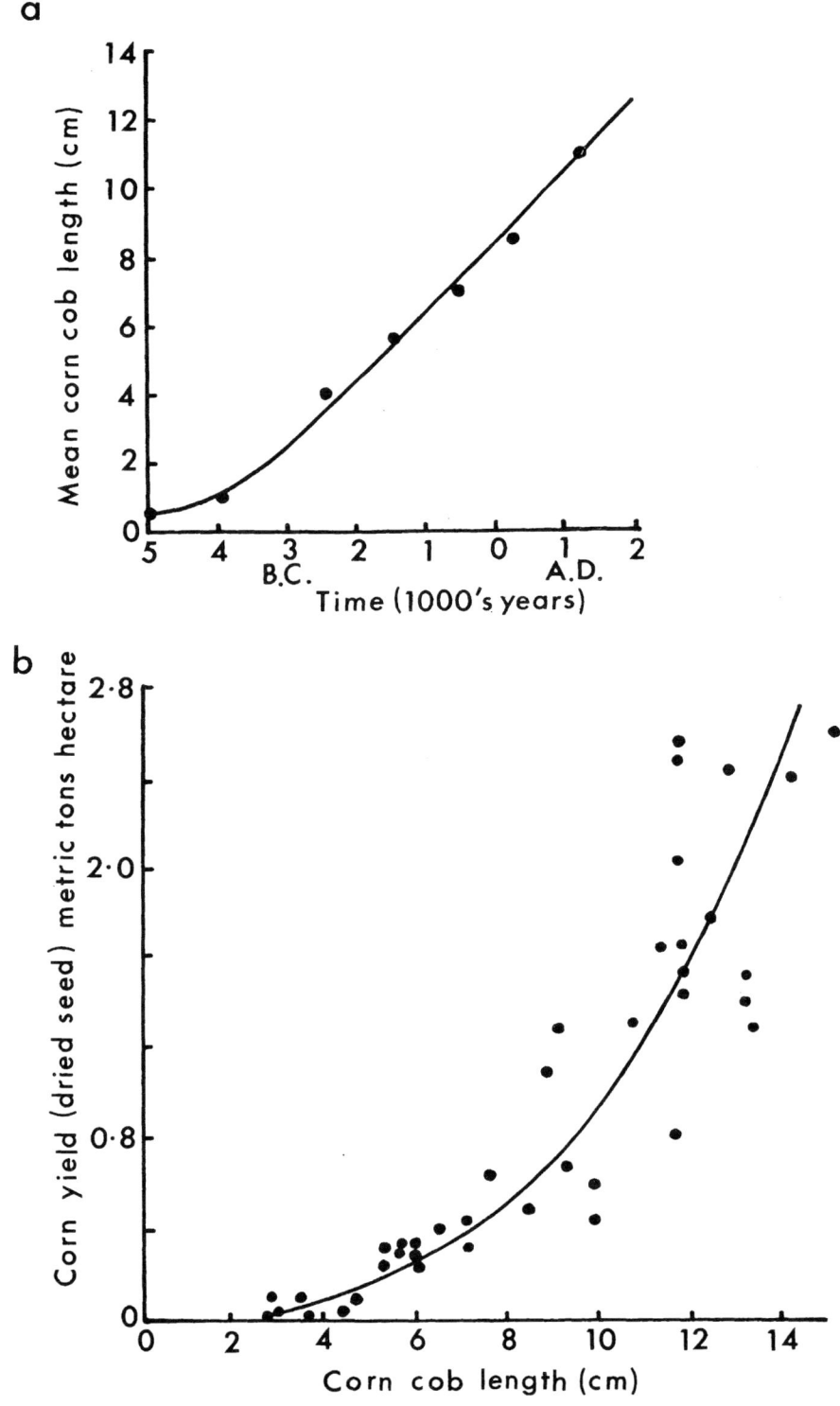

Fig. 48. (*a*) Increase in mean corn cob length through time, 5000 B.C. to the present. (*b*) Mean corn yield per hectare (in metric tons of dried seed) for different lengths of corn cobs measured in the Valley of Oaxaca.

Reconstructions of settlement patterns such as the ones considered here have inherent rigidity because once the initial network is established, succeeding networks are patterned on it. Thus the siting of an initial settlement makes sites immediately around it with similar advantages less favourable simply because they are too close to the first site, and these sites are likely to be occupied only when later infilling of the network occurs. Reconstruction of past settlement patterns can also be no more precise than predicting the most likely locality for a site rather than its specific location, because usually an agriculturally productive area can be controlled from any of several specific sites. Nevertheless, the advantages of certain sites such as Monte Albán itself, and Santa Ana Tlapacoyan are so outstanding that their importance as archaeological sites can be easily predicted within the terms of the reconstruction model described here.

This projection of present corn yield and settlement pattern into the past involves several assumptions which should be clearly stated at the outset. These assumptions can be divided into two groups: those concerning the area cultivated at each point in time and those involved in calculating the population and settlement distribution.

Land Use Assumptions

1) Land yielding less than 200 kilos of corn per hectare at any time was not cultivated.

Present cultivators do not consider it worthwhile to grow corn on land giving a mean yield (including an average of 30 percent fallow) of less than about 200 kilos per hectare. In the Valley of Oaxaca and elsewhere (see especially Hill, 1964, on Chiapas), labour requirements per hectare, especially at weeding and harvesting times, limit the area a family can cultivate to a maximum of 8 hectares. Nutritional calculations suggest that in order to provide 3200 calories per person per day (this amount to provide food and enough left over to exchange for other goods and food), a family of five must grow at least 2.4 metric tons of corn per annum. Since labour requirements limit their workable area to about 8 hectares, they must obtain a minimum corn yield of 200 kilos per hectare from all their land including fallow.

2) All yields and the distinctions made between qualities of agricultural land refer only to corn production.

This assumption is simply a convenient means of simplifying the calculations necessary and is not critical since corn is here used as a basis for exchange. It is valid to say that an area capable of producing a mean corn yield of 2 metric tons per annum can support about twice as many people as an area producing only 1 metric ton a year on average, whether that area actually produced all corn or a combination of corn, cotton and chile, the latter two crops being exchanged for more corn or other goods.

3) The distribution of corn yield among different parts of the Valley has remained essentially unchanged.

This assumption is more difficult to justify and more critical to the argument because corn yield is closely related to water availability (Tables 3-7), and it follows that water availability has also not changed in its distribution through time. The three factors most affecting water availability in the Valley are rainfall, fluvial activity and water use techniques. Of these factors, rainfall appears to have had least effect in changing the *distribution* of the best agricultural land although it may have expanded or decreased the cultivable area in total. From the evidence of pollen analyses, the differential in rainfall among the three arms of the Valley appears to have been maintained during minor fluctuations in moisture availability so that all parts of the valley floor underwent synchronous changes in rainfall (Schoenwetter, Kirkby and Kirkby, 1967).

Reconstruction of past agricultural area also assumes that the distribution of water use techniques has been the same as today since 1300 B.C., although there is no evidence that canal irrigation was practised much before Monte Albán I times (300-1 B.C.) or pot irrigation before 1000 B.C. However, the cultivated land at the two earliest periods considered (1300 B.C. and 1000 B.C.) was mainly that which is underlain by a high water table so that no irrigation techniques would have been necessary to make it productive. The remaining parts of the reconstructed cultivated areas at 1300 and 1000 B.C. are those near streams amenable to being diverted onto fields using the simplest of floodwater techniques, which are considered quite feasible for cultivators at those periods. Sources of error are most likely in the tributary Etla Valleys where present productivity relies on piedmont ridge canal systems.

The major source of difficulty in any assumption that the distribution of water availability has remained unchanged through time is the reconstruction of the alluvial history of the area. This is fully discussed by M. J. Kirkby (1973) who has discovered major changes of river level throughout the time period considered here. From about 800 B.C. to A.D. 1500, there appears to have been a phase of alluviation which ended at about the time of the Spanish Conquest (although it continued near Huitzo in the Etla Valley until A.D. 1700). Alluviation was followed by rapid downcutting and entrenchment of the main streams into the alluvial valley floor, a process which appears to be continuing at the present time. Such entrenchment inevitably entails a decrease in the area that can be floodwater farmed using simple techniques and a decline in the area underlain by a high water table.

Bryan (1925; Albritten and Bryan, 1939) and Hack (1942) have discussed the effects of stream entrenchment and changes in alluviation patterns on the distribution of productive farmland and the feasibility of floodwater farming in the southwestern United States. A similar process probably occurred in the Valley of Oaxaca at the time of the Spanish Conquest. Together with the cultural revolution consequent on the Conquest, agriculture, especially in the Zaachila Valley where entrenchment appears to have taken place first, probably changed from intensive cultivation of crops using pot irrigation and floodwater farming to extensive grazing of newly introduced animals over large areas.

Throughout most of the period which is considered here, however, the main streams appear to have been alluviating with a consequent building up of the alluvial valley floor. The effect of an alluviating main stream on land use and settlement would probably be to move the most productive land out from the centre of the valley towards the margins of the valley floor, and likewise move the villages. Close to the river it is likely that fields would be too often flooded to be productive except for any levees which may have existed, since these would remain both well-drained and well-watered. Alluviating conditions which may be similar to those of the past can be found today in the central Tlacolula Valley. The pattern of land use and settlement in this area is to avoid the area within and immediately around the braided system of the Río Salado which is too frequently flooded to be cultivable (for example, see Appendix III). The most productive land is the high water table area around the margins of the flooded zone (for example, the San Sebastián Abasolo area), where floodwater from tributary streams can be easily managed and diverted onto fields to supplement moisture from the water table.

Shifting of the most productive zone away from the main stream in earlier periods is most likely to have been important in the Zaachila Valley, where a higher proportion of the most-valued land is dependent on the Río Atoyac rather than on smaller tributaries for water; conversely, this would have been least important in the Etla Valley. The Zaachila Valley, therefore, presents particular problems both for the reconstruction of former land use and settlement and for the survey of archaeological sites, since many of those located on the valley floor may have been obliterated by later sedimentation.

Population and Settlement Assumptions

1) The population is close to a maximum for the total possible corn yield at each time period.

This assumption, together with similar assumptions about the constancy of the amount of corn needed to support each family now and in the past and about family size in all periods, is simply a basis for argument, to enable some reconstruction to be made. It serves as a point of reference against which the archaeological data can be compared and is not considered to represent real population levels. (Indeed, it is clear that population never reached the maximum theoretically possible.)

2) All factors other than those generated by corn production are ignored.

This is again a simplifying assumption made for the purposes of analysis. It means that reconstruction is based on a theoretical 100 percent dependence on corn production and enables us to see how far the archaeological data deviate from these theoretical conditions. In particular, this assumption of total dependence of settlement and population on corn emphasises the nonagricultural settlements which show up as anomalous sites in comparing archaeological to predicted site locations. Two other important factors have been ignored here. They are:

a) other sources of food, particularly hunting and gathering. These are probably most influential at the earliest periods and in the Zaachila Valley, which is wide enough for distance from mountain hunting grounds to become a factor in the siting of settlements.

b) links with areas outside the Valley. In the model, the Valley is considered as a closed system, whereas trade and other cultural links with outside areas were important from the earliest times. Sites such as Mitla in the Tlacolula Valley and San Felipe Telixtlahuaca in the Etla Valley, which have little agricultural value but are located on important routes into the Valley, are therefore underestimated.

3) The development of central places.

The settlement hierarchy developed in the reconstruction model is extremely simple and is based on central places being centres of gravity within the settlement pattern. This is relevant to a marketing system although it does not take into account political factors or even differences in crop specialisations. It simply indicates those settlements which were likely to become important by virtue of their convenient location with respect to other villages. In order to simulate the growth of the central place and to conform with the present pattern of the increase in population from all parts of the Valley, the central place has been allowed to have absorbed 0 at 1300 B.C. and 1000 B.C.; 1 in 10 at 300-1 B.C.; 1 in 8 at A.D. 900; and 1 in 4 at A.D. 1970. Since the Valley is physically divided into three components, one for each arm of the Valley, second order central places have been denoted which act in the model as regional centres for surrounding settlements. The number of satellite settlements per second order central place is found to increase through time from less than 10 at 1000 B.C. to 20 at A.D. 1500 and 35 to 40 at A.D. 1970 (the last figure being an actual as well as a theoretical one).

## STAGES OF DEVELOPMENT

### Stage I–1300 B.C.

Figure 49 shows the distribution of land capable of giving a mean corn yield of more than 200 kilos per hectare in 1300 B.C. and the twelve theoretical settlements of 1000 persons each that could have been supported by this agricultural land. Both the land and settlements are concentrated in the Etla and Zaachila Valleys, leaving the eastern sector of the Tlacolula Valley almost unused agriculturally. The estimated theoretical maximum population at 1300 B.C. would have been about 12,000, and the most favourable settlement sites at this time would have been located near the present towns of San Pablo Huitzo, Reyes Etla, Guadalupe Etla, San Lorenzo Cacaotepec, San Jacinto Amilpas, Monte Albán, Tlalixtac de Cabrera, Cuilapan de Guerrero, east of Zimatlán de Alvarez, Santa Ines Yatzeche, Santa Ana Zegache and Santa Ana Tlapacoyan. Of these twelve settlements which are located in the prime locations in the valley, the centre of gravity is at Monte Albán at the meeting point of the three arms of the valley. The richest sites in terms of surrounding agriculture would, however, have been located farther north at Guadalupe Etla and farther south at Santa Ana Tlapacoyan.

### ARCHAEOLOGICAL EVIDENCE: TIERRAS LARGAS PHASE

Figure 49 also gives the distribution of known sites from the Tierras Largas phase (1300 B.C., Early Formative Period). These sites number 10 (compared with the predicted 12), 7 of which can be considered to correspond to predicted sites.

130

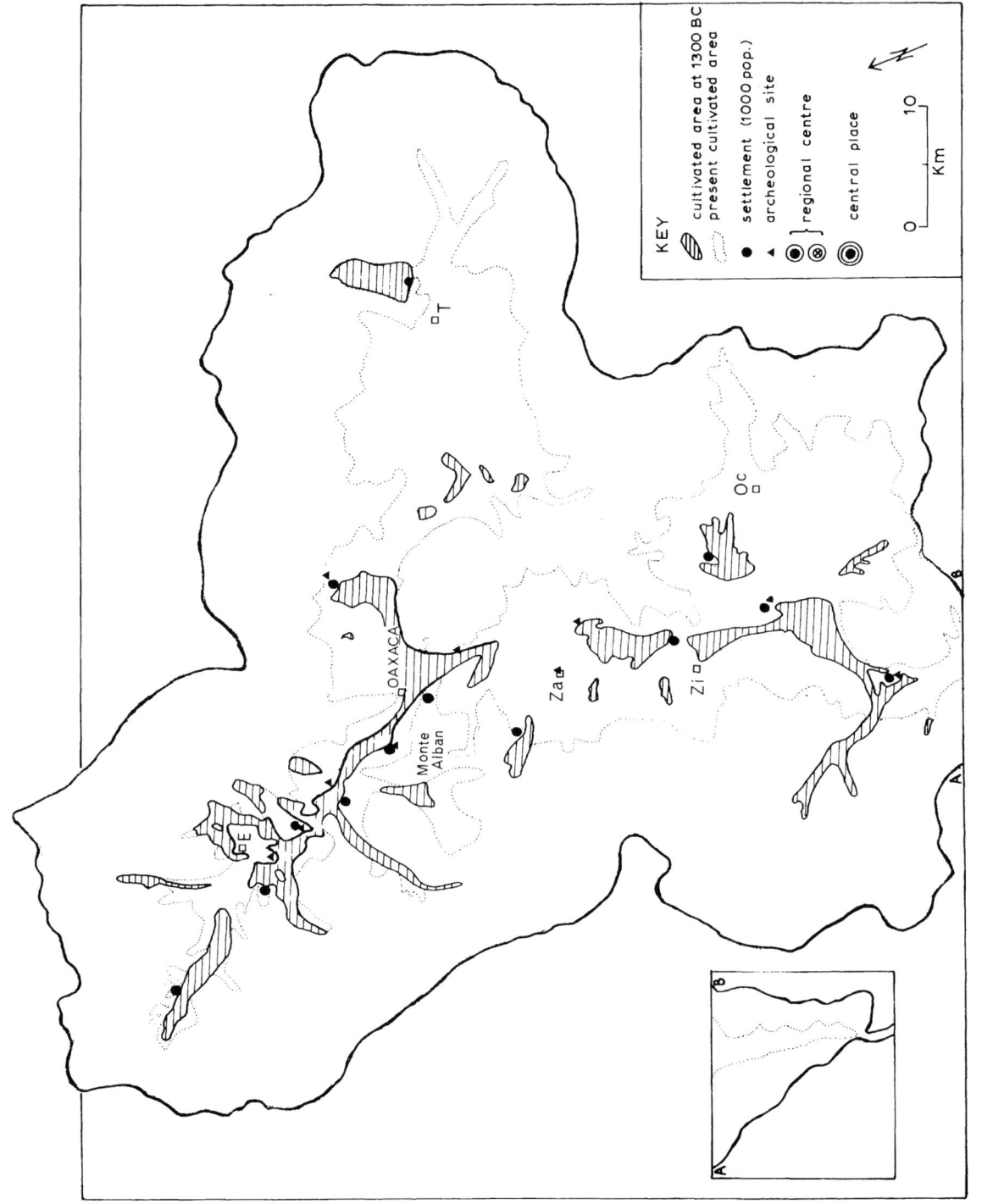

Fig. 49. Predicted area which could have been cultivated, predicted settlement distribution and location of known archaeological sites for 1300 B.C.

The central area around the present city of Oaxaca de Juárez appears to have been controlled from a site to the south, rather than from Monte Albán itself.

The most interesting difference between the reconstructed and the observed archaeological settlement patterns is in the central Zaachila Valley where the archaeological site of Zaachila is not located immediately near any productive land, but is fairly close to another Tierras Largas site near the Río Atoyac at Emiliano Zapata. This early establishment of a site at Zaachila before the land appears to have been productive is especially important in view of the later growth of the site and its eventual elevation to a regional capital. It may have been more productive agriculturally in the past than today, if the Cuilapan stream flowed without interference from diversion works farther across the valley floor to join the Río Atoyac.

The reader should be reminded that our figure of 1000 persons per settlement is one of convenience only; no actual Tierras Largas site so far excavated approached that size (see later discussion).

Stage II—1000 B.C.

Three to five hundred years after the beginning of the Tierras Largas phase, the improvement in strains of corn and cob size (based on Tehuacán data) should have led to a doubling of the cultivated area, thus increasing the population which could be supported to 32,000. This would have changed the ratios of agricultural land between the three valleys by increasing the cultivated area in the Zaachila arm to twice that of the Etla Valley, and enabling the first significant expansion into the Tlacolula arm (Fig. 50). However, the Etla Valley still retained pre-eminence in the proportion of valley floor cultivated and thus in the concentration of highly productive land, both of which are important factors in determining centres of population.

For the first time, regional centres can be designated, though the settlement pattern was still too rudimentary for any real hierarchy to have developed. In the Etla Valley, the richest site and central place coincided at Guadalupe Etla. Increased agricultural productivity in the surrounding area supported two new settlements which were probably subsidiary to Guadalupe or, in any case, would have had very close links since their optimum locations are upstream on the same rivers that flow down to Guadalupe Etla. Similarly, in the Tlacolula arm, increased productivity in the Tlalixtac area should have led to the establishment of a second settlement sharing the water rights to the perennial stream. The agricultural frontier would have moved considerably farther east (with the possible exception of an earlier isolated settlement in the Díaz Ordaz Valley) with villages developing near San Sebastián Abasolo, on the Teitipac stream, and as far as Tlacolula on the Díaz Ordaz stream and Río Salado. Of the seven settlements established by 1000 B.C. in the Tlacolula Valley, the central place would have been at San Sebastián Abasolo, but the idea of a regional centre is scarcely valid for such small numbers. In the southern arm, however, sixteen villages could have been supported at this time, and the central place is at Santa Ines Yatzeche. In a similar manner to the establishment of settlements near Guadalupe Etla, it is expected that one village would be located in the Mixtepec Valley and would thus be upstream of the older community at Santa Ana Tlapacoyan.

ARCHAEOLOGICAL EVIDENCE: SAN JOSÉ PHASE

Figure 50 also shows the distribution of San José phase sites so far known in the valley, which number only 12 compared with the predicted 32. However, all the archaeological sites may be said to correspond with predicted locations, and are sited close to agriculturally productive land at that time. An important new site is located near San Sebastián Abasolo in the Tlacolula Valley, in the same place as that predicted by the model for the regional centre of the eastern arm. Since the Abasolo site was only discovered by searching the bases of wells, it may well be that other sites existed which have been obliterated by later sedimentation. In any case, the number of San José sites known is only a third of the number theoretically possible, especially in the Tlacolula and Zaachila Valleys. This is particularly interesting because in the previous Tierras Largas phase only 12 sites were predicted and 10 archaeological

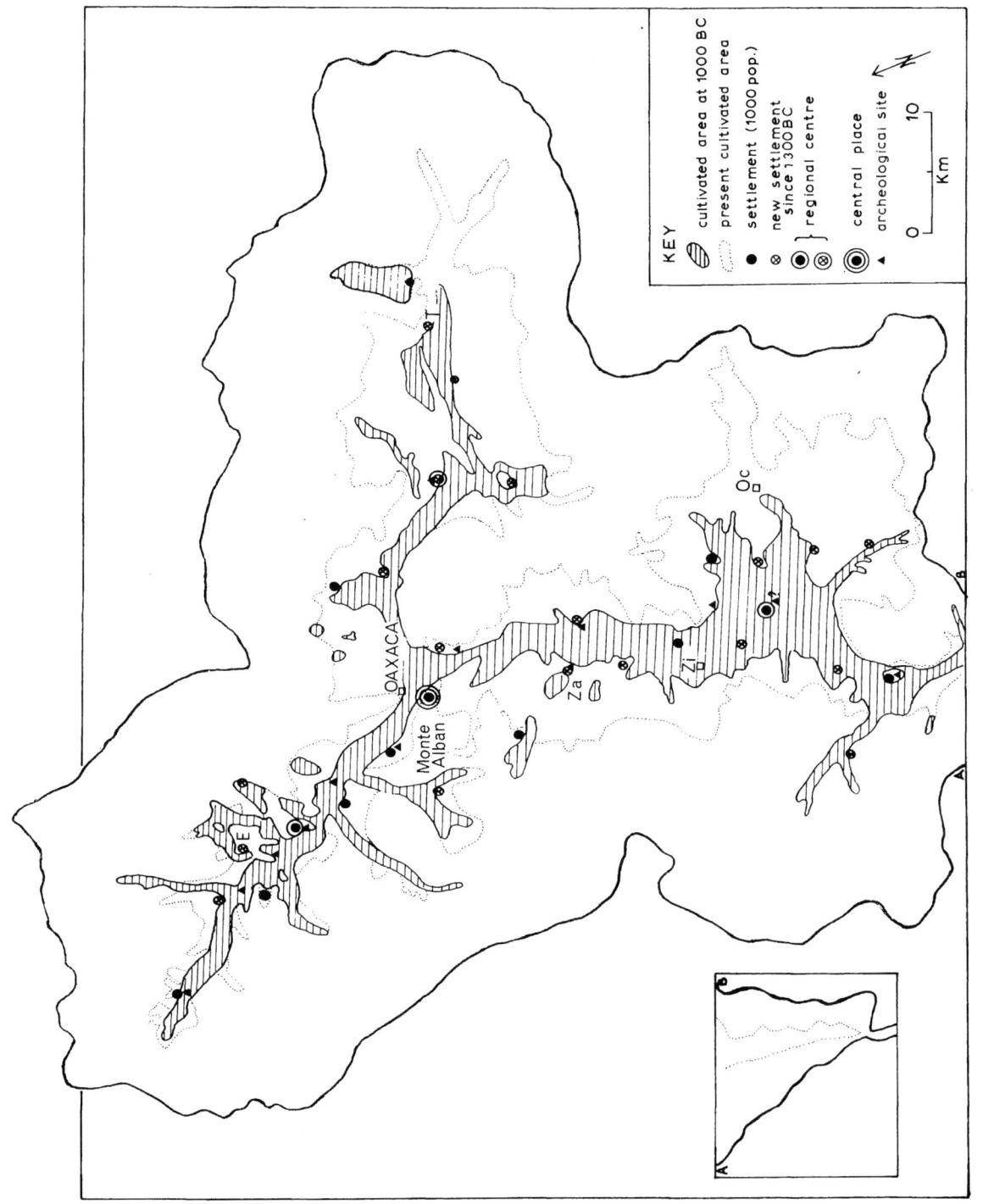

Fig. 50. Predicted area which could have been cultivated, predicted settlement distribution and location of known archaeological sites for 1000 B.C.

sites have been found, even though the Tierras Largas ceramic diagnostics have been recognised for a shorter time than the San José diagnostics, and are presumably more subject to obliteration through deposition and erosion since they are older. The significance of the small number of San José sites will be discussed later in this chapter.[1]

The site of San José Mogote itself is the same as the predicted regional centre at Guadalupe Etla, but there appear to be no subsidiary archaeological sites in the tributary valleys close to San José as predicted. This may indicate that at this time these valleys were relatively less productive than they are today, that is, that canal irrigation as opposed to simple stream diversion was not practised extensively in San José times, although experiments with irrigation may well have been initiated. Such a hypothesis may also be supported by comparing the reconstructed and archaeological settlement patterns for other parts of the valley; for example, predicted sites at Cuilapan de Guerrero, in the Mixtepec Valley and near Tlalixtac de Cabrera are all in localities made productive today by canal irrigation and do not appear to have archaeological sites of the San José phase near them. However, not too much can be made of this type of negative evidence.

## Stage III—300-1 B.C.

By this time, increasing corn yields and increasing cultivable area could have enabled the population to expand to 64,000 which is shown in Figure 51 as 64 predicted settlements each with 1000 inhabitants. The main differences between the predicted settlement patterns of Stage II and Stage III are in the expansion of sites into the eastern Tlacolula arm, into all the tributary valleys in the Etla arm and around the margins of the cultivated area in the Zaachila arm. During Stage III for the first time the present marginal agricultural areas of eastern Tlacolula and Ocotlán are theoretically able to support several communities and become settled agricultural zones. This expansion eastward in the Tlacolula Valley does not affect the location of the regional centre which

remains at San Sebastián Abasolo. In the southern arm, 33 settlements are considered possible and 2 regional centres are designated at Santa Ines Yatzeche in the south and at Zaachila farther north. In the Etla Valley the predicted expansion of settlement into the tributary valleys moved the centre of gravity from Guadalupe Etla farther north to the site of the present distrito head and regional market centre of San Pedro y San Pablo Etla. The central place for the whole valley would remain in the locality of Monte Albán.

## ARCHAEOLOGICAL EVIDENCE: MONTE ALBÁN I

The archaeological pattern of settlement differs from the predicted one not so much in the number of settlements (as it did in the previous stage) since the predicted number is 64 and the number of known sites is 66 (Table 21), but in their distribution (Fig. 51). In the model, an expansion into the eastern Tlacolula area was considered possible, but from the evidence of archaeological sites, expansion took place on a wider scale than that predicted. Instead of a few sites located around the agricultural land, archaeological sites are located as far east as Mitla and Matatlán, more than 10 kilometers from the agriculturally productive land. Similarly, archaeological sites have been found along the edge of the mountains in the southern Tlacolula Valley which are also more than 10 kilometers from land which could have been cultivated at that time.

It would appear, therefore, that in this area settlement was responding partly to nonagricultural factors; many of the Monte Albán I sites established there are hilltop administrative centres, and in some cases their locations may have been chosen for defence. Another nonagricultural site is that found between San Marcos Tlapazola and Magdelena Teitipac.

If the archaeological evidence points to greater use of the eastern Tlacolula Valley than predicted from the reconstructed land use, the other predicted area of expansion, the Ocotlán Valley apparently did not seem so attractive to early settlers. Instead of the predicted 8 sites in the area, only 3 archaeological ones are known, and one of these, like its counterparts in the Tlacolula Valley,

---

[1] Three or four additional San José phase sites have been found since this writing, but the total is still far below the predicted 32.

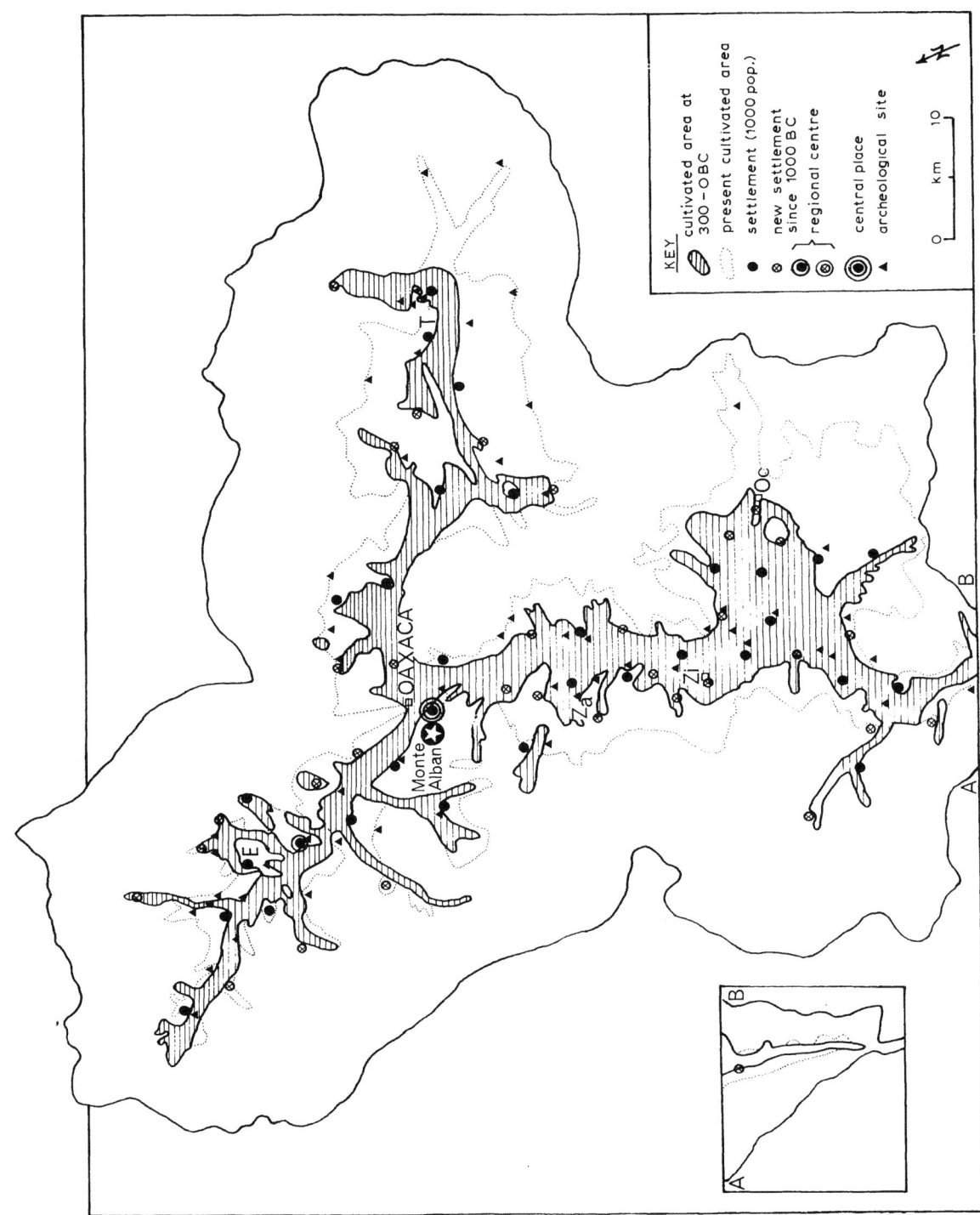

Fig. 51. Predicted area which could have been cultivated, predicted settlement distribution and location of known archaeological sites for 300-1 B.C

TABLE 21

NUMBER OF PREDICTED SITES FROM LAND USE DATA AND KNOWN
ARCHAEOLOGICAL SETTLEMENT SITES FROM 1300 B.C. TO PRESENT

| Date | Number of Predicted and Archaeological Sites | | | | | | | | | | | | | |
|---|---|---|---|---|---|---|---|---|---|---|---|---|---|---|
| | Etla | | West Tlacolula | | East Tlacolula | | Zaachila | | Zimatlán | | Ocotlán | | Totals | |
| | P | A | P | A | P | A | P | A | P | A | P | A | P | A |
| B.C. 1300 | 5 | 4 | 1 | 1 | 1 | 0 | 2 | 2 | 2 | 2 | 1 | 0 | 12 | 9 |
| B.C. 1000 | 9 | 5 | 5 | 1 | 2 | 0 | 6 | 3 | 5 | 2 | 5 | 1 | 32 | 12 |
| B.C. 300-1 | 17 | 18 | 8 | 7 | 6 | 12 | 14 | 15 | 11 | 11 | 8 | 3 | 64 | 66 |
| A.D. 900 | 28 | 30 | 17 | 18 | 7 | 20 | 20 | 20 | 17 | 12 | 18 | 5 | 107 | 105 |
| A.D. 1970 | 47 | 78 | 31 | 34 | 15 | 18 | 37 | 33 | 31 | 30 | 35 | 38 | 196 | 231 |

Note—P = sites predicted from land use data
A = archaeological sites

is located more than 10 kilometers away from cultivable land and was probably connected with mining. Likewise, the Mixtepec Valley, which today is one of the most productive areas of the Valley and according to the reconstructed settlement pattern should have 3 archaeological sites of the Monte Albán I period, does not have any.

In the Etla Valley, the number of predicted and actual sites corresponds (Table 21) and, as predicted, most of the tributary valleys are controlled by at least one settlement. However, whereas in the predicted pattern control is effected from a site in the middle or top of a valley, the archaeological sites tend to be located downstream at the point of entry of the tributary valleys into the main Atoyac valley floor. By this time a substantial settlement had been established as far north as Huitzo, and Monte Albán had risen to its preeminent position as the focal point of the Valley as a whole. Whereas the archaeological pattern in the San José phase did not show any relation to the distribution of perennial tributaries which could have been used for canal irrigation, the settlement pattern during Monte Albán I (with the notable exception of the Mixtepec stream, which may have been applied to land farther downstream by the inhabitants of the Santa Ana Tlapacoyan site) does seem to include many sites whose main agricultural advantage today is derived from canal irrigation.

## Stage IV—A.D. 900

By A.D. 900 the predicted area which could be cultivated was almost double that of 1000 B.C., and expansion in the Etla arm was being severely limited by the narrow width of the Valley itself (Fig. 52). In contrast, the Zaachila Valley particularly, but also the Tlacolula Valley, contained enough valley floor area for increasing corn yields to make vast areas of new land a feasible proposition for cultivation (Table 22). Thus, for the first time the percentage of valley cultivated became less in the Etla arm than in Zaachila, and consequently 64,000 people could be supported in the southern arm compared with only 15,000 in the Etla Valley. This marks a real changeover in the balance of population, and presumably of power, among the three arms of the Valley. The largest increase in cultivable area took place in the Ocotlán Valley, accompanied by a predicted increase of population from 8,000 to 18,000 or from 8 to 18 settlement sites. Elsewhere the increase of agricultural land would have resulted in an overall expansion of the cultivated margin rather than the introduction of new blocks of land as in Ocotlán.

The predicted resulting pattern of settlement is thus generally one of infilling within the existing network rather than an extension of the network into new areas. In the Zaachila Valley, a third regional centre can be designated, near the present Valdeflores south of Zimatlán, so that the southern arm now had three regional centres, corresponding to its three subdivisions into Zaachila, Zimatlán and Ocotlán Valleys. The predicted regional centres, or centres of gravity for the settlement pattern, in the Etla and Tlacolula Valleys remain at San Pedro y San Pablo Etla and

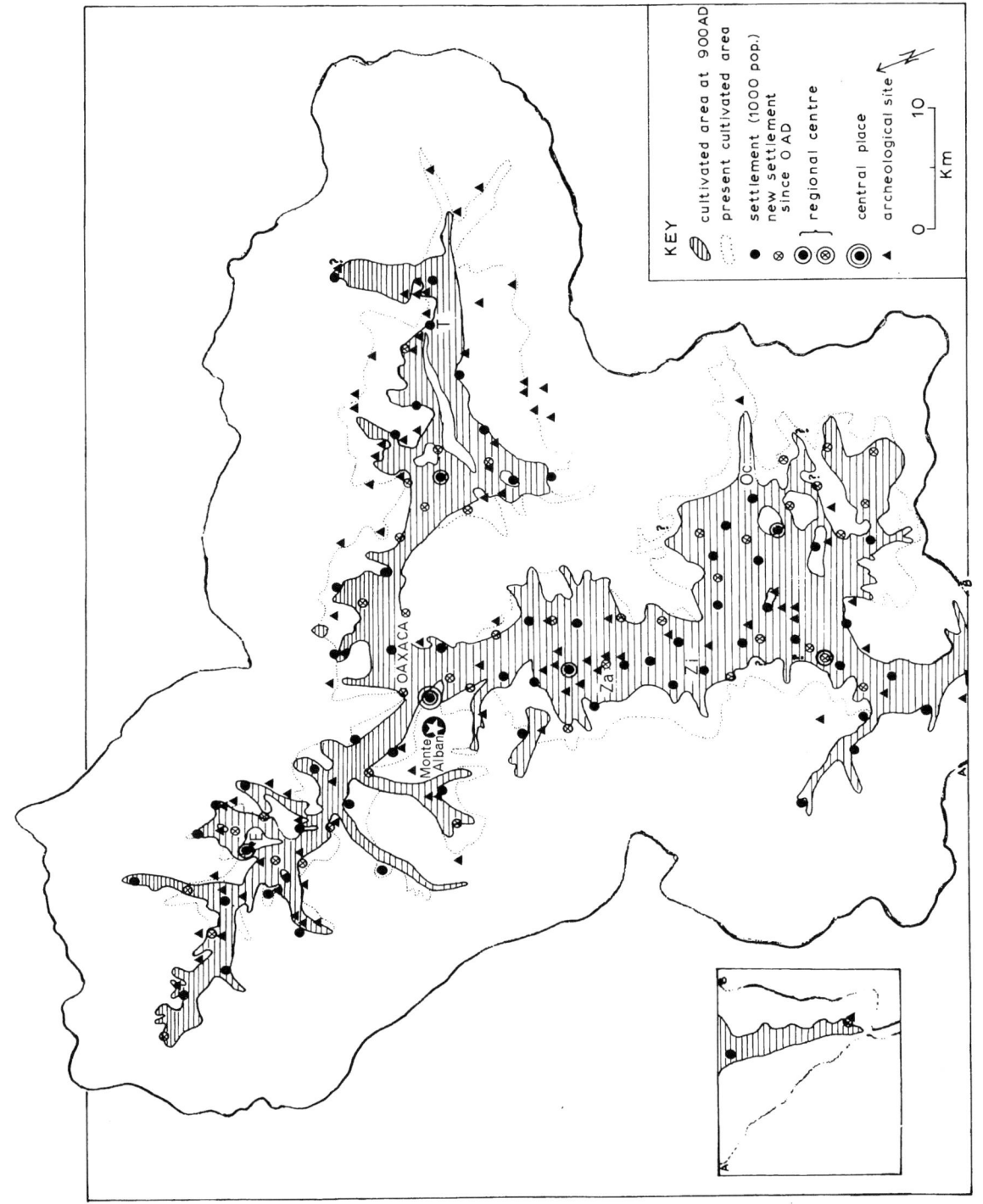

Fig. 52. Predicted area which could have been cultivated, predicted settlement distribution and location of known archaeological sites for A.D. 900.

TABLE 22

PREDICTED SIZE OF CULTIVATED AREA, TOTAL POSSIBLE CORN PRODUCTION, AND POPULATION FOR EACH ARM OF THE VALLEY FROM 1300 B.C. TO PRESENT

| Valley | 1300 B.C. | 1000 B.C. | 300-1 B.C. | A.D. 900 | A.D. 1970 |
|---|---|---|---|---|---|
| | Cultivated Area (km²) | | | | |
| Etla | 81 | 107 | 120 | 133 | 202 |
| Zaachila | 89 | 218 | 330 | 442 | 616 |
| Tlacolula | 33 | 92 | 140 | 187 | 352 |
| Oaxaca | 203 | 417 | 590 | 762 | 1170 |
| | Maximum Possible Corn Production (1000 metric tons) | | | | |
| Etla | 2.4 | 4.3 | 9.1 | 14.9 | 31.2 |
| Zaachila | 2.4 | 7.7 | 17.3 | 30.7 | 67.2 |
| Tlacolula | 1.0 | 3.4 | 7.2 | 12.9 | 30.3 |
| Oaxaca | 5.8 | 15.3 | 32.2 | 58.1 | 163.7 |
| | Maximum Possible Population (1000 inhabitants) | | | | |
| Etla | 5 | 9 | 19 | 31 | 65 |
| Zaachila | 5 | 16 | 36 | 64 | 140 |
| Tlacolula | 2 | 7 | 15 | 27 | 63 |
| Oaxaca* | 12 | 32 | 67 | 121 | 341 |

*Total for Valley including central place at Monte Albán, Oaxaca de Juárez.

at San Sebastián Abasolo respectively. The central place for the entire Valley also remains at or near Monte Albán. At this stage the reconstructed population for the whole Valley would be 121,000 instead of the 64,000 of a thousand years before (Table 22).

ARCHAEOLOGICAL EVIDENCE: MONTE ALBÁN IIIB-IV

The distribution of Monte Albán IIIB-IV sites found by Dr. Bernal (Fig. 52) shows the same tendency of infilling within the existing network as that predicted from the land use data. The number of known sites also corresponds with those predicted—105 compared with 107 (Table 21). The main differences between the predicted and archaeological settlement patterns are those inherited from the previous stage at 300 B.C., namely, the location of archaeological sites at a distance from good agricultural land which presumably owed their establishment to nonagricultural factors. Thus in Monte Albán IIIB-IV times, those sites in the eastern Tlacolula Valley which were established at least 10 kilometers from agricultural land by 300 B.C. continue, and new sites are added. Several of the new sites cluster around the early site between San Marcos Tlapazola and Magdelena Teitipac, which may indicate an increased ability of the social organisation of the Valley to sustain communities with specialist, nonagricultural activities.

The archaeological site distribution exhibits this tendency to cluster in several other parts of the Valley, notably around the regional centre of Zaachila, which by this time is encircled by 6 or 7 satellite communities. Smaller clusters of settlements are found near Yagul, along the Teotitlán del Valle stream and at Santa Ines Yatzeche. A clustering tendency is not predicted from the optimum use of the agricultural land at that time and may reflect the attraction of towns in their own right as economic, social and political centres. The importance of urbanism during the III-B period is demonstrated by the archaeological site on the top of Monte Albán, which was one of the largest and grandest urban and religious centres of its kind in Mesoamerica (Paddock, 1966:233).

By A.D. 900 archaeological sites are located on all major streams which were capable of supplying canal irrigation water (with again the curious exception of the Mixtepec Valley, on whose water the town of Santa Ana Tlapacoyan appears to have held a monopoly since the Early Formative period). In the tributary Etla Valleys several communities are established, thus necessitating some organisation for the sharing of stream water and implying the use of that water.

Stage V—A.D. 1970

The settlement pattern predicted by the model for the present is given in Figure 53 and shows the reconstructed use of an agricultural zone which is now 50 percent greater in area than a thousand years previously. Predicted population that could be supported is 341,000 compared with the Oaxaca State Census returns for 1960 of 280,000 (Table 22). The greatest expansion of agricultural land and population has taken place in the two

138

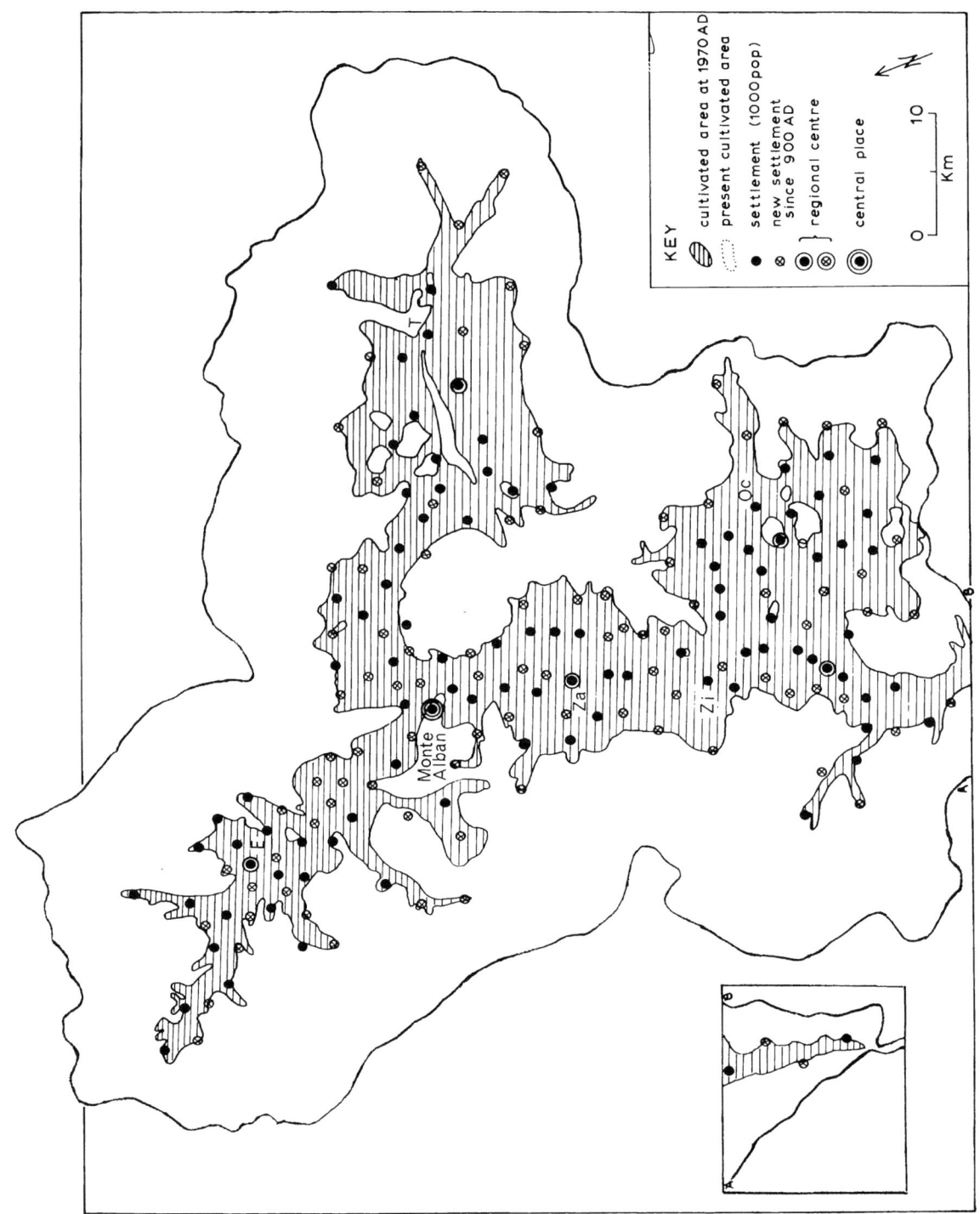

Fig. 53. Predicted cultivated area and predicted settlement distribution for the present.

least developed areas—the eastern Tlacolula Valley and the Ocotlán Valley. The increase in corn yield over the last thousand years would have enabled the long piedmont slope on the south side of the eastern Tlacolula Valley to be cultivated for the first time so that the establishment of new sites is predicted where small tributary streams enter the Valley at San Marcos Tlapazola, San Bartolomé Quialaná and San Lucas Quiavini (in fact, sites at San Marcos and San Lucas were established at least a thousand years earlier, as has been discussed above). Similarly, the extension of the cultivation eastward is predicted to lead to the establishment of agricultural settlements at Mitla, Loma Larga and Matatlán although these were also established over a thousand years previously.

Elsewhere in the Valley the predicted settlement pattern is one of infilling in the network of A.D. 900 which had already established the outline of almost the entire system. Because infilling is presumed to be second or third stage in the Zaachila and Etla Valleys, settlements here are closer together than in the relatively empty areas of east Tlacolula and Ocotlán.

## COMPARISON WITH THE PRESENT

Since it is the present land use that has been used as a basis for predicting back into the past, it is unwise to make too much of the obvious similarities between the actual settlement pattern (Fig. 54) and that predicted from the model (Fig. 53). It is useful however, to point out some similarities between the real and predicted central place hierarchy, and some anomalous village sites.

San Pedro y San Pablo Etla and Zaachila are regional centres that are also predicted, suggesting that the importance of these towns relies heavily on their locations in the centres of agriculturally productive regions; whereas in the Tlacolula Valley, the central place of an exclusively agricultural economy would be at San Juan Guelavía—actually it is farther east, at Tlacolula. Indeed, much of the settlement in the eastern Tlacolula Valley can be regarded as anomalous, because agriculturally it is a very marginal area but it supports several large towns which were also important archaeological sites. In the graph showing the relationship between local corn yield and local population (Fig. 47), the eastern Tlacolula area plots too high since its population today is higher than its corn fields can support.

In the southern arm the two predicted regional centres, in addition to the one at Zaachila, would be located at Valdeflores and Santa Rosa rather than their real locations at Zimatlán and Ocotlán. Santa Rosa is close to Ocotlán and may be regarded as the same central place in terms of the accuracy of this model, but the dominance of Zimatlán over a more southerly regional centre must depend on nonagricultural factors. One possibility is the railway, for it is the lowest point on the line from Oaxaca de Juárez to Ocotlán before it crosses the Río Atoyac, and therefore must serve as the break of bulk point for all the southern part of the valley west of the mainstream. The predicted capital of the whole Valley in the neighbourhood of Monte Albán is, of course, the same as the real Valley (and state) capital at Oaxaca de Juárez, and this has remained the same for all stages considered in the model since it is simply a function of the three-arm topographic configuration of the Valley.

## COMPARISON OF PREHISTORIC POPULATION AND SETTLEMENT DATA FROM THE LAND USE MODEL AND ARCHAEOLOGICAL EVIDENCE

Predicted and archaeological settlement patterns have already been compared for each stage considered here, and the purpose of this section is to draw together the cumulative evidence from both sets of data to see how far they can shed light on three important topics:

1) the development of water use in the Valley through time
2) the development of social and economic organisation
3) how far agriculture and settlement in prehistoric times (as shown by archaeological evidence) approached an optimum use of the agricultural resources of the Valley

In the model presented here, reconstruction of prehistoric land use is based on present agriculture

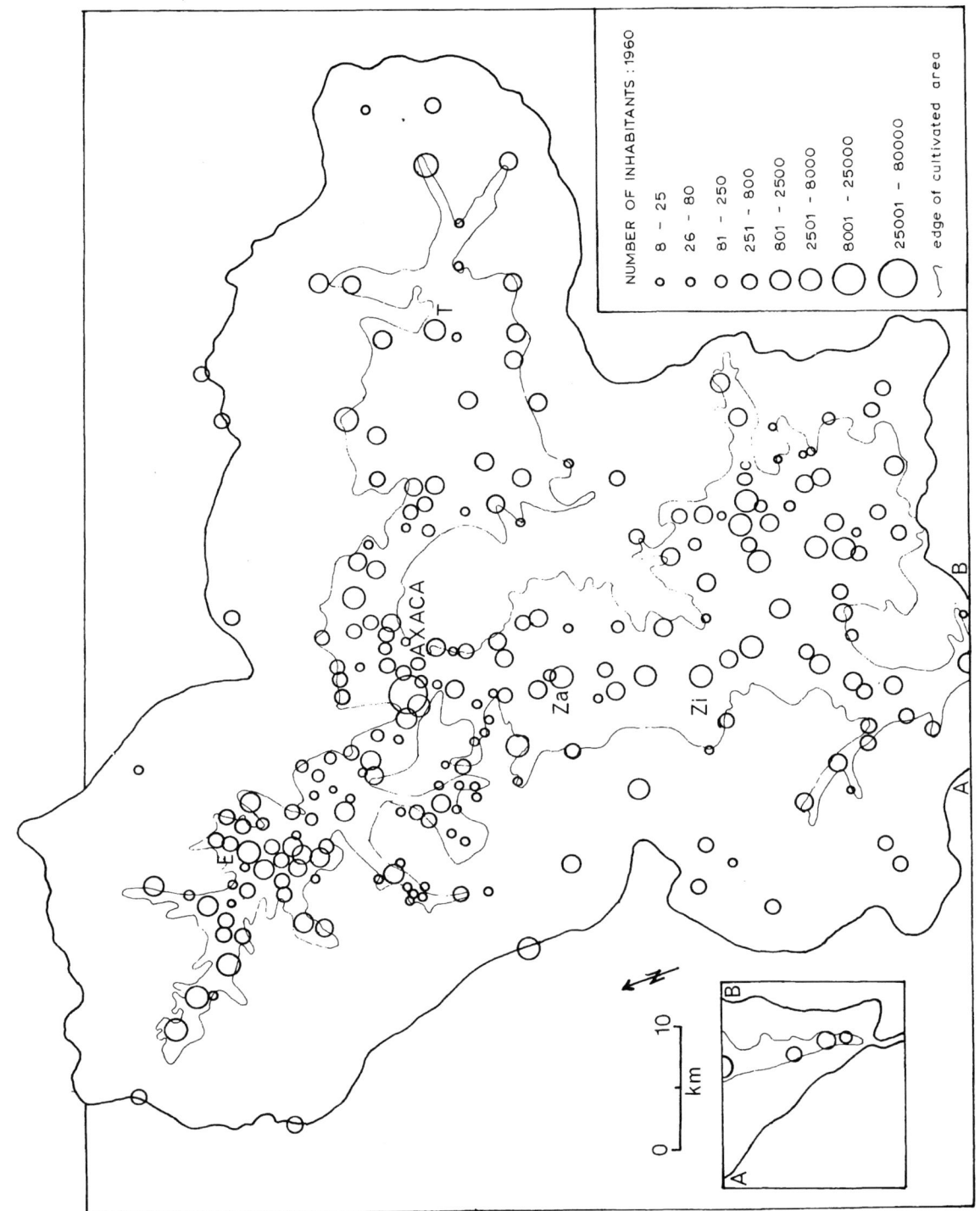

Fig. 54. Present population distribution for the Valley of Oaxaca (based on data in 1960 Oaxaca State Census).

and implicit in the reconstruction is constancy of water use. In the previous chapter it was pointed out that on the basis of the present characteristics of pot irrigation, this water use technique does not appear to have cultural continuity in at least some of the areas where it is practised today. Furthermore, a sequence is envisaged in which pot irrigation developed from a relatively ubiquitous garden plot technique to a highly specialized form of farming at the same time that the Valley's economic and political network strengthened. Since the total amount of land under pot irrigation is generally less than 10 percent, this form of irrigation does not affect the overall productivity of corn on a valley scale and so has had little influence in determining optimum settlement sites in the model. The archaeological site distribution deviates from the reconstructed one in favour of pot-irrigated areas today most noticeably in the case of the Zaachila area at A.D. 900 (Monte Albán IIIB-IV). This could be taken to indicate the possibility (but nothing more) that by Monte Albán IIIB-IV times the growth of towns and the increasingly complex economic and political development of the Valley led to areas specialising in vegetables as they do today, and that one of these areas was around Zaachila.

Less speculative evidence can be found for canal irrigation. The site of Hierve el Agua (Fig. 46) shows that canal irrigation was practised by Monte Albán I times (300-1 B.C.), and study of the present-day techniques involved in canal irrigation (Chapter IV) indicates that the technology and social organisation required should not have been beyond a settled agricultural community of about 15 to 20 households with only the simplest of tools. The assumption that water use has been constant throughout the prehistoric period which underlies the predicted settlement pattern is important in the case of canal (as opposed to pot) irrigation because many areas which are the most productive for corn today are dependent on canal irrigation.

Since the predicted settlement pattern assumes canal irrigation was used from very early times, the deviation of archaeological site data from the predicted pattern can be taken as some indication of when canal irrigation was widely practised. On the basis of comparing the predicted and archaeological distributions only, sites favourable for canal irrigation do not appear to have been occupied until Monte Albán I (300-1 B.C.). At this time, in contrast to the predicted pattern of two settlements on each perennial tributary sharing water, the archaeological data indicate only one site located downstream at the point where a tributary enters the main valley floor. However, in one area—that based on San José Mogote—there was already a large settlement controlling the downstream point of a perennial tributary (San José itself), and here new sites are established upstream of the older one as predicted. It may be, therefore, that both stages of a sequence can be seen in Figure 51, and that in terms of development of a settlement network, the early expansion of San José Mogote by 1000 B.C. (Flannery, 1969) allowed it to lead the rest of the Valley.

That the sequence of expanding water control is from downstream positions first and then upstream sites, as indicated above and discussed in Chapter VII, is further supported by reference to Figure 52 which shows settlement at A.D. 900. By this stage, many archaeological sites have been established upstream of sites founded at least a thousand years earlier, and by this point some social organisation must have been developed either on an inter- or supracommunity level to share stream water among settlements.

This leads to a consideration of what, if anything, can be deduced from the *distribution* of settlements about the development of social and economic organisation on a valley scale. The implication of archaeological sites located away from agricultural land is that at that time the economic system of the Valley was sufficiently advanced to allow some villages to specialise in craft occupation, or in the case of administrative centres, to locate for defence. In order for such villages to be viable, other villages must be capable of producing surplus food, and some system must be in force to enable food to be exchanged for other products or services at an intervillage level. It is between 1000 B.C. and 300 B.C. that villages begin to be sited in locations that imply such specialisation, and the distribution of Monte Albán I sites suggests the existence of a valley-wide social organisation at that time. This is further indicated by the development of a ceremonial centre at Monte Albán which is the natural central place and best site from which to control the whole Valley (Paddock, 1966:91). Likewise the establishment of sites at Mitla and Matatlán may define the limits of political authority centred on Monte Albán or at least the points where trade and other contact with surrounding Indian groups were concentrated.

By A.D. 900 (Monte Albán IIIB) the framework of a valley-wide social organisation or state that was implied for the Monte Albán I period is strengthened and embellished. The central place at Monte Albán has developed into a large urban and ceremonial centre and many more sites are located away from agricultural land, thus implying an increase in specialisation of economic activities and the corresponding trade network. At this time the Valley settlement pattern exhibits as much political cohesion centred on Monte Albán and as much economic diversity as it does today, although the number of sites has now doubled and control has shifted from the summit of Monte Albán to Oaxaca de Juárez, located at its foot.

From the evidence presented in map form (Figs. 49 to 52) and in Table 22, curves can be drawn for the predicted area being brought under cultivation and the predicted population density at each stage from 1300 B.C. to the present (Fig. 55). These graphs show the changing relative importance of each arm of the Valley that is solely dependent on the changing agricultural situation. The Etla Valley shows an early rise to preeminence in agricultural production and population density—a position which is held until about the first century A.D. During this period from 1300 B.C. to A.D. 1 the Zaachila arm and, to a lesser extent, the Tlacolula Valley were in the process of catching up as cultivation expanded on to poorer and poorer land—a resource which was plentiful in both of the larger valleys. By A.D. 1000 this catching-up process was more or less complete, and the Zaachila Valley took over the role of leading agricultural producer and centre of population and kept this lead until fairly recently, when the Etla Valley again had the higher population density. Throughout the period we are considering, from 1300 B.C. onwards, the Tlacolula Valley lagged behind the other two. It followed a similar pattern to the Zaachila Valley with its period of maximum agricultural expansion occurring late, between A.D. 1000 and the present. Likewise, the population peak *relative* to the other two valleys occurred about A.D. 1400, although its highest absolute population density is found today.

This picture of the relative development of agriculture and settlement between the three arms of the Valley is similar to that which can be inferred from archaeological data (Flannery, personal communication) and indicates that in general terms the changing patterns of population distribution and economic leadership through time are closely related to variations in agricultural resources around the Valley. Likewise, there is a good relationship between the number of predicted sites for each period and the number of archaeological sites for different parts of the Valley (Fig. 56 and Table 21). The figure shows that the general relationship between the two is 1:1, with certain exceptions. Two of these exceptions are the eastern Tlacolula Valley from 300 B.C. to A.D. 900, when the number of archaeological sites is greater than the number which might be expected to have been supported by local agriculture, and the Ocotlán Valley during the same period when the number of archaeological sites falls below that expected from the land use model.

The third anomalous group of points is that of the San José phase sites for all parts of the Valley (Fig. 56). The number of archaeological sites dating from San José phase (1000 B.C.) is less than the number predicted on the basis of possible contemporary land use. The problems associated with surveying for archaeological sites in the Valley have already been discussed, and additional sites dating from this period are already being found during the course of more intensive surveys. However, there appears to be no reason associated with the practical business of survey that would lead to a consistent underdiscovery and recognition of San José phase sites, whose number is consistent with those predicted. The implication is therefore that the number of San José phase sites

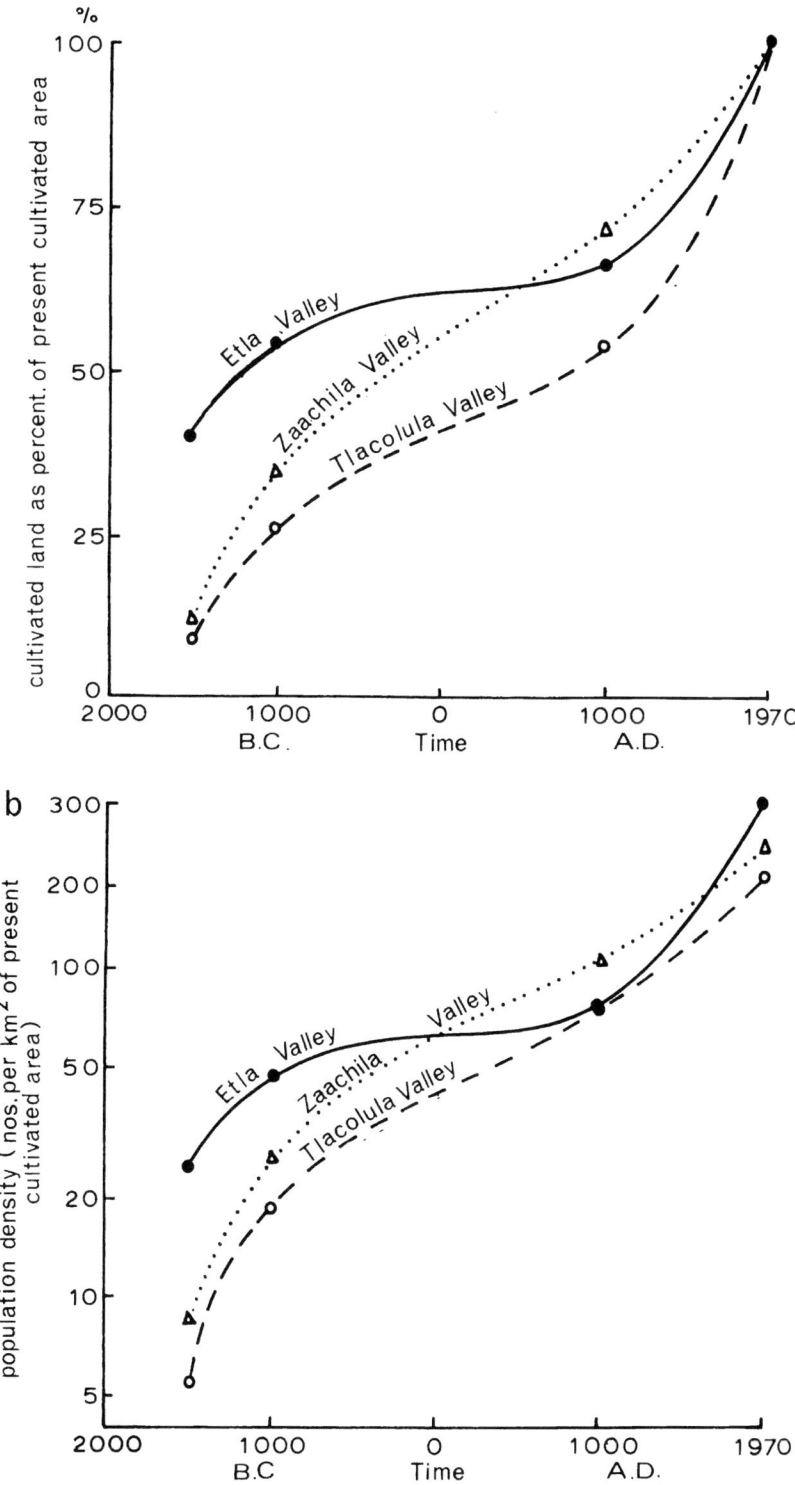

Fig. 55. (a) Increase in cultivated land for each arm of the Valley through time, as predicted from land use data. (b) Increase in population density of valley floor for each arm of the Valley through time, as predicted from land use data.

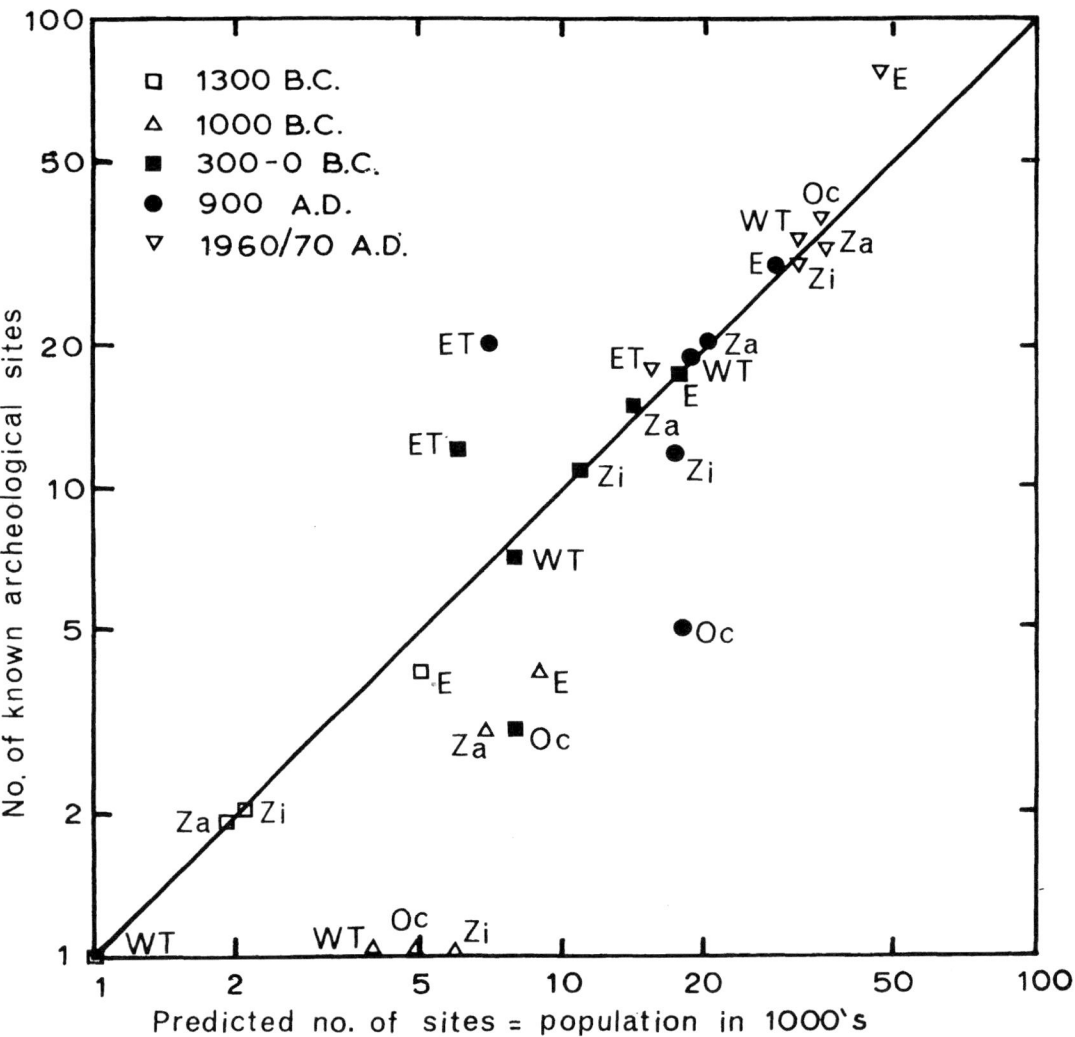

Fig. 56. Relationship between predicted number of sites and numbers of archaeological sites for all parts of the Valley from 1300 B.C. to the present.

is lower than expected because of some unforseen aspect of the settlement pattern at that time; for example, that there were fewer settlements than expected because each one was bigger.

The work of Flannery and Winter (1969) indicates that the settlement hierarchy in San José times may explain the anomalous number of sites. During the San José and Guadalupe phases of the Formative period, one settlement, San José Mogote, grew to huge proportions for that time (10-40 hectares in area from San José to Guadalupe phases) and probably needed to be supported by food produced in surrounding hamlets of 12-20 households (about 1 hectare) such as the site of Tierras Largas. The settlement pattern for the San José area at 1000 B.C., therefore, seems to have been one of a large regional centre, which incorporated economic activities and perhaps high-ranking lineages, having political control over local small agricultural settlements which supplied the central village with food. The implications of such analysis for the subsequent development of urban hierarchies and extension of policical power within the Valley will not be discussed here, but on the evidence of Figure 56 alone it would seem that, in terms of the number of people available, settlement structure was distorted in favour of large centres during the San José phase more than

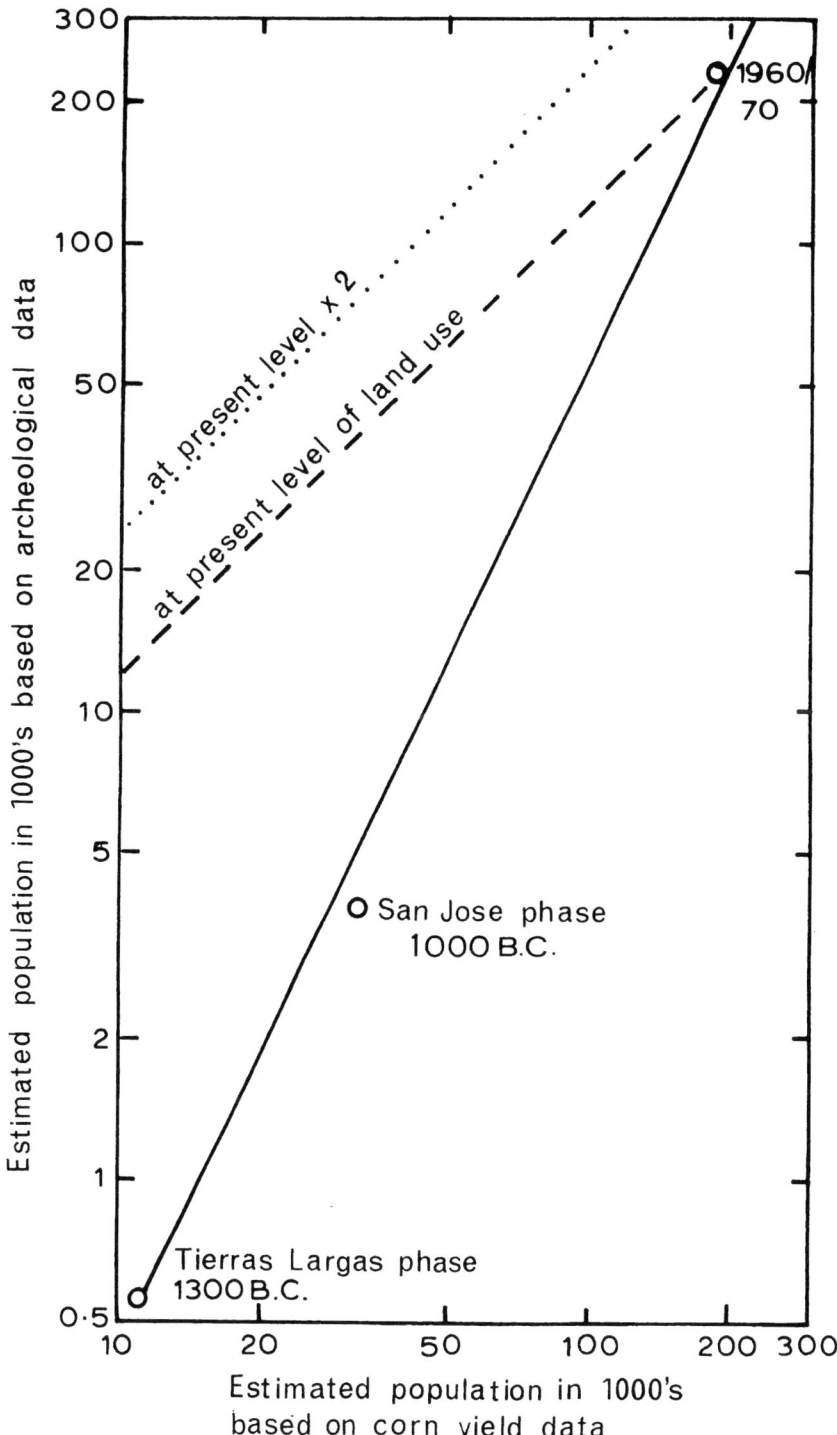

Fig. 57. Relationship between population of Valley estimated from archaeological data and population estimated from corn yield data from 1300 B.C. to the present, showing probable relationship if present effectiveness of land use for food production is held constant through time.

during the later period of urbanisation of Monte Albán IIIB-IV.

Flannery and Winter's data (1969) on the number of households per hectare for settlements of different sizes during the Tierras Largas and San José phases as revealed by careful excavation may also be used to convert the number of archaeological sites in the Valley into rough population estimates for these two phases. Unfortunately, similar good data are not available for the later periods which have been considered here. The number of households for most sites in the Valley during the Tierras Largas phase is considered by them to have been about 6 to 12, or 27 to 54 people, and the larger settlements such as San José Mogot had 12 to 22 households, or 54 to 94 people. During the San José phase, Flannery and Winter calculate that small agricultural settlements had 12 to 16 households while San José Mogote contained 240 to 320 households, or 1080 to 1440 people. Thus most settlements numbered considerably less than the standard 1000 inhabitants assumed for each site in the land use model.

The result is that the number of inhabitants of the Valley calculated on the basis of archaeological data (roughly 550 at 1300 B.C. and 3800 at 1000 B.C.) is always less than the number which it is calculated *could* have been supported by agriculture within the valley (Fig. 57). Thus if today's population and agriculture are taken as a standard (dashed line in Fig. 57), the evidence of archaeological data, as compared with the land use model, is seen in the difference between the dashed and solid lines in the graph (Fig. 57). In Tierras Largas times, the population of the Valley appears to have been smaller than that which could have been supported by a factor of 20 times, and in the San José phase this underpopulation of the Valley is reduced to a factor of 9 times. Although the evidence available is too fragmentary to allow anything more than the most tentative statements to be made, Figure 57 could be interpreted as showing that underuse of the Valley's agricultural resources has declined through time from 1300 B.C. to the present. The degree of underpopulation may have been greatest at earliest times simply because the total number of settlers was initially small, and there are factors other than agricultural productivity which limit the rate at which human population can expand; in other words, the Valley may have been "filling up" during the last millenium B.C.

In Figure 57 it can be seen that populations in the past have numbered less than a population estimate based on the limit of the food they could grow, *compared with the present*. In Chapters VI and VII it was argued that today peasant agriculturalists on irrigated and unirrigated land are in general underusing their agricultural resources, particularly those of their own labour. The present use of resources is therefore not an optimum one in terms of total productivity but is at some level below this optimum. For pot-irrigated land, the level of underuse of resources might be as great as 50 percent; dry-farming cultivators could probably not increase their productivity by this amount. Even so, present underuse of resources can be set somewhere between 20 and 50 percent, thus increasing the level of underuse at 1300 B.C. to a factor of 24 to 40 times, compared with a theoretical optimum. Underuse of agricultural resources, or growing less food than they could, is therefore not simply a phenomenon of peasant society in the Valley today but is likely to have been a feature of social organisation at many, if not all, periods in prehistory (though obviously more data are needed). While underuse today can be specified in terms of man-hours or hectares of land, for the past this underuse is only shown by the fact that populations as indicated by archaeological data were smaller than those which could have been supported.

# IX

# CONCLUSION: THE EFFECT OF CULTURE ON AGRICULTURAL RESOURCE USE

In this study of the resources and agriculture of the Valley of Oaxaca four important conclusions have been drawn:

1) Corn yield per hectare is principally a function of water availability, which at the present level of technology in the Valley means that corn yield is closely related to factors in the physical environment.
2) Whereas the yield in any one field can be related to local water resources, the amount of corn grown by any single household is dependent not only on the size and agricultural quality of their landholding but also on their desire to grow corn. The effect of this desire to grow specific amounts of corn which are less than what could potentially be grown is to make some households grow a minimum amount which is unprofitable—they could obtain greater economic return for their labour by doing something else such as weaving. Other households grow less than their labour and landholding would produce, not because they are employing their time profitably elsewhere but because either they prefer not to work for longer in the fields or because they do not want more corn in return.
3) Although it was considered possible at the outset that crops grown for cash rather than subsistence would be more subject to the desire to maximise profits, the analysis of pot-irrigated crops indicates that this desire to obtain profits does not outweigh a desire to do less agricultural work or to grow, rather than buy, corn to eat. Landholdings which would be more profitably put down to higher proportions of cash-producing vegetables and flowers, therefore, remain largely under subsistence corn which entails less work and is less profitable.
4) Using the present population and land use as a standard, population figures, settlement patterns and area of agricultural land were reconstructed for various times in the past, beginning at 1300 B.C. When these reconstructed patterns were compared with the evidence from archaeological sites in the Valley for different time periods, it was concluded that prehistoric populations appear to have been less than the number of inhabitants the Valley could have supported agriculturally, even taking into account the much lower corn yields that could be obtained at earlier stages of domestication.

These conclusions in themselves raise interesting questions which can be discussed here in a wider frame of reference than just the Valley of Oaxaca. The first question concerns the apparent desire of Oaxacan peasants not to grow as much corn or as many cash crops as they could within the limitations of their labour and wealth (land and capital), despite the fact that they are lacking in many material goods. In Chapter III the social organisation of peasant communities in the Valley was described and the idea introduced that these social institutions operate to provide social security on the one hand and to inhibit wealth accumulation by individuals on the other. If these are the purposes of such institutions as the cargo system and reciprocal exchange by guelaguetza, it is to be asked whether these functions are being fulfilled today; in other words, is wealth leveling being achieved in the Valley of Oaxaca?

While the cargo and guelaguetza systems described in Chapter III are characteristic of communities in the Valley, the rigour with which they are observed, and thus their possible strength in determining social and economic aims, varies considerably between villages. Webster (1968) has described the cargo system in Santa María Guelace, a village of 550 people in the central Tlacolula Valley. Here the cargo system is strong and involves almost total participation of the heads of households as mayordomos, a role from which they take an average of 3 to 6 years to recover financially and which they undertake about 6 times between the ages of 30 and 60 years. Guelaguetza support for these prestige offices and the accompanying fiestas involves almost every household every year in the giving of money or goods.

In other villages the strength of the religious cargo system has almost disappeared although the time-consuming civil offices remain. For example, Zautla in the Etla Valley has now only one important religious fiesta, in January, which is supported by a committee of 15 members plus an alcalde, each of whom need pay less than 500 pesos. The only important device for redistributing wealth appears to be the giving of lavish fandangos, or marriage fiestas, costing up to 5000 pesos instead of buying land for the daughter and her husband (Dennis, 1968).

Villagers do see the cargo system and guelaguetza as a bar to economic advancement, and several have attempted to break down the strength of these institutions by decree. In Santa María Guelace, Webster reports that in 1934 a group of young civil leaders abolished the self-perpetuating burden of mayordomías and introduced a committee which collected a small donation from every family each year for a less extravagant celebration. Four years later the village revolted against this change in the traditional system and a new conservative leadership reintroduced the cargo system which survives today. In Matatlán in the eastern Tlacolula Valley a similar attempt to overthrow traditional institutions is reported to have taken place during the 1930's, and while it lasted, it appeared to improve the economic drive of the village as people spent more time pursuing economic profit and less time maintaining social relations (Barahona, personal communication).

Under the new system, fines were imposed for fiestas, private or public, which continued for longer than one day. As the traditional celebration of weddings, baptisms and saints' days can take up to a week of solid drinking for 20 to 40 people, the number of man-hours released for work was considerable.

In Matatlán, the return of conservative leaders a few years later meant, as in Santa María Guelace, a return to the old system of mayordomías and lengthy fiestas. In Díaz Ordaz, in the Tlacolula Valley, Downing reports a growing desire among the young men not to climb the traditional ladder to prestige, that is to assume cargo duties, but to direct their efforts towards economic success. In this village, often described as one of the more "progressive" in outlook, men avoid being nominated to cargo offices by leaving the village when nominations are due, ostensibly in order to seek their fortune in a city (and thereby make themselves ineligible for the office); they return later when the choices have been made and profess failure to find work elsewhere (Downing, personal communication).

Webster (1968) argues that in the upper echelons of the mayordomía hierarchy, only the richer families in the community can afford to perform, and that for these families the spending of some of their wealth in support of a saint's day thereby makes the rest of their wealth immune to social disapproval. In other words, the cargo system operates to perpetuate social and economic distinctions between households instead of acting as a community wealth-leveling device. This view is also taken by Cancian (1967) who argues that the Mesoamerican cargo system increases social distinctions within a community because wealth is principally based on land and a large landowner can receive sufficient return by hiring labour or entering into sharecropping agreements to enable him to spend his own time on civic affairs and in prestige offices.

However, it is significant that Oaxacan peasants themselves see the cargo system and guelaguetza as functioning to minimise personal initiative and individual economic advancement in order to preserve the community in its present form with lavish public ceremonials and social security for the very poorest households or for any family at a time when its immediate needs are greater than its individual resources. Many peasants, especially the older ones or those living in more remote villages, believe that the cost of the cargo system in economic terms is worth the benefit in social terms, while others see it as a bar to economic progress and prosperity. This attitude is especially prevalent in villages where the cargo and fiesta systems have been abolished, and where prestige is increasingly based primarily on wealth and material possessions. For example, Yucuita, a village which lies in the neighbouring Valley of Nochixtlán, illustrates well the change in attitude toward agriculture that seems to accompany the decline of traditional social institutions, the change from a small subsistence peasant producer to a cash-earning economic farming unit.

It may be that the cargo and guelaguetza systems are not so much effective in themselves as wealth-leveling mechanisms but are symptoms of a traditional attitude which reduces personal initiative if, as it generally does, it threatens social relations. In particular, strong cargo and guelaguetza traditions are associated with characteristically lengthy and frequent family celebrations which are time-consuming for both men and women. A frequent complaint of employers in the Valley is that men and women employees will suddenly disappear for a week at a time with no warning, returning with the confession that they were obliged to attend a family celebration or funeral, or to help another family in a guelaguetza obligation. This may happen every month or so, so that job schedules can rarely be completed in time. Indeed, it seems that a peasant can only become a reliable paid employee *outside* the confines of his own community where he is beyond family and social obligations and also beyond the help they provide in time of need. This necessity of leaving the home community if one wishes to become rich, or at least better off than one's neighbours, is also found in Java where the obligations of village membership require that every personal economic gain be shared with the community (Forde and Douglas, 1956).

The argument being put forward here, that social institutions (whether formal, as in the cargo system, or informal, such as the traditional obligation to help families within the guelaguetza network if you have more than they have and they are in need) can counteract the desire of individuals to obtain greater personal wealth, is one of social versus economic rationality. As such it raises issues which go beyond this study of Oaxaca and affect our whole approach to the study of individual motivation and the structure of societies.

The issue of economic versus social rationality in influencing behavior is not only a theoretical difference of opinion between economists on the one hand and social psychologists on the other, with anthropologists and geographers split down the middle, but determines the methodology used in the study of societies. Thus, game theory analyses of economic decisions at any level can only be valid if it can be shown that the player(s) wish to win the game, that is, maximise their gain. Simon (1957) has argued that although the ideal of maximum economic gain is not possible in reality, actual behaviour in societies can be approximated by a behavioural model based on economic rationality. This is the "satisficer" model which is based on Simon's principle of bounded rationality and states that:

> The capacity of the human mind for formulating and solving complex problems is very small compared with the size of the problems whose solution is required for objectively rational behaviour in the real world—or even for a reasonable approximation to such objective rationality (Simon, 1957:198).

An important consequence of the principle of bounded rationality is that in order for decisions to be made, the choice situation must be simplified; and this is achieved by replacing the goal of maximising with one of "satisficing," or the finding of a solution which is "good enough." The attraction of the "satisficer" model is that it describes human behaviour more accurately than Economic Man because it takes into account three important limitations in real decision-making:

1) the limitations of the human brain for memory and computation,
2) the limitation of information available, and
3) the limitation of time, both with respect to the total amount of time available before a decision has to be made, and the fact that alternatives

are usually examined in sequence without there necessarily being an understanding of the order of the sequence (this is particularly relevant to the planting of crops in Oaxaca).

The effect of these limitations on economic rationality is to make the chosen solution accord more with the perceived situation than the real one and to make the first satisfactory solution the most likely to be accepted. The likelihood of a solution being accepted is determined by a fluctuating aspiration level which corresponds with the level of the known available alternatives (Simon, 1957:253). These same concepts are applied to computer simulation of human information processing, in which decision-making is regarded as a process in which the brain systematically sorts through a series of subroutines until it finds the simplest one; built into the simulation model are aspiration achievements, satisficing, impatience (the limitation of time) and discouragement (Simon, 1967).

Although the principle of bounded rationality as defined originally by Simon (1957) does embrace the concepts of an inability to achieve a desired goal of economic maximisation and the substitution of noneconomic desires for economic ends, he concentrates on the first of these, and the satisficer model has come to mean that:

> The individual is adaptively or intendedly rational rather than omnisciently rational [in the sense of economic gain] (Wolpert, 1964:558).

Thus, although the satisficer model is attractive because it is closer to human behaviour than other economic models, it must be rejected here as a working hypothesis because its underlying assumption is one of economic rationality.

From the data presented in this paper, it would appear that the desire to maximise economic gain is less important for Oaxacan peasants than the desire to achieve social approval and maintain good personal relations within the community. In other words, social rationality appears to be a more effective force than economic rationality. It may then be asked whether this is peculiar to Oaxacan peasants or is characteristic of all peasant communities, or indeed is an important element in all societies, including our own. It can be argued that in western society, which is generally assumed to be the most economically motivated, social institutions representing a less formalised system of balanced reciprocity or guelaguetza exist, such as the dropping of individuals from dinner party and present-giving lists if they do not reciprocate. Likewise, whenever transactions are personal in western society, the price is as likely to be a function of both each individual's bargaining power and his desire to maintain good personal relations as it was found to be by Dewey (1962) in Javanese local markets. If western society is more economic, it is perhaps because it is less personal and thus less of a society in the sense of a social group.

It has, however, been traditional since Malinowski to draw a distinction between western and other societies on the grounds that the high value placed on economic rationality is peculiarly a feature of western society. And as most students of economies are the products of western society, it is not unexpected that the economic aspect of economy has been stressed. In most anthropological classifications of societies, the varying ratio of economic to social rationality forms a major criterion, whether it is implicit as in Firth's (1951) "primitive—peasant—industrial" categories or explicit as in Sahlin's (1965) division into societies characterised by generalised, balanced and negative reciprocity.

The theoretical basis for argument is that simple societies are not governed by the market principle of supply and demand, and therefore formal economics are inapplicable to them (Polanyi, 1957). Their economic activities are not subject to supply and demand because subsistence production is not competitive and is aimed at satisfying the needs of the producing unit only. Therefore, the output is not affected by the production of other similar units such as households. These are nonmonetary economies where there is no generalised medium of exchange, and goods and services are distributed throughout the society, not by a series of money payments but through formal and informal institutions of exchange such as gift-giving and reciprocity. Dalton (1961) and Polanyi (1957) see a sliding scale of effectiveness of economic rationality in determining economy through various types of societies. This scale can be measured in terms of such institutions as the nature of markets and market transactions; the existence of a general medium of exchange or money; and the importance of nonmarket mechanisms for exchange such as reciprocity and redistribution among individual units through the organisation of society itself. At one end of the continuum is the primitive society or tribe in which, according to Dalton and Polanyi, economic transactions can only be understood in terms of social ends or, as Sahlins (1960) states, "The fact remains that primitive economic behaviour is largely an aspect of kinship behaviour."

There is a considerable body of empirical evidence to support the view that in simple societies economic rationality is less important than social rationality. Tribes in Africa have been shown to have agricultural production determined by the traditions of society as a whole with little scope for individual choice. This production provides a fixed quantity of food for daily subsistence with a specific margin for entertainment and occasional huge surpluses for distribution through general feasting (Gluckman, 1965:83). Carneiro (1961) has found that the Kuikuru Indians in the Amazon basin need only work 3.5 hours each day to provide enough food for their households by slash and burn agriculture, and that within the present structure of their society there is no economic gain to be had by working harder so they do not devote any more time to increasing their productivity. Perhaps one of the best examples of the nonpursuit of economic gain is that of the Siane tribe in New Guinea, whose time required for providing subsistence needs was suddenly reduced from 80 percent to 50 percent of the total available to the men by the introduction of steel tools to replace stone ones. The men did not devote the extra 30 percent of their working time to increasing their productivity, which rose only 4 percent, instead they increased the time spent on entertaining, ceremonies and fighting (Salisbury, 1962).

It is relatively easy to see how, in the absence of market exchange and money for goods and services, the principle of increasing productivity to increase economic gain becomes meaningless. The problem of economic versus social rationality becomes more difficult to conceptualise, and certainly to find empirical evidence for, in the type of society with which this study is concerned—the peasant society. Peasant societies are intermediate on the scale from primitive, tribal societies to market-oriented, industrial, state organisations. Their intermediate nature is emphasised by their dual role as producers for subsistence and market economics and the coexistence within them of exchange through money and nonmonetary institutions.

Peasant economy must also reflect the dual nature of peasant society. Bohannan and Dalton (1962) characterise the peasant economy in Africa as one of peripheral markets where the laws of supply and demand operate partially but not sufficiently to remove price differences from one market to another or even within the same market. Likewise, the means of production are so dispersed and traditional that fluctuations in prices do not affect the level of production for a long time. Since most transactions in these markets are directly between producer and consumer, and indeed most peasants are alternately one and the other on the same day, the maintenance of social relations and goodwill is as important as economic gain.

Wealth-leveling mechanisms such as those described for Oaxaca appear to be crucial to the inhibition of technological and economic advance in many peasant societies. The form of wealth-leveling varies from a rigid system of fixed rewards for all members of a particular social class whatever the labour given or harvest produced, to informal exchange transactions and the provision of general feasts and ceremonies which are not obligatory. Epstein (1967) describes the system of fixed rewards within the framework of the caste system among peasants in South India. Under this system, about 14 Untouchable households were attached to 1 Peasant farmer who owned all the land. The Untouchables provided the peasant farmer with agricultural labour in return for a fixed amount of produce which was equivalent to the minimum subsistence level for their households. Since the productivity of the harvest varied from year to year, in bad years the Peasant farmer received exactly the same as the Untouchables (8 *pallas* each), but in good years he received all the surplus (up to 300 pallas) and could use this to give feasts and thereby underwrite his prestige. This system of fixed rewards was therefore based on the average productivity in bad years, and the stability of the system rested on the expectation of good years for the peasant and the threat of bad years for the Untouchables (Epstein, 1967:246).

Throughout Mesoamerica, wealth is pooled through institutions similar to those described for Oaxaca with some variation in the rigidity and degree of formality of the system. In Amatenango in southern Mexico, the giving of an obligatory expensive feast is a direct levy against four rich families who are chosen each year by the village authorities to fill the "honorary" post of *alférez* (Nash, 1966:79). Negative sanctions against those who amass private wealth without being generous with their time and money for the benefit of the community are also characteristic of Latin American peasants. Among the Paez Indians of Colombia, to dispel suspicions of private hoarding a man must give a feast or remove himself from his society (Ortiz, 1967:212).

If peasant societies represent dual societies with dual economies, it is likely that they are particularly subject to the conflict created by economic rationality pulling in one direction and social rationality pulling in the other. From the evidence presented here, it would appear that at least for agricultural production, most peasants desire to conform with locally accepted values and practices more than they desire to "go it alone" in the struggle for economic prosperity. However, this is not so for all peasant cultivators, nor for all communities in the Valley; and it is likely that those innovators who pursue economic gain will be emulated by more and more cultivators as their personal success becomes apparent and well established.

To say that in peasant societies economic and social rationality are providing two opposing and powerful forces is one thing; but until more is known about the processes of decision-making and the means whereby conflicting desires are resolved to allow a choice to be made, accepted, and repeated, we are only at a relatively superficial level of understanding of societies and behaviour in social groups. One future course of action is to try to apply the "face-saving theory" being developed in social psychology (Zimbardo, 1969:15) from experiments ranging from small groups of volunteers in the laboratory to the study of societies or social groups in the real world.

Festinger's theory of cognitive dissonance (1964), which predicts the internal conflict which occurs when a person knows he has freely made a choice which does not lead to his desired outcome, has been shown in laboratory experiments to affect biological and social behaviour. For example, subjects who had voluntarily given up eating resolved their internal conflict by feeling less hungry, eating less at the end of the experiment and actually modifying their physiology to accommodate the situation of food deprivation (Brehm, Black, and Bogdonoff, 1969:34-44). Similarly, experimental subjects (except for those termed Machiavellians) who were induced to cheat reduced their internal dissonance by changing their social attitudes—in this case, their views on conventional morality and cheating (Bogart, et al., 1969:251-63). Although at present these experiments may seem far removed from the reality of conflicting desires of economic advancement and social conformity found, for example, in peasant society in Oaxaca today, they do indicate a second approach to the study of decision-making in these societies.

For example, most agricultural decisions are not simple, however primitive the agricultural technology may appear, The complex task of deciding which milpas to cultivate and when to plant them with corn for subsistence is illustrated in Figures 19 to 21 and discussed in Chapter V. The sources of uncertainty for the Oaxacan peasant are similar to those found by Wolpert (1964:547) in Sweden: personal factors such as health, institutional arrangements such as government policy and landlord-tenant relationships, technological changes, market structure and physical factors such as weather and disease. Wolpert also found that the main variable influencing the effect of these uncertainty factors on productivity was the availability of ready capital to enable the farmer to remain flexible in policy and survive short-term income fluctuations (Wolpert, 1964: 553).

The difference between Swedish farmers and Oaxacan peasants is that sources of uncertainty are greatly reduced for the former through social security, government regulations, and better information, whereas they are reduced hardly at all for the Oaxacan peasant. Similarly, the availability of capital, which allows the Swedish farmer flexibility to survive adverse seasons, does not exist in Oaxaca for most cultivators. The result is that Swedish farmers are more progressive and Oaxacan peasants more conservative in their farming policies.

However, traditional agriculture in Oaxaca should not be regarded solely as a defunct relic from the past which in itself is a bar to progress; it also fulfills a necessary function in providing a body of socially approved "good enough" solutions. From the point of view of a "face-saving theory," therefore, the strength of agricultural tradition in Oaxaca can be understood as a means of reducing dissonance resulting from having to make an important and difficult choice with little information by distorting reality to give an appearance of minimal freedom of choice. In the face of extreme uncertainty, traditional answers serve instead of social security and information services to reduce the sheer work and anxiety of computation and assessment involved in, for example, corn planting decisions.

To conclude this discussion of the relationship between social institutions and the limitations placed on agricultural productivity, the evidence presented in detail here for the Valley of Oaxaca seems to be parralleled by other simple societies and peasant groups. For the Valley of Oaxaca, corn productivity per cultivator has been shown to be a function of cultural as well as physical factors, but the roles which specific wealth-leveling institutions play can only be indicated and not demonstrated convincingly. The theoretical issues raised concern two opposing forces which act on human behaviour, economic and social rationality, and the effects of their conflict must be considered for individuals and social groups. In this respect, the study of decision-making behaviour can also be approached from the theoretical standpoint of a general "face-saving theory," which has been shown to predict behaviour in laboratory experiments and could be extended to the study of behaviour of "simple" societies.

The data presented in Chapter VIII led to the conclusion that if agricultural resources in the Valley are being underexploited by peasants today for the reasons discussed above, they were even more underused in the past. Cultural development in an area can be regarded as waiting on new technological developments or an increase in the area controlled in order to increase the resources available and so support an increasingly complex social structure; or the resources and technology can be viewed as the *result* not the cause of social change. This latter view is suggested by Wolf in the idea that the existence of potential surpluses is not as important to development as the ability of the society to organise their use (Wolf, 1966:6). Thus, efficient irrigation of the alluvium in the Etla Valley during the Formative would have depended not only on the technology of canals and dams but also on the organisational ability of the agricultural communities on a supravillage level.

Paddock (1966:149-51) argues that for the Valley of Oaxaca by the Monte Albán IIIB period, the population had reached the limits set by the agricultural resources of the physical environment, and that because no technological development was forthcoming to increase productivity and the agricultural resources of areas beyond the Valley were unusable because they were too distant in the pre-draft animal era, the grand hilltop cities such as Monte Albán began to decline and eventually be abandoned. Paddock is therefore arguing that at this time the population of the Valley was pushing up against a ceiling imposed by the agricultural resources and contemporary technology.

The implications of this paper are that for today and in the past the general weight of the evidence is against such a view, that populations in the past appear to have been less than the Valley could theoretically have supported, and that today agricultural productivity could be increased by about 20 to 50 percent without any advance in technology or capital equipment. For today, the difference between potential maximum productivity and actual production is seen mainly as a function of peasant social values which place stress as much on community relations as on personal economic advance. For the earliest periods in the past, the degree of underuse of potential resources may have been partly a function of the limitations on rate of expansion of numbers in small groups —limitations such as disease incidence and fertility rates. At all stages of development, resources will probably always be used less than the optimum because of the society's limited ability and powers to mobilise them or to match the ends and the means of its economy. In addition, it can be argued, as Paddock has done for Oaxaca, that resources can be overstrained by societies encumbered by an overelaborate superstructure.

If it is believed that the underuse of resources is related to social institutions and values, as has been put foward here, it follows that social institutions need to be changed before resource use can be made more efficient without the intervention of technological innovation. In other words, economic development cannot precede social development but must accompany or follow it. In Oaxaca this process can be seen today in the increased agricultural productivity which follows or accompanies the breakdown of traditional institutions and values. Once the need to distribute surpluses to the less well-off or the need to gain prestige through supporting communal celebrations is removed by a change in attitude of the individual or the community, agriculture is practised more and more by farmers who view it as a form of investment and less by peasants who regard it as a way of life. The price such communities and individuals must pay for increased economic prosperity is that which has already been paid by the western society they are trying to emulate: increased risk, increased social isolation and decreased social security, all of which aspects of life the present structure of peasant society in the Valley is designed to minimise.

# APPENDICES

# I

## PERCEPTION OF ANNUAL RAINFALL

Peasant cultivators were questioned while they were working in the fields about their memory of past annual rainfalls, and their perception of regularities or randomness in rainfall patterns. Forty-five peasants were questioned from all parts of the Valley of Oaxaca, 20 in 1968 and 25 in 1970. The results from both years have been added together in Table 23 and will be compared with the results of meteorological records beginning in 1926 for the station at Tlacolula, which is the one closest to the fields of most informants. Since the total number of informants is small and the method of questioning was casual rather than rigorous, these preliminary results should only be taken as indicative rather than conclusive.

### TABLE 23
### NUMBER AND PERCENTAGE OF PEASANT CULTIVATORS REMEMBERING PAST RAINFALLS AND BELIEVING IN RAINFALL PREDICTION

|  | Reply | |
| --- | --- | --- |
|  | Number | Percent |
| *Wettest Year Remembered: 1951 | 11 | 55 |
| Other | 3 | 15 |
| None | 6 | 30 |
| Driest Year Remembered: 1954 | 1 | 3 |
| Other | 14 | 31 |
| None | 30 | 66 |
| Belief in a 3, 4, 5 or 7 Year Cycle | 11 | 25 |
| Belief in Autocorrelation with Previous Year | 15 | 33 |
| Belief in no Correlation between Years | 19 | 42 |
| Belief in Jan-June Rainfall of Same Year as Predictor | 42 | 95 |
| Don't Know | 3 | 5 |

*Note—Total number of informants = 45, except for wettest year remembered (n = 20) because the wet year of 1969 "blotted out" the memory of earlier years (see text).

### Memory of Past Annual Rainfalls

Of those informants who could remember a wet year by name (60 percent) the majority named 1951 as the wettest they could remember. Other years mentioned were 1943, 1958 and 1966. If these years are compared with the meterological record for Tlacolula (Fig. 58) it can be seen that 1951 was the wettest year on record (with the possible exception of 1969 which came after the results for this question were obtained). The year 1943 was a dry rather than a wet year, but 1958 and 1966 were both wet years. One wet year which was not mentioned by name was 1936, although it had a higher rainfall than 1966.

In contrast, most informants could not remember the driest year by name (66 percent) and only 4 percent correctly stated 1954; 1967 was frequently suggested as the driest year remembered. The most common pattern of memory is therefore one of peak rainfalls, beginning in 1951 and in descending order of magnitude. In addition, the rainfall of the previous year is remembered. The commonest remembered years are indicated in Figure 58. In general terms these data may indicate that memory of natural events begins with an extreme event which effectively blots out memory of earlier events and acts as a fixed point against which to calibrate later occurrences, and that memory of rainfall may be stepped; that is, the last wet year is remembered, then the year before that *which was even wetter,* and so on. Some corroboration of this possibility was found in 1970, when the occurrence of a very wet year in 1969 appeared to blot out the memory of previous wet years, including 1951.

### Perception of Rainfall Patterns

Informants were asked if they thought wet years occurred regularly every few years, if wet

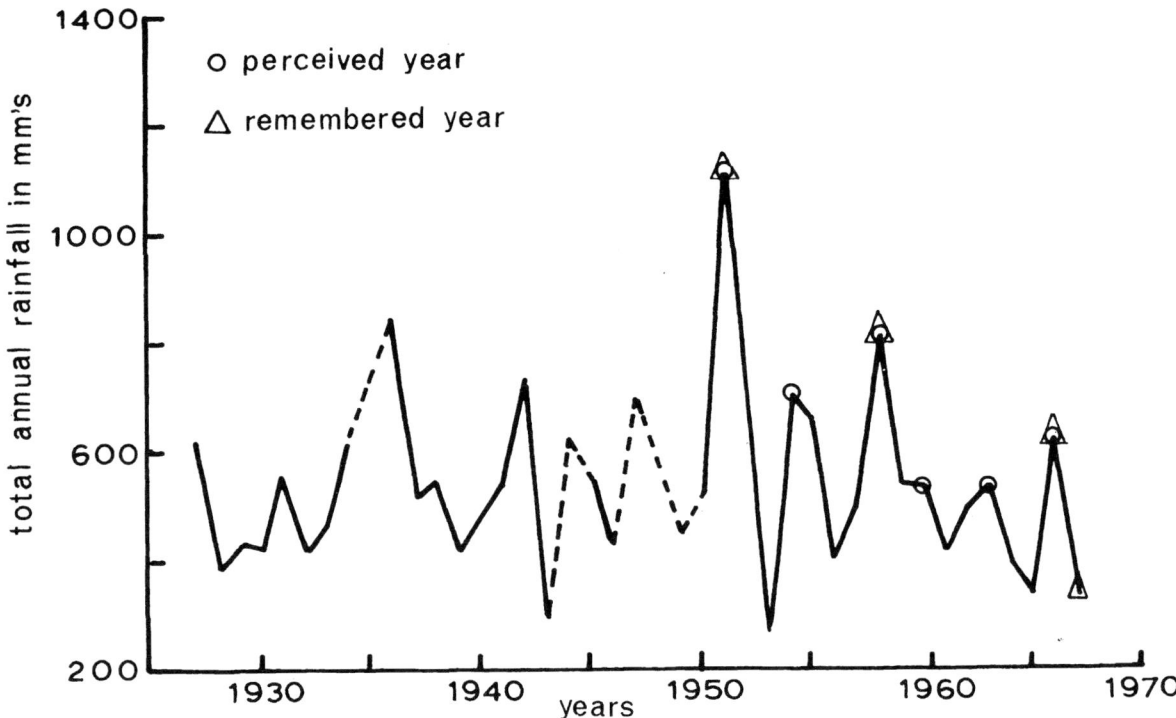

Fig. 58. Patterns of rainfall memory and perception among peasant cultivators in 1968 and 1970 compared with rainfall records made at Tlacolula from 1926 to 1968.

years came in pairs, or if they thought annual rainfall was random and therefore unpredictable. The results are shown in Table 23–58 percent believed that they could detect regularity in annual rainfall; 25 percent of those thought wet years were cyclic, occurring every 3, 4, 5 or 7 years, with 3 years the preferred interval. Another 33 percent of these informants believed that wet years came in pairs, particularly that a really wet year was followed by another, less wet but still higher than average. The other 42 percent, however, thought that there was no correlation in the rainfall of different years, and several mentioned cyclones as more important than the rainfall of a previous year.

Several suggestions were made for the length of rainfall cycles, of which 3 to 4 years was the most common. Such a belief could be interpreted as an idealisation of the time interval between all years with rainfall greater than 540 mm (which were probably good years on average for corn harvests), whose real occurrence intervals from 1951 have been 3, 4, 5, 3, 3, (Fig. 58). Since many of the informants who stated a belief in a cyclic pattern of annual rainfall could not recall specific rainfall years by name, it follows that memory of events does not necessarily correspond to perception of rainfall patterns.

When these two beliefs about rainfall cycles and autocorrelation of rainfall between years are tested against the longer records of the meteorological station at Tlacolula, neither is found to be statistically significant (Fig. 59). However, the belief that early rainfall in a year is related positively to the rainfall of the growing season (June to November) of the same year, which was held by 95 percent of those asked, is supported by the meteorological records. Plotting the rainfall of January to April against the rainfall of May to December produces a highly significant correlation (0.1 percent level). If the spring rainfall is greater than 80 mm, the summer rainfall has an 80 percent chance of being greater than 600 mm, which would be a wet year. If the spring rainfall is low, between 20 and 40 mm, the summer rainfall has a 50 percent probability of being less than

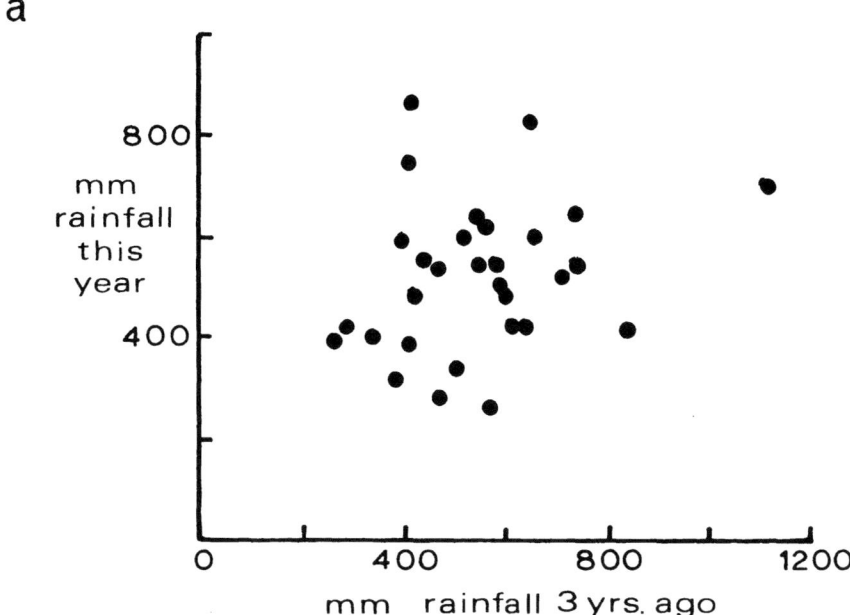

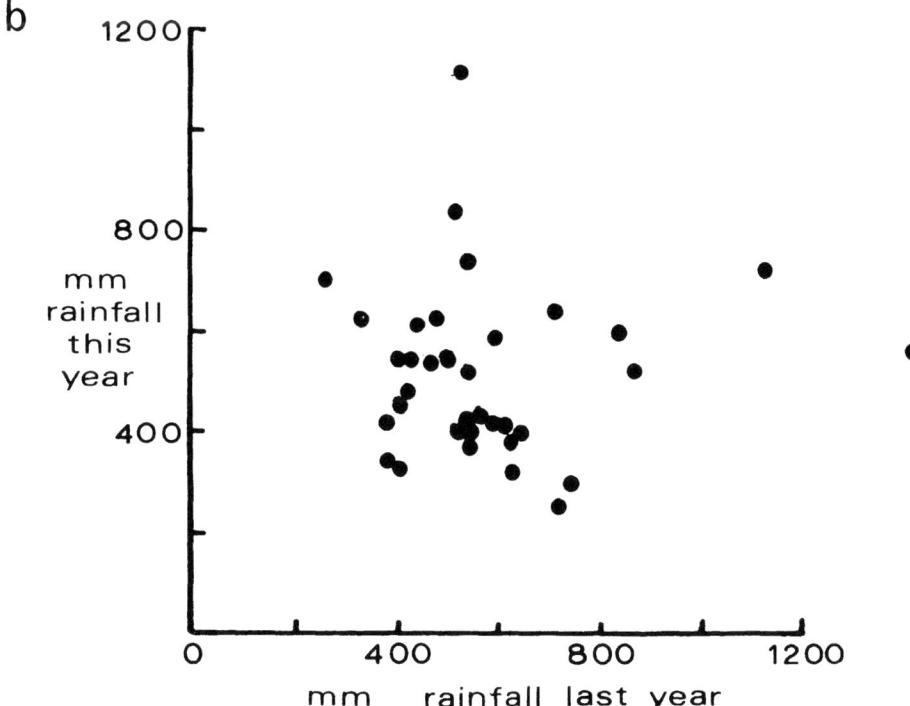

Fig. 59. Annual rainfall for Tlacolula for each year, 1926 to 1968, compared with (*a*) the annual rainfall of 3 years before the given year and (*b*) the annual rainfall of the year previous to the given year.

420 mm, which would be a dry year with crop failure in the more marginal agricultural areas.

From a knowledge of the rainfall of the first 4 months of the year, 50 percent of all wet years and 40 percent of all dry years can be predicted. Without using spring rainfall as a predictor, the probability of the summer being wet (greater than 600 mm) or dry (less than 420 mm) is obviously 25 percent each, so that a knowledge of spring rainfall represents a considerable advantage to cultivators wishing to decide when and where to sow their crops. On the other hand, the expressed beliefs about correlation of rainfall *between* years rather than within years has no statistical validity when compared with the longer record of a meteorological station. Some parallel is seen here with the perception of regularity in statistically random (as far as can be judged) natural events found by Burton and Kates (1964) in the United States. Among residents of coastal areas subject to hurricanes, Kates found that nearly 50 percent of the residents believed they could see regular patterns in hurricane occurrence (Burton, Kates and Snead, 1969:158-159), while 58 percent of Oaxacan peasants saw regularity in wet and dry years. In both cases, the believed regularity of natural events appears to be a result of perception rather than actual experience.

# II

## PRESENT DISTRIBUTION OF CROPS AROUND THE VALLEY

This study has been mainly concerned with the production of corn and the ways in which physical and social factors in the Valley environment influence the cultivation of corn. This is because corn is the most important and most widespread crop grown today and because corn has been equally important in the past both in the beginnings of settled agricultural life in the area and in the subsequent rise of civilisation and the establishment of a powerful state centered in the Valley. Today, however, many other crops are also grown in the Valley, and it is the purpose of this section briefly to describe their distributions.

Areal variations in water availability influence the choice of crops grown along with corn as well as being the prime determinant of corn yield itself. On the piedmont, where irrigation water is usually not available, the combination of crops grown and the proportion of land cultivated rather than left fallow reflect the mean differences in rainfall from one part of the Valley to another. In general, rainfall increases from north to south and from east to west (in addition to marked altitudinal differences) as is shown on the rainfall map (Fig. 8). The effect on crops grown without the advantage of irrigation water is shown in Fig. 60. The piedmont area with the highest rainfall is located in the extreme south of the Zaachila Valley (for example, location 9 in Figure 60) and that with the least rainfall is in the eastern Tlacolula Valley (for example, location 6 in Figure 60).

These variations within one geomorphic unit in the Valley are shown in the proportion of land which can be sown in any one year, ranging from 30 percent in the driest parts (location 6), to about 50 percent in the Etla Valley (locations 1, 3 and 4), and as much as 90 percent in the southernmost and wettest area (locations 8 and 9). Of this 30 to 90 percent of the land which is made productive each year, corn is everywhere the most important crop and generally only two other crops are grown without irrigation in the piedmont. One is maguey which is grown in the drier areas, especially around Mitla and Matatlán, where it seems to thrive on thin caliche soils and where, in any case, its 5 to 10 year growing period minimises the deleterious effect of one or several dry years. The other crop is groundnuts, which are grown in alternate years with corn or may be intercropped with it in parts of the Zaachila Valley.

On the valley floor, a greater variety of crops is found, especially where water in addition to the rainfall is available from streams, wells or directly from a high water table (Fig. 61). The two areas deficient in available water are the eastern Tlacolula Valley and the Ocotlán Valley, both of which have less than 10 percent of their area under irrigated crops (locations 15 and 18 in Figure 61). In contrast, the relatively high water availability in the Etla arm produces a characteristic crop pattern of alfalfa and irrigated corn, with the proportions under each ranging from 30 percent alfalfa and 70 percent corn to the reverse (locations 10 and 11 in Figure 61).

In the Etla Valley, irrigation water comes from streams or directly from the water table through the soil, so that a high proportion of the land can receive at least a little additional water. Where irrigation is afforded by wells, particularly where pot irrigation is the method of distribution, the total land area affected is a small proportion of the cultivated area, generally less than 10 percent. Therefore, although the number of crops grown in a pot-irrigating area may be greater than in the predominantly canal-irrigated Etla Valley, they are confined to a much smaller proportion of the

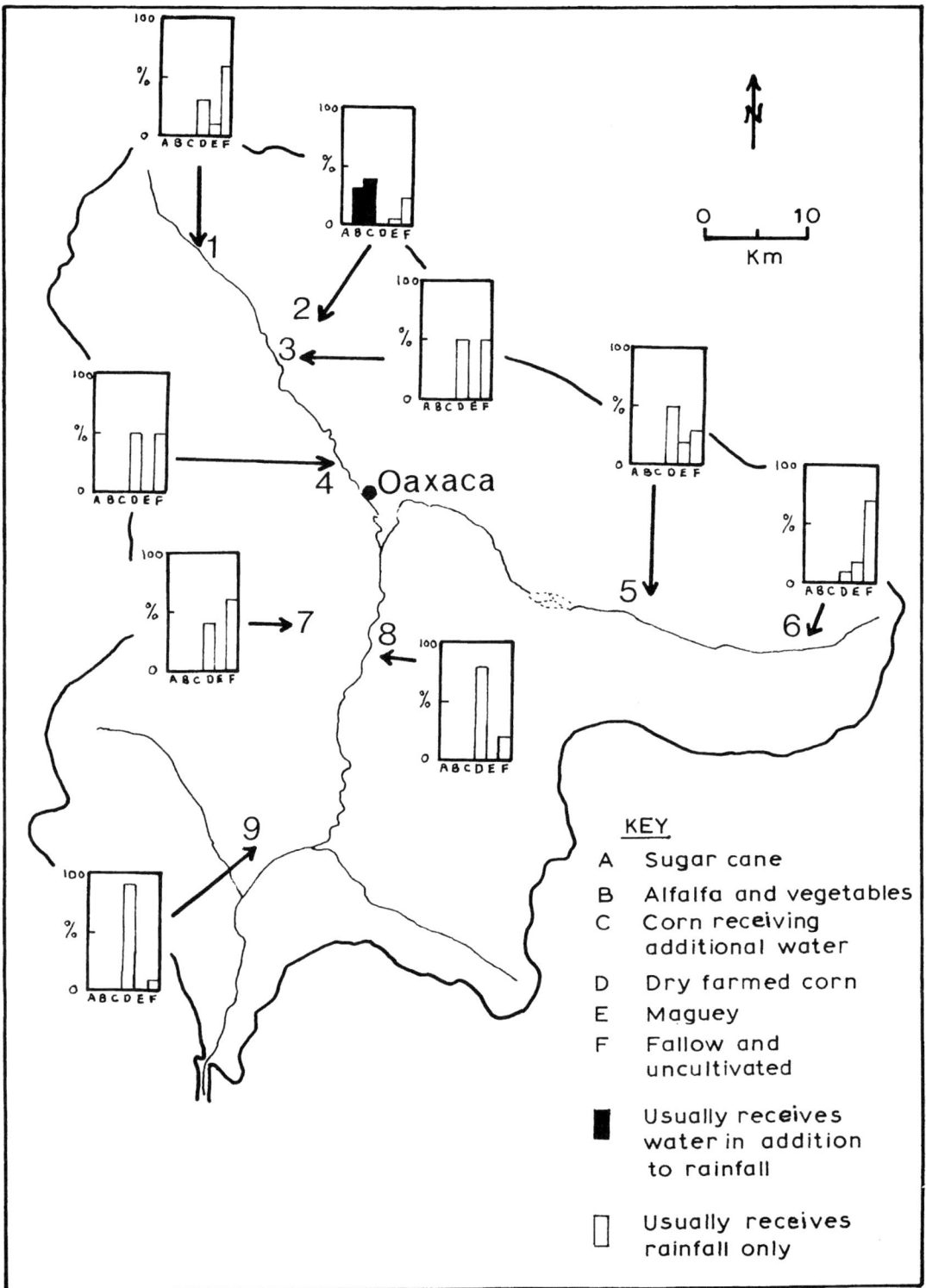

Fig. 60. Measured proportions of areas under different categories of land use for selected points in the piedmont.

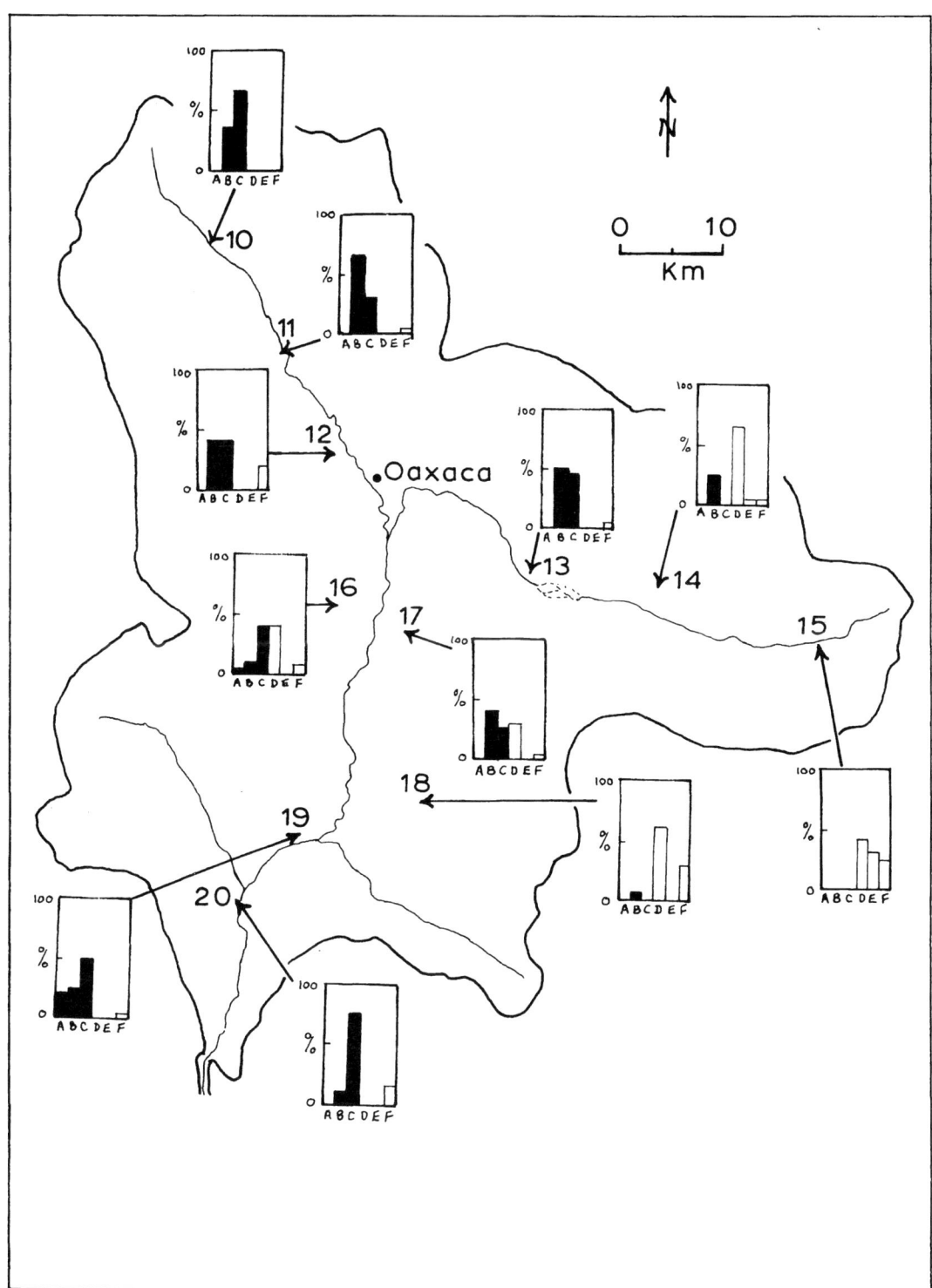

Fig. 61. Measured proportions of areas under different categories of land use* for selected points on the valley floor.

*For key to land use see Figure 60.

fields. A typical crop pattern for pot irrigation is that shown for Zaachila (location 16 in Figure 61), with 10 percent under alfalfa and vegetables such as tomatoes, chile and garlic and 80 percent under corn and groundnuts (about half of which probably receive a little additional water from flood discharges). A second pot-irrigation area is shown at location 13 (Fig. 61), but here the effects of pot irrigation on the overall crop pattern are masked by the availability of water for alfalfa and corn from a high water table.

In comparing the effect of physiographic zone on the proportions of crops that are grown, the main difference between the valley floor and the piedmont is in the higher ratio of fallow and uncultivated land to all crops, whether or not irrigation water is available. Compare, for example, the distributions at locations 2 and 11 for irrigated land in the Etla Valley and at locations 6 and 15 for unirrigated land in both physiographic zones in the eastern Tlacolula Valley (Figs 60 and 61).

For most crops the effect of temperature differences within the Valley floor is negligible, but a few frost-sensitive crops are restricted to the frost-free zone, that is, south of Oaxaca de Juárez, particularly in the extreme south of the Zaachila arm. Sugar cane is grown within this area where sufficient water is available (mainly from a high water table) but is everywhere a minority crop, reaching a maximum of 20 percent of the area near Valdeflores and Santa Gertrudis (location 19 in Figure 61). Farther north, near Zaachila, the proportion of sugar cane falls to 5 percent (location 16 in Figure 61). A newly introduced crop, Turkish tobacco, is also confined to the southern Zaachila Valley in order to minimise the risk of damage from frosts. Its distribution is widely scattered in small plots of 0.25 hectare so that areally it is not yet important, but it is hoped that it will expand enough to support a new tobacco processing plant built near the railway at Zimatlán in 1968. In the southern Zaachila Valley, the rainfall is usually high enough to cultivate the Turkish tobacco except just before and after transplanting, when it is irrigated by sprinklers or pot irrigation.

Castor bean is a widespread crop which is a perennial but grows so rapidly that it is usually cleared out after 2 to 3 years before its size would make its removal very hard work with only machetes. Its beans are crushed to make a light, low-temperature oil which is exported from the state. It was formerly an important local product for use in domestic oil lamps, but these are rarely used today. Small amounts of castor bean can be seen in many areas, particularly around the villages, but it rarely accounts for more than 1 percent of the cultivated area except in the Ocotlán Valley where it may reach 5 to 10 percent and, to a lesser degree, elsewhere in the Zaachila arm.

In addition to the crops discussed so far, many villages and solars are surrounded by fruit trees, especially where additional water is available from canals or a high water table. Common fruit trees include avocados, *zapotes*, peaches, mangos, limes, lemons, pecan nuts and bananas. These trees are important to the diet and income of the owner and are a source of great pride; they are commonly the only crops to be guarded by the younger members of the household.

# III

## LAMBITYECO LAND USE AREA

The Lambityeco area is located in the dry eastern part of the Tlacolula Valley, 2 kilometers west of the town of Tlacolula, where the main valley floor is much wider than it is farther east at Mitla (Fig. 2). The area lies near the centre of the valley and is crossed by the ephemeral stream which drains the Díaz Ordaz Valley. The character of this stream changes within the locality of the sample area from a single channel whose peak flows are efficiently diverted into fairly large-scale floodwater distributary schemes, to a braided channel network that seasonally floods the valley centre and makes it uncultivable during the summer (Fig. 62). The area thus lies at the upstream end of the seasonal swamp centred on San Juan Guelavía, and its predominant water use can be classified as dry farming supplemented by small-scale floodwater schemes which are inefficient in channeling water to and from fields. Within the area itself, the main contrasts are in soil texture and in frequency of flooding, and these are related to the two physiographic zones present—the piedmont and high alluvium.

The piedmont is not part of the valley edge at this point but is situated on the lower slopes of one of the many ignimbrite bedrock knobs that project above the valley floor in this locality. Most of this piedmont slope is formed on gravels rather than bedrock, and the soils developed on them are relatively thin, free-draining sands and silts. In contrast, the soils on the high alluvium are deep clays which become increasingly heavy as the central uncultivated zone is approached. The water table is fairly deep throughout the area, ranging from greater than 10 meters on the piedmont to about 5 to 6 meters on the high alluvium. The main distinction in water availability is in the amount of flooding which increases from the piedmont towards the marshy zone. In the piedmont, floodwater is available only from two small streams draining the bedrock hill. On the high alluvium, floodwater is received both from minor tributaries draining the valley floor to the north and from the old Tlacolula-Oaxaca road, which drains the paved central area of Tlacolula and is more efficiently channeled downstream of the sample areas (Fig. 15). Around the edge of the central depression is a zone of very heavy clay which is liable to damaging floods in wet years and where planting and fallowing strategies are particularly sensitive to flooding conditions.

The marginal dry and floodwater farming practised today in the sample area is in marked contrast to the organisation of floodwater distribution upstream. It is of particular interest because on the piedmont slope are many archaeological mounds and structures which together form the important archaeological complex of Lambityeco (Monte Albán IIIB-IV period) currently being excavated by Paddock (Fig. 62). The site's location may well have been partly determined by the proximity of the well-drained piedmont slope to the course of the Díaz Ordaz stream with its floodwater potential, and to the fine-grained alluvial soils of the valley floor immediately around the piedmont knob. It is not unlikely that water management of this area was more efficient in the past if political control and water rights were centered on Lambityeco rather than upstream in Díaz Ordaz as they are today.

The contrast between the two physiographic zones represented in the area—the drier and stonier piedmont and wetter and finer grained alluvium—is shown in the differences in land use (Fig. 63 and Table 24). The piedmont pattern includes a large proportion of fallow (31 percent), but corn is still

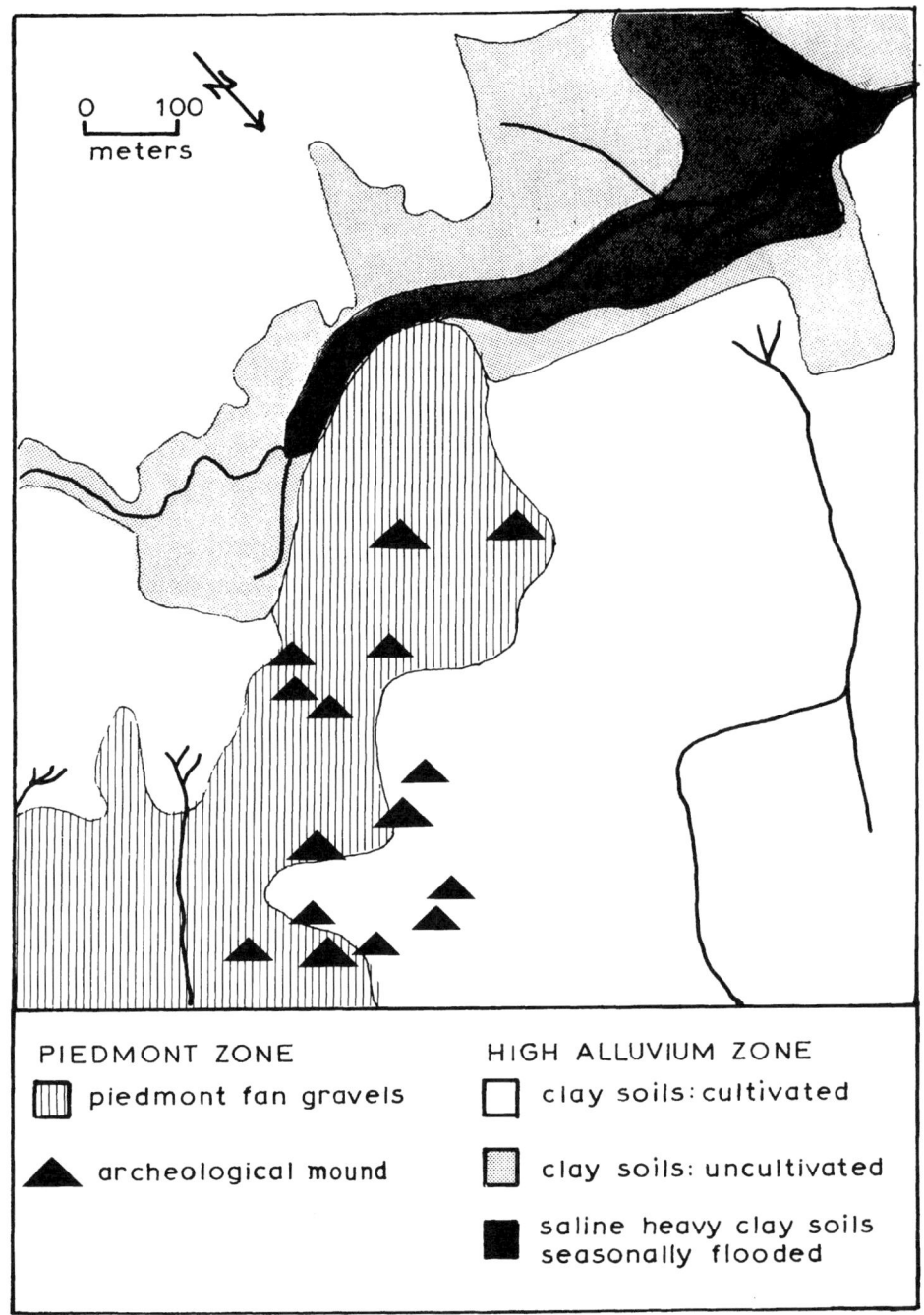

Fig. 62. Physical and archaeological features of part of the Lambityeco sample area.

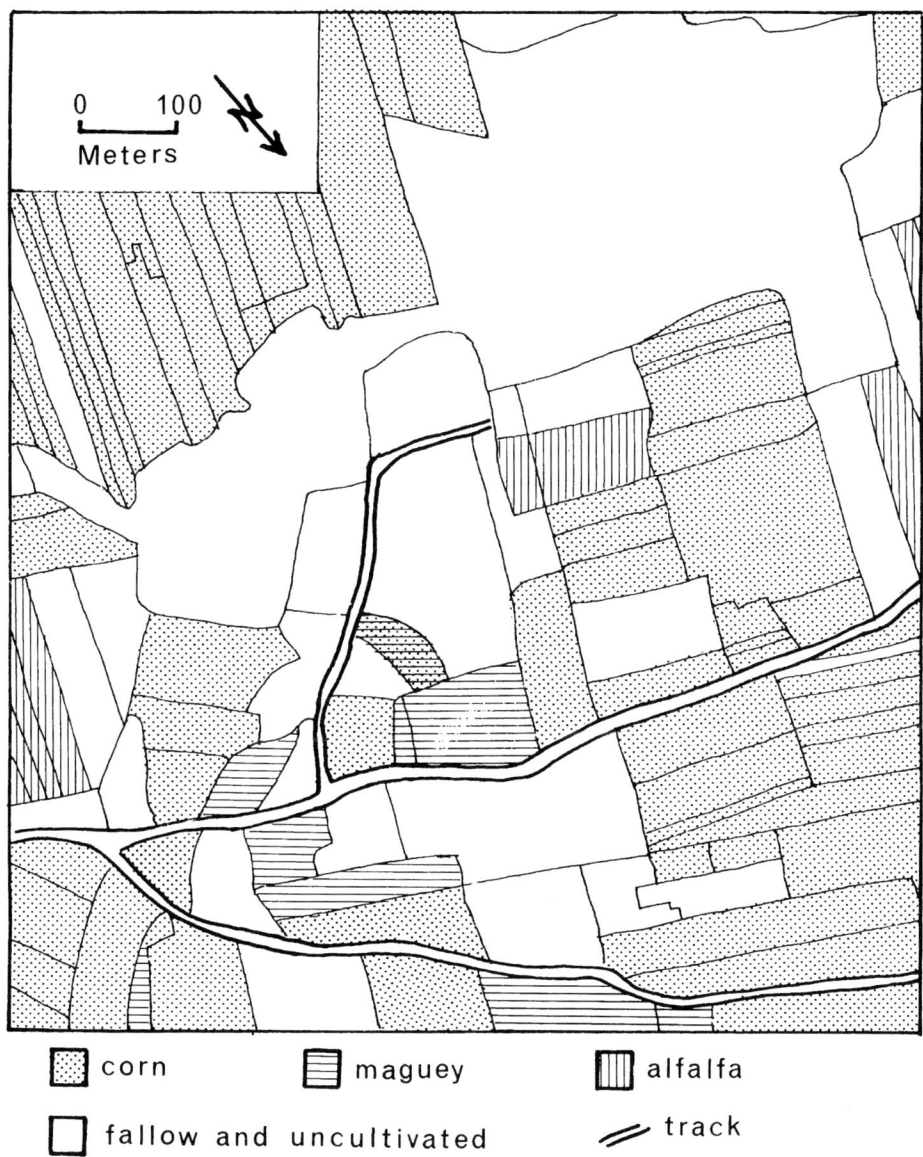

Fig. 63. Land use of part of the Lambityeco sample area in 1970.

the dominant land use (45 percent) and the other crop is maguey (8 percent), a plant which tolerates poor soils and dry conditions. On the alluvium, maguey accounts for only 1 percent of the area and fallow for 5 percent, although 18 percent cannot be cultivated because it forms part of the seasonally flooded and slightly saline central depression. Corn is again the most important crop (54-62 percent) and alfalfa can also be grown on 14 percent of the land with the aid of floodwater and wells with pumps.

In general composition, therefore, the land use of the Lambityeco piedmont is closer to that of the high alluvium than the piedmont zone in Mitla (Table 13), and this reflects the trend of increasing mean annual rainfall from east to west, between the two sample areas. Likewise, the pattern on the Lambityeco high alluvium parallels the low rather than the high alluvium in Miltla. An additional factor here may be that within their own localities, both zones represent the wettest situations available, and both are areas where

### TABLE 24
#### LAND USE OF THE LAMBITYECO AREA BY PERCENTAGE OF PHYSIOGRAPHIC ZONE* AREA, 1966 TO 1968

|  | 1966 | | 1967 | | 1968 | |
| --- | --- | --- | --- | --- | --- | --- |
|  | P | HA | P | HA | P | HA |
| Corn | 45 | 62 | 45 | 59 | 32 | 54 |
| Maguey | 8 | 1 | 7 | 1 | 6 | 1 |
| Alfalfa | 0 | 14 | 0 | 10 | 0 | 7 |
| Fallow | 31 | 5 | 32 | 12 | 46 | 20 |
| Uncultivated | 16 | 18 | 16 | 18 | 16 | 18 |

*P = piedmont, HA = high alluvium.

yields may be expected to decline in wet years from flooding.

The Lambityeco area was first surveyed in 1966 so that land use data have now been obtained for four years. Although a detailed analysis of the area is not given in the text of this study—from the point of view of corn production, the Mitla sample area proved to be more valuable—the results of the work done in Lambityeco are incorporated into the body of the argument (see Figs. 29 and 35). For this reason, the land use data and land use change matrices for the Lambityeco area are presented in this appendix.

The land use change matrices shown in Table 25 are similar to those already described for other areas (for explanation see pages 79-80). The matrices show a consistent trend towards increasing the area under fallow in both physiographic zones; in the piedmont corn is giving way to fallow, and in the high alluvium both corn and alfalfa are declining in favour of fallow land. This trend is probably due to both physical environmental variations and changing economic conditions.

### TABLE 25
#### LAND USE CHANGE MATRICES FOR PHYSIOGRAPHIC ZONES IN THE LAMBITYECO AREA, 1966 TO 1968

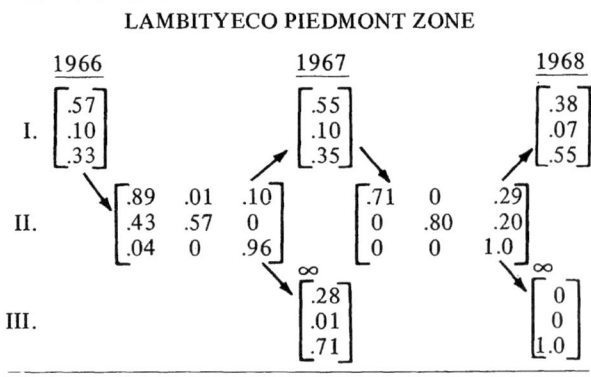

Explanation:
I. measured land use pattern for each year
II. transition matrices for land use change between years
III. equilibrium land use pattern resulting from similar changes repeated indefinitely

$p_{ij} = p$ (changing from crop i to crop j)

For piedmont

    i,j = 1. corn
           2. maguey
           3. fallow

For high alluvium

    i,j = 1. corn
           2. fallow
           3. alfalfa

# RESUMEN EN ESPAÑOL

(por David J. Wilson)

La investigación de la doctora Anne Kirkby se realizó durante los años 1966 a 1970 como una parte del proyecto de la Universidad de Michigan "La Ecología Humana Prehistórica del Valle de Oaxaca" y se trata de la utilización de la tierra y el agua en la región de Oaxaca los tiempos más antiguos hasta la época presente.

En el Capítulo I se discuten los diferentes métodos de campo (geología, geografía cultural y física) que se emplearon. En el Capítulo II se examinan los resursos agrícolas del valle, que está situado en la región montañosa del sur de México a una altura de 1500 metros s. n. m. Kirkby define cuatro zonas fisiográficas: los bajos suelos de aluvión (el área inundada actualmente por el río Atoyac), los altos suelos de aluvión (el área de inundación pleistocena del río, que constituye el fondo llano del valle), el somontano y las montañas. Estas tienen un régimen de lluvia más alto, pero la mayor parte de la agricultura se practica en el fondo del valle, que es una área deficiente en agua (evaporación > precipitacion). Las heladas sólo presentan un problema en las alturas más elevadas.

En el Capítulo III se discute la organización social de terreno, labor y producción. Los terrenos en el valle de Oaxaca son por lo común pequeños y dispersos, con una división entre los terrenos particulares y los ejidos. Dos tipos de labor comunal son *guelaguetza,* una forma de retardada ayuda voluntaria recíproca y *tequio,* que es trabajo obligatorio comunal para la aldea. Este se administra por las autoridades de la aldea eligidas por el muy esparcido sistema de *cargo* tal como en otras partes de México.

En el Capítulo IV se describen las varias técnicas del uso de agua en el valle. La más sencilla, y la menos segura, es la agricultura de secano (temporal). Más productivo es el sistema de cultivo por inundación. Ese sistema utiliza la lluvia, que por medio de pequeñas presas de desviación hechas de ramas y terrazas bajas que retienen cierta cantidad de agua. Riego a brazo es una especie de irrigación que se hace con pozos poco profundos en las regiones del valle donde el agua freática se encuentra a unos tres metros debajo de la superficie (o más bajo en algunas áreas). La irrigación por el sistema de canales se realiza por medio de sencillas presas de desviación o tomas de agua y pequeños canales que corren con la gravedad.

La applicación de estas técnicas varia en las tres secciones distintas del valle de Oaxaca. En la región de Etla (en el noroeste), que tiene una extensión de 202 kilómetros$^2$, se riega más o menos el 50% de la región, la mayor parte con canales. En la región de Zaachila (en el sur), que tiene una extensión de 616 kilómetros$^2$, se riega el 25%, la mayor parte con riego a brazo. En la región de Tlacolula (en el este), que tiene una extensión de 352 kilómetros$^2$, el 33% se riega, la mayor parte con agricultura de inundación.

En el Capítulo V se describe la estrategia para la producción del maíz, que es sobre todo una función de la disponibilidad del agua. La figura 19 es un diagrama de flujo ("flow diagram") para hacer decisiones en cuanto a cuándo y dónde sembrar. Las razas "violento" y "tardón" del maíz pueden utilizarse de acuerdo con el régimen de lluvias (o sea si es un año de sequía o un año lluvioso). Los campesinos usualmente dispersan sus milpas por el valle, el somontano y las áreas montañosas como una forma de seguro. Kirkby da la rendición en toneladas métricas por hectárea para las distintas áreas del valle, y para las distintas condiciones de agua y suelo.

En el Capítulo VI se trata de la agricultura de subsistencia en los terrenos no irrigados; se usa la región de Mitla como ejemplo. La mayoría de las parcelas tienen una extensión de más o menos 2.5 hectáreas. Al usar la coa, los costos llegan a ser más o menos 160 pesos por hectárea, pero un hombre sólo puede cultivar unas 2 hectáreas. Al usar el arado con una yunta de bueyes, los costos llegan a ser 1060 pesos por hectárea, pero un hombre puede cultivar 8 hectáreas. Con un tractor, los costos son 820 pesos por hectarea y un hombre puede cultivar 50 hectáreas, pero es posible que este método no sea factible donde existe una dispersión de las parcelas. En vez de tratar de conseguir lo máximo en la producción del maíz, los campesinos tratan de minimizar la posibilidad de los peores resultados. Aplicación del método de ("game theory analysis") a los diferentes sistemas de producción utilizados durante un período de cinco años demuestra que los campesinos han escogido una solución de conseguir un "maximin" en forma limitada ("constrained maximining solution") en los suelos de aluvión, pero que en el somontano tiendan a "arriesgar" la producción. En los años lluviosos—que se predicen por el régimen de lluvias del mes de junio—ellos reducen los sembríos en los suelos de aluvión y los aumentan en el somontano, mientras que hacen lo contrario en los años de sequía.

El Capítulo VII se trata de la agricultura comercial ("cash farming") en los terrenos de regadío, utilizando Zaachila, Abasola y San Antonio Ocotlán como ejemplos. Andando el tiempo puede verse una tendencia general de suficiencia propia de la aldea hacia (1) riego a brazo especializado de hortalizas en cerca de 10 aldeas y (2) irrigación con canales del maíz en las aldeas del somontano. Riego a brazo da una buena cosecha pero requiere más trabajo; raras veces constituye más que el 10% de la agricultura de la comunidad. La irrigación con canales en Oaxaca funciona debajo del nivel óptimo ya que la ética equitativa de compartir el agua no empareja los mejores terrenos con las mejores fuentes de agua.

En el Capítulo VIII, Kirkby trata de relacionar la agricultura prehistórica con la población. Ella nota una buena relación en Oaxaca entre la producción actual del maíz (en kilogramos por hectárea) y la densidad de la población de la región (según los recientes censos del gobierno mexicano) en las varias secciones del valle. Actualmente, los campesinos de Oaxaca consideran que 200 kilogramos por hectárea son la mínima cosecha para que valga la pena sembrar ciertos tipos de terreno. Una familia de five personas necesita 2.4 toneladas métricas al año, y sólo puede cultivar un promedio de eight hectáreas por lo máximo. Kirkby establece una equación de regresión lineal ("linear regression") que le permite relacionar la rendición en kilogramos por hectárea con los promedios de la longitud de la mazorca de maíz; esto luego le permite calcular las rendiciones en las épocas prehistóricas cuando se sabe los promedios de la longitud de la mazorca.

Dadas estas figuras, luego Kirkby produce cinco mapas que muestran las áreas del valle de Oaxaca en las cuales pudieran producirse 200 kilogramos o más por hectárea (y, por eso, pudiera cultivarse) en los años de 1300 a.C., 1000 a.C., 300-1 a.C., 900 d.C. y 1970 d.C. En estos mapas ella predice lo que, teóricamente, pudiera ser la población prehistórica dada la producción del maíz como el único factor. Los mismos datos de población derivados de la arqueología luego pueden compararse con sus predicciones. Para este propósito, se utiliza el reconocimiento del doctor Ignacio Bernal del valle de Oaxaca (aumentado por datos del proyecto de la Universidad de Míchigan).

Hasta el año 1000 a.C., el número de aldeas arqueológicas representa sólo una tercera parte de lo que teóricamente pudiera mantenerse. Por los años 300-1 a.C., el patrón sugiere bastante irrigación con canales en la zona del somontano, y la ubicación de centros mayores con motivos de defensa. La región de Etla es la más densamente poblada en los tiempos antiguos, pero cede al área de Zaachila hacia 900 d.C., a medida que las razas más grandes del maíz hacen que sea útil una porción mayor de la región de Zaachila. Hacia esta fecha, hay concentraciones de sitios menores alrededor de los "lugares centrales" mayores que no se predicen por el modelo del uso del terreno de Kirkby, y por eso debieran determinarse políticamente. El mapa del año 1970 d.C. se acerca a la población actual, pero todavía representa menos de lo que podría mantenerse con los métodos actuales de la agricultura.

En el Capítula IX, Kirkby llega a las siguientes conclusiones acerca de Oaxaca.

1. La rendición del maíz es una función del agua, no del suelo.
2. La cantidad sembrada es una función de metas fijas que "satisfacen" al campesino, no de lo máximo posible.
3. La conclusión 2 es válida aun para las cosechas comerciales, como se revela en los datos sobre riego a brazo.
4. El valle siempre ha producido menos de lo máximo, desde el año de 1300 d.C. La población ha sido menos de lo que, teóricamente, pudiera mantenerse, y nunca se impulsó la producción a sus límites—ni siquiera durante el apogeo de Monte Albán (700 d.C.).
5. Las instituciones sociopolíticas como el *cargo*, *guelaguetza* y *tequio* refuerzan la tendencia del campesino de buscar la satisfacción, y no lo máximo.
6. Prabablemente para todos los períodos, tanto prehistóricos como recientes, los campesinos de Oaxaca siguen un razonamiento social y no un razonamiento económico. Cuando sí intensificaban la producción, era (a) porque tenían que hacerlo, y (b) porque la estructura sociopolítica había cambiado y podría requerir más producción—no lo contrario, como tantas veces se ha sugerido.

# REFERENCES

Albritten, C. C. and Kirk Bryan
    1939 Quaternary Stratigraphy in the Davis Mountains, Trans-Pecos, Texas. Geological Society of America, Bulletin, Vol. 50:1423-74, New York.

Barry, R. G.
    1969 Evaporation and Transpiration. *In*: Water, Earth and Man. Richard J. Chorley, ed. Methuen. London.

Beals, Ralf L.
    1967 The Structure of the Oaxaca Market System. Revista Mexicano de Estudios Antropologicos tomo XX:333-42. Mexico D.F.

Bogart, Karen, Florence Geis, Marguerite Levy, and Philip G. Zimbardo
    1969 No Dissonance for Machiavellians? *In*: The Cognitive Control of Motivation. Philip G. Zimbardo, ed. Scott, Foresman and Co. Glenview, Illinois.

Bohannan, P. and G. Dalton, eds.
    1962 Markets in Africa. Northwestern University Press. Evanston, Illinois.

Brehm, Mary L., Kurt W. Black, and Morton D. Bogdonoff
    1969 A Physiological Effect of Cognitive Dissonance under Food Deprivation and Stress. *In*: The Cognitive Control of Motivation. Philip G. Zimbardo, ed. Scott, Foresman and Co. Glenview, Illinois.

Bryan, Kirk
    1925 Date of Channel Trenching (arroyo cutting) in the Arid Southwest. Science Vol. 62:338-44. Lancaster.
    1929 Floodwater Farming. Geographical Review Vol. 19:444-56. New York.

Burling, Robbins
    1962 Maximisation Theories and the Study of Economic Anthropology. American Anthropologist Vol. 64:802-21.

Burton, Ian and Robert W. Kates
    1964 Perception of Natural Hazards in Resource Management. Natural Resources Journal Vol. 111:412-41.

Burton, Ian, Robert W. Kates, and Rodman E. Snead
    1969 The Human Ecology of Coastal Flood Hazard in Megalopolis. Department of Geography Research Paper No. 115. University of Chicago. Chicago.

Cancian, Frank
    1967 Political and Religious Organizations. *In*: Handbook of Middle American Indians, Vol. 6. Robert Wauchope, ed. University of Texas Press. Austin.

Carneiro, Robert L.
    1961 Slash and Burn Cultivation among the Kuikuru and Its Implications for Cultural Development in the Amazon Basin. *In*: The Evolution of Horticultural Systems in Native South America; Causes and Consequences. Johannes Wilbert, ed. Antropologica, Supplement No. 2.

Chang, J. H.
    1965 On the Study of Evapotranspiration and the Water Balance. Erdkunde Vol. 19:141-50.

Dalton, George
    1961 Economic Theory and Primitive Society. American Anthropologist Vol. 63:1-25.

Dennis, Philip A.
    1968 Wealth in Zautla. Unpublished dissertation. University of Stanford.

Dewey, A.
    1962 Peasant Marketing in Java. Free Press. Glencoe.

Editorial Porrua
 1969 Código Agrario y Leyes Complementarias. Leyes y Códigos de Mexico; Collección Porrua. Editorial Porrua, S.A. Mexico D.F.

Epstein, Scarlett
 1967 Productive Efficiency and Customary Systems of Rewards in Rural South India. *In*: Themes in Economic Anthropology. Raymond Firth, ed. Tavistock Publications. London.

Festinger, L.
 1964 Conflict, Decision and Dissonance. Stanford University Press. Stanford.

Firth, Raymond
 1951 Elements of Social Organisation. Watts. London.

Flannery, Kent V., ed.
 1969 Preliminary Archaeological Investigations in the Valley of Oaxaca, Mexico 1966-69. A report to the National Science Foundation and the Instituto Nacional de Antropología e Historia. Mimeographed. University of Michigan Museum of Anthropology. Ann Arbor.

Flannery, Kent V., M. J. Kirkby, A. V. T. Kirkby, and Aubrey W. Williams, Jr.
 1967 Farming Systems and Political Growth in Ancient Oaxaca. Science Vol. 158:445-54.

Flannery, Kent V. and Marcus C. Winter
 1969 Land Use in Prehistoric Oaxaca. Paper delivered at Boston Meeting of American Association for Advancement of Science, December, 1969.

Forde, Daryll and Mary Douglas
 1956 Primitive Economics. *In*: Man, Culture and Society. Harry L. Shapiro, ed. Oxford University Press. London.

Gluckman, Max
 1965 Politics, Law and Ritual in Tribal Society. Blackwell. Oxford.

Hack, John T.
 1942 The Changing Environment of the Hopi Indians of Arizona. Reports of the Awatovi Expedition, Peabody Museum, Harvard University, No. 1. Papers of the Peabody Museum of American Archaeology and Ethnology, Harvard University Vol. XXXV. University of Harvard Press. Cambridge.

Herold, Laurance C.
 1965 Trincheras and Physical Environment along the Río Gavilan, Chihuahua, Mexico. Publications in Geography, Technical Paper No. 65-1. Department of Geography, University of Denver. Denver.

Hill, A. D.
 1964 The Changing Landscape of a Mexican Municipio, Villa Las Rosas, Chiapas. Department of Geography, Research Paper No. 91. University of Chicago. Chicago.

Holmes, R. M.
 1961 Estimation of Soil Moisture Content Using Evaporation Data. *In*: Proceeding of Hydrology Symposium No. 2, Evaporation. Department of Northern Affairs and National Resources. Ottowa.

Kirkby, Anne V.
 1969 Primitive Irrigation. *In*: Water, Earth and Man. Richard J. Chorley, ed. Methuen and Co. London.

Kirkby, M. J.
 1973 Past and Present Physical Environment of the Valley of Oaxaca, Mexico. Memoirs of the Museum of Anthropology, University of Michigan. Ann Arbor. (In preparation.)

Lees, Susan H.
 1973 Socio-political Aspects of Canal Irrigation in the Valley of Oaxaca, Mexico. Memoirs of the Museum of Anthropology, No. 6. University of Michigan. Ann Arbor.

Lewis, Oscar
 1964 Pedro Martínez. Panther Edition. Panther Books. London.

Mangelsdorf, Paul C., Richard S. MacNeish, and Walton C. Galinat
 1964 Domestication of Corn. Science Vol. 143:538-45.
 1967 The Prehistory of the Tehuacán Valley. Vol. 11, Douglas S. Byers, ed. Smithsonian Contributions to Anthropology. Smithsonian Institution. Washington, D.C.

Mather, J. R. ed.
 1954 The Measurement of Potential Evapotranspiration, Problems in Climatology. Seabrook. New Jersey.

Nash, Manning
    1966 Primitive and Peasant Economic Systems. Chandler Publishing Co. San Francisco.

Neely, James A.
    1967 Organización Hidráulica y Sistemas de Irrigación Prehistóricos en Valle de Oaxaca. Boletín No. 27. Instituto Nacional de Antropología e Historia. Mexico, D.F.

Orlandini, Richard J.
    1967 A Formative Well from the Valley of Oaxaca. Paper presented at the 32nd Annual Meeting of the Society for American Archaeology. Ann Arbor, Michigan.

Ortiz, Sutti
    1967 The structure of Decision-making among Indians of Colombia. *In*: Themes in Economic Anthropology. Raymond Firth, ed. Tavistock Publications. London.

Paddock, John, ed.
    1966 Ancient Oaxaca. Stanford University Press. Stanford.

Palerm, A. and E. R. Wolf
    1957 Ecological Potential and Cultural Development in Mesoamerica. Pan American Union Social Science Monograph No. 3.

Parson, Elsie Clews
    1936 Mitla, Town of the Souls. Reprinted 1966. University of Chicago. Chicago.

Parsons, Jeffrey R.
    1968 Classic Teotihuacan as Seen from Texcoco. Paper delivered at Annual Meeting of the Society for American Archaeology at Santa Fe, New Mexico, May 1968.

Paso y Troncoso, F. del
    1905 Papeles de Nueva España. 2ª serie. Geografía y Estadística, Vol. 4. Relaciones geográficas de la diócesis de Oaxaca. Manuscritos de la Real Academia de la Historia de Madrid y del Archivo de Indias en Sevilla. Años 1579-1581. Madrid.

Polyanyi, K, C. W. Arensburg, and H. W. Pearson
    1957 Trade and Market in the Early Empires. Free Press. Gencoe, Illinois.

Redfield, Robert
    1956 Peasant Society and Culture. 4th impression 1965. University of Chicago Press. Chicago.

Sahlins, Marshall D.
    1960 Political Power and the Economy in Primitive Society. *In*: Essays in the Science of Culture, G. E. Dole and R. L. Carneiro, eds. Crowell. New York.
    1965 On the Sociology of Primitive Exchange. *In*: The Relevance of Models for Social Anthropology. Michael Banton, ed. ASA Monographs 1. Tavistock Publications. London.

Salisbury, R. F.
    1962 From Stone to Steel. Melbourne University Press. Melbourne.

Sanders, William T.
    1968 Hydraulic Agriculture, Economic Symbiosis and the Evolution of States in Central Mexico. Anthropological Archaeology in the Americas. The Anthropological Society of Washington, D.C.

Schmeider, Oscar
    1930 The Settlements of the Tzapotec and Mije Indians, State of Oaxaca, Mexico. Publications in Geography Vol. 4. University of California Press. Berkeley, California.

Schoenwetter, J., M. J. Kirkby, and A. Kirkby
    1967 Past and Present Environment of the Valley of Oaxaca. Paper delivered at the 32nd Annual Meeting of the Society for American Archaeology. Ann Arbor, Michigan.

Secretaria de Industria y Comercio; Dirección General de Estadística.
    1963 VIII Censo General de Polacion 1960; Estado de Oaxaca, tomo 1. Secretaria de Industria y Comercio. Mexico, D.F.

Simon, Herbert A.
    1957 Models of Man. John Wiley and Sons, Inc. New York.
    1967 Motivational and Emotional Controls of Cognition. Psychological Review Vol. 74:22-39.

Steward, J., ed.
    1955 Irrigation Civilisations: A Comparative Study. Pan American Union. Washington, D.C.

Taylor, William B.
: [1]1969 The Valley of Oaxaca, A Study of Colonial Land Distribution. Unpublished dissertation. University of Michigan. Ann Arbor.

Thornthwaite, C. W.
: 1948 An Approach Towards a Rational Classification of Climate. Geographical Review Vol. 38:85-94.
: 1954 A Re-examination of the Concept and Measurement of Potential Transpiration. *In*: The Measurement of Potential Evapo-transpiration, Problems in Climatology. J. R. Mather, ed. Seabrook. New Jersey.

Veihmeyer, F. J. and A. H. Hendrickson
: 1931 The Moisture Equivalent as a Measure of the Field Capacity of Soils. Soil Science, Vol. 32:181-193.

Weatherwax, Paul
: 1954 Indian Corn in Old America. MacMillan. New York.

Webster, Steven S.
: 1968 The Religious Cargo System and Socio-economic Differentiation in Santa María Guelace. Manuscript.

Welte, Cecil R.
: 1966 Mapa de las Localidades del Valle de Oaxaca. Oficina de Estudios de Humanidad del Valle de Oaxaca. Oaxaca de Juárez, Mexico.

West, Robert C., ed.
: 1964 Natural Environment and Early Cultures. Vol. 1 of Handbook of Middle American Indians. Robert Wauchope, gen. ed. University of Texas Press. Austin.

Williams, Howell and Robert F. Heizer
: 1965 Geological Notes on the Ruins of Mitla and other Oaxacan Sites, Mexico. Contributions University of California Archaeological Research Facility. Berkeley, California.

Wittfogel, Karl A.
: 1957 Oriental Despotism. Yale University Press. New Haven.

Wolf, Eric C.
: 1957 Closed Corporate Peasant Communities in Mesoamerica and Central Java. Southwestern Journal of Anthropology Vol. 13:1-8.
: 1966 Peasants. Foundations of Modern Anthropology Series. Marshal D. Sahlins, ed. Prentice-Hall Inc. New Jersey.

Wolf, Eric C. and Angel Palerm
: 1955 Irrigation in the Old Acolhua Domain, Mexico. Southwestern Journal of Anthropology Vol. 11:265-81.

Wolpert, Julian
: 1964 The Decision Process in a Spatial Context. Annals of the Association of American Geographers Vol. 54:537-58.

Zimbardo, Philip G.
: 1969 The Cognitive Control of Motivation. Scott, Foresman and Co. Glenview, Illinois.

---

[1]The Taylor dissertation has since been published as *Landlord and Peasant in Colonial Oaxaca*, Stanford University Press, Stanford.

Plate 1. Valley of Oaxaca looking south from above Teotitlán del Valle (village in middle foreground).

Plate 2. Eastern end of the Tlacolula Valley looking west towards Mitla showing piedmont and valley floor. Bed of Río Salado is seen in middle foreground.

Plate 3. Central Tlacolula Valley looking south from above the piedmont. The central uncultivated zone crossed by a road is part of the seasonal swamp of the Río Salado.

Plate 4. Part of the weekly market at San Pedro y San Pablo Etla.

Plate 5. Coa cultivation in the piedmont zone: San Gabriel Etla. Note the resulting pock-marked surface.

Plate 6. Series of dry stone trincheras in a piedmont valley which are designed to hold back soil and moisture.

Plate 7. Floodwater farming near San Mateo Macuilxochitl (a) floodwater being distributed along furrows; (b) peak flood discharge half an hour later; (c) destruction of corn and deposition of sediment 12 hours later. (The same bush is marked in each photo)

Plate 8. Series of soil erosion walls of piled branches one day after flooding of milpa in 1966 in the Tlacolula Valley. Position of most concentrated flow was not apparent before the flood.

Plate 9. Pot irrigation field near San Antonino Castillo Velasco. The white scale is 15mm long. A well is indicated in the background.

Plate 10. Pot irrigation in the Zaachila Valley. Well is on the left behind the man.

Plate 11. Modern well and furrow system for irrigating alfalfa near Tlacolula.

Plate 12. Main canal for San Gabriel Etla and San Miguel Etla contouring round and mountain valley side before reaching the top of the piedmont ridge.

Plate 13. Ox-plough introduced by the Spanish at the Conquest and in common use today.

Plate 14. Ox-cart taking zacate from the milpa: Tlacolula Valley.

Plate 15. Clearing a long-fallowed field by burning vegetation and piling boulders (south of San Andres Zabache).

Plate 16. A partly harvested corn field seen in September 1968.

Plate 17. An unirrigated corn field typical of the piedmont zone.

Plate 18. Etla Valley and irrigated piedmont landscape looking west from above San Gabriel Etla. The fields in the lower half of the picture are part of the sample land use area.

Plate 19. San Sebastián Abasolo and the cultivated valley floor including the sample land use area seen from the north.